DATE DUE

OC 25 02			
FE 16 03			
AP 29 0?			
OC 26 04			
FE 1 1 10			

BECOMING A
JEW

BECOMING A JEW

Maurice Lamm

jD | **Jonathan David Publishers, Inc.**
Middle Village, New York 11379

BECOMING A JEW

Copyright © 1991

by

Maurice Lamm

No part of this book may be reproduced in any form without the prior written consent of the publisher. Address all inquiries to:
Jonathan David Publishers, Inc.
68-22 Eliot Avenue
Middle Village, New York 11379

6 8 10 9 7

Library of Congress Cataloging-in-Publication Data
Lamm, Maurice.
    Becoming a Jew/by Maurice Lamm.
    p. cm.
    Includes bibliographical references and index.
    ISBN 0-8246-0350-8
    1. Proselytes and proselyting, Jewish. I. Title.
    BM729. P7L26   1991
    296.7′ 1—dc20

                                                            91-9129
                                                            CIP

Printed in the United States of America

Rabbi Eleazar said: The Holy One, Blessed be He, exiled Israel among the nations only so that proselytes may join it.

Rabbi Yochanan deduced it from this (Hosea 2:25): "And I will have compassion upon her that hath not obtained compassion. And I will say to them that are not My people: thou art My people; and they shall say: Thou art my God." (Pesachim 87b)

I dedicate this book
to my children

David and Yafa Lamm
Judith and Rabbi Yitzchok Young
Dodi Lee and Rabbi Simcha Leib Weinberg

who dedicate their lives
to helping others become better Jews

ACKNOWLEDGMENTS

I wish to thank Herman Wouk, my teacher and old friend, for allowing me to quote from *This is My God*, his classic guide to Judaism. No work exists in English more illuminating to those new to the religion, and I urge that it be read as a companion volume to *Becoming a Jew*. *This is My God*, by Herman Wouk, is presently available in quality paperback from Touchstone Books, a Simon & Schuster, Inc., imprint.

I extend my profound gratitude to one of the finest Torah scholars in America, Rabbi Hershel Schachter, head of the Katz Kollel at Yeshiva University's Rabbi Isaac Elchanan Theological Seminary, and holder of the Nathan and Vivian Fink Distinguished Professorial Chair in Talmud. His critical review of the entire manuscript and his halakhic suggestions and modifications have all proven invaluable.

I cannot estimate how much I owe my wife, Shirley, both for her critical acumen in this sensitive subject and for coping with the ten-year travail that this book required for its gestation.

I thank Ms. Vonda Finley, my administrative assistant, herself a convert to Judaism, for typing the manuscript faithfully and precisely, and for her computer expertise. Also, I appreciate the efforts of Mrs. Adair Klein, librarian at Yeshiva University-Los Angeles for her contributions to this volume.

I thank my publisher and old friend, Rabbi Alfred J. Kolatch, for bearing with me during these many years of toil. I am now five years overdue, and, if not for his patience, I would have given up years ago. His editorial acumen and advice have been invaluable.

Most of all, I thank the Almighty for giving me the opportunity of sharing this knowledge, and the strength to endure the sometimes frustrating process of this volume's production.

CONTENTS

PART THREE

The Protocol

PART FOUR

Responsa:
Answering Questions on Life and Law

PART FIVE

WHO ARE WE?
A CONVERT'S INTRODUCTION TO JUDAISM

PART SIX

Welcome Home

PREFACE

PREPARE TO EMBARK

I

Contemplating religious conversion—with all that is entailed in striking out on a radically different path—clearly testifies to serious thinking, a willingness to change, and courageous resolve. These qualities precisely distinguished the first Jew, Abraham, as he broke with his family's beliefs and, at the behest of God, began a journey which would end he knew not where, but which brought him finally to the Promised Land. These traits are not only admirable, but crucial to the spiritual voyage. They already qualify the candidate for conversion to embark on exploring the Jewish religion and the Jewish people.

The Jewish religion is not simply a calling; conversion to it is not simply a profession of faith. It is a network of profound ideas and rich insights, which during its long history, has generated the fundamental beliefs of all western religion. It has contributed to the civilized world its crowning ideals and its most glorious convictions—among them the idea of one God; a system of jurisprudence; a structure of ethics and morals; the Bible and the Prophets; the idea of a prayerbook and a House of Prayer; numerous ideas, ideals, institutions, and, not the least, a worldview that has dominated western culture for 2,500 years.

It takes aggressive thinking to comprehend this new area of belief, rather than a declaration of faith, and it takes compelling conviction to say, "This is how I see the truth. I must now enter the Covenant of Abraham."

II

If you are ready to join the faith, is it ready to receive you? Yes. But not "by all means."

If you follow the protocol of conversion and make a commitment to fulfill Judaism's expectations that you fashion a religious future, your desire to convert will be honored and cherished. Except for one era in Jewish history, the Jews have never refused admission to sincere converts. A contemporary illustration of this policy of not "shutting the door to converts" is the debate that has been raging in the Jewish world about conversion to Judaism, known as "Who is a Jew?" The protagonists on both sides are more passionate about their views in this controversy than about virtually any other issue in memory. The debate addresses the question of whom the Israeli government should consider a legitimately converted Jew who would then automatically be entitled to become a citizen of the State of Israel under its Law of Return. This law is designed to admit into Israel all born Jews and properly converted gentiles without other requirements.

Out of the otherwise unrelieved blackness of this dispute, we are able to distinguish one illuminating insight: there is an area of calm in the eye of that storm. In the midst of raging passions, eloquent defenses, and fiery protests, there is a tacit and undeniable agreement that is hardly noticed and almost never mentioned, but which is the assumption on which every thing revolves: *The Jewish people unanimously welcomes converts.* The question is "who" is a Jew, not "whether" one could become a Jew.

There is no arguing that today. One small community of Syrian Jews has decided not to accept converts at this time so as to preserve its unity and enable it to survive. But all others, ranging over the whole spectrum of the global Jewish population, accepts Jews "properly" converted.

In fact, the dispute on admission of converts to Israel has

served the Jewish community well in another respect. It has taught subliminally that *it is only by how we define converts that we are able to define our own selves as Jews.* Who *we* are, is what we say about who *you* need to be. The crisis in the Jewish community is actually a crisis of *self*-definition. In an ironic twist of history, converts have become the mirrors of our souls!

You might be upset to learn that the Jewish community is not of one mind as to the protocol of conversion and that in fact several routes to the promised goal are offered. This may seem disturbingly confusing, but that is the stubborn reality. You are welcome—but not by *all* means.

You need to know what options you have. But you also should understand what the consequences of your choices will be. If you choose a liberal protocol, it will not be accepted by traditionalists. It is therefore the rabbi's moral obligation to map the terrain so that you can know in advance where your path will take you. This book will articulate the traditional, historical process of conversion from which other processes in our day have turned. The rabbi you choose to ask to lead you into conversion will undoubtedly feel the same responsibility.

Whichever route you choose to take in order to enter the fold is, of course, your right and solely your decision. God bless you for your noble intentions and for the good qualities you bring with you. By the same token, if most, or even some, of the Jewish people cannot accept your decision because it does not meet their expectations for converts, you should understand that is, of course, their right and their decision. As always, freedom is given—and so is duty.

III

You should also understand what this book does not attempt to do. It does not provide you with a systematic history or chronology of conversions, or an updated psychological analysis of the motivation for changing religions, or a comparative religion table of competing faiths—although it will touch on all these subjects.

Also, it is not designed as a merchandising tool for the Jewish religion, armed with even a subliminal goal of persuading non-Jews to take up the faith. It is descriptive; it has no missionary component. It does not describe Jewish beliefs only to appeal to gentiles in order to encourage conversions, although I do hope that the vitality and the élan of Judaism will shine through the ideas presented.

What this book primarily deals with is the traditional conversion process. It seeks to demystify the age-old ritual; to disentangle it from the web of popular misconceptions; to explain those matters which, to the untrained eye, appear as obscure or irrelevant; and to apply traditional law to new contemporary situations.

IV

THE GEOGRAPHY OF THE BOOK

Part I relates the experiences of converts who have gone through the conversion process, described in their own words. By knowing the delights they experienced and the hardships they confronted, you may well find your own sentiments mirrored in their words. Perhaps it will enable you to feel less isolated in your own circumstances, and perhaps their strategies will be appropriate to your concerns.

Part II defines the idea and framework of conversion—what Judaism requires, the benefits and constraints of joining the Jewish people, and the commitment you need to make in order to participate as a Jew, along with the Jewish people, in effectuating the Jewish enterprise.

Part III delineates the formal process of conversion (the "protocol"), and explains the meaning and relevance of the components of this ritual which have been in force since the tablets were given on Mt. Sinai. These include circumcision, immersion, renaming the convert, the nature of the court, and other aspects.

Part IV, called "Responsa," is the Jewish law section of the book. It addresses frequently asked questions and recurring problems that confront converts. It demonstrates how the Jewish tradition responds to questions about the conversion protocol, specific marriage laws relating to converts, and the interpersonal relationships of the Jewish and gentile families participating in each other's religious celebrations.

Part V presents an overview of what the candidate for conversion needs to know to gain at least a basic understanding of Judaism. It will indicate how to find the light after stepping over the threshold into the House of Israel, and will include a series of introductions to the beliefs and practices of the Jews.

Part VI is entitled "Welcome Home: We are Keeping the Lights On." It speaks to the convert and also to the possibly disaffected Jewish mate of a new convert. It may surprise you to learn that converts are actually "returning" to Judaism.

The final portion of the book contains a bibliography, appendices, and the index.

• • •

I began this work with some misgiving, because of both the historic ambiguities of the subject of conversion and the passions aroused by my colleagues in the public forum as to its application in the contemporary world.

I have tried, however hesitantly, to light a candle for those who want to become the children of Abraham. That is how I view my obligation as one of his descendants.

Maurice Lamm
Palm Springs, California
January 1991
Shvat 5751

FORE WORDS

Entering the covenant of Judaism requires learning new ideas, and assimilating new ideas requires learning a new vocabulary—the basic vocabulary of Judaism. This is especially true when studying Judaism, for two reasons. First, the convert needs to learn "new" terms for unique Jewish concepts which have no parallel in the western lexicon. Second, there is a need to learn new definitions for old and familiar terms, which have become culturally embedded in a Christian society and which now need to be understood afresh in a Jewish context.

I. NEW MEANINGS OF OLD WORDS

"B.C./B.C.E."—"A.D./C.E."

Judaism counts the years of the calendar on a universal scale—from the biblical account of creation according to the dates counted literally in the Bible itself. The year 1991, for example, is the Hebrew year 5751, which is the number of years from God's creation of the universe.

When Christianity rose to power in the western world, it began to date history from the birth of Jesus, according to the Gregorian calendar. Hence, history was divided into B.C., "before Christ," which identifies years prior to Jesus' birth, and A.D., "anno Domini," or "in the year of the Lord," which signifies years following Jesus' birth.

Judaism could never consent to divide history along these lines, of course, but it also would not divide universal history to celebrate any individual—even to draw the line at Abraham's birth, or Moses'. Nonetheless, the Jewish community had to accommodate its *secular* business and social calendar to global usage. While Judaism is not "of" this world—its beliefs and mission transcend material reality and "global interests"—it is very much "in" this world. Therefore, it divides history according to the exact dates of the Gregorian calendar, as do all nations, but refers to the historical divide as "before the common era," B.C.E., and the "common era," C.E. Thus, in Jewish terms, we are living in 1991 C.E. The Jewish *religious* calendar, however, makes no recognition of this secular accommodation to the secular world—retaining its universal format and continuing to count its years from Divine creation.

"Sabbath"

Jews introduced the world to the natural intrinsic rhythm of a seven-day week, the climax of which is Saturday, called *Shabbat*, after the fact that on this day God "rested," *shavat*, from the work of the six days of creation. (Genesis 2:3)

With the arrival of Christianity came a desire to break with Judaism, the mother religion, and to find a reason to designate a day other than Saturday as a special day within the seven-day week. Sunday was chosen. The Muslim faith, centuries later, found the same need in order to develop its own individuality, and moved the Sabbath to Friday.

Needless to say, the original Sabbath, or Shabbat, referred to in this book, is Saturday.

"Night" and "Day"

The twenty-four-hour day in the western calendar runs from midnight to midnight. It is so arranged for the sake of precision and uniformity. But it is an artificial imposition on the clock. The natural division of days follows astronomical events—the rising and setting of the sun, the appearance of the stars. In ancient times, before mechanical clocks were in everyone's possession, there was no way for the public to determine the precise middle of the night.

The Bible records the beginnings and ends of Sabbaths and Holy Days in accordance with natural phenomena, universally perceived, and begins the day with the setting of the sun and ends it that way. Thus, the Sabbath begins on Friday night at sunset. (Actually, to avoid inadvertently violating the Sabbath, it is observed from eighteen minutes before the start of sunset.) The Sabbath ends with the appearance of the stars (later than sunset, again to avoid violating the holiness of the day). It does not begin at midnight Friday, nor does it end at midnight Saturday.

Judaism counts the beats of time by a different drummer. The subject of time counting is detailed in Part Five.

"Bible"

The Jewish vocabulary does not recognize terms such as "Old Testament" and "New Testament." To Judaism, the *Torah*, which is the Hebrew Bible, is first and last, God's Revelation of His will to His people. This revelation of God is true for all time. The appearance of no person, no religion, and no edict may supersede it or render it extinct.

Christianity's declaration of a "new" testament or "new" covenant cannot retire the Bible by calling it the "old" one, inevitably subordinating the "old" to the "new." The Church Fathers deigned the Bible to continue to exist as the "Old" Testament rather than discard it altogether for no reason other than that they regarded it as a book of prophecies that foretell Jesus' career centuries later. Entire libraries have been written attempting to "prove" Christian fulfillment of the Jewish prophecies. This robs the Jewish Bible, Torah, of any intrinsic value, and the whole idea is utterly irreconcilable with the Jewish belief in the eternal validity of God's covenant with Israel.

Therefore, all references to the Bible in a Jewish framework, refer to the Torah which begins with Genesis and ends with the second book of Chronicles. For further elucidation see "Torah" (below) and the basis of these concepts in Part Five.

"Faith"

In common parlance, "faith" has become interchangeable with "religion." In the western religious vocabulary, both terms signify purely spiritual belief. The Jewish "religion," however, is not primarily a matter of faith. The dominant note in Judaism is deed—what is called *mitzvah*, the commandment to perform a certain deed—which is expected to be the vehicle for a wholesome faith. The *mitzvot* (plural of mitzvah) are embedded in Jewish law, called *Halakhah,* and form the substance of Judaism.

While Christianity repudiated the Law and considered it harmful from its very inception, Judaism called it a "delight" of the Lord and made its observance the litmus test of Jewish survival.

Mitzvah and Halakhah do not imply a skein of charming folkways or even good conduct, but specific and precise mandates of Jewish law. When a non-Jew converts to Judaism, he or she does not convert to the Jewish "faith" but rather accedes to the Jewish "covenant"—the convert "enters into the Covenant of Abraham, our Father."

II. NEW WORDS FOR NEW IDEAS

The following terms are described in their context when they first appear in the book. The brief explanation here provided is to serve as a general introduction to the Jewish vocabulary.

Torah

In its narrow sense, Torah refers to the Five Books of Moses spanning the beginnings of Jewish life from Creation to the death of Moses. Often, Torah includes all Scripture—the Five Books of Moses, the Prophets and the Writings, referred to collectively as *TaNaK*—an abbreviation of *Torah, Nevi'im* (Prophets) and *Ketuvim* (general writings). Sometimes, Torah is broadened to signify all Jewish learning—to include the entire corpus of Jewish tradition, the Written Law and the Oral Law encased in the Talmud, together with all its commentaries. Sometimes, it simply represents all of Judaism, as in "The Torah Way of Life." Torah is thus not accurately identified as Bible.

Halakhah

From the root definition "to walk," it takes on the meaning of the "Jewish Way." More specifically, it signifies the binding legal component, as opposed to the narrative and more spiritual realm, of the tradition that is generally referred to as *Aggadah.* Halakhic Judaism refers usually to that Judaism which pays very serious attention to the strict observance of Jewish law, in addition to its ethical content.

Mitzvah

Mitzvah is the irreducible, "organic" substance of the relationship between man and God. Mitzvah refers to the commandment issued by God, who is the Command-er—the *Metzaveh*—as written explicitly in Torah, or derived by the Sages from the Torah implicitly. Mitzvah is thus the distillation of God's mandate—whether of a moral or ritual nature—and not, as in common parlance, merely "a good deed."

Ger

From the root meaning "stranger" (as in the biblical phrase "the *ger* who lives in thy gates") which refers to non-citizens who lived under Jewish governance and who had certain rights, privileges and prescribed duties. From early times, ger has been used for "religious convert," a stranger to the religion. The feminine is *giyoret*, the plural *gerim*, and the process of conversion, *gerut*.

Part One

PERSONAL EXPERIENCES:

Seventeen Jews Reflect on Their Conversions

INTRODUCTION:
INSIGHTS FROM LOOKING BACK

"Why did you convert?" That is probably the question most frequently asked converts by born Jews. It does appear to be a natural question to pose to one who makes a radical change in life-style: "Why did you need to do this?"

Perhaps it is simple curiosity. Perhaps it is because Jews seek an affirmation of their own values and are reinforced when "strangers" say nice things about them and their religion. It is much like a little girl who knows she is pretty, but asks if she is because she wants to be flattered. The convert in turn asks in disbelief, "Why are you asking me this? Can't you believe a gentile would actually want to convert to your religion? Don't you realize what a treasure you have?"

The statements that follow are by gentiles who deliberately chose Judaism. They are new Jews—Jews by choice. They describe here the inner experience of their conversion: both the values they found or were looking for, and those they did not find as they turned to the Jewish people. At this point, we are not concerned only with the immediate reason for the conversion—whether it was for the sake of marriage, out of conviction, or to satisfy family—but with the meaning they discovered in both the process of the conversion and in the substance of their newfound faith. The comments are in the form of published articles, personal letters, and oral conversations. In them, you might find articulated a sentiment, a thought, a fear, that is familiar and has crossed your mind. Certain of the behaviors described are uniquely the individual's and not necessarily valid for every convert. Not all of them solve their problems in a similar way; neither have they necessarily chosen the right solution, even for their own situations; nor are all their concerns shared by other converts.

The new Jews represented here come from no specific, single persuasion or social group, or economic or academic level of society. They are men and women, professionals, tradespeople and homemakers, married and single. Most of them are young (or were young when they wrote these statements) and college educated. They hail from many different regions of the country, and from a large spectrum of religious beliefs—from atheism and agnosticism to Roman Catholicism and evangelical Protestantism. Their statements were written over a long period of time—some in the early fifties, others in the early nineties. Some of their sentiments are remarkably similar despite the fact that, in confronting these obstacles, there is a wide variety of thresholds. From each of these statements, we are able to get good insights into the wide variety of reasons that a considerable number of gentiles have decided to become Jews. I have done little editing in order to retain the specific flavor of their individualities.

The inclusion of these insights from those who have already run the gamut of converts' feelings and have concluded them successfully, will have served its purpose if, after reading them, a potential convert will be able to say: "Others have trodden this path; I am not alone. My feelings are not isolated."

A CORRECTED COSMIC ERROR

Adele Milch

Adele Milch's statement is excerpted from a series of articles under the rubric of "*Gerut*: Responses from Converts," in *Moment* magazine.

My colleagues may have been non-Jews in the past and are now Jews. I, on the other hand, believe that I have always been Jewish, although born through mysterious circumstances to non-Jews. I am what one of our friends, a reputable biologist and student of the *Kabbalah* [Jewish mysticism], identifies as a "corrected cosmic error."

My family is Polish Catholic and I grew up in what was then a Slavic immigrant neighborhood—Seventieth Street and Second Avenue in Manhattan. I didn't learn English until I went to school at the age of six. My first social contact with Jews was in high school (although my mother always went to a kosher butcher, because Polish peasants believe "Jewish meat" is superior). My Jewish classmates were mostly from middle-class, cultured homes and lived in the West Side's "Golden Ghetto" of the 1950s. They came from a life-style which enchanted me. I was soon hooked, and, during those four years, my accent changed from Polish to New York Jewish and I soon became a "Jewish type."

During my college years, I was an avid reader and soon found Christianity as a religion to be intellectually unacceptable. Since I was no longer able to make the required "leap of faith," I soon stopped my Catholic religious affiliation, which was eased by moving out of my parental home at twenty-one. My family is basically anti-Semitic and my dating was with non-Jews.

My husband and I met in our early twenties. We were co-workers and were mutually attracted by the other's rebellious and irreverent attitudes towards society and life. It was several months before he discovered, much to his dismay, that I was a non-Jew and I discovered he was Jewish. Even though we both knew it was destined for us to live out our lives together, Bob was a non-religious Jewish intellectual who was very much aware of historical continuity and so delayed our marriage by three years. His parents, typical ethnic types who discover Judaism only when intermarriage threatens, wanted me to convert before the marriage. I refused on principle. Children were to be no problem because neither one of us wanted any. . . .

The actual catalyst for my formal conversion took place in the summer of 1969. Bob and I went to Poland, where I was enrolled in a seminar at the University of Warsaw. The university was always planning interesting trips for its foreign students and one of them was to Auschwitz. And so it was, one sunny August day, that my life took a completely different turn. Seeing photos at Yad Vashem is difficult, but actually being at Auschwitz, which is kept up perfectly by the Polish government, is an emotionally devastating experience. The exhibit which finally made me weep openly was the one where thousands upon thousands of baby shoes were piled up in a room-wide display case. That trip culminated in a visit to Israel which totally finished me as a goy. That winter, I made the decision to have children and they would have to be Jewish. By March I was pregnant and we went to see Rabbi _____.

I guess you can categorize our family as right-wing Conservative now, although, if it weren't for the *mechitzah* [the synagogue divider between men and women in Orthodox congregations], I would be quite comfortable in a modern Orthodox *shul* [the familiar term for synagogue, usually an Orthodox one. The word is a derivation from Yiddish.]. Both Bob and I attended conversion lessons conducted by a young rabbinical student and his wife for eight and a half months and this ended up making Torah Jews out of us.

Studying with _____, who dealt with the good and bad of Judaism and the Jews, was a singularly important growth experience for Bob and me because it showed us that Judaism provided not only the highest of intellectual stimulation, but also the most satisfying of emotional experiences. It provides for the two-year-old and it provides for Einstein. I can't emphasize how important it is, if you want quality conversions, to be able to provide this kind of highly individualized and personal instruction and caretaking. I started my new Jewish life not only with a guaranteed marriage contract, but with a fully kosher kitchen and a theoretical knowledge of 613 mitzvot. [A mitzvah is a commandment or religious obligation, and the total number of mitzvot, only a small fraction of which are applicable today, number 613.]

However, it took years to be able to perform the mitzvot comfortably. It is very difficult for a highly urbanized couple to be able to completely rest for a whole day. It took years to be able to ignore the phone on Shabbat. And, four years after my conversion, I would still crack sometimes on *kashrut* [the dietary laws] outside the house.

I have a story, however, which will explain how I came to have strength, and will indicate how effective our Jewish training was *vis-à-vis* our firstborn. One day, my mother-in-law and I, along with our oldest son, who was four at the time and already a *meshugeneh frummy* [extremely Orthodox], were out for the day. Around lunch time, we passed a McDonald's on the highway and my mother-in-law urged us to stop off. Inside, Grandma ordered a round of hamburgers. The two of us gulped ours down while my son would not touch his. Grandma naturally said, "Eat, darling, eat." And my four-year-old son replied, "I don't eat *traif*" [non-kosher food, from the Hebrew *trefah*].

Now, as a family, we maintain kashrut both inside and outside the house, maintain all aspects of Shabbat, and celebrate all the holidays enthusiastically. We don't drive on Shabbat except to shul, or as the case may be, to the Hillel *minyan*. Both our boys take their share of religious responsibility seriously. Our eight-year-old could lead a goodly part of a Sabbath service. Our two-year-old can sway sideways, knows when to respond Amen, and is hooked on *Havdalah* candles.

We do not send our eight-year-old to the local congregational Hebrew school, as we find it inferior (although no worse than most), and he is too advanced in his studies for it. Bob teaches him Hebrew reading, writing, conversation and ethics (they are now working on *Pirke Avot*) [a popular book, *Ethics of the Fathers*, which is a small tract from the Talmud and contains ethical and moral insights of the Sages of 1600 years ago and more], *davening*, history, and the essentials of every holiday. Right now the whole family is undergoing rigorous *Pesach* [Hebrew for Passover] practice.

There was one woman who was unique and an example of what the rabbis should aim at. She was a non-Jew who had once been married to a nonpracticing Jew. After her divorce, she continued her interest in Judaism which had also been sparked by her fundamentalist Protestant background. She worked as a head nurse at the V.A. Hospital in Northport, New York. She found her way to the North Shore Jewish Center because of Rabbi _____. She was soon adopted by an elderly religious couple, studied with Rabbi _____ and eventually converted under Orthodox auspices because she decided to make *aliyah*. [Technically, it means "going up," and refers most commonly to "going up" to the Torah Scroll reading during services, but it is now used to mean "settling in Israel."] Today she is a head nurse at the Hadassah Hospital. This is the kind of quality convert we should be aiming at. What we need for the survival of Diaspora Jewry in America is quality, not quantity. . . .

> *Note:* Adele Milch converted after marriage. She learned the need to become a Jew in Auschwitz and Israel, to practice traditional Judaism from her rabbi, and to become a fully observant Jew from her child. Here is a saga of a Polish Catholic raising Judaism beyond the level of a born-Jewish family. She obviously has strength of character and a strong, supporting spouse.
>
> —ML

PUSHED AWAY AND HELPED IN
Shoshana Lev

Shoshana Lev's story appeared in the December issue of *Direction*, published by the University of Judaism (the west coast branch of the Jewish Theological Seminary) in Los Angeles. It is based on a talk she delivered to a University of Judaism class on Contemporary Jewish Issues.

I was raised in the Roman Catholic church. I attended Catholic schools, elementary school through university. Until I went to law school, I had never attended a non-religious school. . . . There could be no compromise: the Church has a set of dogmas, a manifesto of faith, and the Catholic must believe all of it. There was no place for me in the Church. . . .

I passed through Christianity, from the dogmatism of Catholicism to completely undogmatic Quakerism, through atheism and agnosticism, meditation, and yoga, and still could not find a vehicle for religious expression. One day, I picked up a copy of Leon Uris' novel *Mila 18* and made a shattering discovery: at age eighteen, I didn't know that Hitler had exterminated six million Jews. I had always assumed that concentration camps and prisoner-of-war camps were the same thing, and that Hitler was just another tyrant. I learned about anti-Semitism and genocide. I wanted to know what it was about the Jews and their beliefs that made others want to exterminate them. So I went to a Jewish bookstore and there found a little volume by Milton Steinberg called *Basic Judaism*. At last, I felt I had found what I had been looking for: here was what I believed. . . .

For the next four years, I continued to study, and I started looking for a rabbi who would convert me. Everywhere I went, I was regarded with suspicion by the Jews I met, who couldn't understand why I wanted to convert. The rabbis I spoke with were either too busy, uninterested, suspicious, or told me to settle my marital situation before they would convert me.

I mentioned my dilemma to Mrs. Bloom, one of the instructors at the university. She was very interested in my problem and introduced me to her Reform rabbi. He sent me to the Bureau of Jewish Education and, within a very short time, performed the conversion ceremony. I had finally, at the age of twenty-two, become a Jew. One toe in the door. . . .

In Los Angeles, I enrolled in what was then the Yeshiva Teachers College. One Orthodox rabbi who was my teacher approached me after class one night saying, "I understand you want to have an Orthodox conversion. I'll arrange it." And so he did.

For the next few months, I continued to study. I was tested by the Orthodox Bet Din. I was then taken through the conversion ceremony, including immersion three times in the *mikveh* [Hebrew for the ritual pool used for immersion]. The rabbi wisely told me that I should not try to do everything at once. He counseled me to start with Shabbat [Hebrew for Sabbath] and kashrut [the laws of keeping kosher] and assume one practice at a time. For the most part, I have followed that advice, but I cannot call myself Orthodox.

There is a well-known Jewish maxim that says the convert should be pushed away with one hand and helped in with the other. This was not my experience with Judaism before I converted. Until Mrs. Bloom offered her help, I had been firmly pushed away. There is a lesser-known counsel offered by Maimonides that says that once the convert becomes a Jew, the conversion should never again be mentioned; the convert has become a Jew in all respects and must be treated as such. Would that it were so!

You continue to be called a convert by many Jews. Some indicate that they expect you to drop Judaism and flee, flying into the arms of Christianity when anti-Semitism touches you. You are seen as a religious fanatic by some, and by others as a talking dog; it doesn't matter what the dog says, the fact that it talks is amazing enough.

I was a great favorite of my Greek professor at the University of San Francisco until I converted to Judaism. He told me, "But surely you understand that only those who believe will enter the kingdom of heaven!" He refused to speak to me. My advisor in the philosophy department, my friend for four years, avoided me and refused to come to my wedding, telling another student to let me know how disappointed he was in me. . . .

Surprisingly, my parents did not react very negatively. My father prefers that one should be moral and believe in something. My mother, who had a Jewish grandfather amidst her scores of Catholic ancestors, believes that since I was born on his birthday, it was somehow meant to be. She has come to accept my religion, although she is mystified by my religious practices. Being a convert, I could, as the Halakhah [Hebrew for the whole body of Jewish law] enjoins me, forsake my family, consider myself a *"bat Avraham Avinu"* [a daughter of Abraham, our Father] and forget from whence I came. Because I continue to love my family, I toe a fine line. I go home for Christmas and down-play my Judaism around my family. But when I am in my own home, I practice Judaism and am at peace with myself.

> *Note:* Here is another instance of conversion being sparked by "What made others want to exterminate them?" Shoshana's decision to convert earned her rebuff from her past and from the future she chose. Sometimes, but not always, that is indeed the situation. Shoshana handled it well. It is also good that she continues to respect her gentile family, because the Halakhah never enjoins rejecting one's relatives. There is a chapter on this question in Part IV, "Responsa."

—ML

THE FIRST TIME IN THE SYNAGOGUE WAS CONFUSING
Boaz McNabb

> Brian, who changed his name to Boaz, has undergone a Reform and then an Orthodox conversion. He is a sophisticated, sincere person who works in city government, in a job that his father held before he died. He lives in a small, predominantly Protestant community in Southern California which views good-naturedly Boaz's new and strange religious observances.

The first time I went to a synagogue it was to a Reform synagogue in Riverside, California. I think I had a nice feeling, particularly because it was similar to a church setup—lots of English, of course, and lots of singing—and singing is very attractive to me. There was a little confusion because of a bit of a Hebrew mix. The first time I went to an Orthodox synagogue it caused a good deal of confusion—one, because everybody's doing something else, or so it seemed, and two, a fear that either I might be discovered or somebody might ask me to do something or other. I wasn't sure how I would react to such a thing.

As to my feeling when I entered the mikveh: The first thing I remember is that there was no distinct feeling of a spiritual high. I remember feeling strange—taking off my clothes and parading myself down into a body of water in front of somebody watching intently. The second thing I remember is after I surfaced from the mikveh, I was asked to say a *berakhah* [Hebrew for blessing, which Jews make before fulfilling a commandment and at other specific times.]. Now which berakhah do they want me to say? Ultimately, I started "Barukh atah Ha'Shem" (Blessed art Thou) and then they guided me along. Whew!

My first Pesach *Seder* [the Passover meal] was the most wonderful Seder I've ever had. It took place before I was Jewish. . . . We had been invited by our friends, and they welcomed me with open arms. They explained all sorts of things to me. They let me participate a little bit because I could read a little bit of Hebrew. Just the story telling that went along with the actual script of the *Haggadah* [the book for the Passover service read at the Passover meal on the first two nights of the holiday] was wonderful. And though I've heard more detailed explanations now as to why and how, and I understand more, there's nothing that can ever replace that first Seder. . . .

A funny thing happened on the way to the Bet Din—I missed my appointment! [The Bet Din is the court of three that presides over the conversion process.] The reason I missed my appointment was that I was told that, as soon as the conversion process is completed, the convert is already obligated to be doing certain mitzvot. And one of the mitzvot, of course, is the mitzvah of the fringes, the *tsitsit*. [Tsitsit refers to the fringes placed at the four corners of the prayer shawl that Jews wear at services. This will be discussed further in this book.] And so, I had this appointment and I was driving to Los Angeles from Palm Springs. I get to Fairfax Street in order to find the fringes, and, lo and behold, I don't directly know what I'm looking for! I was too embarrassed to ask for help. Finally, it was beyond my appointment time, and I rushed to call Rabbi ____ and the phone is constantly busy. Finally, I got hold of somebody at the office and apparently there were other people to be converted that day and I was told, "Sorry, it's too late. You'll have to come another time." So I missed the appointment at

the mikveh to become a Jew because I was too busy trying
to become a Jew!

> *Note:* Boaz notes his confusion the first time he entered an
> Orthodox synagogue. This is quite natural; it is strange and yet
> exciting. His ability to grow intellectually and religiously is attested
> to by his wife in a letter quoted later in the book.
>
> —ML

I WAS A ROMAN CATHOLIC PRIEST

Abraham Isaac Carmel

Abraham Isaac Carmel was born in London, England, in 1911
as Kenneth Charles Cox. He was ordained as a Roman Catholic
priest in 1943. Because of his doubts about the divinity of Jesus,
he left the priesthood after a few years. He converted to Judaism
in London, after very long preparation. After conversion, Mr.
Carmel taught Jewish studies at a well-known Orthodox day
school in New York, the Yeshiva of Flatbush.

The passages quoted here are from *Conversion To Judaism*,
by David Max Eichhorn, published by Ktav, 1965, who excerpted it from the American edition of Mr. Carmel's autobiography,
So Strange My Path, published by Bloch Publishing Company,
1964.

. . . As time went on and I maintained my serious reading,
I discovered more and more sound reasons for returning to
the original faith out of which both Christianity and Islam had
grown. I retained a profound respect and admiration for Jesus
and his followers, and I fully recognized the many praiseworthy
episodes in the history of the Church. Beyond this, however,
I could not go.

The notion of the Eternal King of the Universe becoming
a human baby, beautiful as I felt it to be, was to my thinking
outside the bounds of acceptance. The idea of directing any
form of worship to a created being, no matter how saintly he
or she might have been, became utterly repugnant to me. And
as my appreciation of the infinite nature of God developed,
so did I find all forms of religion which failed to conform to
a strictly monotheistic standard unworthy of credence.

Coincidentally with the increasing direction of all my fervor
to God Himself, I became aware of a knitting together of my

personality, so to speak, and the assumption of an inner unity and power such as I had never previously known.

Nevertheless, I realized that this monotheistic conception by no means represented Judaism in its entirety. My research had shown me, in fact, that Judaism, while monotheistic in a strict sense of the word, was less a creed than a way of life; every action throughout the livelong day was linked in one way or another to Judaism. If I was to be a Jew, I could not merely believe in one God and leave it at that. The Unitarian Church did as much. On the contrary, I would have to live in the manner prescribed for Jews when the Law was given to Moses on Sinai. The dietary laws and those concerned with observance of the Sabbath were fundamental. Moreover, it was essential that I be circumcised. . . .

. . . First and foremost among the features of Judaism which my studies had taught me to admire, I think, was its intense practicality. Thoughts of the world-to-come were not permitted to distract the Jew from fulfilling as completely as possible his mission here on earth. Jews did not simply sit passive and wait for the Messiah to come, for if they did so He would not come. His coming could only be hastened by mitzvot— their own good works. A hymn along the lines of "O Paradise, O Paradise, 'tis weary waiting here," could find no place on a Jewish tongue.

Then there was that splendid, robust principle of assuming undivided personal responsibility for one's actions. I had so often felt that the dual aspect of religious life among Catholics: devout piety and the commission of mortal sins seeming to share so paradoxical a co-existence, stemmed from their undue reliance on the sacramental system, whereby much personal responsibility to God was either absolved or transferred to others—priests, saints, or the Virgin.

Judaism, by contrast, insists that its follower shall give his whole heart, soul, and mind to the Eternal Creator. The Jew must stand upright on his own two feet before the Judge of all. He has no patron saints to plead his cause, no Father Confessor to grant indulgences, absolutions, or dispensations. He is, in the fullest sense, the "master of his fate, the captain of his soul." He neither has, nor asks for, any intermediary to bear his brief before the Judge of Heaven. Each man is his own barrister. He must plead his own cause, with a sincere heart that is truly repentant, to God alone.

Judaism does not and cannot offer any season tickets to Heaven at reduced prices. Every pilgrim travels under his own steam, so to speak. The Jew believes that he, as all men, has sufficient willpower, assisted by prayer, to resist any evil inclination. He does not require an extravagant sacramental system, born of human ingenuity rather than of Divine revelation, to snatch him from the fires of God's anger.

And a Jew either gives all to God or does not bother with external religion at all. He does not bargain with God for special terms. Whatever his failings may be—and many Jews do fail grievously, it cannot be denied—he at least does not whine about God's asking too much of him. He strikes his breast and confesses, "I have sinned and fallen short." Even on the great Day of Atonement, it is clearly understood, however, that only the sins directly against God are thus forgiven. Sins committed against his neighbor are forgiven only after he has begged his neighbor's forgiveness, and he must, if necessary, ask often.

The Catholic Christian, on the other hand, can harm his neighbor, go to Confession, make a sincere act of contrition, and receive forgiveness forthwith. He can still complacently go his way without begging pardon of the injured neighbor.

These and many other outstanding characteristics of Judaism filled me with eagerness to embrace it with all speed.

> *Note:* Abraham Carmel was an unusual man whose idealism had become legend in his time. The factors that prompted his disaffection and subsequent rejection of Catholicism—the regression from pure monotheism; the removal of responsibility from people for their own actions; the otherworldliness that induced spiritual passivity; the separation of faith from deeds; and Judaism's strong opposition to these elements, are those ideas which, to a lesser extent, have motivated many converts to Judaism.

—ML

I'VE COME HOME

Frances Price

Mrs. Price's story was excerpted from *Conversion to Judaism* by David Max Eichhorn, p. 61, which was reprinted in turn from the *Women's League Outlook* of the National Women's League and then reprinted in the *Jewish Digest* in April 1958.

It is not as a convert to Judaism but as a very proud Jewess that I write. Even though I was born into the world of the gentile and have only comparatively recently become a Jew, I hesitate to use the term "convert," since I feel in no way converted to Judaism. What I really feel is that I have "come home."

Coming into Judaism is a stimulating experience. One does not find it the end of a search, but at the beginning of a mental and spiritual journey. Judaism does not say, "I am the way." The convert must seek and find Judaism with all its traditions, its ancient, yet ever new teachings, and its depths of spiritual truth. . . .

My entrance into Judaism dates from the beginning of my small son's religious education. . . .

When our son was five and had reached religious school age, I sent him to a synagogue near our home. My mind began to turn toward Judaism, not only for him but also for myself. I must admit that it was a purely academic thing with me. What makes a Jew a Jew? How does a Jew think? What are his traditions? These and many other questions nagged at me and, for the sake of my child's religious training, I wanted to know the answers. My quest for Jewish knowledge began. . . .

I have been asked by Jews and gentiles alike, "What do you find in Judaism that makes you seem so happy and satisfied?" "How can you possibly like being Jewish and living 'kosher' with all that entails?" By such as probe more deeply, the question put is, "What in Judaism is most important to you?"

The last question is a difficult one to answer. But, if I had to choose just one word to express all my feelings, that word would be "tradition," which to me is Judaism in its glorious entirety. Tradition is the heart, the soul and the body of Judaism.

It is Torah, with all that glorious word implies. It is the Holy Days, the glow of the Sabbath candles, the rituals in the synagogue, the wearing of the *yarmulka* [Yiddish for traditional headcovering worn by men] and the *tallit* [prayershawl worn at services], the *mezuzah* [Scriptural verses encased and fastened to the doorpost of Jewish homes, symbolizing the protection of the Almighty] upon the doorpost, the Hanukkah lights, the *sukkah* on the lawn [the fragile structure symbolizing the desert hut which Jews used after the exodus from Egypt is erected for the *Sukkot* holiday that follows the High Holy Days.]. It is the firm structure of religious observance without which Judaism would be a weak, hollow shell. Everyone worships God in his heart, but truly religious people need tradition as a specific blueprint for daily living. The sensations of the soul are not enough. The eyes must see and the hands must feel.

Jews, scattered abroad, bearing untold miseries and cruel afflictions, could not have endured had it not been for the mental and spiritual discipline of our tradition. The laws of the fathers have made the children strong and our tradition has kept them steadfast. Tradition has kept Hebrew in constant use as the universal language of the Jew. It is reflected in the poetry and song of the rites of the synagogue. It is in the joy of the student as the voice of the rabbi teaches him the ancient way of life. The chant of the *chazzan* [the cantor who leads the singing of the service] takes us back to the early days of our people, to pray and to dream and, sometimes, to cry with bygone generations.

And when I speak of tradition, I include our dietary laws. So very many people seem to feel that my having a kosher home is "old fashioned," "too religious," and almost anachronistic—out of tune with modern living. This attitude rather amazes me.

To me, following a kosher routine is one of the highlights of my Jewish life. It is one of the most important parts of this tradition of ours. It is my mark of distinction. It gives me a feeling of satisfaction to eat foods that bear the stamp of formal religious approval. I like knowing, when I serve meat at my table, that the animal not only was free of disease but felt no pain when it was slaughtered, and that the slaughtering was done by one both technically and religiously qualified. Surely, a law that has been upheld through the ages, benefiting our people for so many centuries and keeping them united and distinctive, must still be upheld today regardless of the habits of the world around us. . . .

Very early in my studies with the rabbi, he indicated to me how grievous my lot might be in my new affiliation. He told me that, from the time I entered Judaism, I would be exposed to the prejudices of uninformed non-Jews. I have since learned that, despite this persecution and ignorance, Judaism displays an amazing tolerance toward those not of the Jewish faith. It does not encourage those who have found God in other ways to change their religion. It welcomes all who come into its fellowship of their own free will, but it claims no monopoly on salvation.

How can I help but raise my head in pride as I pass by the mezuzah on my doorpost and enter the warmth and the beauty of my Jewish home, wherein lives my Jewish family?

No, I was not converted. I came seeking. I was informed. I was welcomed. I was convinced. I was home.

> *Note:* What initiated Francis Price's interest in Judaism was the realization that her child needed to inherit a faith, a way. But evidently what matured her interest were both the passionate feeling that ideas had no life of their own unless they were acted out, and the compelling beauty of a rich Torah tradition which she and her family could continue.

—ML

THROUGH SOME ACCIDENT OF BIRTH, I WAS NOT BORN TO JUDAISM

Constance Head

The piece that follows was excerpted from *The National Jewish Monthly*, published by B'nai B'rith, March 1981. Dr. Constance Head is Professor of History and Religion at Western Carolina University and author of several books.

When I was thirty-nine, I became a convert to Judaism. The event was the culmination of many years of seeking, pondering and trying to force myself to believe the doctrines of Christianity, which I never accepted, yet felt guilt in rejecting. I teach history and religion, and I have a Ph.D. and a divinity school degree from a Methodist university. I came to Judaism not through marriage, for I am, and will most likely remain, single. I came not through the influence of friends, for when I made my decision to seek conversion, I had no close Jewish friends. The nearest Jewish congregation is fifty-three miles from my home. I came into Judaism because, while there is a measure of truth in all of the great religions, I believe that Judaism is the truest of them all. Not for everyone perhaps, but for me.

During the years before my conversion, I always dreaded the question, "What religion are you?" This is an inquiry frequently made in the South, where Christians of various sorts are eager to proselytize. "Oh, I'm not anything," I'd say.

It's terrible not to be "anything," but I was not about to claim I was a Methodist just because I'd been baptized as an infant. Then, gradually, I began to admit how I really felt. "I guess I'm more Jewish than anything else," I'd say. And when I did, I felt a warm wonderful glow of rightness. In my heart, I was Jewish; only through some accident of birth, I was not born to Judaism.

I was drawn toward Judaism for many years before I converted. I postponed the decision as long as I did because of geographic location, fear of family reaction, concern about the security of my teaching position as a professor of religion. But there came a time when none of these complications seemed so important as moving ahead to be what I must be. . . .

Nominally a Methodist, my mother disliked going to church. "Somebody has to stay home and cook dinner," she explained to me when I would ask her why she didn't attend—an answer that never seemed logical to me. But she had a warm-hearted attitude toward the Bible and, when I was about five, she began to teach me Bible stories. I loved stories of every sort, but nothing, absolutely nothing, could compare to the world of ancient Israel. My mother opened the door to a land of vast fascination. On summer nights, my mother and I would lie on a quilt in the backyard. "Just look at the thousands and thousands of stars," she said, "so many that no one can count them. It is like what the Lord promised Father Abraham, that his descendants would be more than the stars of the sky." I remember the zest she put into the tale of Elijah and the contest on Mount Carmel. " 'Go look again!' he told his servant, and the servant climbed the mountain again, and after seven times, he finally came down and said, 'I see a leee-ttle teenseytinsey cloud, no bigger than a man's hand, rising out of the sea.'" . . .

When, behind our garage, I found pieces of broken cement blocks with a few letters stamped thereon, I was sure I'd found fragments of the Ten Commandments that Moses had dropped coming down from Mt. Sinai. At that point, my mother injected some geographical information, and I began to realize that the Bible lands were far away. But, near or far, nothing detracted from the fact that the people of the Old Testament were my friends to be loved.

Then there was the New Testament—somber and sad. It centered around Jesus, a perfect young man with absolutely no faults or human weaknesses, who went around working miracles, but who, for some incomprehensible reason, had to die on a cross. He then arose on Easter morning, but soon after went off to Heaven, promising to send his replacement, which turned out to be the Holy Spirit, who was quite invisible. The whole scheme was baffling. . . .

After completing my undergraduate studies, I went to divinity school, not with the intention of becoming a minister, but with the hope of teaching Old Testament on the college level. I also studied church history and theology. The more I learned, the more discontented I became. After completing my divinity degree, I switched to the graduate program leading to a Ph.D. in history, rather than religion, for, as a non-believer in Christian doctrines, I felt there was no hope for me ever to be employed teaching religion.

I like history and, if I was not completely satisfied with my change in academic direction, I was resigned to it. I graduated and obtained a teaching position at a state-supported university. Along about this point, I abandoned all pretense of being aligned with any Christian church. When asked my religious preference, I began to say I was "nothing." . . .

I began to think more and more about Judaism. I was not happy being "nothing." I believed in God and felt close to the biblical heritage of ancient Israel. I read a great deal about Judaism; I thought and pondered, and a few more years slipped by. . . .

Ultimately, I set out to seek the rabbi of the nearest Reform temple. I can well imagine his surprise at my arrival in his office. In good rabbinic tradition, he tried to discourage me, but I was not easily discouraged.

"Why don't you become a Unitarian?" he suggested, after we had talked a while, and I had told him of my doubts about Christian doctrines.

I did not want to be a Unitarian, although it is a good religion and one toward which I feel warmly. "But they don't have four thousand years of tradition!" I protested. Although I am rarely at a loss for words, I found it very hard to explain to the rabbi that I really wanted to be Jewish, that I felt Jewish, that as a student of history and religion, I had come to believe that Judaism has what no other faith has.

It is well that Judaism does not take in converts too rapidly. In the months that followed my inquiry, I had time to think about my decision. There are two questions I believe a person needs to ponder when faced with any life-shaping decision, particularly relevant to the matter of conversion: One, is this decision one that I can be proud of, that I can acknowledge before everyone, without hesitation? Two, is this decision one I am willing to live with for the rest of my life?

To both questions, my answer was a clear, unhesitating yes. I let it be known that I was planning to convert. While my new friends at the Reform temple were pleased, I found a different response from some of my gentile associates. "Don't you feel odd with them? Out of place?" they asked. My answer: "All my life, I have felt out of place. No more so there than anywhere else—less so than in many places." Then: "How could you do such a thing? How can you deny your roots?" My answer: "No one chooses the faith into which he is born. God gave us brains, and He expects us to use them."

"You're not a Christian? Oooooh!" (An expression of total shock; this from some of my Bible-belt, fundamentalist Christian students.) "When Jesus comes again and takes us up in the Rapture, you're going to be left behind." . . .

Last year, there was an incident. A new term started; there was a new crop of students. On the first day, a newcomer asked me outright, "Are you a Christian?"

"No," I answered. "I am Jewish."

The young man rose and started toward the door, and as I faced that act of bigotry, I felt a great kinship to the Jews of every age in history.

"You will not leave this room!" I told him. "You may drop this course if you wish, but today, you're going to learn the

decency not to display your prejudice so openly! Sit down!"
He sat.

Somehow, we got through the class hour. Then I went into
my office and wept—not so much because my feelings were
hurt, but out of the general sadness that our world is so full
of hate and ugliness, masquerading, sometimes at least, under
the guise of religious zeal. Yet, even in my stunned sadness,
I have never felt gladder to be Jewish.

> *Note:* Purity of motive, strength of mind, pursuit of idealism
> are the foremost qualities of the Jewish "Woman of Valor," which
> Solomon celebrated. To that extent was Constance Head by
> an accident of birth not born Jewish. Few converts have this
> opportunity or this challenge, but in varying degrees, all con-
> version calls forth personal heroism. Note also the powerful force
> of tradition, after reason has used all its ammunition.

—ML

WHEN CONVERTS FEEL REJECTED
Dorothy Foster Friedman

> Dr. Friedman has taught British and American literature at
> Missouri Western College and the University of the District of
> Columbia. She now coordinates a tutoring program at the Uni-
> versity of Maryland. The excerpt that follows was drawn from
> *The Jewish Spectator*, Spring 1980.

"Study Shows Converts Feel Rejected," read the headline
in the *Baltimore Jewish Times*. . . .

I read the newspaper clipping reflectively. It pointed out that
a new study of converts by Steve Huberman, sponsored by
the Union of American Hebrew Congregations, reveals that
average American converts to Judaism are rejected by their
gentile families and friends and also by Jews. Conversion has
been for many, therefore, a doubly alienating experience. One
convert reported, "I will always know that I am different." Others
feel that they are expected to wipe clean from their minds
any past experiences associated with Christianity, even happy
memories.

While over ninety percent of the converts studied were converting because of marriage to a Jew, presumably in the hope

of establishing a Jewish family, they feel they can never expect to be accepted into the larger family of the Jewish community, no matter how often they attend services, how fervently they pray, how deep their commitment to Judaism.

My own experiences have been different. I do feel at home being Jewish. And yet I can sympathize with the responses of my fellow converts, for I know how easy it would have been to feel as they report they feel after the hostile experiences I, too, have known.

At the time of my conversion, I was single, divorced, with a nine-year-old daughter to raise alone. I had turned to religious experience as a means of coping with the pain of daily existence. In Judaism, I found a way to express these feelings and a pattern of life and thought compatible with my own intellectual and emotional state. There was no immediate prospect for marriage, but I had dated several Jewish men and had many close friends who were Jewish. One of these friends, who himself felt cut off at the time from a full sense of his Jewishness, said to me very seriously, "Look, if you convert, there will always be people who will stare at you when you walk into the synagogue and will say, 'What's this *shiksa* doing here?' " The word struck hard, for words like shiksa and *goy* always hiss or groan with the force of centuries-old fear and hostility toward a gentile-dominated world which necessitated defensiveness. . . .

Judaism as a larger whole and as a way of life had much more to offer in a positive way, I decided, than the hostility I might receive from some individuals in the Jewish community. To commit myself to Judaism and to value actively my participation in religious and social expression, I would have to refuse to be rejected.

To *refuse* rejection is by no means easy. I do not mean by this a passive turning of the other cheek, a stance which strikes me as basically alien to Jewish thought and tradition. That was only a first step, a holding action, so to speak. As one convert reported in Huberman's study, even regular attendance at Jewish services did not deter some Jews, who never entered a synagogue, from saying: "Once a goy, always a goy." . . .

In light of my experience, these are my suggestions to other converts:

1. Find Jewish friends with educated hearts. There are many

who will accept you because they have learned to accept themselves and to value their own Jewishness.

2. Pursue Jewish activities you can participate in comfortably and wholeheartedly. In my first basic Hebrew class, I met several Jewish people who were in adult life growing toward a desire to participate more fully in their religion and were learning Hebrew for the first time, as I was. We could share the difficulties in learning the language, but we could also share an appreciation of Judaism. There were Jewish singles activities in my area and, at an informal lecture series, I met my future husband. My teaching adult classes has become a significant part of my life.

3. Recognize your anger when you have difficulty fitting in. There will be times when this happens. Slowly, it dawned on me that not even all rabbis have educated hearts. I had to learn to deal with my anger realistically. Sometimes, it made more sense to withdraw from people or groups who were abrasive. I learned that questions about why I converted were not always invitations to bare my soul. You won't withdraw in anger if you are aware of what you might encounter.

4. Take time to explain to non-Jewish friends and to your family the reasons why you have converted, and be careful to do this in a way that does not denigrate their choices. Continue to send holiday cards and presents to them if that has been your habit, and maintain the same close contact, recognizing that *you* have changed.

5. Appreciate the good experiences you have and forget the rest.

> *Note:* There is no doubt that rejection is an emotion new converts will almost certainly have to confront, and for which they should be prepared. Dr. Friedman's suggestions are good ones. Please know that "goy" is not a term of opprobrium. It means "nation" and, in the technical sense in the Bible, it is properly applied *only* to the Jewish nation. It follows then, as you will read later, that the only real goy is a Jew!

—ML

JEWISH SON, GENTILE MOTHER
Edward Finnegan

Edward is a bright person who publishes books and lives in a university community in the Midwest. He married into a prominent Jewish family. He converted to Judaism and his brother followed suit. A portion of his family history unfolds in the following quotation from a letter he sent me. He is very sensitive and committed to the Jewish people, as is his wife.

. . . Some background on my family: My father was born in New York City to Jewish parents. They were non-religious—no one went to Hebrew School, and my father does not even know his Hebrew name (or if he was even given one). I think his father fancied himself an atheist. I learned that in her later years my paternal grandmother began going to the synagogue. In the last month of 1987, I met, for the first time, one of my father's cousins. He informed me that he had become a Christian and had gone so far as to study for the Episcopal priesthood! So much for Jewish roots.

My mother was raised in rural Oregon. Several of her ancestors were Protestant ministers. My father met my mother during World War II when he was stationed in Oregon. . . . While my father was Jewish, there was nothing Jewish in my childhood. Jews were the people in the first half of the Bible. About the only thing I can remember that had any Jewish content was my younger brother's obsession with the Holocaust—he brought home a lot of books and I remember looking with horror at the photographs in them.

My marriage: Sarah must have told me early on in our dating that she was Jewish. This didn't really have much of an impact on me. Although I was a philosophy graduate student and had an interest in religion, I had little appreciation of the great depth of social and cultural content of Judaism. I had this rather unsophisticated view of Judaism as being a theological variant of Christianity (i.e., everything but the New Testament).

In retrospect, I can see that Sarah's parents were, to put it mildly, dismayed at her interest in this non-Jewish boy. They were always courteous to me, but I am sure they were praying that this whole relationship would just disappear. . . .

At the time, I did not sufficiently appreciate how upset Sarah's parents were with the prospects of our getting married. Because I had been raised in a family in which religious belief had played a rather minor role, I could not recognize how important these matters could be to other people (especially Orthodox Jews who had survived the war). . . .

The *prospect* of conversion was quite acceptable to me; the *reality* of the conversion was quite another matter.

For some unknown reason, I had not been circumcised at birth. Even though it was a routine practice in my day and nearly every other male I knew had been circumcised, my parents did not do it. Sarah's father informed me that in order to convert, I would have to undergo circumcision. The prospect of surgery was not at all pleasing to me. I offered to convert to Reform Judaism (just cut off a little, please), but this was totally unacceptable.

The social, philosophical, theological and cultural aspects of becoming a Jew (as far as I could appreciate them at the time) did not trouble me at all. Conversion, for me, became a medical concern with all the attendant problems that the prospect of any surgery entailed. Although I studied for conversion with a rabbi, the subject uppermost in my mind was the fear, pain and uncertainty of an operation. . . .

My parents have never indicated to me any disapproval with my conversion and have always spoken with real affection for Sarah. However, there is no doubt that my conversion (and my brother's later conversion) has never been a matter that my mother has been able to understand or to be entirely happy with. For her, given her upbringing in a rural western community, Jews have always seemed foreign—outsiders. She may well have, initially, seen our conversion as being some sort of rebellious phase, a rejection by the children of the parents.

There has always been an undercurrent of hostility in her attitude regarding things Jewish. This hostility only surfaced since our marriage. By and large, it is exhibited in little throw-away nasty comments: "Oh, do you people put cheese on your pork chops?" etc. Even after all these years of marriage and after having Jewish customs explained by me, my brother, my wife and my father, she still tosses these things out.

The focus of all my mother's hostilities and anger has been on the Christmas holidays. Initially, Sarah and I would go to my parents' house on Christmas day where they exchanged gifts and had a big dinner. I must emphasize that Christmas

has never been a particularly religious holiday for my parents—
no talk of religious matters, no manger scene, no baby Jesus,
etc. For them (or for my mother, since she is the dominant
force in the household), it is a family holiday and time for gift-
giving, a tree, lights, an elaborate dinner, etc.

After a few years of these visits to my parents' house, Sarah
became increasingly uncomfortable. She felt that by visiting
my parents on this day, we were somehow, ourselves, celebrating a Christian holiday. Sarah's discomfort became a source
of conflict in our marriage. Although I had no desire to celebrate
this holiday, I felt that Christmas was important to my parents
and that our refusal to be with them on that date would be
interpreted by them as a real affront. All of this put me in
a most uncomfortable (and stressful) position: I was a Jew,
my wife was a Jew, and we did not celebrate this Christian
holiday. On the other hand, my mother was not Jewish and
did celebrate Christmas and, moreover, had a deep emotional
involvement in celebrating this day. I recognized at that time
that Christmas had become, for my parents (or, rather, for
my mother), more than a holiday—it had become the focus
for them of a lot of unresolved problems and hostilities that
they had with their sons and with their daughters-in-law. I found
it exceedingly difficult to walk the line between respect for my
parents and things that they might find important in their lives
and my religion and the feelings of my wife. . . .

At this point, the problem of Christmas appears to have
been resolved: we don't go to their house for the holiday, but
we do call them and wish them a happy holiday and we do
go visit them before the first of January.

> *Note:* Edward's deep sincerity, his respect for his parents with
> whom he disagrees, and his love for his wife, Sarah, are very
> evident from his full letter. Both of Edward's deep concerns are
> replicated in most converts. The apostle Paul dispensed with
> circumcision because of this very difficulty in gaining new con-
> verts. The problem of the Christmas conflict affects virtually every
> convert, and is discussed in the Responsa chapter, Part IV.
>
> —ML

I JUST KEPT LOSING MY PLACE

Kathy Tennell-Wanderer

Kathy is a deep-thinking, deep-feeling woman who was married to a prominent Jewish psychologist in Venice, California, when she wrote this letter. She was planning to settle in Israel and make it her permanent residence. Since that time, she has divorced and decided to remain in the United States.

My non-Jewish family and friends were tremendously supportive and encouraging about my decision to convert to Judaism. I am fortunate. I know it doesn't always happen that way, and my husband and I have really put our family and friends through the test—we are planning to emigrate to Israel. Though I know our loved ones don't look forward to our departure, they are still very supportive, and I think they look forward to visiting us there.

During the year's span before my final conversion, my family and friends were eager to know what I was learning and how it applied to my life. They really made it easy for me to develop and present my Jewish identity. My brother gave me the Star of David I wear around my neck. My close Catholic friends were present during my final conversion and later on surprised me and my husband with a beautiful wooden, hand-carved, Seder plate [the large Passover plate on which are placed the many symbols of the departure from Egypt] that they made themselves. To this day these same good friends call to wish us "Happy Shabbat."

Quite frankly, I have always found it terribly interesting that the only negative responses we have received concerning our choice of an Orthodox life-style has come from two Jewish friends. Neither of them is religiously observant; but they are Jews. It seemed to me the more my husband and I developed our religious life-style, the more uncomfortable it made these people feel and eventually we drifted apart.

Finding a place for myself within the Jewish community and being comfortable in the synagogue was a gradual process and took a lot of practice and time. Although I was learning Hebrew, I wasn't able to follow the service without getting completely lost, even in English. I was also a stranger to the community and not always able to sit next to someone I knew who understood my dilemma and could show me the place in the prayerbook. I was uncomfortable asking for constant help if I didn't know the person next to me. So I would stare blankly at the pages, stand up and sit down with everyone else, and go through the motions. It was only in these situations that I found I didn't want to disclose the fact that I was a convert. I was afraid someone might say "You don't belong here." Of course, that never happened—it was just my own fear. And after all, I was there to talk to God. Only I couldn't concentrate; I just kept losing my place. After several frustrating attempts at attending synagogue, I told myself that I had satisfactorily completed my conversion and—as I was practicing Judaism at home—was a bona-fide Jew. However, I knew that I had need for further study.

I bought a copy of Rabbi Donin's *To Pray as a Jew* and with the understanding and help of my husband, I began to learn how to pray. I studied the services for daily and Sabbath prayers and, when a holiday approached, I would study those special services. In this way, I prepared myself for going to the synagogue. I learned when to stand, how and when to bow—but, most important, I learned where these prayers came from and what they meant.

It's been three years since my conversion and the days of feeling alone and overwhelmed. I have developed wonderful friendships within my community and continue to study so that my Hebrew has improved. I attend synagogue regularly and can walk into the sanctuary without a feeling of dread. I still lose my place occasionally, as *everyone* does, but I pray to God, and I take my time and if I have a particular thought or a special prayer to put forth, then I depart from the service and join in again later.

The turning point came for me in synagogue one Sabbath morning as I noticed the woman next to me nervously turning the pages of her prayerbook with trembling hands. I gently touched her arm and then pointed to the page number in my own prayerbook. From that moment, I followed each word on every page with my finger until the end of the service. I could tell right away she had relaxed and was following along with me. When the service was over, she hugged me and said that she had not been to synagogue in many years and because I had helped her she felt comfortable and at home again. Could

she sit beside me again next Sabbath? Now, there is no doubt—
I belong.

> *Note:* Kathy's concern about not feeling comfortable in the
> synagogue when you first convert is an authentic, understandable
> feeling replicated in virtually every new convert, and also in many
> old-time born Jews. She overcame it the only way it can be
> overcome—by study and the support of friends. Also a common
> feeling: when you try to follow a traditional Jewish life, non-
> observant Jewish friends, as well as non-Jews, might very well
> not understand.

—ML

THE LONG, WINDING SEARCH
FOR THE TRUTH

Richard Kajut

> Richard Kajut, formerly a Protestant minister, is now living
> in the deep South as a committed Jew. He is not only perceptive
> in terms of his conversion, but very creative. His poetry on Jewish
> spiritual issues has been published extensively by *The Jewish
> Spectator*.

The decision to break with my former Christian faith was
the culmination of a lengthy process of religious search and
intensive self-examination of my personal beliefs. There was
no flash of lightning which prompted my choice to convert.
Ironically, it was the desire to know more about the character
of Jesus the man, the historical Jesus, which eventually led
to the renunciation of my Christian heritage.

I had been active in the Church during my youthful and
adolescent years. When I reached my high-school years, I began
to harbor some vague notions of suspicion about the credibility
of the theological concept of the Trinity—God in three persons—and, more specifically, how the Master of the Universe
could manifest Himself, completely, so to speak, in this man
called Jesus. The seeds of my disaffection had begun to sprout.

During my college years, I spent many spare hours in the
religion stacks of the university library pulling texts on the "historical" Jesus. Schweitzer led me to R. H. Charles, Charles
to Albright, and Albright to A. Powell Davies. I graduated soon

to Joseph Klausner and Abba Hillel Silver. . . . A whole new world of understanding the *zeitgeist* of the early first century opened before my eyes: apocryphal and pseudepigraphal theology, the Roman occupation, Greek mystery religions, Sadducees, centrist Pharisees, apocalyptic Pharisees, Essenes, Zealots, Hillel and Shammai. . . . If I was to serve the one God of Moses and the Prophets in the manner I was drawn to Him, I could do it only as a Jew. Like *Avraham Avinu*, Abraham, our Father, by rational inquiry, I had come full circle to the doorstep of the *Ribbono shel Olam*, the Master of the Universe. . . .

The first Jewish service Cathy and I ever attended was a Yom Kippur service in a small Reform temple. We were not, at that time, attuned to the all important distinctions between the Reform, Conservative, and Orthodox movements. The temple was, at any rate, the only center of Jewish activity in the small town to which we had recently moved.

The service was starkly simple and "comfortable" for us, even as Christian strangers. Mixed seating, the absence of much Hebrew, and hospitable congregants, made it not too unlike our familiar church setting. There were just enough of the trappings of our naive expectations of a synagogue to give the service a distinctive Jewish flavor—such as the Ark of the Torah (*Aron Kodesh*), the candelabrum (*menorah*), and pulpit (*bimah*), and the superb ethical selections in the prayerbook with prayers devoted exclusively to God Almighty and no other. This is what we had come looking for—but not for long.

We spent one year undergoing our Reform conversion. We learned to read a little Hebrew, superficially studied the high points of the Jewish calendar year, and comprehensively covered 4,000 years of Jewish history. . . .

Six months after our conversion, we began to wonder. . . . Our final decision to take a hard look at what Orthodox Jewish living meant came when a close friend of ours from a more traditional Jewish background informed us we could never be accepted as Jews by the religious authorities in the State of Israel with a Reform conversion. This was our first encounter with the "Who is a Jew" question. We had never been informed that in the eyes of the Halakhah and Orthodox Jewry, we still were not Jewish. We had come to identify ourselves as such, and now we learned our identity was transparent. . . .

Fortunately, our Reform rabbi was a sensitive and unusual

person. We explained to him our growing sense of dissatis-
faction with the intangible dimensions of Reform Jewish living
and our desire to know what Orthodoxy demanded of potential
converts to really be considered Jews. He immediately directed
us to a dynamic young rabbi in a neighboring city. We were
on the road to a Torah-true life-style, never to look back again.

Devekut, cleaving, embracing. I cannot think of a more apt
description of the unfulfilled longing I had so as to be able
to link the waking hours of my day with God's intimate Divine
direction. Although I cannot truthfully say that I fully understood
the dimensions of the halakhic demands on the observant Jew,
I can truthfully say that I consciously sought the structure of
the Halakhah to physically put me in touch with the parameters
of living with *kedushah*, holiness. I wanted the possibility of
maintaining an ongoing relationship with God from the moment
I parted my eyelids in the morning until I closed them in sleep
in the late hours of the night. I do not pretend to have been
able to live up to all of the inherent possibilities the Halakhah
affords the Jew to "walk with God." Many years of learning
and striving are still in store for me, and the rest of my life
will be spent in pursuit of this ideal. But isn't that what it is
all about?

Question: Did Cathy and I experience any difficulties in being
accepted by the Jewish community?

Absolutely and unequivocally, no. Cordiality and curiosity
gave way to open embracing and encouragement as soon as
our fellow congregants discerned our honest commitment and
devotion to Judaism. I believe with all my heart that an individual
only takes away from a relationship what he or she gives of
himself or herself to it. . . .

Converts should also try to learn to be graciously forbearing
with more unlearned friends, congregants and neighbors who
sometimes may unintentionally slight or embarrass them with
questions or remarks concerning his or her non-Jewish background. The curious and prying as well as the honestly interested (often at inopportune moments such as a social
gathering) will always be with us. These are the keys to
successful integration which must be kept in hand for a lifetime
of service.

Question: Was circumcision a difficult or painful process in
the conversion?

No. I was already circumcised and only required a *hatafat*

dam b'rit [the symbolic re-circumcision by drawing a droplet of blood for the purpose of entering the Covenant of Abraham]. It brought only a minor, short-lived discomfort. I expected more pain and embarrassment than I experienced. When I was undergoing this process in the steps toward becoming a Jew, I had the distinct feeling that all involved were engaged in a holy task, which alleviated any sense of personal awkwardness.

Following is one of many poems by Richard Kajut that appeared in *The Jewish Spectator*:

Jew That I Am
I live absurdly,
Jew that I am.
Camus would marvel at me.
Beckett should write me in a play.
Shabbat, Mashiach,
Tefillin, my prayers;
Kashrut and mikveh,
Fasting appointed days.
And even beyond these,
transcendent, unexplained,
my love for a land
and an ancient walled city,
my lean, hungry eyes
never seen.
I am a servant of the ages.
Part of a people with a dream.
A Jew living absurdly
in love with his God.

Note: Richard Kajut is a gifted young man and an ardent idealist. Few people can duplicate his odyssey with such conviction. Also, few people can handle rejection with such ease, unless supported by such idealism. What most converts do finally learn is that even friendly, well-intentioned people can cause awkward and embarrassing situations.

—ML

ON NOT BEING HALF AND HALF
Miriam D.

Miriam D. was born and lives in the Philippines where a gentile girl's becoming Jewish requires much more courage than almost any other place on earth. The handful of Jews live in a sea of Christian, Muslim and Far Eastern religions. To adopt the Jewish faith is to be willing to become an outsider, to be suddenly vulnerable in a closed community of tightly-knit old friends and intertwined families. Nonetheless, Miriam's decision to convert and then to join her husband and in-laws (with the help of an American rabbi's wife) in making an elaborate, kosher wedding appeared to be a natural and unremarkable social event. She is married to M., a born Jew, who also was raised in the islands and whose family members are very highly-respected citizens.

I come from a Catholic family living in the Philippines. We went to Mass together as a family until I was over twenty. Later, however, my sister and I would continue going to Mass with my parents primarily on holidays. I was considered the more religious of the two, so when I told my parents that I wanted to convert to Judaism, they could not understand why I had to do this. Their reaction was not simple anger—but just as any parents who worry over and want the best for their child are angered and frustrated when they see the child wanting to change the parents' religion. They questioned themselves: Where did we go wrong? I calmly told them that I wanted to marry M. and that it was very important for me to convert, so that we could have only *one* religion in our future home. My mother then turned to me and said, "Well, if you are going to be Jewish—be a *good* Jew. Don't be half-and-half. Be a whole Jew." I knew it. I got their blessing.

On our first Christmas after the conversion, my relatives asked me all types of questions—Could they invite us to dinner? Could they give us presents? etc.—as they really wanted to do the right thing. To date, we still go to my aunt's house for the Christmas eve dinner. My husband always brings fireworks to entertain the children until it is time for them to open their presents. My family and relatives have been very good about respecting our beliefs and religion to the extent of preparing special fish or dairy meals on dishes especially reserved for us at our gatherings. We have not felt any pressure from them as I have always answered their questions directly from the start. On Christmas day, my parents go to Mass on their own, pick us up afterward, and we all go to an eggnog party with family and friends. . . .

My first shul experience: The first time I went to synagogue was my most frightening experience! M. and I had already made arrangements with the rabbi for my lessons. I was going to start after Pesach. However, the rabbi suggested to M. to start bringing me to the services to acquaint myself with the holidays that were coming up. So, one day, M. announces that we are going to synagogue—for Purim, the Feast of Esther! He mentioned that the children would come dressed in costumes as is customary on this happy holiday. No other specifics were told me. There I was, very serious and attentive, watching everything going on during the service when all of a sudden everyone started making weird noises—actually, while the prayers were going on! I could not understand this! I asked myself: How in heaven can anyone pray here with all this commotion? To be honest, I was in shock and thought this was really the Jewish way of praying. I am not sure a convert should start shul with Purim!

I never experienced anyone in the Jewish community giving me a feeling that I was "not accepted" as a Jew. However, strangely, I have felt this from my non-Jewish friends and associates. Many have told me that to them I am not a real Jew because I am a convert.

My kosher Philippine wedding: To have a kosher wedding meal served for 400 guests where I live is like asking for the moon and stars. For one thing, it was difficult arranging for live chickens to be delivered to the synagogue for kosher ritual slaughter—but anything is possible if one wants it to be possible—especially if God wants it, too. I am fortunate to have a mother who works in a private bank restaurant that operates from Monday to Friday. Since our wedding fell on a Sunday evening, we had the whole of Saturday night, after the Sabbath ended, to clean and burn the ovens of the kitchen to make them kosher. The rabbi, with the help of the cooks, did exactly that and, on Sunday, the cooking was done and supervised. The food was then transported to the Polo Club, which also provided new dishes, and the wedding was on "go." The Yacht Club, where the wedding was held, earned great ratings for the food they served that evening, better than the usual non-kosher meals they serve! My wedding cake was made from Crisco vegetable shortening as we cannot get parve [non-dairy] butter here. To be honest, it wasn't that fantastic, but, by the time we cut the cake, everyone, including us, was in high spirits and nobody paid attention to the cake but to the Jewish dancing and the merrymaking of a typical Jewish wedding—not so typical in an Asian island on the brink of storm.

> *Note:* Conversion, even in such an unlikely place as the Philippines, can be intelligently facilitated by cooperative, understanding families. But even such families need strong-willed and committed young principals. This is a graphic demonstration of "Where there is a will, there is a way."
>
> —ML

ON BEING CALLED "CONVERT"

Mary Lynn Kotz

Mary Lynn Kotz is the author of several books including *Upstairs at the White House: Passion for Quality, George Wiley and the Movement* (with her husband, Nick Kotz) and *Marvella: A Personal Journey*, as well as numerous magazine articles.

This selection first appeared in *Moment* magazine, in an article entitled "Jews by Choice," p. 29, based on a conference for Jews by choice in Manhattan.

. . . "We knew," they said, "that this was what we needed and wanted. It was like coming home." And person after person repeated that phrase, which I had thought was mine alone: "coming home."

There was pain in our stories, too. Everybody kept remarking, with some surprise, about the similarity of their feelings, saying "Yes, that happened to me. . . . I didn't know anyone else felt that way." Another theme began to emerge: "I felt so alone."

We talked about feeling unwelcome, at first. About rabbis who discouraged us at the outset. Some of us were rejected by our own families. (Some of us were afraid to *tell* our families.) And many were not accepted by the family of the spouse who was born a Jew.

Most of us hated the word "convert." "I do not want to

be forever thought of as a convert," one woman said. "I am a Jew." And that rang a bell with me. We all want to be accepted. We all want to be thought of as "no different." Your people are my people. . . .

As voiced by the group of Jews by choice in New York and borne out by statistical studies conducted by the UAHC, the most far-reaching and difficult problem the Jew by choice must face is the second-class status he or she is often accorded by the Jewish community—the fact that many born Jews have trouble thinking of the convert as a "real" Jew.

How painful it is for us to hear the word "goy." It implies an outsider, who can never become one of us. It refers to my brothers, whom I love. Many times I have heard it wrongly applied to me. (I wonder, when they call me "shiksa," if they know that the word "shiksa" means "abomination"?)

And how many times have I heard, from born Jews—whom my rabbi calls "Jews-by-chance"—"Why on earth would you want to become Jewish? Jews have suffered too much." . . .

But I knew nothing about contemporary Judaism. I didn't know I could "get in." Ever since my childhood, I had *known* I was a Jew. What I didn't know was that you don't have to be Jewish . . . to be Jewish. I later discovered that I was not alone; most people, including many Jews, think of Judaism as a closed society.

Most Jews think of themselves as having been *born* Jewish. And most believe that "Jews do not seek out converts." Because of that statement, and the way it has become embedded in the lore of our people, many people have no idea that a person can *become* Jewish.

Not knowing the dreadful historical reasons for Jews not reaching out—the edict of Constantine, the Crusades, the Inquisition—non-Jews have come to feel that they are excluded, that they are not welcome.

And that's too bad—not only because Judaism is such a rational, viable, sensible religion, but also because the seeds of anti-Semitism are often sown in feeling excluded. And in feeling envy.

Jews used to reach out. From the very beginning, reaching out to seek and welcome converts was an active part of the Jewish tradition.

There is an old Rabbinic statement, "Where were the Ten Commandments given?"

"In the desert."

"Why in the desert?"

"The desert unreels. Open. Free to everyone. So is the Torah. It is there; it is open to everyone."

. . . "According to the Rabbis, Moses had ten names. Of all those ten, why did He call him Moses? The Rabbis wrote, "Because the name 'Moses' was given to him by Pharaoh's daughter, Beta, who became a convert. And because of that, the name 'Moses' is more precious to God than the other names."

Even in the fourth century, after the edict of Constantine proclaimed Christianity to be the official religion of the Roman Empire, Jews continued to reach out for converts—and risk capital punishment. And during talmudic times, the Rabbis were favorable both to conversion and to converts.

We who chose Judaism were called "those who seek shelter under the shade of God." And the Rabbis wrote that "they shall flourish like corn, they shall blossom like wine." Another verse: "More precious to me are the names given by converts than all the wine that was poured on the altar of the Temple."

But during the Crusades, and again beginning about the fifteenth century all over Europe, to seek converts became impossibly dangerous, and a new Jewish tradition was born— that of *not* reaching out. When Jews today say, "Jews don't seek out converts," they forget that it was only the cruelest of repression that stopped the practice. . . .

> *Note:* Again we read of the discomfort caused by legitimate fears of not being accepted. It is entirely likely that this is a problem that will be solved in time, especially considering the growing openness of our society and large number of new Jews. Perhaps, also, as Ms. Kotz avers, Jews could help this process along by not calling Jews by choice "converts."

—ML

BEING HONEST WITH YOURSELF
IS NEVER CHEAP

Bruce James

Bruce James is a free-lance writer in Washington, D.C. The
following excerpt is taken from the *Baltimore Jewish Times*
article, "Jewish by Choice."

"You're a convert? Gee. That's interesting. If you don't mind
my asking, why did you do it?"

I suppose every convert to Judaism is asked the question
and I've gotten used to it, but there is another comment I
often hear that is disturbing:

"You're a convert? There must have been a girl."

Oy!

A lot of people just can't believe that there is something
in the Jewish religion worth having—something that someone
from the accepted, middle-class WASP world would want. So
when a Jewish person makes this comment, I have to be patient
and explain why I converted and how much value there is
in being Jewish.

I doubt that my parents will ever understand why I converted.
All they see now is a yarmulka on the head of a son who's
not the same person they watched grow up.

But I am the same person. Yes, I keep my head covered,
pray three times a day, put on *tefillin* [phylacteries on head
and arm worn by men during weekday prayers to symbolize
God's lordship over our minds and hands, thoughts and actions]
keep a kosher home and stomach, keep Shabbat [the Sabbath]
strictly, and observe other laws that, in my parents' eyes, link
me with the most fanatic and backward cults in the world.
When I come home, it's not as if their son came home, rather
it's as if they received a visit from someone from another planet.

Still, it is doubtful that I could have become an Orthodox
Jew without the important training I received at home. My
parents gave me a firm belief in God, a dedication to honesty
and consistency, and a love for all people. Without these values,
I would have been lost in an agnostic world full of contradictions
and ethical conflicts.

I was sixteen when I decided to become a Jew. But, even

at fourteen or fifteen, I was very religious, active in my church and giving thought to someday becoming a minister as had my great-great-grandfather. I was developing ideas that were different from standard Christian doctrine: not knowing any alternative, though, I decided to use them in a Christian context.

But all that changed one Friday night. My church confirmation class made a field trip to the synagogue in my hometown, Colorado Springs, Colorado. After the service, the rabbi stayed on and answered our questions.

One student asked if the color of the rabbi's skullcap meant anything. No, he said. He has one to match his blue suit and others to match different articles of clothing. Another person asked him why they had somebody else (a cantor) sing the service. "Because he has a better voice than I have," he answered quickly with a grin.

But I was cocky, and still believing that Jesus was Messiah, I baited the rabbi:

"Has the Messiah come yet?" I asked.

"No," he said. "Look at all the suffering in the world."

"When will he come?"

"Certainly not until we get better for him."

"Then why should he come?"

"Exactly."

I was stunned. Obviously, his answers to my questions were brief and oversimplified. But he hit me with one of my own theories that had no source in Christian doctrine: man plays a key role in the salvation of the world. The world is not doomed to destruction, and man may be, ultimately, perfectible.

I continued my studies of the New Testament. I was disturbed that the enlightenment of Jesus was fizzled by the narrow-minded doctrine of the Apostle Paul. Yet, when I finished my confirmation training, I was at the top of my class. On a test of Bible knowledge, the average score was twenty to forty points. I scored an eighty-eight, double the next highest.

Then my minister asked everyone in my class to write a statement of faith. This would be used when the church elders considered our applications for membership in the Presbyterian Church.

I prepared my paper with the same glee that Martin Luther must have had when he wrote his attack on the Catholic Church. First, I attacked the way the Jewish ideas of Jesus had been cast away by Paul and other Church leaders and substituted with customs and values from pagan religions—often without benefit of any symbolic tie-in—all to make Christianity more marketable. Then I attacked the dualism of Christianity. The devil got the blame for everything, I wrote with tongue in cheek, but where would Christianity be without the devil? What would motivate people to do good if not for the threat of eternal damnation?

One of the elders eventually read my piece. He told me that I had some interesting ideas. And he recommended me for membership. I couldn't believe it. Didn't the Church have any standards? I should have refused membership at that point. But, at the time, I felt I really had no choice but to accept.

One day, I just stopped going to church. But that didn't send me to the synagogue. I didn't know anything about Judaism. But I did know that I didn't like the way Christianity had developed. In my mind, what had begun as a Jewish cult, in a short time, became a religion that preached love and fought wars.

One day, just by accident, I started reading Chaim Potok's *My Name is Asher Lev.* Although some people call the book anti-Jewish, I became captivated with the idea that Jews have laws and live by them. That little bit of inspiration sent me back through history to learn at what point Christianity had abandoned Jewish values, what Jewish values it had abandoned, and why Jews have persisted in maintaining these values for 2,000 years. Before long, I was telling people—actually promising people—that I would become a Jew.

People ask me when I first knew I had to be Jewish. I don't remember any one particular event. I have a feeling that there was a voice talking to me every night as I slept telling me that I was destined to become a Jew. The more I heard it, the more convinced I became.

I really do believe that I was meant to be a Jew. There is a Hasidic thought that all righteous converts were at Mt. Sinai with every other Jew, born and unborn. . . .

Being honest with yourself and consistent to your principles is never cheap. I had to give up my dream of being a newspaper reporter because American newspapers don't hire people who can't cover a breaking story whenever it happens. [If it happens on the Sabbath, one may not violate the holiness of the day.] And I've had to risk breaking up the good relationship I've had with my parents. Although there is great tension, fortunately I am still on speaking terms with them.

The conflict with my parents came to a head one night when they visited me. My mother was crying as she asked me if the Bible said I was supposed to honor them. "You've rejected your religion. You've given up your career. I suppose next you'll reject your country [and leave for Israel]. When are you going to reject us?"

It's hard to deal with such arguments. They come from an emotional level it's best for me to stay away from. The Torah says that, even if your parents do not observe God's commandments or even curse God, you are never to show disrespect to them. So I listened to them as they vented their frustrations and kept quiet most of the night. I did explain to them my problem. I can't break God's commandments in order to honor them. It may disturb them that I won't eat their food from their plates. But I can't change that law just to please them.

But still I love them. . . . My father and mother taught me how to love all kinds of people . . . to give freely of myself and of my possessions. In a way, they gave me my first lessons in the laws of *tzedakah*, charity. Because of it, I'm a better Jew.

Many Jews have come to me and said that I know so much more than the average Jew. I don't see that as a point of pride; in fact, I find it very sad. When I was studying with my rabbi, I was sure that I knew enough to be converted. But my rabbi waited. I think his goal was to convert me when he was sure I knew enough that I realized that I needed to learn a lot more Torah.

Finally, I went to the mikveh to be immersed in its waters and complete my conversion, and I felt elation and joy I've never felt before. Many people will never understand why. But, all at once, I had the very positive feeling of completing one difficult assignment successfully, and having another challenging assignment before me. The Boss liked my work and now He was giving me a new challenge He knew I could handle.

Thanks for Your faith in me and all of us.

Note: Bruce James demonstrates a clear-minded, arrow-straight progression from the early teens to adulthood, overcoming all obstacles. What is disturbing is his relationship with his parents. He is thankful for their values, and dutiful in respecting them, yet he is true to his own self. Is there not some way to make the process less painful?

—ML

I DO NOT MISS ANY RELIGIOUS ASPECT
Karen S.

Karen hails from the Midwest, is university-trained and is married to an attorney who is a born Jew, the son of two Holocaust survivors. Both come from different, but very well-established families.

. . . Neither my family nor I were exactly what you would call Christian before I converted. We were Christian by heritage only—we never went to church, and never practiced religion at home. We celebrated Christmas as a family holiday without any real religious meaning, much as we celebrate Thanksgiving.

Christmas, however, has been a bit difficult for me. I do not at all miss celebrating Christmas in my own home. But, because it is a time of year when my family gets together, I miss being a part of that. We haven't found it convenient to travel to Wisconsin (where my parents live) at that time because we usually go to Los Angeles to my husband's family for Hanukkah. I do not miss any religious aspect of Christmas, because we never had that, but even now I miss the family get-together. Easter, on the other hand, is no problem: there is nothing to miss. We never went to church on Easter, which I understand even the least devout Christians usually do. . . .

One of the first services I attended was in a small Orthodox shul in Georgetown. I loved the atmosphere. It was casual; children were running around, and people were more or less independently going through their prayers. It felt comfortable—like a family. . . .

I feel very accepted by the Jewish community. My Jewishness doesn't seem to be an issue at all. Our kids go to a Jewish nursery school and everyone just assumes we are all Jewish. It happens to be a Conservative synagogue, and very often I know more about Judaism and its laws than other parents. . . .

I have one funny story about the reaction of a friend of my

parents when he was told I converted and married a Jew. This friend happens to be Chinese and, when he heard I was Jewish, he said: "Well, that's a very good thing—Jews are the Chinese of the west." He was giving Jews credit for being as smart and resourceful as the Chinese!

> *Note:* Karen is spared some of the problems of conversion because she had no early involvement with religious practice. She has converted from a secular Christianity to a traditional Judaism.

> —ML

I HAD NOT THE SLIGHTEST TREMOR OF RELIGION

Roger Owen

> Roger Owen is an Englishman who works as a journalist for the BBC. His conversion odyssey is in part unlike most others and is worthy of being read by prospective candidates. The superbly written piece that follows was excerpted from an article in *Commentary*, November 1987, "Becoming a Jew." It generated both an angry and a laudatory response. Whatever the reader believes about the validity of Owen's methods or insights is not as important as the problems and ideas he raises. This selection is not included as instruction for the convert, so much as for sensitizing the reader and preparing them for this possible scenario.

One morning in the summer of 1978, and in the manner prescribed by Jewish law, I became a Jew. Such an event is something one does not easily forget, and in my case the occasion was made especially memorable by its setting and circumstances.

My conversion took place in New York during my first visit to the United States. The final ceremony was performed somewhere in the Flatbush area of Brooklyn, in a neighborhood with an evidently large population of Orthodox Jews—not the kind of district which British visitors normally have cause to seek out.

And because, among other formalities required by Jewish law, it included a ritual immersion, that ceremony was held in the local mikveh, or ritual bathhouse, which was also a new and strange environment for me to find myself in. Finally, some of the things which happened there that morning, though no doubt routine occurrences to the three rabbis who supervised my conversion, struck me at the time as being extraordinary and mystifying.

Nine years later, however, it is not only the exotic or alien nature of that experience which makes it stay in my mind. I was to discover that the actual process of my conversion had engaged my interest and also aroused my feelings in ways which beforehand I would not have thought possible.

The project, I have to say, was one about which I had felt not the slightest tremor of religious or transcendental sentiment. Nor did it at any stage engender such emotions. I had undertaken it with reluctance, only to meet the needs of my future wife's parents, who had been literally sickened at the prospect of her marrying a non-Jew. I approached the matter, therefore, with diffidence and embarrassment—indeed with some sense, from my own point of view, of its absurdity. Yet, to my surprise, the nature of the experience itself was such that these feelings were changed into interest and respect—into admiration for the three rabbis, and what they stood for. It would be overdoing things to say that I came to mock, and stayed to pray. But in the days that followed my conversion—once I had found time to make sense of the multiplicity of impressions the event had made on me—I realized that it had contained meanings and expressed truths which I had neither expected nor sought from it. In a dim, approximate, and unspiritual way, it had acquired a kind of authenticity.

At home in England, it seemed that a conversion to Judaism was certain to be a wearying and lengthy process, so I had decided to look elsewhere. Because of my misgivings about the propriety of what I was doing, I wanted to get the business over with quickly. . . .

In a way, the very speed of the act seems to me in retrospect to have been a necessary ingredient of its style, contributing to the powerful impact it made on me. The whole transaction, including its formal procedures, and the manner and spirit in which these were handled, was brisk and businesslike; its outward forms neatly and economically embodied the meanings I chose to draw from it. These I took to include certain perceptions about the world and about human behavior, which, in spite of their antiquity, I as a proselyte was to find novel and refreshing. They were unmistakably present that morning in the mikveh, in those events which I found—at the time—so bewildering. . . .

One day, my future wife's brother came to the hotel where I was staying. We sat in its courtyard drinking coffee. It was obvious that he, too, was in the role of emissary. . . . Could, therefore, the question of a conversion at least be discussed?

I went through the motions of argument. The children—were there to be any—would be Jewish anyway, as the offspring of a Jewish mother. We intended to live in Israel where a Jewish education would be guaranteed. How, anyway, could I promise to keep the Jewish obligations or mitzvot when my future wife (or he for that matter) was far from observant herself? Jewishness, I argued, was a condition, and not just a religion, one from which I was excluded by birth and national feeling. A conversion would imply beliefs which I did not hold. It would be a dishonest procedure, as his parents knew, without meaning to me and, in consequence, I felt it ought therefore to be of no significance to them. It would not change the real world.

My future brother-in-law ignored all this. He looked at me steadily. "Do it," he said with great vehemence and urgency. "Just do it." And then he added, in a tone of high moral seriousness as though his proposition would be self-evident to all good men, *"You don't have to believe it."* This remark would not, I imagine, meet with rabbinical approval, but it seems to me now that there was something very Jewish about it. He was asking me to perform a good deed, something which, in its way, could be construed as a mitzvah. Judaism, as far as I know, urges but does not demand that people *feel* good about doing good. . . .

Tutored by my future wife, I began a modest course of study. We read the *Shulchan Arukh*, Joseph Karo's sixteenth-century codification of Jewish law. I learned by heart a number of prayers and she explained the significance of the Jewish festivals. We dipped into Maimonides. As Passover was due, I was taken through the Haggadah, and I followed the first of the nine seders I have since attended with some understanding and interest. I was charmed by the way it involved children, and moved by the contemporary parallels which lay in its pages, and which, I supposed, had always done so. I realized too—to qualify the remarks I shall be making below about the appearance of the mikveh—that, for Jews, it is in domestic matters that religious and aesthetic feelings come together; for example, in the seder, or in the lighting of the Sabbath candles. . . .

Shortly afterward, we flew to New York. Two weeks later, I went to keep the appointment arranged for me at that mikveh.

On the morning concerned, I made my way to Flatbush by subway. I carried a briefcase which contained the accouterments required for the ceremony. These included a blue velvet yarmulka with silver trimmings, perhaps a shade frivolous, I felt, for so solemn an occasion. I also took with me a set of phylacteries, or tefillin, the ritual objects containing passages from Scripture with which observant Jews bind the left arm and head during prayer. These items were the property of my wife's nephew who had just had his Bar Mitzvah. The briefcase was my own, though it bore the letters "BBC" stamped over its lock. . . .

I had never seen the inside of a mikveh before (nor for that matter have I done so since) and so had little idea of what I would find there. This one was a small, single-story building of rather worn appearance. Naively, knowing of its religious purpose, I had half-expected to see there some signs or artifacts of an elevated or pious character—perhaps a menorah or some volumes of the Talmud. Inside, however, its anteroom was devoid of ornament. On its otherwise bare walls there was only a large notice which said "MIKVEH, $5.00—SPECIAL, $10.00."

In front of the notice was a row of massive and aging hair dryers. I was early, so I sat down to wait on a bench next to these silent machines. Judaism, I told myself, as I waited nervously for the three rabbis to arrive, pays little attention to those aesthetic concerns which, especially on solemn occasions, inform the practice of some more "spiritual" religions. I knew this in theory; now this utterly functional setting brought the idea home to me. A mikveh is a place used routinely by observant Jews—for example, by women for their monthly acts of cleansing and purification; hence, the hair dryers. This was indeed the place where I would be pronounced a Jew. The appearance of the mikveh, however, matched the events that followed, some of which were indeed prosaic in character. . . .

I was then taken—almost in escort—to the changing rooms where I was given a loose white gown of some linen-like material. Clad only in this, I made my way to a small tiled bath, and, under the direction of the rabbis, descended its steps and immersed myself three times in its waters. The rabbis stood in front of me on the side of the bath looking down at my actions with close interest. As my head rose out of the water for the third time, I could see from their gestures that a discussion had broken out, though from its vehemence, and in those acoustics, it sounded a bit like a fight. I looked up at them, fearful that something had gone badly wrong, and that my enterprise was in trouble even at this late stage.

"You touched the side," one of them at last explained brusquely. "We think you touched the side the last time, so you'll have to do it again." I did it again, this time satisfactorily. And then, or perhaps it was earlier (for the chronology of some of these events is now confused and dream-like), I stood with the waters of the mikveh up to my middle, and repeated in Hebrew after the presiding rabbi some of the prayers which my future wife had taught me by heart in the preceding weeks.

I was told to get dressed. I scrambled into my clothes. My hands were trembling. There was a mirror in the changing room and I looked at myself briefly with disbelief. I hurried back past the hair dryers and the large notice to where the rabbis were waiting. I opened my briefcase. A prayer shawl was placed on my shoulders, and somebody put the blue velvet yarmulka on my head. I saw that its style was a matter of indifference to them; it served. My head and left arm were now bound with phylacteries.

"You never laid tefillin before?" asked the old one incredulously, as he watched my nervous and muddled efforts to put them on in the prescribed manner. I had practiced several times the night before, but I lied (gratuitously, I am sure), mumbling something sanctimonious about not being sure that I had been entitled to do so—I was afraid of being exposed as the impostor I felt myself to be. Help was provided. The proceedings continued with more prayers, which I repeated adequately, conscious, though, of my English accent and again of the deep improbability of my appearance and situation. Suddenly, I found myself being congratulated. It was all over. . . .

In the days that followed, I began to realize that the ceremony I had just been through had confronted me baldly and without false delicacy with a way of looking at the world which was fundamentally different from my own and which, on inspection, turned out to have an enviable degree of power and coherence. Of course, I had done some reading in preparation for my conversion and was not completely ignorant, I thought, of the distinctive nature of Judaism. But those attitudes with which I had some modest theoretical familiarity now leaped at me. I had seen them reified in the appearance of the mikveh and witnessed them in performance in the behavior of the rabbis. The small crisis in the bath, and even their indifference to my fancy yarmulka—all these, it seemed to me, vividly asserted the same proposition, one which I had known intellectually, but had not so far really felt: in Judaism, obedience to the Law is what matters. In the weeks following the ceremony, that simple idea struck me with subversive force.

Perhaps, at the time, my own understanding of this notion was itself a simple-minded one. Bemused and in turn fascinated by the way the rabbis had devoted their attention to what seemed to me to be trivial matters, it is likely that I was making too much in my own mind of the prescriptive and behavioral elements in Judaism, and doing so, furthermore, at the expense of its spiritual content, its foundation in faith. I had perhaps taken the importance Judaism attaches to obedience to the Law, and accorded it a paramountcy even greater than that which it properly enjoys. I was thus myself seeing the religion in terms which were excessively mechanistic. What is more, in focusing just on the *idea* of obedience to the Law, and on that idea's psychological effects, I was scanting the Law's concrete substance, its myriad actual duties and obligations, its content and its rationale.

Still, this perspective, in spite of its distortions and over-simplifications, provided me with a means by which I could attempt to organize and "read" the events which had taken place. With some temerity, I found myself invoking what I judged to be a "Jewish" way of looking at things as I reflected on my recent experience. At a strict theological or scholarly level, what ensued in my mind, I dare say, is dubious or at least incomplete. Nevertheless, this was indeed the way in which I approached the matter. And it gave the whole business, to my own satisfaction at least, a certain coherence.

For example, the course of action I had undertaken had much about it which had seemed to me dishonest. Was I selling out? Had I compromised my integrity and been untrue to myself? Were the concessions I had made to my future wife's family unreasonably large ones? Was my action inspired by magnanimity and tolerance, or merely by an unprincipled desire to avoid trouble, the product of my weaknesses and not of my strengths?

All nonsense: so the conversion itself, the manner in which it had taken place, seemed to be telling me. Such preoccupations I now deemed to be non-Jewish. The inspections of my inner condition had been fruitless, since they had led to no serious outcomes in my behavior. I could have stopped the whole business at any time if I really had been deeply concerned by them, instead of trying to have it both ways. It occurred to me that my thoughts could be regarded from a behavioral point of view— and this, it seemed, was a point of view which my conversion so clearly expressed—as part of the surface noise or chatter which modern people feel obliged to emit, especially when they are uncertain of themselves, and wish to assert their uniqueness: a kind of posturing. *This* world, however, of which I had been given so compelling a glimpse, had no place for such fancies. It was clear and confident in its purposes—ones which I saw displayed with unaffected poise and assurance. The rabbis knew exactly what *they* were doing, and why. But it was not only the insidious attraction of their moral certainty that touched me. Their point of view, I realized, if I had understood it correctly, was a very intelligent one. . . .

It goes without saying that Judaism is grounded in the idea of a transcendental God, an idea which the Jews were indeed the first in history to promulgate and champion. But as a religious system, Judaism, I was convinced, is on the whole a matter more of law than of faith. Certainly in every tiny respect the conduct of my conversion seemed designed to fix this truth in my mind. Since obedience to the God-given Law is the first requirement, it follows that motives are of secondary importance, and so too is inwardness. Right behavior might lead to a desirable inner state, but it is anyway virtuous in itself.

The utility of this point of view made an impression on me. It was more theoretically elegant than, though very different from, some of the ideas on which I myself had been brought up. I thought, for example, of the Christian concept of pride— T. S. Eliot's characterization of Thomas a Becket, agonizing about doing the right thing for the wrong reason. So far as I could tell, Judaism was mercifully free of this kind of agonizing. . . .

These thoughts are wide of the mark. My conversion, when

it became known, was perhaps the cause for a short time of some amused gossip at the bar. My many Jewish colleagues, their careers not evidently damaged by anti- Semitism, looked at the matter with a mixture of curiosity and embarrassment. The most I had to endure were their facetious jokes ("Oy vey, so you're one of us already?"). These jokes have left no scars, though they might indicate the presence of some in those who made them.

But . . . if my father-in-law's observations showed some mis-apprehensions about the nature of the country I lived in and the organization I worked for, I found them all the more poignant. They came, I realized, from the heart of Central Europe, from the Hungary he and his wife had left in that fateful year 1933. His family had suffered grievously in the Holocaust. He saw my action as one that aligned me with the past sufferings of his people and as the guarantee that I would be obliged to share those sufferings in the future. In Israel, where I now live (and I live there by right as a Jew, by virtue of the Law of Return), the possibility that I might be called upon to do so is real enough.

> *Note:* Roger Owen has written brilliantly and with tongue in cheek, as befits a British journalist. Often, his words are over-stated, his opinions exaggerated, and his images too graphic, because they are designed to shock. I have tried to bring them into balance in the chapter on Immersion. Despite that fact, there is much meaning that he derives and conveys— almost despite himself.
>
> —ML

"MOTHER IS DYING; CONVERT BACK TO CATHOLICISM"

Molly Lyons Bar-David

The author is writing about the conversion experience of a friend, Devorah Wigoder, a Catholic lady who converted to Judaism and resides in Israel, and wrote of her experience in a book entitled, *Hope is My House*, Prentice-Hall, New York, 1967. The article that follows appeared under the title, "In the Home of a Convert," published in *Jewish Affairs*, p. 41, March 1967, South Africa.

To be a convert to Judaism in Israel is a role so common and so accepted that no one ever thinks of such a person as a stranger in our land, and so no one guards one's tongue on that topic. But some cases, like Devorah's, are unusual.

Born with the name of "Jane McDwyer," Devorah was schooled in a convent and brought up in a Catholic family so religious that her brother became a priest and one of her sisters a nun.

Like the nun Pat who risked her life amid rebels in Africa, Devorah faced the defense, threats and hunger of our austerity years.

What brought her to Judaism at the start was her contact at the university with all groups. Learning what the Nazis were doing (before the burning of Jews became known), she was startled by the lack of action to curb it [based] on the ancient Catholic attitude that the fate of Jews would be to suffer until they became Christians. For that reason, her kind father was so eager about missionary work. Devorah began to study the Old Testament and became a follower of Judaism. Her decision to convert came when the United Nations voted for the establishment of Israel's statehood. The Wigoders came to Israel to marry and remained here to live.

It takes courage to face the test of a convert. In New York, Devorah's mother was gravely ill in the hospital. A telegram arrived for Devorah from her priest brother, urging her to come and to reconvert to Catholicism and thus ease her mother's heartache on her death bed.

It was just after the Sinai campaign and Israel was threatened by Russia.

"How can I leave my children with such a Communist threat?" Devorah in near-tears asked of Geoff. "And how can I break my mother's heart by not returning to Catholicism? I'd better stay here, though I want so desperately to see Mother now." . . .

"You MUST go," asserted Geoffrey. "And reconversion to Catholicism is a challenge you must face yourself, choosing between your mother's agony and your feeling for Judaism."

Devorah flew off that evening for the United States and prayed in her heart all night long, torn with emotions for her mother and her Jewishness. On arrival at the airport in New York, her brother, the priest, and another priest, waited for her to rush her through the ritual of reconversion before her mother's passing.

"Wait, I want to be alone before I go to Mother," she said determinedly. Devorah went into her room, relaxed, changed her clothes and then set off alone to her mother.

She entered the hospital, tiptoed to her mother's bed and looked upon her sleeping, saintly face with love.

Her mother awoke.

"Jane! Jane! My child!—Jane, what is this radiance that glows around you?"

"It is the Jewishness in me, Mother."

"If that is so, then God bless you, my saintly child!"

The mother and daughter clung in love, and wept together in the joy of consolation.

The next day, the aged mother passed away in peace. Devorah sat down to write her vital, moving book, *Hope is My House.*

> Note: The courage of both the Jewish daughter and the Catholic mother of a priest is heartwarming. The Jewish people can only be strengthened by such conviction.

> —ML

"THE WHOLE THING SEEMED IMPOSSIBLE"
Mary Ruth Gehr

Without the help of Divine intervention, Ms. Gehr's long odyssey across the unimaginable distance from her grandparents' missionary activity with Indians in the remote mountains of British Columbia to the mikveh in Toronto, would strain the imagination. This letter to my publisher, Rabbi Alfred Kolatch, dated Feb. 9, 1990, is a historic document.

My grandfather, the Rev. William Allan, baptized me. My grandmother Mary, after whom I had been named, had come to Canada with her husband from Scotland to teach the Indians in the mountainous remote interior of British Columbia. While in Chilliwack, their first posting, Grandad received his calling to the Methodist ministry.

The little Quebec town, Beloeil, in which I grew up was dominated architecturally by churches. . . . My parents' social life has always revolved around church activities. The main message that I absorbed, both at home and at church, was never, "Go and convert the heathen!" but rather, "Love thy neighbor as thyself."

I started to read a *Life* book from my parents' shelves called *The World's Great Religions*. As well, I started to read all the Christian theological writers on my parents' bookshelves. Heated discussions with both my mother and my agnostic, Jewish, hippie tenth-grade teacher made me realize that my belief in God was unshakable, but that my belief in Christ was an intellectual construction.

In my second year at university, I took a course in comparative religion. It was the research papers for this course which were finally to open my eyes to the historic arrogance of the Christian Church, particularly vis-à-vis the Jews. While writing the first paper, the full implication of Jesus' claim in the Gospel of John: "I am the Way, the Truth and the Light—no man can come to the Father but by Me" began to hit home— not even my broad-minded parents could ignore it completely.

The second paper was a study of Jewish Messianism. I started the research for the paper wondering why the Jews ignored the obvious prophesies foretelling the coming of Jesus, the Messiah. By the time I had completed it, I was shattered by the realization of the total distortion of the Hebrew texts by the Christian Church.

I headed off to a music camp and met Ronnie Gehr, a young South African engineer who, though he was not observant himself, did not laugh at religion, also did not smoke or drink, and happened to be Jewish. I soon found out about his desire that his children be raised as Jews. I had no trouble with that, although the idea that I might become Jewish myself seemed impossible. I was, after all, an observant Christian still!

Ronnie's uncle, a Conservative rabbi, soon convinced him that I too must be Jewish for the marriage to be healthy. The news hit me like a bombshell, but I sensed that while the numerically strong Christian Church would hardly miss me, the numerically small Jewish people really needed me. So I decided that there was nothing to be lost in starting to study, to see if Judaism was as incomplete as Christianity said it was. On the advice of an Orthodox friend of Ronnie's, I read Herman Wouk's *This Is My God* and Rabbi Donin's *To Be a Jew*.

I was referred to a Montreal rabbi who ended up being totally intimidating. Everything Jewish seemed strange and frightening when I was alone. . . . However, I slowly began to observe a little bit here and a little there, and in the following summer spent in Toronto, Ronnie taught me how to read Hebrew.

I grew to love the observant life-style that allowed me to give voice to my inner religious self, and to share that self with other religious Jews (the United Church has virtually no ritual outside of the church walls, except grace before meals).

I fell in love with the *Siddur*, studying it as I would a masterpiece by Bach, learning the meaning of the Hebrew, analyzing the structure, memorizing some of it, and chewing on its meaning as I davened.

Slowly, the religious isolation of the past ten years started to drop away. I was also impressed by the basic tolerance of Judaism's approach toward non-Jews. Judaism actually discouraged converts, declaring that "the righteous of all the world have a share in the world-to-come." This, since talmudic times! Christians, by contrast, had only stopped persecuting anyone who disagreed with them (even other Christians) within the last hundred years or so. I realized that the chosen people concept actually freed Jews from the sin of religious imperialism. Oh, the joy to be religiously observant without being narrow-minded as well! Furthermore, I liked the simplicity of Jewish theology—that God would forgive and accept anyone who repented of his or her past misdeeds. Above all, I could genuinely pray for the day when "God would be one and His Name one"—where I could never have wished for the whole world to worship Jesus. I was particularly moved by reading Jewish history. What an enormous shock it was to read of the romantic Crusades from the point of view of those who were on the receiving end!

I must confess that my parents' vehement opposition to my proposed conversion took me aback at first. . . . I began to realize how profoundly painful it is when a child rejects the traditions of her early home. . . . But, as they worked through their own anger and fear, they never stopped trying to listen to and learn from us, and so the relationship has remained a very supportive one.

Ronnie, on the other hand, discovered that he had let an unexpected genie out of a bottle. Although he came from a militantly Reform home, he was strongly advised to organize an Orthodox conversion for me for the sake of his future offspring, should any want to emigrate to Israel. I had been trained at home in a rigorous honesty, and thus felt honor-bound to live up to my promise to obey the Law of Moses. Ronnie, however, was torn between his loyalty toward me and his profound skepticism concerning any observance, planted in him by his mother. Nontheless, for my sake, he accepted the basic minimums of kashrut and Sabbath observance, and was prepared to attend shul with me. We settled on a "Conservadox" minyan.

I became Miriam Ruth, the ger, at the community mikveh in Toronto in March 1978. I became Mary Ruth Gehr at the Reconstructionist Synagogue in Montreal (Orthodox synagogues were still too intimidating) in June of the same year. My father, bless his worried heart, arranged for, and paid for, a kosher reception. Ronnie's family was very accepting of me as a person, but relations with Ronnie's mother became ever more strained as we grew increasingly observant (she was much more comfortable about daughter Susie's marriage to a non-observant Catholic). However, his father's increasing involvement in temple affairs paralleled ours.

We eventually joined an Orthodox shul . . . where the cantor organized an enthusiastic group of young couples and set to work increasing our level of observance through a regular study group. Trips to the mikveh and tighter observance of Shabbat soon followed, as did our first daughter, Carolyn.

The death of Ronnie's father helped him to make Jewish observance his own. Suddenly, he discovered that the strict observance of the Jewish mourning laws helped him to grieve, and now he found himself laying tefillin regularly as he said Kaddish. He has hardly missed a day since.

Two major problems followed. With the birth of my second child, I found myself, especially in December, trying to integrate Christian symbolism into my Jewish understanding of life. Just defining the confusion in my own head was very difficult. Added to that was the strain of an eight- week visit by my bereaved mother-in-law.

I suffered a nervous breakdown. After some time, I found a wonderful psychiatrist who enabled me to trust myself again, and I was finally able to assure myself once again that I really wanted to be a Jew. I certainly believed as a Jew—only the Christian symbolism had not lost its emotional force.

Carolyn was another challenge. An intense, brilliant child, she loves her maternal grandparents and cousins and is intrigued by Christmas. In the summer that she turned seven, after having spent a week with her cousins, she started to question why I became Jewish, and why she must be different from them in areas such as kashrut. I explained to her then that I became Jewish because Judaism needed me, and her, in order to survive, and that Judaism was too precious a religious language for us to let it die. I pointed out that Christians do have Christmas, but we have Pesach, Shavuot, Rosh Hashanah, Yom Kippur, Sukkot, Hanukkah and Purim, and above all, Sabbath. We make a point of celebrating all these holidays in ways that are exciting to the children. She accepted this explanation, and now, immersed as she is in a Hebrew day school, is again proud to be a Jew.

Note: Mary Ruth's saga is remarkable on several counts. First, are the courage and headstrong will to undertake this "impossible idea" which are hallmarks of a thinking and caring person who is committed to truth. Second is her ability to overcome her husband's family's reluctance to appreciate her becoming so observant. Third are her insights—that chosenness inhibits religious imperialism, that Jewish theology is quite open to the legitimacy of non-Jews entertaining opposing ideas, that the conquering Crusaders look vastly different from the view of the conquered, and so on. Very important is her observation that one should not lose sight of the danger when young children relate to the natural family and are attracted to the former religion, as was Carolyn. Mary Ruth Gehr is a true ger, and truly Ruth.

—ML

SUMMARY: WHAT THE CONVERTS ARE SAYING

We began this book with the conversion experiences of seventeen Jews who were new to Judaism so that the reader could find kindred souls or ideas and locate his or her own feelings in the words of one of these alert, perceptive individuals.

Among the writers are two former Christian clergymen, two professors, three journalists, a variety of men and women from different walks of life with assorted intellectual abilities, from different regions of the world—the Deep South, the Northwest and Northeast, the West and Midwest, from the U.S. and England and the Philippines.

They drew their inspiration to explore Judaism from different wells. Some were shocked out of their inertia by the horrors of the Holocaust, through some act of anti-Semitism, or by evidence of the sheer survivability of the Jewish people in the face of persecution. Others came by way of reading descriptions of Jewish life in books by Leon Uris and Chaim Potok. Three came from disaffection with the religion of their childhood and actively searched the roots of Christianity in order to discover Judaism. Some were impelled by prospective mates, others by their children, and still others received their inspiration indirectly through the noble souls of gentile parents. They were then brought to Judaism by the spiritual leaders of the whole religious institutional spectrum of American life.

In these letters, we learned a veritable glossary of Hebrew terms: Torah, Halakhah, Shabbat, Sukkot, Pesach, mikveh, shul, chazzan, tallit, tefillin, yarmulka, mezuzah, kosher, aliyah, and others. In Part V there are ten special chapters designed to provide a snapshot of the major ideas and ceremonies of the Jews, including the Holocaust and Israel. There are, of course, more elaborate chapters in this volume on the philosophy and the halakhic requirements of conversion.

Conversion to Judaism is not for timid souls. The convert's plan for new learning and new living will almost surely be intruded upon by one of the problems described above. It might come from the strained relations with parents who perceive the convert's success to be their failure. Perhaps it will derive from rejection by many familiar personalities that fill the past who feel betrayed, and from the ubiquitous, untutored souls who will associate with your future. Unexpectedly, on days which you have come to love as a youngster, but which your decision in maturity has made critical—the holidays, both Jewish and Christian—family ties which were meant to bind only become knotted and strain on your good-natured desire to celebrate.

On the other hand, these testimonies teach us that if, as a new Jew, the convert develops strength of character and the firmness of will to create a life, a family, a marriage, on a new spiritual base and a new philosophy of living, then that person will prepare for these eventualities and although the hurt may linger the courage of decision will fortify the soul.

What we discover is that the seventeen new Jews had qualities and ideas in common that enabled them to succeed. One important quality is strength—a stiff-neckedness that truly qualifies them to become members of the covenant. They have withstood rejection of close friends, even rabbis; alienation from beloved families; and the tribulations of newness—entrance to a tight-knit, family-oriented, long-established community that knows itself to be the chosen people and in permanent covenant with Almighty God Himself.

We began with this chapter, filled as it is to overflowing with problems, portrayed in the graphic grays and blacks of reality, for yet another reason: it follows the advice of a wise, old Jewish custom of first parading the obstacles of joining the Jews before prospective proselytes, before telling them how truly glorious is "coming under the wings of the Almighty."

In testimony to that custom, we should note, the spiritual triumph of these Jews. It is to be found in a phrase which insinuated itself, in different expressions, in virtually all of their statements:

"I have come home."

Part Two

THE FRAMEWORK

1
Paradoxes of Jewish Conversion

AN INTRODUCTION

God loves the convert. In the Bible, He instructs the Jews no fewer than thirty-six times to do likewise—with mixed success. Why this special love for converts—even more difficult than the nearly impossible demand to truly love one's neighbor?

One answer may be to counteract the convert's isolation—witness the Bible's term for convert, ger, which originally meant "stranger." The natural isolation of being a stranger is probably compounded because the Jewish community began as a family—headed by patriarchs and matriarchs—and from its inception has been family-oriented and close-knit. In addition, it has always known itself to be a people chosen by God for a special mission to humanity.

Another is a historically conditioned response to newcomers. "Remember you were 'strangers' in Egypt," the Bible reminds us. Loving the convert thus calls on all Jews to continuously recall the feeling of being alien and to respond to "strangers" in a positive way.

Still another is that loving the convert is an expression of admiration for a person who has the strength of character that it takes to act on one's feelings, even to the extent of putting one's future at risk. Whichever may be the primary motive, it is not a matter of suggestion or courtesy but a command issued by God to His people: Love the convert.

• • •

The purpose in writing the first chapter of this book composed entirely of paradoxes is not to seek answers, but to accomplish three goals:

First, to convey to the reader that the subject of conversion is complicated—in terms of judging the candidate's internal motivation; of the variables of the reality that will confront the convert and how they will be viewed by Jewish law and tradition; and of predicting the future success of the convert's religious practice. The Rabbis, who were the teachers and also the jurists of the Jewish people, concluded many of their deliberations on this inscrutable subject by leaving it to the judgment of local Sages—"according to how the eyes of the court see it"—opting for individual rabbinic assessments of often unique circumstances, rather than rigidly adhering to generalized assumptions.

Second, its purpose is to teach, at the very outset, that Judaism is not a simple faith, content with simplistic answers. It is, after all, a religion with a very rich legal tradition; a history so complex it has spanned centuries of global dispersion and confronted almost every conceivable reality; a veneration for learning and wisdom and sophistication. To expect of this religion a yes-or-no, quick-and-easy answer to a complicated problem is to do it a grievous injustice.

Third, front-loading this book with questions, without providing answers, will open up a subject that is as closed to many today as it has been for centuries, and will begin to demystify what has been a virtual secret for the community-at-large. There are no magic incantations that transform a person from Christian to Jew. The symbolic components of conversion are not the outlandish abracadabra of fraternal organizations; the process is not a hidden formula. The determination of the candidate's acceptability is not made by whim. Judging matters of "Who is a Jew" requires sympathetic understanding, sharp insight into people, and wisdom to protect the future of the Jewish people. I hope these questions may help begin this process.

Alas, there may be a by-product of our questions: it may assure potential converts that they are not alone in not fully grasping the conversion process. Perhaps more important than having all the answers is knowing which questions to ask, and being willing to search for the answers. Many native Jewish people do not know the answers to these and other questions about Judaism.

• • •

Does Judaism encourage converts? If so, why are there no missionary movements within modern Judaism? If it does not, how can the Torah speak of loving the convert—which implies, at the very least, attracting him? And how does it speak of idealism and personal transformation and the pursuit of truth? Do not those with passionate convictions naturally seek to convince others of the truth they have found?

Yet, we find no systematic philosophy of missionizing in Jewish literature and there are no such examples in Jewish law. Apparently, missionizing is not a mission of the Jews. Yet, history does record numerous instances of conversions of non-Jews to Judaism. And it does register the decrees of a number of hostile host countries forbidding Jews from proselytizing gentiles—which itself is an indication of Jewish missionizing. Further, while it is true that Jews have not missionized on a large scale, especially during the last 1600 years, the Jewish tradition does warmly accept non-Jews and pointedly demands that they be accepted and treated without condescension and it does chastise those Jews who act prejudicially toward converts.

Judaism has no theological problem with accepting converts. Jews are a people, not a race, and they open their arms to all sincere, upright human beings whatever their color, from wherever they hail, and no matter which beliefs they once embraced. In fact, in terms of Jewish law,[1] the Jewish people is technically considered *goy*, a people, not *mishpachah*, a family—which deals only with blood lines, "admitting" only those "outsiders" who contract for marriage. When non-Jews convert to Judaism, they are considered no different from native Jews and, like them, are children of Abraham and called *b'nai b'rit*, "children of the covenant." And they are members of the "chosen people."

Yet, these teachings notwithstanding, history is pockmarked with social upheavals in a number of Jewish communities, and these have caused leading rabbis to reject even apparently authentic converts.

For one thing, as a people persecuted for so long, Jews often have had to pay dearly for the privilege of accepting a convert from the host country. Was a pogrom by furious Christians or Moslems or Parsees worth the privilege? Another reason for a temporary suspension might be the incomprehensibility of it all. Having been for centuries the butt of vicious hatred, perhaps Jews could not imagine why anyone would freely choose such a fate—especially since the Rabbis preached the doctrine that non-Jews could achieve salvation *without* converting to Judaism. Indeed, they taught that the pious and just of *all* peoples have a "share in the world-to-come."

Question: the convert is almost always referred to in superlatives—he is either greater than the most righteous born Jew or, according to one opinion, "a blight and a scab" on the corpus of Jewry. On one hand, there is the fact that eminent scholars, prophets, even King David himself—and hence the future Messiah—are descended from converts; on the other, there is a nagging fear that at some point one convert or another will bring down the sky on all Jewish heads. That is one reason why many Jewish leaders seem to have applied the Talmud's counsel (regarding another matter) toward potential converts: "Draw them close with your right hand and keep them at a distance with your left." Such poignant ambivalence reveals the trauma in the historic experience of the relationship of Jews with converts.

Equally curious: despite the existence of converts throughout Jewish history, there is no major text on the practice and protocol of conversion except for six pages of a late, minor talmudic tractate. To this day, the subject of conversion is something of a closed book.

But other questions about conversion are more pertinent and demand openness, candor and clarity. What is the attitude of Jewish law to conversions today? What exactly is the approved process of conversion? Who are the authorities who regulate and legitimize it? What should be the convert's relationship with the family from whose religion he or she has separated? Should a convert to Judaism also celebrate Christian religious holidays in a spirit of cooperation? Must the ethnic component of Judaism—the folkways and the foods of the Jewish people—be adopted together with their religious norms? Is liking Jewish people an integral part of liking Judaism? Must one identify with the history and goals of God's people or is a relationship with God alone sufficient?

Is conversion motivated solely by marriage legitimate? And, if so, should religious demands be made of the Jewish spouse? Should Judaism insist that the gentile become an observant

Jew even if the native Jew has not yet shown an inclination to become a practicing Jew? How, indeed, does a Jew become truly Jewish? Is it a factor that should be taken into consideration in judging the spouse's candidacy for conversion? If a marriage is to follow conversion, when exactly should the conversion take place? And what is the legal status of the convert in the Jewish community?

Does Judaism believe in infant conversion—when one obviously cannot speak of commitment? What is the optimal time for child conversions? Who is obligated to make the decision—the child, the parent, or the Jewish community?

How important is the protocol, the formal process of conversion? Is not a sincere, verbal declaration of commitment sufficient? Are circumcision and immersion in a ritual pool absolutely obligatory, or may there be modifications and adjustments, depending on specific personal circumstances? Which process will be accepted by all Jews—by the rabbinic courts of Israel and England, Romania and South Africa? How long must the process of study be? What beliefs are part of the required commitment? What must a person minimally accept of the practices of the Jewish faith in order to be considered an adherent?

In a real sense, the subject of conversion touches the very essence of the Jew's existence—not only his experience, but his very identity. One Sage taught that the receiving of the Torah at Mt. Sinai was itself an act of conversion. All other questions—how Judaism expresses its faith in God; how it handles love and death and pain; what ethical demands it makes of its adherent— are peripheral to this central concern: Who is a Jew and who is not? What is a Jew? How does one become a Jew?

The whole framework of conversion must become an open and public part of the Jewish heritage. If most Jews do not comprehend the concepts and processes of conversion, how can gentiles be expected to understand them? And if gentiles do not understand the process, how can they make intelligent inquiries that lead to a commitment to Torah?

In this chapter, we pondered theoretical questions. In the next, we will focus on the more complicated matters of the whole framework of conversion, and integrating beliefs into life-styles.

Note to Chapter One

1. Rabbi Hershel Schachter, "Gidrei yuchasin ba'uma ha'Yisraelit," p. 225, published in *Or Ha'mizrach,* Nissan 5747 (April 1982).

2

Welcoming the Convert:

A NOD OR AN EMBRACE

The convert is not only to be welcomed, but loved. The love of neighbor, considered by Rabbi Akiva the fundamental principle of all Torah, is not merely extended to embrace the convert as a "new neighbor." There is a separate commandment given the people of Israel to love the convert, the ger." The Hebrew word for male convert is ger, for female giyoret, which the Rabbis of the Talmud derive from the original biblical term ger, meaning "stranger."

This concept of loving the convert, who is both stranger and neighbor, is unique in Jewish literature. Indeed, on the level of legal obligation, it ranks even higher than love for parents, and while one owes this person no special gratitude for deciding to convert—the decision is the convert's own, for his or her own reasons—the obligation to honor and respect the convert is at least equal to that accorded parents.

There is little doubt that the love for the convert derives from the special admiration for spiritual heroism. He or she has demonstrated an impressive strength of character and mind—even if the motivating factor might be marriage—in a society of acculturated, assimilated, and easily adjusted personalities. This praise for the convert, which begins in the Bible, continues to be expressed in law and literature and history despite centuries of dispersion and uprootedness and tenuous living. Some of the major personalities in post-biblical, medieval, and modern times hail from convert origins or were themselves

converts, their genealogies unblushingly listed by a very proud
tradition. The very Messiah is glorified as descending from the
convert, Ruth. Prayers for the welfare of the convert are inserted
in the most important of our daily prayers, the Silent Devotion,
recited three times every day, and the convert is bracketed
with the *tzaddik*, the *hasid*, the elder and the scholar, and
with righteous and saintly Jews of all time.

That love is demonstrated not only by legislation, but by
the dynamics of the historical process itself. The practice of
conversion has persisted in spite of Jewish legal obstacles
caused by historical forces, such as the destruction of the ancient Temple. This cataclysm led to the sudden termination
of the Temple sacrifices required of each convert. It also broke
the chain of Rabbinic ordination that began with Moses, which
might have disrupted the Rabbinic court that presided over
conversions.[1] The Rabbis made strenuous efforts to facilitate
the practice of conversion in the face of these internal obstacles
"in order not to close the doors to converts." This effectively
demonstrated that religious conversion was meant to transcend
all the obstacles.[2] The attitude is best exemplified by the per-
sistence of conversion in virtually every age and every major
city in defiance of the bloody threats and the persecution of
host nations, often in contravention of the edict of local rabbinic
authorities who were trying to protect the population by tem-
porarily suspending the whole machinery of conversion. Records of the threats by the dominant cultures are easily available,
as are the rabbinic edicts that comply with these threats, and
these are matched by the undying insistence of gentiles to convert during these dismal times.

In effect, conversion proved itself to be as stubbornly and
as mysteriously durable as Jewish history itself, and it became
a stabilizing necessity of the religious spirit under most
conditions and in virtually all the generations of the Jewish
record.

This is not to say that Jews—prominent Jews, even rabbis—
never made disparaging remarks about converts.

After all, conversion introduces new people into what some
may feel is a socially closed circle. Further, Jewish law requires
that converts be accepted as honorable citizens with equal
privileges before the law. On top of that, the law, repeated
in every book of that most sacred book, the Bible, mandates
unquestioning love for them. That combination of emotions

and obligations might very well make some people uncomfortable—no matter how great or good the convert. Add to this the fact that not all converts are *ipso facto* lovable, and that the history of converts includes some who have caused the Jewish people grave misgivings, and the few negative statements sprinkled in the literature can be accepted without shock as inevitable.

Indeed, what is most pleasing is that alongside some of the harsh statements about converts in the ancient literature, one discovers strenuous attempts, in every generation, at interpreting those statements in order to ameliorate the feelings of converts, and also to make sure that fellow Jews understand their biblical responsibility to the new "stranger in the gates."

Moreover, tracing these negative comments back to their origins makes one realize that various communities differed in their response to converts, based on their own experience with them.[3] Thus, the Sephardic community always appeared more hesitant to accept converts. One does not have to dig too deep into history to prove this: witness the decision by contemporary rabbis of the Syrian community in the United States to accept absolutely no converts (regardless of the Bet Din or the Torah scholar that approves of the specific conversion) as a way of combating further inroads of intermarriage into their vulnerable small community. This pattern is not seen in Franco-German life generally, and their scholars, having had a different set of experiences with converts and host nations, appear more eager to accept the convert. In a similar attitudinal difference, the Palestinian community leadership was generally more restrictive than was the Babylonian.

While there were differences in the degree of openness and warmth with which Jewish communities embraced the convert, the law was uncompromising. There are three, clearly distinct legal prohibitions found in the Torah that protect the convert from ever slipping into a second-class citizenship: Leviticus 19:33-34; Leviticus 19:35; and Deuteronomy 24:17. Together, they guarantee the convert equality[4] before the law—and even protection from pejorative epithets, gossipy innuendoes, or solicitous condescensions.

Surprisingly, then, there is no theological compulsion to convert the world. Judaism is not a closed system, in which one is worthy only if one is "in." It is not belonging to a particular belief system that assures a person eternal reward; it is behaving according to a value system that redounds to the benefit of the whole society that is a guarantee for finding favor in the eyes of the Lord. One who is already Jewish still needs to act out that Jewishness. That is his or her assurance of finding merit in God's eyes. A moral Christian or Moslem will also receive reward—equal to that of an observant Jew and greater than that of a non-observant Jew. No person needs to be saved by any miracle of grace. The Jew converting the gentile, therefore, does not get some heavenly credit for "saving a soul."

There is therefore no mandate to convert gentiles, although it is a mitzvah (as we note later on) that the court accept the righteous candidate who wishes to become Jewish. Hence, this very people which has given the world its greatest literature, Scripture, and has historically demonstrated the strongest tendencies to express its values in legal form, has produced virtually no literature and only few laws on the subject of conversion.

"Rectifying the world" is indeed one of God's primary purposes in ordaining the worldwide Jewish dispersion that has endured through all Jewish history since the Exodus. But that by no means implies a mandate to actively missionize by direct confrontation. It is, rather, to serve as "a light unto the nations," attracting others by becoming noble human beings ourselves. Some teach by lecture and blackboard, others by serving as an example and role-model. Jews have conceived of their mission to be not the former, didactic teachers, but the latter— exemplars of what humans should strive for and the destiny that awaits those who adopt such aspirations. This is as worthy a goal as any people can have. (But a difficult one, as we have come to learn.) In this regard, the Jewish people is like a family— a family does not missionize for relatives; it attracts prospects for marriage.

A very keen insight into the drive to proselytize was made by Maimonides in the Introduction to his great work, *The Book of the Commandments*. In analyzing the foundations of Judaism, he says that the love of God implies two aspects: the cognitive—striving to know God—and the affective—loving God in an almost romantic way, as it is portrayed in the Song of Songs. Such love naturally implies that you want to tell everyone about the wonders of the object of your love. It is this impulse which motivated Abraham and Sarah to convert all the men and women they could influence. How could it be otherwise?

Of course, this powerful psychological impulse is a natural derivative of any strong love or strong belief. In this sense, reaching out to the ger is indeed an obligation, a mitzvah, one encoded in that great and fundamental mitzvah to love God. And, of course, there is no doubt that the universal impulse in Judaism is founded partially on this natural need to bring the love of God to all others.

Nonetheless, even this natural drive did not impel the Rabbis to roam the world looking for converts. Different conditions did encourage this activity for specific periods, but it has never been the central historical thrust of the Jewish religion, as it has been in Christianity, in which converting the heathen to the faith was considered a major achievement.

Historically, the Jews have actually missionized only during specific eras. One example occurred in 125 B.C.E. when John Hyrcanus, the Hasmonean king, subdued the Idumeans and wrongfully compelled them to observe Jewish rites. This was an historical aberration in the long record of the Jewish people, utterly uncharacteristic of its basic nature. Undoubtedly, this was politically motivated rather than religiously inspired, but it constitutes a sad day in Jewish life that was never to be forgotten. Judaism legislated against the possibility of that dismal practice from ever recurring. We have been, and continue to be, so much the object of coerced conversions that we recoil from ever imposing or even attempting to persuade masses of gentiles by "softspeak" or bribery to take on our faith.

In our times, some Jewish religious leaders have proposed missionary activities. The debits and credits of such an activity, though sincerely intended, must take into consideration the following concerns:

Will there be a net gain in the spirituality and in the piety of the Jewish community? If we lower standards of entrance into Judaism, will Jews generally, like water, tend to the lower level? Will a gain in population serve the religious survivability of our people? Will there be a significant loss of Jewish energy in the attempt? Will it have a negative effect on heretofore friendly Christian communities? Will it inspire counter-missionary activities? How will it affect the character of the Jewish community?

One conclusion that appears to be warranted by Jewish history and by current religious and communal needs is that, while Jews should warmly welcome sincere converts and should encourage them in their expressed desire more than has ever been done before, they should not institute a community-wide missionary program (which, in any case, the community is not capable of doing successfully).

This must be said with certainty: regardless of its stand on proselytizing, Judaism welcomes the sincere convert with open arms to become a partner in its past and in its future, in its history and in its destiny. A handshake will not do. Only an embrace. Welcome.

Notes to Chapter Two

1. According to the Tosafists, Yevamot 47b and Gittin 88a, but in disagreement with Rashba, *ad loc.*

2. See Avner Shaki, "Hatokef b'Yisrael shel Giyur Reformi b'Chutz la'Aretz," pp. 161-179, in *Dine Yisrael*, edited by Zev W. Falk and Aaron Kirschenbaum, vol. IV, Tel Aviv University, 1973.

3. The two basic schools of thought in medieval Europe, the Franco-German Ashkenazim, functioning in a Christian-dominated society, and the Spanish Sephardim, under Moslem rule, arrived at differing attitudes based on the same sources. See the interesting article by Ben Zion Wacholder in *Historia Judaica*, October 1958, vol. XX, Part Two.

4. It should be noted that equality before the law does not mean identity in obligations and permissions, but in rights. Thus a ger may marry a *mamzer,* but not a *Kohen.*

3

The Conversion Protocol:

A FIRST GLIMPSE

THE IDEA BEHIND THE PROCESS

Judaism is unique in terms of what it requires of those who wish to join the Jewish people—as the tradition phrases it, "to come under the wings of the Divine Presence." The requirements set by Judaism represent a radical departure from religious conversion as it had existed in the past. It demands that those who want to enter the Jewish fold give up their former faith completely.

In the classical period in Greece and Rome, conversion meant that a person could retain his original faith-commitment, but would supplement it with the ideas or practices of a newfound religion, and then perhaps modify his standard practice somewhat to accommodate the change. The Greeks considered the civilized universe, as opposed to the chaos beyond it, as a multi-racial, multi-national society. "Those who refused to accept this structure were considered enemies of man. . . ."[1] In that society, the transition of religious conversion was smooth. There were no family upheavals, no communal disruptions, no socially dislocating leaps of faith. Consequently, conversion triggered no state interference which might outlaw it or curb its vehemence.

Conversion in Christianity was patterned after the Jewish model rather than the syncretism of the classical Greek period. To Christianity, religious conversion was considered not merely an accretion, but a splitting-off. It was a radical event requiring a transformation of faith—commitment—rejecting the old without reservation, and embracing the new in its totality, with its God ideal and its salvational system and the rituals that symbolize those beliefs. Conversion, in this sense, signaled the entrance into a new faith-community, and it changed the character of the convert's faith and his life-style.

Conversion to Judaism—the process which Christianity adopted and made into one of its foundations—requires a commitment, qualitatively different not only from that required by the ancient syncretistic faiths, but also from that required by the Christian religion that derived from Judaism.

At the fundamental level, Judaism has always insisted on a commitment so new that the convert must be regarded as a "newborn child," not only in spiritual-emotional terms, but also in legal and technical forms. That means nothing less than that the convert enters fresh into this world, with no encumbrances of old times, with no family associations in regard to inheritance rights, and also with no ties to the church into which he was born, all of which could encumber his present status as a new Jewish person.

This raises some legal problems as to property rights, and socio-psychological ones as regard the convert's interpersonal relations with his or her natural family, and these were handled by the Rabbis with both admirable compassion and technical deftness. But the convert is born of a new people, in the metaphoric sense of the word "born" and it is a tribute both to the convert and to Judaism that a person could embrace a new life and could, even in mid-life, actually be considered to start anew.

This new birth is the nature of the personal change which Judaism expects and the revolutionary quality of the conversion upon which it insists. That Christianity was not willing to accept the totality of this transformation is demonstrated by the fate of the Jewish conversion ritual of circumcision. This "radical" act, on a very sensitive part of the body, denotes the very serious nature of conversion, and it is this very symbol which Christianity rejected—as it did not reject the immersion component of the Jewish conversion ritual—precisely because its radical nature would prove an obstacle in its attempt to convert the heathen world to Christianity.

Moreover, it should be emphasized that the convert is expected to cleave both to a *covenantal* community, and to a *faith* group.[2] The *faith* relationship speaks of belief, truth, commitment and love and fear of God, whereas the *covenant* relationship speaks of these values as they are made concrete by the duties and deeds which enable the Jewish people to put faith into practice. (Paul's emphasis on faith over works cuts a deep chasm between Judaism and Christianity.[3]) The covenant mandate speaks primarily of obligations to *do good*; the faith mandate requires primarily a *belief in truth*. The former is the more demanding of the two for it entails a covenant between people and God and between person and person. "Your people will be my people, your God my God," says Ruth, the archetypical convert to Judaism, and that remains the most eloquent expression of Jewish conversion to this day. Adopting Judaism means adopting the Jewish people as the convert's people, Jewish history as the convert's own history, Jewish destiny as the convert's own destiny.

One should not underestimate the difficulty of this demand. While it is plausible to ask of the prospective convert an acknowledgment and a love of God, is it realistic to require a commitment to love a people? Yet that is exactly what Judaism does require. The love of the Jewish people is not conditional upon the love of every single Jew. It may be that a person may not "like" all Jews; but it is a religious mandate to "love" all Jews.

THE PROTOCOL

The conversion process requires a symbolic affirmation of both components of the covenant—the relationship with God and identification with the people. We call the formal process "protocol" because protocols are procedures that must be completed prior to the final establishment of an agreement or covenant, and because "protocol" implies an accepted "correct" procedure. The act of entering the Jewish fold establishes a covenant with God and all components of the process leading to it are parts of the "protocol."

1. The protocol begins with the potential convert's first legal pronouncement of intent—a commitment to God and to the

Jewish people—before a three-man rabbinic court, called "Bet Din." This undoubtedly will be preceded by the candidate for conversion acquainting himself or herself with the nature of Judaism.

2. The Bet Din's formulaic response to every convert is astonishment, as expressed in these words from the Talmud:[4]

> What reason have you for desiring to become a proselyte? Do you not know that the Jews at the present time are persecuted and oppressed, despised, harassed and overcome by afflictions?

The court then reviews the current state of the Jews of the world. But, since converts are dear to the Jewish people,[5] the court is cautioned not to overstate the case, and is required to balance the discussion of afflictions with an equally compelling description of the joys of being Jewish and the rewards for becoming a member of God's chosen people. Judaism encourages the convert to approach becoming a Jew with eyes wide open. Being acquainted with the hard realities of Jewish existence is as important as the knowledge of lofty Jewish ideals.

3. For males, there now follows the act of circumcision, which symbolically demonstrates leaving the old faith and entering the new. It is the distinguishing symbol of Judaism, for males, since the days of the first Jew, Abraham, who initiated the rite. It is also the one symbol for which the Jew has most suffered at the hands of numerous persecutors.

4. The preliminary statement, which began the whole process, now needs to be reaffirmed through a series of questions and answers put to the candidate by the Bet Din based upon the candidate's studies. The potential convert now makes a declaration of unqualified commitment which is the crux of the process and requires the presence, the evaluation, and the full acceptance of the court of three. It is designed to take place immediately prior to the immersion as the last act of the admission procedure to become a Jew.

5. For females, and also as the second requirement for males, Judaism requires immersion in a specially designed ritual pool of water. This ceremony is traced to the conversion of the Jews at Mt. Sinai. Archaeologists have discovered immersion pools, mikva'ot, atop Masada, and indeed, they are found in cities all over the world. The mikveh image of purification has fired the imagination of all western religions and it has survived

in different transmutations in the form of an initiatory rite for religious faiths, ancient and modern.

When the convert leaves the water, he or she emerges into the fresh air newborn to Torah and to the Jewish people.

Notes to Chapter Three

1. Arthur Darby Nock, *Conversion: The Old and the New in Religion from Alexander the Great to Augustine of Hippo,* Oxford University Press, Oxford, 1933, p. 12, as quoted in "Gerut: Laidah U'Mishpat" by Aaron Lichtenstein, in *Torah she'Baal Peh,* Mossad Ha'Rav Kook, Jerusalem, 1971. See also Paul Johnson, *A History of the Jews,* Harper & Row, New York, 1987, p. 134.
2. This theme is developed fully in chapter 6, on Covenant, and chapter 10, on Immersion, on the subject of the different symbolic significances of circumcision and immersion. The landmark Hebrew essay, "Kol Dodi Dofek," most easily accessible in Pinchas Peli's *B' Sode Ha'Yachid Veha'Yachad,* "In Aloneness, In Togetherness," published by Orot Publishers, Jerusalem 1976. Also see Rabbi Hershel Schachter's essay, "Berurim b'Inyane Yuchasin;" in the Jubilee volume dedicated to Rabbi Soloveitchik, vol. I, published by Mossad Ha-Rav Kook, Jerusalem, 1984.
3. See "Kefirah b'Am Yisrael be'Inyanei Giyur," by Rabbi Shlomo Goren, in *Shanah b'Shanah,* edited by Rabbi Aaron Ha'Levi Pichnik, published by Hekhal Shlomo, Jerusalem, 1983.
4. Talmud, Yevamot, 47a.
5. As described in Yevamot 47b and in the codes, *Mishneh Torah,* Hilkhot Issurei Bi'ah, 14 and *Shulchan Arukh,* Yoreh De'ah 268, 2, but applied to the condition of contemporary world and local Jewry.

4
Honoring Motives

Is going through the formal process of conversion—study, circumcision, and immersion—enough to simply transform a gentile into a Jew? Are subjective considerations—intent, motivation, and commitment—also determining factors in deciding the eligibility of the gentile to become a Jew? And, if so, what must be the nature of the intent? What must be the quality of the motivation? To which practice is commitment necessary? In short: How much of a Jew does the non-Jew have to become before he or she becomes a Jew?

CONVERSIONS OF CONVICTION

In our jaded society, our vision is often clouded; we no longer see the possibility for personal growth, spiritual growth—let alone a reaching for the sky. We instinctively doubt that anyone can seriously consider changing his or her life-style or daily behavior simply for the sake of an ideal or a belief.

But a more careful searching into the modern soul will reveal many idealists among us who transcend their surroundings in search of a more meaningful life. And there are authentic and sensitive people among us who are repelled by contemporary values. Their disillusionment with the current state of human affairs triggers a passionate seeking for a faith more promising, more absorbing, more compelling.

The history of humanity is replete with stories of those who converted to other faiths and thereby enriched themselves and their adopted people in astonishing ways. Spiritual revolutions in the souls of special men and women have impelled them to strike out in new directions they once never thought possible. Their courage and determination in overcoming their own spiritual inertia and inevitable social ostracism are the sure marks of a unique kind of heroism. In seizing upon an idea and putting their lives behind it, they often have had to reject their personal histories and endure the blandishments of family and friends in an attempt to express a new and overwhelming insight. They are proof that human beings are capable of the most radical and surprising changes.

Now, such change is not necessarily a deep-seated reaction to some early childhood psychological trauma, as popular Freudianism would have it. Nor does the radical nature of religious conversion necessarily imply that the process leading to the decision was sudden, impulsive, and involving, as William James maintained, a "surrender of will"—some transcendent coercion or unanticipated illumination that induces a passive acceptance of the will of God. An authentic decision of faith can, and often does, proceed from contemplation, insight, study, rational analysis, experience, and the exercise of free will. These are some of the ingredients of the spiritual "soup" over which a soul creatively broods and in which an ultimate decision slowly and patiently simmers.

At the precipice of change, it is often a leap of faith—a radical split-second decision, a sudden insight, a flash of light—which helps the person across the divide. This leap of faith requires an agility of mind, but, more than all else, a willingness to risk vulnerability and even ridicule, what Winston Churchill calls "the nerve of failure"—and it is often considered a failure by those who have known the convert all his or her life. But conversion to Judaism is little more than immature impulsiveness if it is not preceded by searching, study, agonizing introspection, and deep reflection. It is not a business for the timid.

CONVERSIONS OF ACCOMMODATION

While it is true that many convert out of conviction—more than most people think—they are vastly outnumbered by those who convert for convenience or accommodation. Once, as in the case of the "Rice Christians," the convenience was material—conversion for the sake of more food, a better job, or entering into a higher social class. Today, mostly, this accommodation is associated with prospective marriage, when conversion serves the purpose of appeasing volatile in-laws and also prevents future children from seeing more conflict in their parents' home than is necessary. Conversion to another faith, in this sense, is a marriage of convenience to facilitate the convenience of marriage.

The western world is fertile ground for such conversions. Blended communities have, in some ways, made mixed marriages commonplace, whereas, only a decade ago, they were anomalies to be ignored or barely tolerated.

Naturally, those who convert for accommodation purposes are apt to be authentic and idealistic, but often the conversion is without significance, because the accommodation is without meaning. The democratic consciousness today is dominated by three ideas which make a hospitable environment for the growth of accommodation converts.

The first is pluralism, at least in its popularized, marketable version. The welcome competition of faiths in our society was expected to induce a powerful encounter of commitments—allowing the faithful to see their own perceptions in the light of other and different values. Largely, this has succeeded. But often it succeeded only in producing friendly differences in "lifestyles," and the kind of social amenities that skate harmlessly, but also meaninglessly, on the surface of faiths whose living waters had turned cold and frozen over. Pluralism spawns a pick-and-choose religious consumerism. Unencumbered by ancient memories and the glue of family loyalties, by metaphysical convictions and the long investment of hope and sacrifice, a change of ideology becomes as easy to accept as a new fashion in clothes. In this society of ideological and geographical mobility, neighborhoods flow into one another and neighbors comprehend and accept their mutual differences with virtual indifference. This often parades as tolerance.

A second element is our popular definition of pragmatism. People do what has to be done in order to make life more livable. Of what use, they ask, are the old theologies and the inherited codes if they cannot make a person more comfortable, more happy? Is not religion made for people, rather than people for religion and, therefore, is not God made to serve people rather than people God? And, if that is so, why not simply relieve ourselves of the excess mental and cultural baggage? The rigidities of our formal past are gone and, in any case, they are irrelevant to the flux of American social mobility.

A third factor which facilitates the increase in conversions of accommodation is our thinly disguised narcissism. This legitimates and elevates self-concern to the extent that we have exalted beyond reason the satisfaction of personal needs and feelings. "Taking care of number one" has become our central function, and we casually and unblushingly embrace it as a new "value." We speak of "self-fulfillment" with the same reverence the old-time religions once reserved for sacraments. We have canonized self-concern and beatified the hedonists amongst us; sociology has become our iconography. For making a cult of self-centeredness, we have developed what has been elegantly termed "the culture of narcissism." (Of course, we tend to forget that Narcissus drowned as a result of his self-love.)

Given these dominant factors, religious *destinies* have become reduced, as in job applications, to "religious *preference*." "The religion of your choice" has an all-too-tolerant ring to it. But, upon reflection, it is seductively simple. It involves "choice," yes; but "religion" hardly. The climate has become conducive to religious quick-change experts, and conversion out of the need to accommodate a mate or family comes as easy as a change of spouses with no-fault divorce. Our society takes a happy and light-hearted attitude to a change in "preference"—whether of aesthetics or of spirit. Face-lift or faith-lift?

THE IDEAL MOTIVE: FOR THE SAKE OF HEAVEN

Acknowledging the authority of Torah and observing its traditional precepts do impose a serious burden, but, if the person converts out of conviction, an authentic desire to love God, he or she will not find it onerous. The genuine desire to embrace Judaism for its own sake, "for the sake of Heaven," was considered the sole legitimate ground for conversion permitted by the Rabbis.

Historically, it is the only motivation that "worked" for the Jewish people. The authorities rejected conversion for ulterior motives as unworthy, and indeed harmful, to the religious development of the Jewish people. They cite examples through the ages that amount to a litany of troubles. Those ulterior motives range from materialism to marriage, but they were all rejected as grounds for becoming a Jew. The Torah, even as God Himself, was not to be used as a means, only a goal.

It is instructive to discover how the Rabbis dwelt on the subject of motive, not only for the masses but for their most popular leaders, whom the Bible itself praised.[1] The motives of the greatest of biblical converts were subjects of much speculation and even heated debate through the ages. The study of the lives of Abraham and Ruth provides indication enough of the complexity of motivation even in ancient times.

A classic example of this genre is the analysis of Jethro, the High Priest of Midian and the father-in-law of Moses. The Bible is silent about Jethro's reasons for converting. In the Bible, Jethro's words are clear but sparse. The Rabbis extrapolated from those few remarks and squeezed every nuance of meaning and implication from them. The great medieval Bible commentator, Rashi, quotes the Talmud, which questions Jethro's motivation: *Mah sh'muah shama u'va*, "What news did he hear that he came and turned proselyte?" What exactly prompted him to "come" to the Jewish people? This is not a question about immediate cause, but about the deeper insight which led a High Priest to join another people.[2]

THE PREDOMINANT MOTIVE:
FOR THE SAKE OF FAMILY

But today, while truly successful conversions from pure motive occur more frequently than most people would imagine, they surely represent the minority of conversions. How does modern Judaism deal with the often mixed motivations behind so many of the conversions confronting American rabbis today? Must Judaism even today accept only converts of conviction but not of accommodation?[3]

The good news is the startling possibility that the very complexity of the social and religious situation of our day might hold not only great fear, but great hope. When we search deeply into the nature of today's convert, we often find authenticity even in converts of accommodation—the prospect of his or her growth in Judaism, despite his own belief to the contrary, perhaps even becoming a "returnee" to Jewish observance; the great opportunity for keeping families together and also close to the tradition; the hope of a child of this union turning to the serious study of Torah; even the possibility that a convert's enthusiasm, or that of his or her children, will reinvigorate a sometimes somnambulant Jewish community.

Perhaps there is even a glimmer of hope from an unexpected source: the gradual subsiding of the intergenerational conflicts regarding intermarriage which prompted modern conversions motivated by accommodation in the first place.

A growing number of contemporary rabbis, in reviewing the state of modern society in light of the age-old halakhic requirements, are coming to believe that perhaps the marriage motivation should *not* be classified in the category of ulterior motive. There are a number of reasons, halakhically valid, which are prompting a reconsideration of opening the doors to Judaism wider despite the obvious risks attendant upon such a policy.[4]

Not the least of these considerations is that people in our open society can grow from accommodation to conviction. Experience today teaches us not to be cavalier with those who adopt a new religion without what we consider to be the *right* reason. Often, they begin the long road of conversion for reasons of accommodation, yet, in the end, arrive at remarkably deep levels of spiritual conviction. The Jewish tradition has long known of such means of discovering the truth in many areas. Habituating oneself to honest *practices*—even for the wrong *motivation*—may lead one to honesty. Feigned love often evolves into authentic feeling. If a person studies Torah, even without pure intent, he is likely to end up studying it out of genuine devotion.[5]

It is for this reason, and others too technical to treat in the body of this text, that strenuous Jewish communal efforts are being exerted to bring the accommodation convert into a more serious consideration of the Judaism he or she adopted.

What is heartening is the sincerity of large numbers of people converting to Judaism today, who do so "for the sake of Heaven."

Conversion generally will result from a complex of multiple motivations—to marry; to raise children in a one-faith family; to avoid conflict with parents. A desire to establish a home in a unified religious commitment for the purpose of bringing up children as Jews obviously savors more of sincerity than of personal gain, and must be for Heaven's sake.

The Jewish people searches for converts of conviction. But, it recognizes the great potential in those who are sincere, who are family-oriented, who love God, who work "for the sake of Heaven," and who are therefore candidates for moving from accommodation to conviction.

Notes to Chapter Four

1. In accordance with this principle, they noted that no converts were accepted during the reigns of King David and King Solomon, because the motives doubtless were power or wealth or social advancement. But they also confirm that, as Maimonides wrote in his monumental code of law, Hilkhot Issurei Bi'ah, 13:14-15, "This is the 'secret' of the failures of both Samson, 'a savior of Israel,' and Solomon, '*yedid ha 'Shem,*' the 'friend of God. . . .'" It is inconceivable that these great leaders married gentile women. Surely, we must assume, their wives had been converted prior to their marriage. But the problem was that it soon became apparent that, in fact, their wives converted only for the sake of marriage and power, and by a court of laymen—rather than rabbis—who did not enforce the current practice that converts were not to be accepted during these years. The law considered them to be legitimately converted until, with the passing of time and events, their original intention would be discovered. But, as their true motives finally were revealed, their conversions were invalidated, and both leaders technically were held to be in consort with heathens. The Book of Judges 14:3 and the first Book of Kings 11:4 therefore considered the wives still to retain their former status of gentile.

2. See Appendix 1.

3. If so, what will it do with this host of people and their marriages, which almost always will take place, with or without benefit of conversion? And what shall we say of those accommodation converts who might have grown into conviction converts? And how does it measure genuine conviction infallibly, and what are the criteria?

   The problems of motivation abound and, in our day, they are multiplied and exacerbated by the heady freedom of our open society, which has loosed the bonds of family, religion and community. Unfortunately, solutions that possibly could be used are considered by some too dangerous, by others too radical, by still others insufficiently authoritative. For the mass of the religiously illiterate Jews, they are hidden in footnotes in the tomes of the law, in small-scripted super-commentaries on the back pages of the Talmud, and in hundreds of closely written responsa dating from the Middle Ages—the province of scholars and rabbinic courts. But people need answers to pressing problems. And both the Jewish partners and their sincere prospective non-Jewish spouses are most often decent people from decent families, and have their own integrity and their own genuine motivations, although probably inadequate Jewish knowledge, experiences and identifications.

4. See Appendix 5, "The Marriage Motivation: A Brief Review."

5. The talmudic phrase is *mi'toch she'lo li-shmah ba li'shmah.*

5

To Join or Not to Join

THE JOYS AND BURDENS OF BEING JEWISH

The formal response that the Bet Din makes in behalf of the Jewish community to the gentile's customarily enthusiastic request to be converted is astonishment, disbelief: "You can't mean that." It is a cold splash that emphasizes a sobering fact: being a Jew is no joy ride—it is often a painful experience. This hesitation does not meet the convert's expectations at that moment of decision—it surely does not fan the fire of his exuberance by enumerating the glories of Jewishness and strengthening his resolve.

The tradition clearly describes the entire process of receiving converts:[1]

> When a gentile comes forth for the purpose of becoming a proselyte and, upon investigation, no ulterior motive is found, the court should say to him: "Why do you come forth to become a proselyte? Do you not know that Israel is at present sorely afflicted, oppressed, despised, confounded, and beset by suffering?" If he answers: "I know, and I am indeed unworthy," he should be accepted immediately. The great commentator, Rashi, amplifies: "I am not worthy enough to share your troubles, and would it were that I could reach that level."

> After teaching him a short selection of fundamentals of the faith and of major and minor laws, we inform him of the punishment for violating the commandments. How so? The

> court should say to him: "Know that before you came to this religion, if you ate prohibited animal fat, your punishment was not excision from the people; if you violated the Sabbath, your punishment was not stoning. But now, after you convert, if you eat prohibited fats, you are liable to be excised from the people; if you violate the Sabbath, you are liable to be stoned."

Telling someone who, in good faith, wants to embrace Judaism that he is liable for the death penalty (although it hasn't been practiced in thousands of years) does not sound quite like a Jewish Welcome Wagon. But if this statement of the Rabbis is meant to be straightforward and not oriented to attract converts, it is also not designed solely to discourage or forestall them. Maimonides adds: "And we do not magnify [the mention of punishments]; and we do not detail for him [even the punishments just recited][2] because this might cause him to hesitate or to turn away from the good path to the bad path." Judaism will not sell itself to a prospective convert; but it will also not sell itself short. It warmly welcomes all sincere converts; and so it must reassure them, soon after it discourages them, that being a Jew has huge benefits, as well. Therefore the bad-list of the agonies must be balanced by a good-list of the joys— a roster of benefits equal to the roll call of risks.

For this reason, immediately after listing the troubles, Judaism counts the blessings that accrue to a gentile who accepts Judaism:

> And just as we teach him the liabilities of the commandments, so we teach him the reward of the commandments. And we teach him that, with the observance of these commandments, he will merit the life of the world-to-come; and that there is no completely righteous person but the wise ones who perform these commandments and know them.

> And we explain to him: "Know that [a place in] the world-to-come is kept for the righteous—and that they are Jews. But that which you see—that Jews suffer in this world— it is [in fact] a good thing, hidden away for them because you can't gather much good in this world."

At this point, the prospective convert is faced with alternatives, both of which offer substantially the same result—the world-to-come; he or she can opt for remaining a righteous non-Jew and receive it, or become an observant Jew and receive it. Which will the convert choose?

In essence, the response to the convert articulates the wisdom of the ancient talmudic advice, offered in another context: "Bring them close with the right hand and keep them distant with the left."

These statements are placed at the very outset of the process and are formally delivered by the community's representative, the Bet Din, with the specific intention of informing the candidate the balanced truth—some of the woes and some of the joys— about the state of the Jews and their religion.

It would require a complete history and philosophy of the Jews to do justice to a listing of all the delights and disappointments of Jewish living. It is not our intention to provide such an exhaustive description but, following the style of the talmudic Sages, to touch upon the subjects lightly so that the reader may become acquainted with them, but not be overwhelmed.

The Burdens of a Jew

Some of the woes of being Jewish are unfortunately obvious:

The Jews are the permanent minority of global society. With over five billion people on earth and only thirteen million Jews sprinkled thinly over the whole spinning globe, it is easy to understand why we are the perpetual "strangers in the gates" of every city, historically outcast to its perimeters or choked into the ghettos of its bowels—unwelcome, unprotected, and often savagely driven out.

If this sounds coarse, it is because life as a Jew was coarse. If this sounds like a generalization, it is because it was always true. The Jewish people has been an object of jealousy and hatred throughout most of its history, and it has suffered not only at the hands of butchers in concentration camps, but also at the hands of the "good people," such as Christian crusaders, Papal inquisitors, Muslim sheikhs, and third-world potentates who never met a Jew. And, of course, they are scoffed at and turned away by the "old boys" at the club. Measured against the Nazis, these hometown bigots are only tumbleweeds blowing on the desert floor, but their persistent and ubiquitous presence is a constant reminder of the universal Jewish condition.

Converts need to know that conversion means being associated with a pattern of ethnic behavior that is out of sync with the style of the prevailing majority, thereby making them vulnerable to prejudice, possibly to social isolation, and at the very least, to petty gossip, annoying innuendoes, and all the verbal firearms in the arsenal of the local gentry.

But one should not mistake these as just the stale idiosyncracies of our society. Often in our history, these malignant little prejudices have diseased a whole society, metastasizing uncontrollably until they destroyed both their bearers and their victims. It is unfortunately true that, in terms of the risk-benefit ratio, the risk has often outweighed the benefit, and has made being a Jew a difficult and sometimes unbearable burden.

The convert should understand also that, with conversion, one becomes vulnerable to rejection by old friends, and possibly to only partial acceptance by new ones.

Also difficult to bear is the whole skein of new religious practices. They are many, and alien to the life-style the convert is leaving; they often take a toll on one's time and one's patience. Then, too, at the beginning, the convert feels ignorant of the proper way to observe the laws and may begin to doubt the wisdom of deciding to join the Jewish people. One may feel intimidated attending services, community meetings or parties, fearing that he or she will be called upon, or tested, isolated or humiliated, or made the subject of whispers. In fact, this is one reason why many Jews wonder what possesses otherwise intelligent gentiles to want to convert to this fate. "Can anything be worth this?" they ask themselves. It is a question which must occur to those who choose to become Jews, and it is worth pondering.

Is It Worth Bearing the Burden?

There are two obvious questions that might occur to a convert at this point: First, who needs to put up with these difficulties? If it is spiritual salvation that the convert is seeking, he now knows that the righteous gentile shares with the observant Jew the same reward in that future world-to-come. There is no religious requirement for the gentile to be "saved" and no obligation to become Jewish.

Second, is this an effective way of selling this religion? Surely, it is not—that is, if Judaism is to be sold. But that is not at all the purpose of conversion. The Bet Din's response to the convert is designed to be an authentic, unadorned description of the condition of the Jewish people as it exists today and as it has prevailed throughout most of Jewish history—nothing more, nothing less. It is meant to convey a truth, and the truth admits of no romancing, no glorification, no pretty words designed to attract people to the faith—and also no pugnacious, xenophobic attempts to stave off newcomers with tales of horrors.

The Joys of Jewishness

It is well, therefore, that the reader, in keeping with the Halakhah's spirit as well as its dictum, should also be aware of the joys of *being* a Jew before *becoming* a Jew.

The waters of Jewish joy issue forth from many wellsprings. Taken together, they become the headwaters that have refreshed the Jewish spirit in every age, buoyed the hopes which the agonies of existence have withered, and enabled the Jewish people to flow mightily through history, fertilizing arid civilizations and producing scholars, rabbis, leaders and artists whenever they appeared. Terrorists have indeed caused havoc, but they have been vanquished time and again. The Torquemadas and Chmielnickis and Hitlers and Stalins are entombed in the black caves of the earth; but whenever at the Passover Seder another Jewish child ritually poses the Four Questions, their graves sink lower into the abyss of human history.

Many are the wellsprings that enabled Jewish life to flower. The Torah faith of the Jew emphasizes more meaning than magic, more earthly well-being than spiritual reclusiveness, more community vibrancy and growth than individual salvation, more reason than leap of faith, more deed than belief, more "vitamins" than "tranquilizers." The joy of this religion is enhanced by its structure and form; an actionable law rather than an amorphous mass of beliefs. The joy of its tradition is that it is long-lived and time-honored, enriched by a universe of ideas and a cultural diversity unknown to any other religious or philosophic system. It knows exuberance and solemnity, contemplation and protestation, humor and pathos.

The Jewish ethic speaks of tenderness and loving-kindness, but boasts a muscular morality that never turns the cheek. The paradigm is the comparison of the major religions at the dawn of their civilizations:[3] Buddha, upon seeing death, sickness and poverty, retreated from the real world to a life of contemplation; Jesus saw his time as the "end of days" and developed a perfectionist ethic of surrender; Mohammed simply fled reality and began to prophesy from the bush.

Moses went out of his residence in Pharaoh's palace, saw two men fighting, and lunged to intercede and strike a blow for justice. Hence, the Jewish perpetual and ubiquitous presence at the forefront of every social progress movement, in every major revolution, in virtually every country of their exile, from the ancient Egypt of the Hyksos to the civil rights movement in rural Alabama.

The joy of being Jewish derives from pride in the people's unflagging creativity—monotheism, the Bible, the synagogue concept, the idea of a prayerbook and, of course, its immense role in the formation of democracy, religious freedom, and human rights. This joy celebrates Judaism's emphasis on the development of the mind and its intellect which manifests itself in the overwhelmingly disproportionate number of Jews in the sciences, the arts, the professions, the sheer numbers and diversity of Jewish Nobel laureates, the size of its college population. And it derives from the Jews' success in the act of survival, not only a triumph of endurance in the fury of endlessly changing environments but also a constantly creative life-enhancing state. Feudal lords beat Jews as serfs; communists exiled them to the frozen wasteland as capitalists; crusaders burned them as infidels; but Jews knew their mission and their lot clearly, and they stood, collectively and at all times, in the center of immensities and in the conflux of eternities, and called upon the God of Israel.

There was a sort of agony implicit in our joy. The downside of every achievement was proclaimed vigorously by our detractors—our intellectualism made us "elitist"; our determination to succeed made us "pushy"; our religion made us "strange"; our tight families made us "clannish"; our feeling of chosenness made us "insufferable." They forced us to bare our backs, broke their sticks over our spines, then called us "passivists." The world asked us to build them towers of civilization and then tried to hang us on the scaffolding: the Christians took Jesus, the Jew, and then began to crucify the Jews; Charlemagne, the king, invited the Jews to inaugurate a new industrial class in France and then accused the Jews of mercantilism and expelled them; the Axis Powers unleashed a Holocaust and forty years later, in a riot of brazenness, the Jews are taunted for being fixated on persecution; some lunatics incredibly declare that the bloodletting never even happened; many even say, "Let bygones be bygones; let's forgive and forget." Indeed.

The joy comes also from a sense of belonging to a well-defined, close-knit group, whose motto is: "All Jews are responsible for one another." At the end of the conversion process, the newborn Jew does *not* become a "member of the *faith*"—some spiritualized entity facing heavenward—but a member of the *people*, brothers and sisters locked arm-in-arm and sharing the destiny of people halfway across the globe. The Jewish people is an extended family—sometimes very extended—and the tightness heightens our pride in those of our people who bring glory to the name of God, but also intensifies our shame for those Jews who desecrate the Name. For better or for worse—the cohesiveness and the quarrels are all in the family.

The joy and the agony merge most indistinguishably in the one concept of the chosen people which has characterized the Jew since Abraham struck the covenant with God. Chosenness, which describes the Jewish relationship with God, is a consequence of our mutual choosing. It is a profound concept, difficult to articulate, easily corrupted by counterfeit and heinous imitations, such as Nietzschean racial superiority, and easily mistaken for chip-on-the-shoulder snobbishness. It requires study by new Jews.

Chosenness is both burden and glory, agony and joy. The Jews have been chosen for service and for servitude. The most evident contemporary illustration is the State of Israel. A country the size of New Jersey, with the population of Chicago, receives as much news coverage as the Soviet Union.[4] Is Israel a superpower? Does it have oil? Can it threaten the whole world? Yet the west has a fascination and preoccupation with Israel—either a blind love or a burning hatred. But almost no one is neutral about the Jews.

The French philosopher Montesquieu once observed, "Happy is the nation whose history is boring to read." Jews who one day glory in their chosenness to bring a message of goodness to the world, on the next day moan that Israel is the cynosure of the world's ills and of some of its decadent imaginations. Only a thin membrane separates the joy from the agony of the chosenness of the chosen people.

These are but a few of the pluses and minuses of the Jewish

equation. The choice is yours. Garibaldi once said to the Italian patriots that he did not promise them victory, but only a good and honorable struggle. God does promise the Jews ultimate victory: "The eternity of Israel will never be proven false." But a good and honorable struggle will absolutely be required.

"Why did Israel have to suffer exile?" ask the Sages. "To win converts to Judaism," they answer.[5] Ultimately, the joy will overcome the agony.

Notes to Chapter Five

1. Maimonides, *Mishneh Torah,* Hilkhot Issurei Bi'ah, ch. 14.
2. Bach to Tur, Yoreh De'ah 269.
3. Dr. Yehudah Bergman, *Ha'Yahadut: Nishmatah ve'Chayehah,* ch. 9, *"Ha'Yahadut Vea'Enoshiyut,"* Reuben Mass, Jerusalem 1935.
4. See Thomas L. Friedman, lead story *New York Times Magazine,* February 1, 1987.
5. See Pesachim 87b.

6
Entering Into the Covenant

The formal term for becoming Jews by choice is "entering into the covenant." It is the unique covenantal relationship with God that a gentile enters into in order to become a child of Abraham. It is therefore important for the prospective proselyte to understand the nature of the Jewish covenant—what precisely is the definition of "covenant," what and whom the covenant binds, and how it affects the *b'nai b'rit*, or "children of the covenant," the Jewish people.

A covenant is an ancient legal instrument that formalizes a relationship between persons and is the basis of the structure and governance of society, the *polis*. Judaism originated a new concept of "covenant" (*b'rit*). It dared to introduce the incredible idea that people could strike a covenant which could bind not only one person to another, but a flesh-and-blood person to Almighty God, the King of Kings. This covenant is the creative and unique contribution of the Torah.[1] Nearly two thousand years later, Christianity, in seeking to replace Israel as the chosen people, would introduce a replacement covenant, or new "testament," which would strike a new formal relationship with God.

Because it defines the elemental relationship between people and God, the covenant idea is the most fundamental, seminal, and consequential concept in all the Bible—and the covenants recorded in the Torah are thus the main events of the Jewish religion.

Of all the important covenants in the Torah, two are central to the faith: the covenant with the Patriarch Abraham, and the covenant struck at Mt. Sinai at the moment of Revelation, the giving of Torah. These two covenants are of diverse qualities and they express different emphases. The Patriarchal Covenant is personal and intimate—between God and a single great man, Abraham. It created the underpinning for the grandest and most significant covenant, the Sinaitic Covenant. The covenant at Sinai is public and formal, between God and the descendants of Abraham—600,000 members of the House of Israel and their progeny.

THE TWO COVENANTS

The Patriarchal Covenant

The narrative description of the Patriarchal Covenant is simple: God chose Abraham and his descendants as His eternal people, and He chose also the land which He promised them. At first, Abraham was called Abram (*av ram*), a great father, but a private person—brilliant, original, kind, self-sacrificing, powerful, magisterial. This singularly superior, pre-eminent personality underwent a complete internal transformation.

Astonishingly, the Torah does not describe his voyage of discovery. It does not provide us with even one detail of Abram's early life which might give us some clue to understanding why God chose to enter into a covenant with this one individual in all the world. It does not speak of an intense inner struggle, flashes of insight, bolts of creativity. It records simply: "And God said to Abram . . ." (Genesis 12:1).[2] It is as though this report were intruding into the midst of a dialogue or event, without even the benefit of an introduction; without God's ever "appearing" to Abram before speaking with him, as He had appeared to Noah and Adam before He spoke to them; without even a sparse description of who this Abram was, or which personal attributes qualified him to talk with the Lord of the Universe.

Characteristically, it is the Midrash (Rabbinic teachings that elaborate the biblical narrative) that addresses the question of how this human being discovered so lofty and fundamental a concept—and even the Midrash does so only in passing. It describes Abram, the child of Terah, the foremost manufacturer of idols in his day, as smashing the statues in his father's shop. Abram was always to be found "arguing with his neighbors, protesting that they were not following the truth . . . saying that all images deserve to be destroyed and smashed into pieces in order to save the people from error. . . ."[3]

In another source,[4] the Midrash quotes Rabbi Isaac as saying that Abram's discovery of God as the Master of the Universe was similar "to a man who was traveling from place to place when he saw a building in flames [the world being consumed by vice].[5] 'Is it possible that the building has nobody to look after it?' he wondered. Then the owner of the building looked out and proclaimed: 'I am the owner of the building.' In similar fashion, when Abraham our father asked, 'Is it conceivable that the world is without a guide?' the Holy One, Blessed be He, looked out and proclaimed: 'I am the Guide, the Sovereign of the Universe.' "

Abram's internal transformation after receiving the word of God propels him to a new and exalted religious stature, ultimately elevating him to such heights that he is no longer simply a private person of immense capabilities, but the greatest public leader in the history of ancient religion. The internal metamorphosis called for an external change—a change of his *gestalt* in the eyes of the world. No longer will he be called *Abram*, "a great father," but *Abraham* (*av raham*), meaning "father of a multitude," the progenitor of descendants who will mold the world for millennia to come.

Abram's wife, *Sarai*, undergoes a parallel transformation, a radical soul change during which she grows spiritually alongside her husband. To conform with her new mission, her name is changed to *Sarah*, "princess," signifying her growth from citizen to "sovereign," from mother to matriarch. The covenant is made by God with *both* Abraham and Sarah, and thereafter Patriarchal Covenants are struck with both husband and wife, and Jewish men and women are all parties to the covenant.[6]

Abraham undergoes the ceremony of circumcision at the command of God as a symbol of the covenant. It is for the express purpose of conversion, and he and Sarah begin to proselytize others. Judaism begins to spread among the masses. The Bible record is clear about the "souls they made in Haran," referring, as the Talmud puts it, to the male converts "made" by Abraham and the female converts "made" by Sarah—"made" because their conversion created new beings akin, as it were, to God's creation of the human being.

In Jewish tradition, Abraham is every convert's "father" and, according to Jewish law, the convert is referred to in official matters, such as marriage and divorce, as the child of "Abraham, our father." That is the sense of the question that a twelfth-century convert put to Maimonides: "Am I permitted to recite the phrase "God of our fathers" in my prayers, since it is an obvious untruth?" Maimonides answered, in a florid and eloquent declaration, that all Jews—born Jews and Jews by choice—are partners in the covenant with God and spiritually Abraham's children.[7]

Jewish law here expresses the proselyte's reality. Converts are Abraham's "children," and enter into the "Covenant of Abraham," because they have retraced Abraham's daring steps in their lifetimes—capturing a new idea, having to smash old idols, suffering the fate of having to be "alone" in their views (tradition says that Abraham was called *ivri*, Hebrew, because Abraham stood on one side, *ever*, and the whole world stood on the other), and going through the pain of circumcision as adults.

The Sinaitic Covenant

Though Abraham formally converted and was circumcised as an individual, it was not until the Jews departed Egypt and arrived at Sinai that the whole people converted formally.

Unlike the intimate revelation of God to Abraham at the founding covenant, the Revelation at Sinai and the covenant ratified there were witnessed by hundreds of thousands of people who left Egypt. This covenant was held as a massive public forum rather than as a private audience with a chosen leader. It was to be a national referendum on the Jews' contract with God.

The Rabbis of the Talmud elaborated on this aspect of the Revelation by means of parable, metaphor and poetic imagery. They said that the Revelation was enacted in the desert because it belongs to all civilization; it was not heard by Israel alone but by all the inhabitants of earth; the Heavenly voice divided itself into the seventy languages of the world so that all might understand its universally significant message; the souls of all the unborn generations in Israel were assembled at the foot of the mountain.

This was the setting for the conversion of the whole Jewish people and for its covenant with God.

THE TEXTS OF THE SINAI COVENANT

The Proposal of the Pact (Exodus 19:3-8)

> And Moses went up unto God, and the Lord called unto him out of the mountain, saying: "Thus shalt thou say to the House of Jacob, and tell the children of Israel: Ye have seen what I did unto the Egyptians, and how I bore you on eagles' wings, and brought you unto Myself."

> "Now therefore, if ye will hearken unto My voice indeed, and keep My covenant, then ye shall be Mine own treasure from among all peoples; for all the earth is Mine; and ye shall be unto Me a kingdom of Priests, and a holy nation. These are the words which thou shalt speak unto the children of Israel."

> And Moses came and called for the elders of the people, and set before them all these words which the Lord commanded him. And all the people answered together, and said: "All that the Lord hath spoken we will do." And Moses reported the words of the people unto the Lord.

Israel must observe God's law. In turn, God agrees to accept Israel as His Holy Nation. The Jewish people accept the agreement, and Moses transmits this message to God.

The Revelation (Exodus 19:9-11, 16)

> . . . And Moses told the words of the people unto the Lord. And the Lord said unto Moses: "Go unto the people and sanctify them today and tomorrow, and let them wash their garments. And be ready against the third day; for on the third day the Lord will come down in the sight of all the people upon Mt. Sinai."

> . . . And it came to pass on the third day, when it was morning, that there were thunder and lightning and a thick cloud upon the mount, and the voice of a horn exceeding loud; and all the people that were in the camp trembled. And Moses brought forth the people out of the camp to meet God. . . .

The Lord accepts the nation's offer "before the eyes of all

Israel" and conveys the commandments to them face to face. The Revelation takes place in the midst of a thunderstorm of exceptional power and grandeur, accompanied by an eruption of nature—lightning, thunder, earthquake, fire, and the piercing sound of the ram's horn.

The Covenant is Presented; the People Respond (Exodus 24:7)

> And he took the Book of the Covenant, and read in the hearing of the people; and they said: "All that the Lord hath spoken we will do, and obey."

The following day, Moses formally reads the people "The Book of the Covenant," the *Sefer Ha'B'rit*. When the people formally respond, "We will do and we will obey," they emphasize that they first will fulfill the action required by the contract and only then, they add, will they try to understand the mandate—to which they are in any case committed unflinchingly (Exodus 24:4-18).[8]

The Covenant is Ratified; the People Convert

> And Moses took the blood [of the oxen, half of which he placed in a basin and the other half of which he poured on the altar] and sprinkled it on the people, and said: "Behold the blood of the covenant, which the Lord hath made with you in agreement with all these words."

The two contracting parties receive the blood, half and half, and are united in a solemn bond by mutual agreement. The Sages maintain that, before participating in the sacrificial blood sprinkling, the people had to perform the immersion. This is hinted at earlier when Moses "sanctified the people and they washed their garments" (Exodus 19:14). This was what the law required of all who were to bring sacrifices. The immersion at Sinai was the concluding ceremony of conversion for the entire people.

The Sinaitic Covenant is considered the most important single public convocation in Jewish history and the central event of Jewish theology.[9] It is the most comprehensive expression of the distinctiveness of the Jewish people. Only by grasping the covenant at Sinai can we have an appreciation of the uniqueness of Jewish morality, Jewish destiny, Jewish peoplehood, and the place of Torah in the collective Jewish mind.[10]

This covenantal event has no parallel in human history— a pact by God with an entire people. It is not refuted subsequently or even questioned by any reputable Jewish scholar for centuries. It does not rest, as do other religious covenants, upon the testimony of individuals—whether of prophets, priests, philosophers or saints—or miracles performed by religious mystics. It is also not primarily a consequence of sudden Divine inspiration, of heroic leadership or of some inherited dogma.

It is, in its essence, nothing other than the simple fulfillment of the first covenant, that ancient pact with Abraham. Simple proof of the primacy of this covenant is that early Christianity never considered claiming that Jews had no covenant—that was unthinkable. They dared not tinker with the Jewish formula for religious significance and spiritual meaning. Rather, they claimed that the Sinaitic Covenant was "superseded" and that henceforth Christians, and not the Jews, were bearers of the Divine covenant. The power of the covenant idea was too intense to be dismissed by any contemporary personality or movement; it could only be "improved" upon—slightly altered to serve other purposes.

CONDITIONS OF THE COVENANT BETWEEN GOD AND MAN

The covenant was not merely a promise, nor even only a Divine promise. It was a workable, enforceable, dynamic contractual agreement that bonded the King of Kings with His chosen servants. This set the tone of their relationship for all time. This covenant has to be a recognized, actionable, legal instrument that clearly itemized the demands and expectations of both parties. In order for it to be effective, it needs to meet the following conditions at a minimum.

It is Bilateral

The covenant between human beings and God is a bilateral pact of free and independent parties. God is free, of course—independent of humans, although in need of their human testimony.[11] But, in a profound philosophical sense, people are also independent of God—witness Moses, Jonah and Jeremiah who say "no" to God's urgent calling—although obviously human beings exist by the grace of God.[12] As free agents, both God and man are within the legal ambit of the covenant; both are indispensable to making and also to ratifying the covenant;

and both are under rigorous obligation to fulfill their portion of the agreement. The Sinaitic Covenant is a consequence of a "negotiated settlement" between two "equal" parties.[13]

In the words of Rabbi Joseph B. Soloveitchik: "It is a meeting of finitude and infinity, temporality and eternity, creature and creator . . . they bind themselves together and participate in a unitive existence."[14] At Sinai, the Bible records the fateful meeting as "*God* went *down* upon the mountain . . ." and "*Moses* went *up* the mountain . . .". The two covenantal parties meet on the mountain and the covenant they strike endures eternally.

It is Indestructible

The God-man covenant cannot be terminated by either party acting alone. Neither party can withdraw from the agreement at any point in history or for any reason whatsoever. God accepted that limitation upon Himself by entering this contractual agreement. It is true that one party might not perform according to the expectation of the other, but that would not invalidate the covenant. It would be its violation, but not its abolition.

Indeed, even a superficial reading of the Prophets proclaims this biblical truth, "And Jeshurun [Israel] waxed fat and kicked." The Jewish people has backslid on the icy roads of history after virtually every uphill advance. For that, the Jews were punished—but never irrevocably banished. God may have "hidden His face" for a time, but never did He withdraw from His covenantal relationship with the Jews.

A graphic illustration of this binding, yet irrevocable, nature of covenant are the two metaphors most frequently used in ancient Jewish writings to describe the Israel-God relationship. They are the parent-child relationship and the husband-wife bond. Why are two such quite different metaphors necessary? The answer of the Jewish teachers is insightful: the relationship of husband and wife is utilized to emphasize the *intimacy* of the partners to the covenant; the bond between parent and child is to illustrate its *indissolubility* even when that intimacy lapses. Husband or wife may ultimately betray their most intimate partner. But, unlike a marriage relationship, the God-man covenant could never end in divorce. That is why covenant is also illustrated by the parent-child bond—the most indestructible human relationship possible.

It is for All Jews—Jews by Chance and Jews by Choice

Both covenants, the Patriarchal and the Sinaitic, remain in force for all Jews—those who lived then and those who live now. And the covenants permanently embrace all persons who "enter into the covenant." Those who in subsequent generations decide to enter the covenant are considered to have been spiritually present on that mountain and in those days. Indeed, the early ancestors of converts might well have been there before a later descendant in the genealogical record decided to defect.

While only the Jewish people are bound by this covenant, which they accepted at a specific location and at a specific moment in history, Judaism is not and has never been exclusivist in either ethnic or territorial matters. All gentiles throughout the ages could have become parties to the covenant—as though they themselves had stood at Sinai—as soon as they converted formally.

These words sound noble, but the whole enterprise of conversion took no mean effort. It takes little imagination to realize what an immense achievement it was for this embattled people to have kept open the gates to Judaism in the face of every impulse to slam the doors shut forever. "Who needs this trouble?" must have been the anguished cry of every generation that suffered because it was hospitable to non-Jews. But the religious principle remained unshaken: "Do not shut the door in the face of converts."

The Distinctions

There are several significant, yet subtle, distinctions between the Patriarchal and Sinaitic Covenants:

The Patriarchal Covenant is designed primarily to bind God, not Abraham or his descendants. It is unilateral—God chose, God promised. Forever. There is no *quid pro quo* expected. In fact, Abraham is given only three simple obligations—believing in God, not marrying out of the faith, and circumcision.[15] This is a clear guarantee to the Jewish people that God assures its survival, that Jews remain God's chosen people—even though they occasionally backslide, anger Him, violate His commandments. His covenant with Abraham is unconditional.

The later Sinaitic Covenant is contractually bilateral— binding the two parties to *reciprocal* action. This means that while the Jews will always remain God's people, if they sin, they will be punished; if they violate His trust, He will violate theirs.

Further, the Patriarchal Covenant addresses itself to the vital essence of the religious *persona*—the person of faith and his or her inward experience with God. The Sinaitic Covenant relates to a person's external behavior which God mandates. Abraham teaches how to *feel* Jewish; Sinai teaches how to *act* Jewish. The Sinaitic Covenant legislates and enacts the Patriarchal Covenant. Whereas thinking and feeling are matters for the individual, the actionable component of religion is mandated in detail and must be followed.

Despite differences in content and style, both covenants are permanently entwined. The Patriarchal Covenant does not create a people; that must wait until Sinai. Conversely, the Sinaitic Covenant needs the Patriarchal—at Sinai, God says: "I remember the covenant with Abraham, Isaac and Jacob."[16]

TWO LANDMARKS OF THE SINAITIC COVENANT

If prospective proselytes want to appreciate the spiritual aspirations of the Jews—their religious program and their shared destiny—as they enter the fold and become members of the covenant, they need to probe more deeply and to grasp the practical religious consequences of the covenant.

As we bring the Sinaitic Covenant into sharper focus, it becomes clear that it actually comprises two separate critical moments—one takes place at the Exodus, immediately *before* the Jews depart from Egypt; the other occurs *after* they depart, at Sinai itself. Tradition teaches that, before leaving Egypt, all Jewish men were circumcised—the first step in conversion. The second step in the conversion process, the immersion of both men and women in a mikveh, was taken in preparation for receiving the Torah at Sinai.

The first part of what is comprehensively called the Sinaitic Covenant occurs three months before Sinai at the final stage of the Egyptian slavery when God promises, "And I will take you unto Me for a people and I will be your God." This first component expresses the reciprocal quality of the Sinaitic Covenant between the Jews and their God.

The second component of the covenant takes place at Mt.

Sinai and is the peak moment—the zenith—of the emerging formal relationship between God and the people. The Bible records: "And he [Moses] took the blood of the covenant . . . and he said: 'This is the blood of the covenant that God struck with you with all these words.'" It is said that all Jews were there—past, present and those yet unborn. Abraham's descendants were there, masses of Egyptians who fled with them and converted were there; Ruth the convert was "there"; Rabbi Ben Bag Bag, the converted talmudic Sage of the third century was there; the King of the Khazars who converted in the eighth century was there; Ovadiah, the noted convert of the twelfth century, was there; a young woman who converted in Los Angeles last year was there.

At the Exodus in Egypt: The Peoplehood Pact

Before the Jews could gather to meet God and receive the Ten Commandments, they were hurled together by the forces of history. Already at this early stage, as they prepare to break the shackles of the Pharaoh, Jews discovered the desperate need to seek the shelter and company of other Jews to protect themselves against the slings and arrows of hostile nations. The individual needs to be bound to a whole people. Physical and political conditions will not permit him to escape the fate of his people.

Already here, at the very beginning of the people's history, the Jew finds himself alone. He realizes that if he is to keep God's law in the face of a disbelieving world, he will be chosen—to be pursued for much of his existence. The glorious promise to be God's own people empowers him and enables him to endure the crisis—but he need only look into the fierce eyes of the armed horsemen bearing down upon him at the edge of the sea to realize that the head-splitting pressure on him only muffles the thunderous promise to be God's people. The Jews' only security is to stay close to brothers and sisters. This is the peoplehood component of the covenant—a basic ingredient of the glue that held Jews together for centuries. Thus, the Jews embraced their fellow Jews even before they embraced God and His Torah.

The Beginning of Community

This historic moment, so expressive of the lonely man of faith, is actually an extension of the spiritual history of the earlier Patriarchs and heroes. Grandfather Abraham was also alone in the midst of a sea of zealous idolators when first he found God, and God him.[17] His son and grandson, Isaac and Jacob, found themselves in frightful loneliness at critical junctures in their search for truth. Joseph, in the midst of a society that adored him, was alone because he was genuinely a man of faith. The need for community was implanted in the minds of Jews from their earliest national memory. From that time to this, the Jew has persevered in this shared fate.[18]

It is at this juncture that the Jew by choice joins Jewish history—seeking fellowship with the Jewish people. The convert is no spiritual hitchhiker, getting on at a crossroads with no concern for the road already traveled. He or she does not become just a believer in Judaism but a part of the people, sharing the people's ancient experience and its promised future.

It may appear paradoxical that those who are born Jews opt more quickly and in greater numbers to the call of community life than of the synagogue and its reaching for God; while the Jew by choice very often comes to Judaism with an easy affinity for the faith, but no easy association with the community. Of course, the convert comes from a "faith"—generally Christianity—and expects that he will be entering another "faith." But soon he learns that Judaism is not merely a faith. It is a blend of God and people and land and Torah and holy tongue. It is not a "Jewish church," a place for prayer—it is the "House" of Jacob, a place for living.

This sharing of the Divine fate as a community of the faithful promotes a number of positive values:

It permits no distinction between the fortunate and the suffering. In whatever condition Jews find themselves, they need to be at one with other Jews. Queen Esther of the Bible may be wrapped in royal robes in the Palace hallway while Mordecai, covered with mourner's sackcloth, waits anxiously in the courtyard, but both are equally considered the oppressed. When one Jew is beaten in a cave in Ethiopia, another Jew in a Chicago skyscraper must feel pain. A Jew in Kansas City is expected to sacrifice time and funds to protest for the Jew in Moscow not permitted to emigrate to Israel. This is neither startling nor even remarkable. For Jews, it must be second nature—its roots after all derive from our very first experience as a people.

This sharing component of the first part of the Sinaitic Covenant—the peoplehood pact—is the basis for that landmark legal and philosophical pronouncement of the Talmud: "All Jews are guarantors for one another." As partners in suffering, no Jew can afford, either physically or spiritually, to lead a life of hermetic isolation.

This is forcefully illustrated by a question recorded in the Midrash of a child born with two heads. To what portion of the parents' inheritance is he entitled—that of one child or of two? In an ancient Jewish court, they decided upon a test: apply hot water to one head and watch the reaction of the other. If the second is pained, the two-headed child is one child. If the second does not react to the pain of the first, they are two people. The application is clear: the Jews, spread over many nations, speaking many languages, heirs to widely divergent cultural influences, are they one or many? Are they a divided people or do they share the same soul and live a unitive existence?

Being "guarantors for one another," our brothers' keepers, is not idealistic poppycock, an exalted but hardly ever reachable goal. In Judaism, such ethereal phrases need to be snatched from the sky and molded in the clay of reality. "Love your neighbor" in Jewish law conveys a practical strategy in how to deal kindly with even a criminal neighbor. The ideal of taking responsibility for others is translated into specific positive acts expected of Jewish people in daily living.

The English word "charity," for example, is derived from the Latin *caritas* meaning to help someone less fortunate. The Jewish term for charity is *tzedakah*, which derives from *tzedek*, meaning "justice"—and it implies a very practical redistribution of wealth, not dependent on how empathically one is disposed toward the troubled. (This contrast is elaborated upon in Chapter 23.) Being helpful, in a Jewish framework, is not a moral directive to do a favor for those less fortunate, but the fulfillment of a religious obligation mandated by God. This accounts in great measure for the success of Jewish institutional charity. In Jewish terms, this bespeaks the concept of "Divine Fate," the *goral* component of the covenant.[19] It is one of the major consequences of the peoplehood covenant.

At the Revelation on Sinai: the God-Man Partnership

The Jews, already having come together in a common bond of mutual protection, now stand poised as one people at the foot of Mt. Sinai prepared to face God—to dedicate themselves to live in His presence, obey His will, follow His precepts, and pursue His moral ideals. Here they wait in solidarity, for the express purpose of receiving His Law, being elected by Him, and being elevated to the stature of a "Priest People" capable of becoming a light unto the nations. The togetherness of Sinai is of a people come together to share common ideals rather than for common protection.

This spiritual feat is best characterized by the Hebrew term *ye'ud*, which means "Divine Destiny"—participation in the fulfillment of a God-given mission. Ye'ud was a voluntary exercise of the will, an accomplishment of incredible spiritual growth for this slave people, which was to prepare them for their ultimate contribution to the morality of human society.[20]

From this second aspect of the Sinaitic Covenant flow fundamental Jewish concepts—in a sense, the entire body of Jewish religiosity. Some of these concepts are invaluable to the convert's appreciation of Judaism because they are natural and familiar to western ears, the unspoken assumptions of the western mindset—but they differ in subtle, yet fundamental ways from their Christian meanings. These Jewish concepts become more understandable if one realizes their origin in the covenant. The subjects are both broad and profound and therefore can only be touched upon in this volume. More extensive study of these ideas is surely desirable.

CONSEQUENCES OF THE COVENANT

Jewish Morality

The authority of Jewish morality does not derive from an intrinsically superior value that people ascribe to it. Naturally, Jews hold that what proceeds from God is good. But the obligatory character of Jewish morality derives from its origin— the historic, public, corporate agreement that was made by our ancestors with God in the boundless and timeless spaces of the no-man's land of the Sinai desert. Moral good is defined as the fulfillment of the Jews' part of this covenant. Moral evil is the abandonment of the agreement between the Jews and their God. This is what historically has impelled Jews to keep these laws—regardless of their value or relevance in any particular age.

The Talmud itself recognizes this dilemma of an absolute morality and unhesitatingly offers the unvarnished truth that indeed, in certain instances, there appear to be incomprehensible leniencies, and a detail of Jewish morality here or there might seem inferior to that of other religious or ethical systems. The Rabbis, in such cases, surround the law with creative stringencies in order to avoid the appearance to converts of Jewish permissiveness—"so that it should not be said that they are coming from a higher level of holiness to a lower one." The morality of other systems may be very high as well, but those systems are not the result of the public covenant with God at Mt. Sinai. (This wisdom should deflate the self-conscious air of some Jewish people who believe their moral decisions are inherently superior—without reference to their obligatory nature as a mandate accepted by their ancestors.)

Regardless of the comparative value of Jewish morality as judged by the standards of other religions or of contemporary secular humanism, Jewish morality is binding upon Jews— simply because of its covenantal character.

Religious Conduct

The rituals and symbols of Judaism are derived from the same covenantal authority. These observances are not practiced because they are considered intrinsically superior. Fundamentally, all human symbols are arbitrary; they do not possess a specific, intrinsic "good" nature, and they are not necessarily connected in a one-to-one relationship with specific spiritual or metaphysical events. They are norms of conduct that were freely agreed upon and carried out as a result of a covenant struck at Sinai between God and the Jewish people or because they were promulgated by the Sages. They are norms of conduct agreed upon by covenant, voluntarily entered into, and then ratified.

This is exemplified best by the biblical rules of sacrifices brought in the ancient Temple. The Prophets could denounce with impunity the practice of the insincere offering of animal sacrifices by a donor lacking in integrity. The sacrifices are mandated by the Bible, but they are not intrinsically holy. If the bringers violate the Divine covenant by their hypocrisy, the sacrifices are without value.

This is also the basis for what might appear to be a contradictory view of Judaism toward icons. The golden calf described in the Bible is considered an idol; the intricately carved cherubim described in the Bible are part of the Holy Ark and considered sacred. The latter is accepted because it falls within the covenant—God so instructed and the people so accepted. The former is rejected because it is outside the covenant— an alien intrusion, an abomination, and hence an idol. Neither has intrinsic value—only the value given it by God in His Torah, the covenant of the Jews. That is what Jews accepted when embracing the "Divine Destiny" at Sinai.

The Land of Israel

In the Patriarchal Covenant, God obligated Himself to give Abraham's descendants, the Jews, the Holy Land, Canaan, as an everlasting inheritance. He repeated that promise in the Sinaitic Covenant. It is for this reason, and for this reason alone, that the Land of Israel occupies a place of dominant significance in the Jewish religion. This is abetted by many other good and cogent reasons—religious and nationalistic. But its critical significance derives neither from its value as a place of refuge for persecuted peoples nor from its symbolic utility as a homeland serving nationalistic interests and sentiments— important as they both are. Its value rests fundamentally, and eternally, as a provision of God's covenant, that it is a land "promised" to the descendants of Abraham.

While this is not fully appreciated in non-Jewish circles, it is a never-to-be-compromised principle of the Jewish people, and, as such, it needs to be appreciated if Jews are ever to be truly understood in the global arena. Israel is an invaluable and irreplaceable segment of the Jewish *soul* and collective psyche, much as is the Torah. We believe that God chose the Jewish people, and chose to give them both the Torah and the Land of Israel. Neither is dispensable.

The value of the covenantally promised land, therefore, transcends even the historically sanctified affection and need for a Jewish homeland. That is why Theodor Herzl's attempt to substitute Uganda for Palestine in the early days of political Zionism did not enrage religious Jews so much as it provoked disbelief and laughter. Herzl's suggestion might have been politically expedient, but it was not within the covenant and thus held absolutely no significance for the Jewish people. Herzl, coming from a secular background and profoundly committed to relieving the political plight of his people, sought any land so long as it provided refuge. It made much good common sense.

But this was not what the Jew had waited and hoped and prayed for for millennia. The Jews looked for Divine protection, a spiritual cloud over their heads, as they trekked through the wilderness of the globe. They needed an affirmation by God that His agreement with the Patriarchs was still in force. They needed a fulfillment of the covenant, not only protection from persecution. Only the Promised Land itself could be the answer. When, in 1948, the State of Israel declared its independence, it was spoken of by Jews as the "beginning of Redemption." Israel to Jews today is at once Holy Land and homeland, motherland and refuge—and it is perceived as the beginning of the people's long-awaited redemption by God.

The goal of Judaism is that the spiritual energy that propels the Jew through history derive from both elements of the Sinaitic Covenant—the Exodus and the Revelation. Similarly, the convert must strive to experience both "Divine Fate" and "Divine Destiny" which, together, forge a community whose solidarity results not only from being clamped together by severe external pressure, but also from being bonded with the internal glue of love. The Jewish people has been and continues to be a fraternal, purposeful amalgam of "guarantors" covenantally obligated and personally committed to mutual caring and a common striving for a moral life under God.

KEEPING THE COVENANT

The prospective convert's commitment to practice Judaism must be articulated at two stages in the conversion protocol: in the initial statement of intent to enter the Jewish covenant—prerequisite to the total process—and in the declaration recited at the climax of the conversion ceremony, immediately prior to immersion in the ritual pool.

Some converts embrace Judaism in a sudden dawning of consciousness, a shock of recognition, a leap of faith. More likely, however, this commitment will come at the end of extended soul-searching—a slow process inching gradually toward realization of the truth.

Whether it is one or the other, a combination of the two, or a result of external pressure, conversion is a radical life decision requiring enormous courage and personal strength. It calls for even more: an extraordinary sense of tact to avoid disappointing family and close friends and constantly needing to explain, justify, and interpret the decision to enter the Jewish covenant to everyone—old cronies and bump-into acquaintances, gentiles and also Jews.

But *entering* the covenant, arduous as it may appear, is not as demanding as *keeping* the covenant. Making a pledge to keep the covenant calls for the convert to know explicitly what is required by Judaism.

Before Making a Commitment to Act

Because the Jews constitute a covenant-community rather than a faith-community, the decision to convert is a decision not only to *believe* in the Jewish idea of God, but to *act* on that belief. When one "enters into the covenant," the convert's personal Sinai, one accepts the Divine mandate requiring distinctive behavior. This is called "acceptance of the yoke of the commandments."

What does this entail as a practical program? First, it necessitates *acknowledgment* of the authority of Torah, the five books of Moses, and the oral interpretation of that law by the Sages of the Talmud and the Codes of the Halakhah. These two components are called the "Written Torah" and "Oral Torah" and together they comprise the body of Jewish law. The Rabbis rule that the candidate for conversion may not willfully reject even one of these laws. By this they mean, basically, that the convert may not deny the Rabbis' authority to establish a particular law. Thus, the commitment to practice is referred to as *kabbalat ol ha'mitzvot* the "acceptance of the *yoke* of the commandments," rather than by the more tepid phrase "observance of the mitzvot." It is a recognition that, although the laws may sometimes be restrictive, they need to be accepted as authoritative notwithstanding any difficulty in keeping them.[21]

Second, accepting the "yoke" entails a decision that goes beyond acknowledging the authority of the law. That acknowledgment must be translated into practice and acted upon. The convert's commitment to Judaism must include a commitment to observance. This is true not only for moral laws, but also for the laws of ritual practice.

Of course, the conversion candidate may feel disposed to observe the tradition, but lack the emotional stamina to keep it and not just let it slip out of consciousness. This does not by itself cast doubt on the conversion. There is an inherent recognition in the laws of conversion that people can and do grow. What is important, therefore, in addition to the desire to keep the covenant, is to design living conditions that will be conducive to growing in the observance of Torah—such as a willing mate, a vibrant Jewish community, a nearby synagogue, positive Jewish friends, a caring rabbi. On the other hand, if there is no intention to keep the Sabbath or the dietary laws, it indicates no desire to grow after entering into the covenant, and the conversion may not be validated.

Preparing for Commitment

It goes without saying that study preparatory to entering the covenant should be as extensive and intensive as possible, and should be as unhurried and as filled with Jewish experiences as possible. (The candidate should, of course, become familiar with the outlines of Judaism before taking even the first step of meeting with a rabbi.) But a truly profound appreciation of Judaism takes a lifetime and no candidate for conversion could reasonably be expected to be acquainted with all of Torah before entering the fold. But, if one cannot digest the whole menu, one should at least taste the distinctive flavor of Judaism.

Realizing this, the Rabbis proposed that we inform the prospective convert of the essential beliefs—the uniqueness of God and the prohibition of idolatry—some of the major and minor commandments and some of the punishments and rewards, "and we are not overly strict with him," being aware of the Torah's complexity and its unfamiliarity to a newcomer.

For this reason, the teachings must be selected carefully. The Rabbis provided parameters for such study and urged that it be taught in a manner that would "make it dear to the convert." The actual subjects with which the Rabbis minimally required familiarity are few, but they are meant to be only the coils which form the springboard of further instruction. They are outlined and discussed more fully in Part V.

Please turn to that section and the chapter on a convert's bibliography to view the universe of subjects with which the convert should become familiar before undertaking the formal conversion discussed in the next chapter.

Notes to Chapter Six

1. See the excellent treatment of the Israelite covenant concept and the qualities of comparable covenants among Near Eastern nations in Nahum Sarna, *Exploring Exodus*, pp. 134-144, Schocken Books, New York, 1987.
2. See Nachmanides and the interesting insights of *Or Ha'Chayim ad loc.*
3. The Midrash is quoted at length in Maimonides, *Mishneh Torah,* Hilkhot Avodah Zarah, 1, 3.
4. Genesis Rabbah 34:1 and 38:1.
5. Isidore Epstein's editorial comment on this excerpt from Genesis Rabbah, in Soncino Press, p. 313.
6. In Abraham Besdin's *Shiure Ha'Rav,* see "The Covenantal Community,"; also Joseph B. Soloveitchik's Nov. 1973 lecture on *Chaye Sarah, Ha'Mevaser,* Yeshiva University, New York, 1973.
7. *Teshuvot Ha'Rambam* 293 to Ovadiah, Ger Tzedek, edited by Joshua Blua, vol. I, Mekitzei Nirdamim, Jerusalem, 1958.
8. "Understanding the Covenant," by Jose Faur, *Tradition,* vol. 9 #4, Spring 1968. It is a seminal article on the theological components of covenant.
9. Because it is freighted with so much significance, the Sinaitic Covenant is virtually the only concept that is fully developed in the Bible and that is constantly used in its original meaning, retaining its original force and the binding nature of its conditions. In this sense, it is unlike the idea of monotheism itself, the most fundamental Jewish concept and the warrant of Jewish existence which, in the Bible, paradoxically, remains an undeveloped concept.
10. All covenants are important events—but pre-Sinaitic covenants are with-

out the equivalent legal authority and post-Sinaitic ones are admonitory. It is only at Sinai that the covenant *par excellence* is framed.

11. "You are My witnesses, and I am God" (Isaiah 43:12). The Jerusalem Bible, translated and edited by Harold Fisch. The Midrash records the bold interpretation of Rabbi Shimon, son of Yochai: "If you are My witnesses, I am God; if you are not My witnesses then (if one could say this) I am not God" (Yalkut Shimoni to Yitro 19, 271).

12. See Sol Roth's *The Jewish Idea of Community,* ch. V, Yeshiva University Press, New York, 1977.

13. In Jewish law, the Sinaitic Covenant is treated as a standard civil agreement. The validity of this God-man covenant rests upon the same juridic terms as that of a civil contract between people:

   1. Free negotiations must lead to ratification, unfettered by the obviously disproportionate status and power of the two parties.

   2. There must be a mutual assumption of duties—by God no less than by man.

   3. Both parties must fully recognize each other's equal rights—in terms of this covenant, the Jews' rights are parallel with God's.

   4. The inalienable rights of each of the parties may be surrendered only by the mutual consent of both.

14. See his profound landmark article, "The Lonely Man of Faith," by Rabbi Joseph B. Soloveitchik, in *Tradition,* vol. 7, #2, Rabbinical Council of America, New York, Summer 1965.

15. Yevamot 100b.

16. Walter S. Wurzberger, "Covenantal Imperatives," *Samuel K. Mirsky Memorial Volume,* pp. 3-12, edited by Gershon Appel, Yeshiva University Press, New York, 1970.

17. *The Rabbis of the Midrash,* vol. II, edited by H. Freeman, (Soncino Press, London, 1951) portray this graphically: "Rabbi Judah says: 'All the world is on one side, and he [Abraham] is on the other side" (*Bereshit Rabbah* to Lekh Lekha 8:2). Even Joseph, as Pharaoh's viceroy, had to eat at a separate table: "And they set [the table] for him by himself, and for them (his underlings) by themselves . . ." (Genesis 43:32). Later, Balaam, the gentile prophet, sees into the early Jewish character with stunning perception as the Jews wander in the desert: "It is a people that shall dwell alone, and shall not be reckoned among the nations" (Numbers 23:9). Decades of *ad nauseam* repetitive United Nations votes condemning Israel confirm this prophecy doggedly, unremittingly.

18. See Appendix 2 for a discussion of the covenant and the social contract.

19. The Torah, in referring to other Jews, uses the term "brother," not "friend." "To whom can a Jew turn?" asks Maimonides. "To an idolator who hates him and pursues him?" Sharing the same goral has made us into "blood" brothers—we are brothers not only because we are children of the same father, God, but because at the outset of our existence as a people we threw our lots into the same destiny. The terrifying circumstances in which the Jews found themselves during the formative years in Egypt and which have continued on and off to this day have shaped the intense feeling of Jews for peoplehood to the point that it has become an integral part of their collective consciousness.

20. Curiously, the unity of "fate" preceded the unity of "destiny"—goral before ye'ud. But that appears to be only an expression of our humanity. First, we worry about our ability to survive and only then about the desirability of being idealists.
21. The Halakhah, in saying that the conversion is not valid, does not imply that if the convert cannot psychologically or physically carry out some detail of the law, or does not understand it or have the time to observe it, he has invalidated the conversion. The intent is that if the potential convert denies, as a matter of personal philosophy, the _right_ of the rabbis to decide the law as it applies to all Jews including himself, he would thereby undercut the authority of all Jewish law and would indeed invalidate the entire conversion. In addition, as Rabbi Shlomo Kluger holds, in his responsa, _Tuv Ta'am Va'Da'at_, vol. III, part 2, #109 (Grossman Publishing House, Israel, 1980), it invalidates the conversion only in a situation in which a convert demands that the court confer upon him the status of Jew while allowing him to exclude observing a specific law.

Part Three

THE PROTOCOL

7

The Formal Process

Becoming a Jew is a decision which triggers not only conflicting emotions, but hard thinking—exploring the fresh and
unfamiliar terrain of Judaism and then reaching deep into the
substance of the soul to reshape a worldview nurtured since
childhood. This new and revolutionary thinking that is needed
to undertake a sea change in life requires a powerful statement—
a ceremony of formal declaration. That is the role of the elegantly
simple—some would say stark—yet meaningful ceremony that
announces the admission of a convert to the family of Jews
whose spiritual ancestors stood at Mt. Sinai to receive the
Torah.

The conditions for such a formal conversion, stipulated by
the Rabbis in the Halakhah, Jewish law, as referred to earlier,
are simple and fundamental:

A rabbi receives a request for conversion from a prospective
convert. If he is convinced that the desire is sincere and without
reservation, and also that it has a good chance of being successful, he introduces the conversion candidate to Judaism
through self-education and life experiences.

After completing this stage satisfactorily, the applicant appears before a qualified three-man court, known as a Bet Din.
The court then proceeds with searching and inquiry into the
candidate's motive, goals, and knowledge, with the intention
of eliciting the quality of the convert's commitment to Judaism
and the Jewish people. Upon the successful conclusion of this

critical segment, the male candidate undergoes circumcision or, if already circumcised, the drawing of a drop of blood. This in turn is immediately followed, for both men and women, by immersion in a pool of water, required of all converts without exception. There is then a second formal declaration of commitment to Judaism. The gentile candidate emerges from the water of the immersion as a full-fledged Jew.

THE NEED FOR A FORMAL PROCEDURE

But why is a formal procedure the *sine qua non* of entrance into the Jewish fold? Why is not a declaration of faith sincerely made in the presence of a Torah scroll and a large congregation sufficient to induct the prospective candidate into Judaism?

Indeed, for many Reform rabbis a declaration of verbal commitment made sincerely after an adequate period of study and guidance is all that is required. The commitment is expressed in a Temple ceremony that is both eloquent and moving.

But such a conversion procedure is not acceptable to Orthodox and most Conservative Jews, and has never been formally considered legitimate by any other group of rabbis in any century of the long record of Jewish conversion. It will not be accepted by the Chief Rabbinate of the State of Israel.

Conversion is too transforming an experience, too much a life-determining act, to be accomplished by a simple declaration no matter how touching, or by sincere words however eloquently stated and in however sacred and austere a setting. It needs to be confirmed by the seal of a sacred event; to be expressed by symbols replete with centuries of meaning; made unique by the sanctification of a specific moment in time; mandated by some action commanded in the Torah and experienced by the totality of the Jewish people at Sinai, and shared by every Jewish convert as the climax of his or her personal odyssey.

Words Affirm

The attitude of the Jewish people is that this rebirth of the soul to a new "life" requires an act both definitive and transforming, one that will bind the person to Abraham and to the ancients who stood at Mt. Sinai and will confirm the commitment required by the Sages and hallowed by millions of earlier converts. Nothing less will do.

Words are words. Surely when they are made solemnly and in conjunction with a sacred act, they are valuable. But words by themselves are not validating because they are, after all, only words. Words can affirm; they cannot authenticate.

The convert now moves from months of amorphous soul-searching and studying to the final formal act that makes it all concrete. The convert reenacts, in his own life, that historic moment of Revelation that transformed human civilization. At that event, the Jews as a people received the Torah and responded "we shall do and we shall understand." Then they underwent circumcision and immersion. In microcosm, the convert as an individual, responds to God's charge with the intent of "doing" and "receiving" and then undergoes circumcision and ritual immersion. These symbols confirmed the bilateral covenant at Sinai between God and the whole Jewish people; they now confirm God's covenant with this new Jewish soul.

Actions Authenticate

The flesh-and-blood marriage of husband and wife is an appropriate metaphor for the celestial "marriage" of God and Israel. In earthly marriage, deep love, respect, affection, and moving words of devotion, do not call forth the responsibilities and rights of married life unless they are accompanied by a binding covenant that formally sets forth those emotions, pledges and duties. Love is too precious to be left to words.

Indeed, that is how every nation sees the process by which it naturalizes aliens. No immigrant, regardless of how much he loves democracy, believes in capitalism, adores liberty, and respects the people of the United States, can become an American citizen without studying the foundations of its government, waiting the required legal period, and swearing allegiance—something the natural citizen is not required to do—to uphold the Constitution of the United States. All the protestations of love are to no avail unless they are confirmed by a binding covenant—or they remain only protestations.

Thus Judaism, which touches every aspect of life—marriage

and family and education and death; which inspires historical and geographical loyalties; and which demands disciplined behavior in all experiences of living—food and sex and community—could ask no less.

Whichever route converts choose to take is their own decision and will be determined by their beliefs and needs. But they should be aware of the consequences of their actions and not be taken aback later should an Orthodox or Conservative rabbi refuse to participate in a marriage ceremony based on this conversion, or should some difficulty arise relative to living in the State of Israel as a Jew. The requirement of formal conversion itself will not be compromised by the traditional community.

The experience of this carefully crafted moment, the enactment of a spiritual embrace, marks the beginning of participation in the ultimate Jewish destiny. The formal religious conversion, culminating the long spiritual odyssey toward becoming a Jew, marks the beginning of Jewish living.

Formal is Not Pro Forma

The convert's long, personal journey into the unexplored regions of the Jewish religion reaches its climax with formal, precisely defined procedures of conversion. Superficially viewed, the two steps of unbounded searching in the convert's quest for knowledge, and then the constrained formality of the conversion ceremony, appear to be contradictory. One is spiritual, subjective, lonely, intimate—the mind roaming in the domains of meditation and imagination; the other physical, objective, public, formal—navigating the world of court action, precise procedures, measured movement. From a deeper perspective, however, the process is not disjunctive. In fact, it is a continuous natural flow characteristic of all Jewish ritual. That flow expresses the unique character of Jewish conversion. To appreciate it fully, one needs to understand the process in greater detail.

The final procedure is indeed formal. Witness the fact that whereas the first stage is a lonely one with no required definitive guide or instructor, the second requires that everything be accomplished in the presence of a court of three, especially the formal statement of commitment at the end of the soul's journey.

While it is formal, it is anything but *pro forma*, routine, mechanical, dry. The commitment made before the court is not merely a declaration, a catechismic recital, an encyclopedic spewing-forth of undigested facts and formulas. In no place in traditional literature can one find prescribed test questions or rigid affirmations for the convert to repeat. There are instead, probing questions into the convert's soul regarding God-belief, symbols and practices. But most characteristic are questions eliciting the practical prospects for successful religious living in the long future.

Just as the questions are not rigidly formulated, so the court's responses are not rehearsed. There are no graded marks, no pass-or-fail scores, no questions—only an evaluation, a profoundly subjective estimate by the members of the court regarding the sincerity of the candidate for conversion.

Two Phases: Exploring and Affirming

The first, amorphous phase is the heart of the process—without which the conversion process is vacant and posturing, while the second, formal phase is its ratification. That is why the ceremony calls for two commitments—one at each phase. But unmistakably there is another dimension in the relationship of the two phases. As Rabbi Aaron Lichtenstein[1] notes, the two are interlocking components of the same process—not only essence and confirmation.

The first stage aims at the convert's personal growth in his relationship with God, the "I" of the convert addressing the "Thou" that is God. To that end, the person develops his own thoughts by letting them fly hither and there, alighting upon an idea here, an insight there. It is a soaring of the soul into realms never before experienced—light, free, formless. There are, of course, guideposts established by Judaism for the study of its basics. But the first forays into unexplored territory are usually in the nature of a personal odyssey, and their aim is to connect with the Almighty through a diversity of ideas the convert may encounter—this concept, that holiday, an illumination of a biblical personality, a talmudic business case, an ethical problem solved.

The second stage aims at the convert's connection with the Jewish community—called *Knesset Yisrael*. The community, in the person of the rabbi, accepts the application for admission; as represented by the Bet Din, it queries him or her; and then it decides on the conversion. The community is not a medium between man and God, but a full partner in the relationship. Connecting with the community is a goal unto itself. The convert's "I" goes out to meet not only the Divine "Thou," but also the human "thou," fellow man, as the proselyte joins the Priest People. That is why, after ascertaining the motive, the candidate for conversion is immediately asked, as in the Maimonidean formulation described above, "Do you not know that our people is in a loathsome condition, oppressed, prostrate, torn, and in agony . . . ?" It is a statement about the community, even after the convert's motive for coming to Judaism has been determined to be pure—for the sake of heaven. It is a dual "Thou" that the convert confronts: the "Thou" of God and the "thou" of community.

The Process Reflects Judaism's Nature

The two phases also have an educative function. In this sense, far from the second stage being "merely" confirmation—a sort of mechanical letdown from the dizzying peaks of personal striving—it is an exalted affirmation of the striving, and this formal aspect conveys the more significant teaching.

It forcefully strikes the chord of the unique religious thrust of Judaism and that chord should resonate in the convert's life as a Jew. It is the Jewish emphasis on deed, mitzvah—on the value of the religious symbols originating in the written Torah and developed through the Oral Law by centuries of rabbinic interpretation. It is the Jewish emphasis on the fact that faith is not sufficient unto itself, but must be translated into structured observance. The convert is suddenly confronted by laws, do's and don'ts, courts and *mohalim* (those who perform circumcision) and mikveh (the pool for immersion). It is the definitive, first-step exercise of Judaism-in-practice to be considered. In this respect, it is not less than exalted spiritual teaching; it is not only the confirmation but the enactment of the first stage.

The formal stage of the conversion process is characteristic of Judaism in yet another distinctive way. As Judaism believes in bonding ideas to realities, so it tends to isolate moments and events and to sanctify them. It does not allow them to pass by unnoticed. Only by freezing the moment does it survive. Man is, as the theologian Harvey Cox words it, "*Homo festivus*," "Celebrating Man." Freedom, for example, is celebrated on

Passover, but its ideas live on by the vehicle of matzah and wine and bitter herbs.

The formal conversion is a celebration of the successful efforts of the convert in anticipation of entering into the covenant. He or she has reached the top of a personal Sinai. There is a feeling of fear of the uncharted future, of awe, of mystery— intermingled with the joy of having found a faith. The conversion stops the clock and holds the final moment. It celebrates a soul transformation by means of an unusual, unique, meaningful, never-to-be-forgotten act of acceptance, circumcision and im- mersion. It is a source of relief and exhilaration.

"The soul comes to the gate, and the court says: 'Now take these steps and enter the portals and become part of the Jewish household.' "[2]

IS RELIGION THE ONLY PASSPORT: WHAT ABOUT ZIONISM, MORAL HEROISM, LOVE OF JEWS?

As Judaism is not monolithic—it is not to be described as a community of the "faithful," but as a "House" of Israel, which incorporates many aspects of civilization—an important concern is whether an association with the Jewish people other than religion can effectuate a legitimate conversion. For exam- ple, can an ardent Zionist substitute Zionism for religious con- version? Can offering one's life in the Israeli Army grant one membership in the Jewish people? More to the point: A Christian suffered through the tortures of Nazi concentration camps because a great-grandfather happened to be Jewish— can that not serve as a satisfaction of conversion requirements? Further, a righteous gentile secularist who loves the Jews, can he not become a fellow Jew, even without a belief in God and a commitment to observe Torah laws?

A significant question disturbs those candidates for conver- sion to Judaism who are not willing to commit to the strict observance required by Jewish tradition: Is it conceivable that a newcomer to Judaism should be required to be more knowledgeable and observant than most native-born Jews? Yet, clearly and unequivocally, that is indeed the requirement of Jewish law, the Halakhah.

It is important to understand that never in the millennial universal history of the Jews have rabbis, scholars, or community leaders recognized any way to authenticate Jewish identity other than by religious criteria. Jewishness is a religious designation, and Judaism is the religious criterion. Zionism is a political movement, though it is properly founded on very high religious ideals and it can seek to establish standards of conversion which determine who will be an Israeli citizen, because Israel is a national entity. Nationalism, Zionism, and fraternalism are all exalted concepts, but they are not religious criteria. And, if they are to serve as shibboleths for Jewishness, the character of Judaism will be altered and will inevitably cease to exist as a religious entity. There is no peoplehood if there is no Godhood. Fighting in the Israeli army is a highly commendable, self-sacrificing, valorous act—but it does not relate at all to becoming a Jew.

This is an extract from a moving speech by former Israeli Prime Minister Golda Meir:[3]

> I am not religiously observant, but, had it not been for religion, we would have shared the fate of all those peoples who have disappeared. We are fortunate, indeed, that there are still synagogues in Moscow, Odessa and Leningrad serving as the only center for Jews to come to, at least on Simchat Torah, as an outlet for their feelings of Jewish identity. I would like to tell you that in 1948, when I attended synagogue on Rosh Hashanah and Yom Kippur in Moscow, I did not stir from my place the whole day. I thought to myself that, had I stayed longer at my post, I would have gone to synagogue not out of duty, as the representative of the Jewish State, but I, Golda Meir, my place is in the synagogue along with other Jews.
>
> Above all else, in my view and that of the overwhelming majority of the Knesset, the survival of [the people of] Israel comes first, before the State of Israel, before Zionism. . . . Any price is worth paying for the security of the State of Israel, so long as it is realized that its role is to preserve the Jewish people. Otherwise, it is pointless. . . .

Similarly, no one can gainsay the Holocaust survivor's ordeal. One must laud, with the highest encomia, those noble Christians who willingly suffered the agonies of the Jews as they would those of their own families. Surely, there are few more commendable acts than to have expressed such love in the superhuman dimensions it demanded—to have provided food and shelter for a person whom society considered subhuman, and to have done so at the risk of losing one's life in the very act of offering the kindness. The full history of such righteous heroic Christians has yet to be written.

But such heroism cannot be made into a standard for conversion. Religious conversion must be available and consistently applicable to all people—saints and other people. Such heroic living is an ideal for living on the highest moral plane known to man—but for all that it does not make one a Jew. The Jewish religion affirms that the heavenly reward for this is as great as any Jew can achieve through his own religious observance. But suffering in concert with Jews, or extraordinary kindness on their behalf, makes no statement about God, about Torah, about Yom Kippur. Conversion is a pledge for future religious behavior. It does not relate to the experience of the past.

Becoming a Jew is not an honorary degree, the Chief Rabbi of the British Empire, Lord Immanuel Jakobovits, writes, any more than the honorary degree at college graduations, *honoris causa*, can make one an honorary physician who may practice without meeting proper qualifications.

Similarly, religious conversion has no room for secularists who refuse to recognize one God and to act on that belief. Now the thoroughgoing secularist often has the highest ethical and moral standards; he may be the most charitable person in the community. Would that such qualities were adopted by all members of the religious community. But Jews survived and grew because of an association with God with whom they entered into a mutual covenant. No one can enter into the covenant by denying the other party to the covenant. It makes sheer mockery of the Jewish people, the people created by Torah, to permit denial of Torah. Goodness cannot replace Godliness; it must strengthen it. But the paradox of proud secularist Jews standing foursquare amongst a people that makes a commitment to God a condition of entrance, is everywhere to be seen.

ON KEEPING HIGH STANDARDS FOR CONVERSION

How can the conditions for conversion of Christians be more demanding than those asked of born Jews?

First, it should be noted that the presence of nonpracticing Jews in fairly large numbers is itself testimony to the priority of Jewish internal missionizing over the often-discussed desirability of missionizing others. Second, it is testimony to the breadth of the "House" of Israel, that it includes such diverse "residents" as secularists and pietists, Hasidim, secular Zionists, and atheists, all co-existing under the talmudic rubric of "A Jew, though he has sinned, is a Jew." This concept affirms that all Jews belong in the household and that, to the Jewish people, no Jew is ever lost, no matter how far he or she has strayed.

But insistence on high religious standards for conversion is what the Jewish survival instinct, supremely successful these thousands of years, has taught the Jew. The quality of the Jew is great survival insurance. He or she should not be expected to compromise that quality for the sake of adding large numbers. That is why the talmudic Sages, although deeply desirous of proselytizing gentiles, refused to compromise on the more stringent practices even if compromise were the only way to attract converts. Century after century, scholars, finding themselves in the most despairing conditions, still insisted on total commitment from prospective converts.

True, a majority of conversions throughout history might have failed. But the minority of successful ones have helped to elevate the quality of Jewish life and have provided the Jewish people with scholars, saints, rabbis, heroes, and communal leaders. Converts of questionable quality attenuate, rather than reinforce, the Jewish community.

The analogy to nations is again appropriate. The alien requires greater familiarity with the country of his new loyalty than the native-born citizen. An immigrant who pledges to respect all the laws of a country except for one will not attain citizenship. But a native who is a criminal cannot formally be disowned, though his liberty can be restricted. Conversion is a process of religious naturalization. It requires full allegiance and superior knowledge of the laws, and will not brook an "all-but-one" acceptance of the Torah's values and commandments.

Perhaps the most compelling analogue is the adopted child. Parents accept and love their natural child, whether he be healthy or severely handicapped, a first-rate scholar or a juvenile delinquent. One cannot erase the picture of the loving, pleading mother of Sirhan Sirhan after his assassination of Robert Kennedy. Yet, a couple adopting a child will research every aspect of his biological and psychological past—questioning, weighing, testing—in order to be sure of the child's physical and mental health and potential for successful upbringing. That is their right; nay, their obligation.

Judaism adopts a convert with similar doubts and concerns. Its demands are no less compelling. The covenant of the people is bilateral. All Jews indeed are guarantors for one another. The prospective convert must search the beliefs, traditions and character of the Jewish people and be satisfied with the adopting parents. No less do the prospective parents need to search the character of the new child.

Former Israeli Prime Minister Menachem Begin made a historic utterance on the subject:

> Our people should have by now numbered 200 to 250 million souls. . . . Why have but thirteen million survived? There are only two reasons for that: slaughter and assimilation. And who knows if assimilation did not take what slaughter had spared—many millions in each generation? Were it not for the prohibition of intermarriage, we would have disappeared long ago. . . . What are your grievances against the Halakhah which determines who is a Jew? . . . We interpret the laws of Israel, for well over twenty years, in the light of English Common Law. If, in the days of Queen Elizabeth I, a British judge passed a sentence, Israeli judges are still bound by that precedent. . . . What is wrong, what is sinful, with the idea that in the fateful matter, Who is a Jew, we should be bound by the interpretation of the Jewish Common Law— pardon my expression—the Jewish Halakhah which is in force thousands of years? What free man can be insulted by that?

> I propose the following rule to the entire Knesset without distinction of party. Here it is: That Judaism not be forced on any person, and no person be forced on Judaism. Is this compulsion? . . . Suppose a person does not submit to traditional conversion and is still classified as a Jew; isn't that compulsion? Yes, that would be a compulsion imposed

upon the entire Jewish people for generations without end; upon millions no longer living, upon those who are alive, and upon millions yet unborn.[4]

The options offered a free people are often dizzying and perplexing. The problem is not political, but personal and spiritual. In conversion, the Jewish people joins the convert, just as the convert joins the Jewish people. Insistence on an authentic process is the court's obligation to the Jewish community and to Jewish destiny.

Notes to Chapter Seven

1. Aaron Lichtenstein, in "Gerut: Laidah U'Mishpat" in *Torah she'Baal Peh,* Mossad Ha'Rav Kook, Jerusalem, 1971.
2. Aaron Lichtenstein, as in endnote #1.
3. As quoted by Rabbi Immanuel Jakobovits in *The Timely and the Timeless,* Vallentine, Mitchell and Co., London, 1977, p. 204.
4. Jakobovits, *ad loc.*

8

The Court of Admission:
BET DIN

Formal conversion to Judaism requires authorization by a Jewish court. This three-man Bet Din represents, in a manner of speaking, the whole Jewish people into which the convert seeks entrance. It has the power to authorize or deny the application to join its ranks.

THE BET DIN'S FUNCTION

The Bet Din determines the validity of the conversion. In order to make this judgment, it needs to exercise its fundamental responsibility of weighing the chances of the conversion's success—determining the variables in this very personal and intimate process of spiritual rebirth and the likelihood of its endurance. It must assess the genuineness of the motivation, the commitment to observe the precepts of Torah, the influence of the candidate's future environment on his or her potential for observance—such as the mate's religious practice, the extended family, and the nature of the Jewish community in which the convert will reside. To a great extent, the destiny of the Jewish people rides on these courts of conversion. Whether we fashion a diluted Judaism or an intense one will be effected by the three-man Bet Din. It is an awesome responsibility.

While the duty for probing these matters is the court's, the onus for proving worthiness and sincerity rests solely on the prospective convert. The duration of study, therefore, depends on the convert's interest, time, power of concentration, self-confidence, and—in a marital situation—on the strength and motivation of the Jewish mate.

THE BET DIN'S CREDENTIALS

The Bet Din consists of three individuals, as it does in regard to cases other than conversion—at least one of whom must be an ordained rabbi expert in the subject of conversion. Some Sages of the Talmud derive the requirement of a Bet Din from the biblical verse, "You shall have one manner of law, as well for the proselyte as for the home-born. One law shall there be for you and for the convert" (Leviticus 24:22). Others derive it from the verse, "And thou shalt judge righteously between man and his brothers and the convert . . ." (Deuteronomy 1:16). This much is certain: there is to be no difference in the legal process as regards Jews and converted gentiles. As the rules of justice for cases between one Jew and another require a court of three presiding in session during daylight, so, too, in all cases between converts and Jews. In matters of the conversion protocol as well, the process is identical—neither more nor less strict—so the Halakhah requires three Jews, knowledgeable about the conversion procedure, to oversee the protocol, and it must be held only during daytime.

A problem arose over the requirement of ordained Rabbis.[1] While there are many rabbis today who are traditionally ordained, the historic chain of ordination technically linking present-day rabbis with Moses is considered to have been broken. But if there are technically no ordained rabbis today whose lineage stretches back from student to teacher to Moses, what will happen to the conversion process which requires it? Shall Judaism therefore no longer accept converts because the law cannot be fulfilled as completely as the Sages determined it should be?

The Tosafists, medieval French scholars,[2] therefore ruled that the biblical insistence that conversion be a "statute forever throughout your generations" (Numbers 15:15) takes precedence. The requirement of historic ordination had to yield to the biblical mandate on conversion that it be available "for your generations"—able to be practiced for the entire duration of Jewish history. Conversion was not a policy emanating from one period in history or one country—it is part of the warp and woof of the Jewish religion. The rabbis of the court were to be considered as "messengers" of the early Rabbis who were ordained in the chain still tied to Moses.

Today, therefore, a rabbi with a traditional ordination who is thoroughly conversant with the requirements of the conversion protocol can select two other rabbis or, in their absence, two knowledgeable and observant laymen, and form a valid Court of Admissions. This milestone decision of the Sages which secured the perpetual right of people to convert to Judaism was motivated by a standing concern of the rabbis—the fear that we might somehow "shut the door in the face of converts." That was never to be countenanced.

THE EMPOWERMENT OF THE BET DIN

The authority that the Sages gave to the members of the Bet Din is truly remarkable. The entire process was placed in the hands of the Bet Din—"according to how the eyes of the Bet Din view it." The evaluation of the candidate's sincerity, the testing of his or her knowledge, the assessment of potential for success in becoming a Jew, all were entrusted to the judgment of the court. Complexities naturally arise from the obvious fact that people are so unlike, their worldviews so diverse, their spiritual insights so radically different. The Bet Din's ability to judge so many variables might tend to make it susceptible to error. Yet, the Halakhah cut a wide swath in these matters and allowed great latitude in this very critical area.

Even the decision on qualifications for membership in the Bet Din provides wide latitude, especially considering that this is a process designed to make people Jewish, with all the attendant responsibilities and obligations. It permitted the court to be staffed by one rabbi and two laymen, not requiring absolutely—even in this era when the chain can no longer be traced to Mosaic ordination—three traditionally ordained rabbinic specialists in the laws of conversion.

The Bet Din's latitude was historically and halakhically required simply because the door to gentile conversions had to be kept open, the system of conversion had to be available in every generation and in every corner of the worldwide dispersion of the Jews. That is why so much depends on who the members of the Bet Din are, why it behooves the religious community to insist that all three members be rabbis, that, if they are laymen, they be practicing Jews, and, if there is only one rabbi, that he be at the very least expert in his knowledge of the Halakhah of conversion. This is why the dispute between the Orthodox and non-Orthodox is so vehement when it relates to the subject of conversion—it is primarily a dispute on the subject of the acceptability of the rabbis for service on the Bet Din.

Far and away the most effective Bet Din is one sponsored by a rabbinic body, a religious institution, a city or school. In such a case, the certificate of conversion is recognized forthwith by rabbinic authorities without further investigation. Examples of such courts are the Bet Din of the Rabbinical Council of America in New York, and the Bet Din of the British Commonwealth in London. Potential converts should be aware in advance of the acceptability of their conversion by Jews the world over.

ITS CONVERSION FUNCTION IS A MITZVAH

The Halakhah, in addition to formulating the two principles that conversion *must* last for all generations and that the court must always act to avoid closing doors to converts, held that the very court process is itself a mitzvah.[3] The scholars of the French school, such as the Tosafists, held that since *not* accepting proselytes is unthinkable, and since the Bible expressly ruled that it must be available throughout the generations, accepting converts is a positive commandment. Indeed, the blessing that the circumcisor, the *mohel*, recites at the circumcision of a convert refers to "God who has sanctified us with His commandments and commanded us to circumcise converts." And, because presiding over a conversion is a mitzvah, the Bet Din was ordered not to tarry in its performance.

Once it saw that a gentile was acceptable for conversion, it needed to proceed forthwith in arranging for the formal conversion.

In his *Book of the Commandments*, Maimonides[4] speaks of the love of God that results from studying about God and the great pleasure that people derive from it. He reasons that the logical extension of the mitzvah of loving God is teaching others to love God—by persuasion and never by compulsion—just as when one loves someone they praise and even exaggerate their beloved's personal qualities. It is thus an implied mitzvah to bring others under the "wings of God's presence" as did Abraham, our father.

It is remarkable that, despite the Rabbis' insistence on the permanence of conversion and their insistence that the act of presiding over a conversion is a mitzvah, bringing gentiles into the covenant did not trigger a zeal to missionize gentiles. But, absent a major overt drive to proselytize, the decisions of the Rabbis nonetheless constituted a very powerful statement of the Jewish attitude toward qualified converts. The Talmud sums it all up:[5]

> And Rabbi Eliezer said that God exiled the Jews among the gentiles only so that they should attract converts to themselves.

WHAT WILL THE BET DIN ASK THE CONVERT?

The questions the Bet Din will ask are designed to determine the sincerity of the convert and the likelihood of religious observance, and whether the degree of knowledge he or she has accumulated will be adequate to the observance of the mitzvot. Honesty and integrity are quickly recognizable and are considered, along with kindness and compassion, to be the hallmarks of the children of Abraham and foremost among the desirable traits that qualify those entering the Covenant of Abraham. But these values are also qualities that characterize all good people—Jewish and gentile. The convert needs more.

The Jewish people are the "People of the Book" and converts having only a generalized belief in a benevolent Creator accompanied by "spiritual feelings" and loving their neighbors,

fundamental as these obviously are, need to be enriched by
what is specifically and uniquely Jewish. Regardless of the teacher, the nature of the local community, and the family's demands,
the convert is under a religious obligation to learn and know
the ideas and facts as well as the hopes and dreams of the
Jewish people. Serious study is needed for the conversion to
be warranted. Indeed, such study should enable the convert
to rise above the level of knowledge and observance of the
general Jewish community.

The questions will focus on:

1. The idea of one God.
2. An understanding of Torah as coming from God.
3. The authority of Jewish law (the Halakhah) and an
   understanding of the covenant and of religious obligations.
4. The Jewish idea of the Messiah, and the distinction from
   other systems of belief.
5. The concept of Reward and Punishment.
6. The obligations of ethical living, chesed.
7. The requirement of giving charity.
8. The observance of the Sabbath.
9. The observance of the Day of Atonement, Yom Kippur,
   and, specifically, whether the convert will fast on that day.
10. The prominent observances of a variety of major Jewish
    holidays.
11. Knowledge of the major aspects of kosher laws.
12. Familiarity with the major prayers, such as *Sh'ma Yisrael*,
    the *Amidah*, and the major blessings—especially the bless-
    ing for immersion in the mikveh.
13. For men: familiarity with putting on the tefillin.
14. For women: familiarity with the laws of the monthly im-
    mersion, *niddah*.
15. Interest in continuing to study Torah.
16. Whether the children will be given a Jewish education.
17. The place of the Land of Israel in Jewish life.
18. (If marriage to a Jew is being planned) whether the convert
    would leave Judaism if the marriage were ever to be ter-
    minated.

Notes to Chapter Eight

1. For a deeper understanding of the subject, note the dispute of Rashba in his novellae to Yevamot 49a, and Tosafot, *ad loc.*, in which Rashba holds that there was never a requirement for ordination for the Bet Din on gerut. Also, see Rabbi Hershel Schachter, "Kuntres Ha'Semichah" in *Or Ha'Mizrach*, Nissan-Tammuz 5748 (1988), vol. 36, #3-4, pp. 198-213, ed. by Shepansky, Shmidman and Gopin, which elaborates on a theme of Rabbi J. B. Soloveitchik.

2. Tosafot, Yevamot 46b-47a, and Kiddushin 62b.

3. See *D'var Avraham*, vol. 2, ch. 25, who assumes that it is only *hechsher mitzvah* such as *shechitah*. The fourteenth-century rabbi of the Spanish classical school, Rabbi Shimon ben Zemach Duran, asked why conversion should not be counted among the 613 mitzvot that comprise the religious life of the Jew. The great codifiers, Maimonides, Nachmanides and Rabbi Moses of Coucy, did not include it, implying that it is indeed a mitzvah, but was delivered as *Halakhah le'Moshe mi'Sinai*, the oral law given to Moses on Sinai (while only mitzvot written in the Torah are formally counted). For "Halakah le'Moshe mi'Sinai," see *Zohar ha'Raki'a* to *Sefer Azharot* (Vilna, 1879), *Essin* 40; *Encyclopedia Talmudit VI*, col. 426, Jerusalem, 1954.

4. Maimonides, *Sefer Ha'Mitzvot*, Mitzvah 3, quoting the Sifre.

5. Pesachim 87b.

6. A united Bet Din was attempted in Denver in the late 1980's. While it appeared to work, in fact it brought an irate and total rejection by the national Orthodox community.

9

Circumcision:

GENESIS OF A NEW LIFE

Every male among you shall be circumcised. And you shall be circumcised in the flesh of your foreskin and it shall be a token of a covenant between Me and you (Genesis 17:11-12).

THE FOREMOST SYMBOL

Circumcision is foremost among Jewish religious symbols—so intimately identified with "Jewish" that the term "uncircumcised," originally intended simply for one who was not a member of the covenant,[1] became an epithet for those who are religiously objectionable such as the "rebellious heart" or "the stubborn ear."[2] Eventually it became a term of opprobrium for impurity in virtually every area of life. The Torah thus refers to "uncircumcised lips," "uncircumcised ears," and an "uncircumcised heart." Moses, urging a spiritual revolution, demands that the "foreskin of the heart be circumcised" (Deuteronomy 10:16).

No one with the slightest knowledge of Judaism can overestimate the significance of this sign of the formal relationship between earthbound human and awesome God. Paradoxically, this symbol of the loftiest spiritual bond known to man is expressed on man's physical being, on the organ which represents the quintessential earthiness of his existence, his most private part.

Circumcision is the first commandment addressed specifically and uniquely to the Jews. While there are other symbols of the covenant, circumcision remains the most powerful and, in the Bible, the most pervasive.

The punishment that the Bible records for intentionally violating the mandate to circumcise is nothing less than complete excision from the Jewish people. It is one of only two positive commands in the Torah that evoke this response. That alone bespeaks the strength of this symbol as the mark of identification of all Jews.[3]

The Talmud refers repeatedly to the fact that the Torah itself, with its numerous mitzvot, is linked to the covenant only three times, whereas the single mitzvah of circumcision is bracketed with the covenant at least thirteen times. Maimonides says that this fact by itself indicates the primacy of this single ritual, circumcision, in the struggle for Jewish survival—and with this statement he concludes the entire chapter on circumcision in his *magnum opus* on Jewish law. The medieval scholar Meiri goes so far as to say that to reject circumcision is to reject the very essence of Judaism and is virtually equivalent to apostasy.

THE FIRST SYMBOL

Circumcision is not only the foremost symbol, it is also the first of life's religious celebrations. It is, furthermore, the only mitzvah not voluntarily entered into by the individual. The child traditionally is circumcised before self-awareness dawns—on the eighth day of life. There is no waiting for his voluntary assent or for the religious maturity officially reached at age thirteen with the Bar Mitzvah.

A contemporary scholar[4] explains the unusual nature of this pre-awareness mitzvah by analyzing the blessings to be recited at the celebration of the circumcision. Immediately before the act, the circumcisor, or mohel, pronounces a benediction citing God's command to circumcise. It is recited *before* the performance of mitzvot, as all benedictions are recited before the eating or the performing. But the Rabbis added a special parental blessing for this event, "Who has commanded us to bring him into the Covenant of Abraham, our father," to be recited not before the act, but afterwards. Why so?

He answers:

> You may ask about this mandate of the Torah to circumcise a child on the eighth day: "It is understandable that the obligation to circumcise falls on the father, but in fact it takes place on the body of the child. In which case, it becomes problematic as to why the Torah does not require that it be done by the child [rather than by the father] when he comes to the age of religious maturity at thirteen or even later?"

> The reason for this is that if circumcision were like all other mitzvot—simply an individual requirement—the Torah would indeed have waited until he was thirteen. But this mitzvah is of the very essence—through it, the Jew enters into the sanctity of the Jewish community and comes under the wings of the Divine Presence. The Torah therefore declared that as soon as the child is born he should enter the Holy Covenant. . . .

The reason the parent's blessing is recited only afterwards, unlike other mitzvah blessings, is because this mitzvah is the very essence of the Jew-God relationship, and it is as though the child himself were expressing gratitude to God after bringing him into a sacred relationship with the Almighty—and all prayers of gratitude are recited *after* the act.

Circumcision is of such a fundamental nature in the Jewish religion that it was not to be delayed thirteen years, waiting on the intellectual consent of the youngster, as were the other commandments.[5] He adds:

> Further, if the operation were postponed until the boy grew up, he might not then submit to it; [whereas] the young child does not experience much pain. Another reason is that the image of the child has not yet taken a firm root in the parents' minds. The parents' love for the newborn child has not grown as great as it will be for a one-year-old. The parent's very love for the child might lead him to neglect the law if he were allowed to wait two or three years. . . .[6]

Rabbi Samson Raphael Hirsch, the leader of nineteenth-century German Orthodoxy, has another instructive view of the parental blessing unique to the circumcision rite. He holds that the obligation to circumcise devolves upon the father first because it is intricately bound up with the paternal requirement to teach a child. Hence the blessing, "to bring him into the Covenant of Abraham," refers to teaching the child the ways of the covenant. Education for a Jew's taking on the responsibilities of the covenant must begin at birth. If the father tarries in this duty unnecessarily, the Jewish court is required to arrange for the circumcision.[7]

In that case, why was Abraham's circumcision, the very first, delayed until he was ninety-nine years old? The number ninety-nine signifies "ancient, near the end." Rabbi Shlomo Goren, former Chief Rabbi of Israel, maintains that this makes the statement that Jews may not shut the door in the face of converts who are circumcised as adults. Instead, Jewish people must encourage converts by the example of Abraham, the first Jew, who was circumcised not only as an adult, with all its attendant sensitivities, but at a very advanced age.

Another implied lesson is that circumcision which is always the *opening* religious statement in the life of a Jewish male, performed on day eight, was in Abraham's life the *culminating* declaration. For this first Jew who practiced circumcision, it became the crown of a religious career, one of the greatest in the annals of history and literature.

As circumcision is performed on a youngster as a precondition to his relationship with Almighty God, so the male convert to Judaism undergoes circumcision as a mark of an irreversible relationship *before* he enters the faith, as a precondition, while only anticipating becoming "a newborn child" in the family of Jews.

STRUCTURE OF THE OBSERVANCE

An expert in circumcision describes the procedure for adults as follows:

> "The adult is circumcised in an operating room with the customary precautions. The surgical team scrubs as they would for any other operation. The mohel makes the first and last incisions; the major part of the *b'rit milah* [circumcision] is performed by a urologist, although there are some mohalim who are trained to do this type of circumcision by using the same technique as with an infant. Here, too, physicians are

needed to administer anesthesia and suturing."[8] [Questions of anesthesia and other aspects of the circumcision are discussed in detail in the Responsa portion of this book, pp. 362-364.]

Divided into its component parts, the procedure of circumcision, or b'rit milah, consists of the following four steps:[9]

1. The removal of the foreskin.
2. The denudation of the *glans penis* until the corona is uncovered.
3. Suctioning the blood for hygienic purposes.
4. Bandaging the wound. (Mohalim have practiced the art of bandaging over a period of 3,200 years, long before suturing was developed.)

For persons who had been circumcised as children as a standard surgical procedure, the religious requirement is only the extraction of a drop of blood—*hatafat dam b'rit*—which is painless and effortless, although it is somewhat awkward for adults. The act of circumcision is generally a matter of concern to converts. Adult men may think twice before undertaking this radical step of circumcision. There is no doubt that the surgical aspect of the circumcision, for men who had not been circumcised as children, can be its most formidable component. It is understandable both because of the general fear of surgery and also because of its inevitable association with one's masculinity.

While one cannot gainsay the actuality of such fear, the convert needs to understand that circumcision could never have become a requirement of a religion like Judaism if it were in any way hazardous to the physical health or the psyche of the average person. Jews do not believe that anything which a good and all-wise Creator demands can be harmful to His creatures. However, before one undergoes the procedure, he should satisfy himself that all the medical aspects are carefully scrutinized and that every hygienic precaution is taken. Fortunately, the contemporary procedures of modern surgery offer us more preventive protection than at any other previous age.

There is no lengthy religious service associated with circumcision for the convert. There is a blessing made prior to the circumcision, and two lengthier ones recited immediately afterward, over the ceremonial cup of wine. This brevity is understandable in light of the fact that the circumcision is only one constituent of the total procedure, while the crescendo of the conversion ceremony must await the immersion.

Some rabbinic authorities do suggest some festivity after the circumcision. Those who hold that Jethro converted formally base this view on a biblical verse describing the joyous acceptance of Jethro into the Jewish people. Exodus 18:12 reads: "And Aaron and all the elders of Israel broke bread with Moses' father-in-law before God." The Rabbis interpret this as the festive meal (*se'udat mitzvah*) celebrating a mitzvah—in this case the mitzvah of "entering into the covenant" and accepting all the mitzvot incumbent upon a Jew."[10]

WOMEN: IN THE COVENANT AS IN CREATION

Women are equally part of the covenant with God, although no physical symbol of the flesh was required of them. Rabbi Joseph B. Soloveitchik, the renowned contemporary scholar, notes that God's covenant was struck not with the first Patriarch alone—but with Abraham and Sarah together.

Man and woman are both included in the covenant, just as they are together included in creation. Adam alone would never have been accorded the title of Man. Human experience is a dual one. The covenant cannot be carried on by Ishmael, who represents only Abraham. It requires Isaac, who represents both Abraham and Sarah. No covenant is possible without her.[11]

Indeed, after Sarah's demise, Abraham makes no significant religious advance or statement, and nothing of great import happens to him except the arrangement of Isaac's marriage to Rebecca. This is done only in order to secure the continuation of the covenant requiring both husband and wife, Isaac and Rebecca as Abraham and Sarah. All the Patriarchs were partners with their wives in the covenant with God, sharing the Divine covenant as well as the marriage covenant.

DEEPER LEVELS OF MEANING

The ideas implicit in the circumcision symbol are many layers deep. In every age, it inspired ever-deeper speculation into its meaning. The study of the literature is itself an exciting adventure in interpretation, although not all biblical commentators savored a mortal's imaginative exploration into God's motives on a subject so basic as circumcision.

Ibn Ezra, for example, holds that circumcision is so basic, so unalterable, so much a part of the Jew, that it is in the category of laws that are beyond reason, *chok*. A *chok* requires adherence, not rationalization—it admits of no second-guessing and should simply be followed. But his opinion, especially in regard to circumcision, is an isolated one. Most Jewish thinkers have grappled with the idea and have tried to shed light on it to the ultimate benefit of history and philosophy, and of all who wish to understand this complicated aspect of Torah.[12] Following are some of the interpretations of this rite offered throughout Jewish history.

Circumcision Has a Motivating Function

The fundamental idea behind circumcision is most graphically expressed by the two aspects of it that set it apart and make it strange to the western imagination: first, its locus on the sexual organ—its very physicality; and second, the irrevocability of the act.

The fact that a spiritual covenant was to be expressed in an unalterable physical act affecting the sexual organ engendered much speculation as to its moral significance. A lively debate ensued among medieval thinkers.

Maimonides,[13] who, in addition to being a great rabbi and codifier of the law, was also a leading thirteenth-century physician, offered an unusual hypothesis. He held that circumcision serves a morally utilitarian purpose—a natural diminution of sexual passion would result from severing the foreskin and act as a physical inhibitor of sexual abuse. Other thinkers disagreed vehemently.

Nachmanides saw it as a physical expression of a purely spiritual "sacred covenant," *b'rit kodesh*. This reminder of man's spirituality, not his physical wound, would restrain his elastic libido and channel the excesses of his sex drive.

Rabbi Yehudah Halevi[14] maintained that circumcision is a behavioristic strategy: man would be conscious of this evidence of his Jewishness and symbol of the covenantal relationship with his Maker, and this consciousness would help him control his lusts.

Abravanel similarly refers to its behavioral value.[15] He notes that the symbolic mark is much like a personal coat of arms which draws the bearer's attention to the pride of his birth and the obligations attendant upon his family's tradition—the *noblesse oblige* that in fact distinguishes much of Jewish ethical behavior.

God and Man are Partners in the Creation of Humanity

The Midrash raises a disturbing question: "Why was not man created as complete as God wanted him to be?" If He desired that man's flesh be circumcised, why did not the All-Powerful Creator simply create him already circumcised, as He created him with two eyes and ears?[16] The Rabbis answer that what appears to be the Creator's incomplete work is actually His invitation to man to become a partner in his own self-creation by completing what God had begun.

This is symbolic of the whole religious enterprise which promotes the idea that man must strive to become *shalem*, a whole being—not spiritually fractured or bifurcated in heart and soul. Perfection, *shlemut*, demands human participation in the Divine scheme.[17] It is, therefore, only after his circumcision that Abraham finally reaches the state of wholeness.[18] Participating in the Creator's plan makes him an equal partner in the binding covenant with Him.

Circumcision Creates a Bond

Maimonides[19] holds that hidden within the rite of circumcision is another compelling idea:

> It gives to all members of the same faith, all believers in the Oneness of God, a common bodily sign, so that it is impossible for any stranger to say that he belongs to them . . . and then attack them.

There are two separate threads intertwined in this explanation of circumcision: first, that it binds all like-minded believers in the one God. The commonality of belief strengthens the ties of the people to one another in a sort of spiritual *landsmanshaft*. The effect of this idea ought not be minimized. Experience teaches that a purely spiritual nexus can be dismissed or at least ignored with relative ease. But a physical mark binds those who bear it in a way that generates mutual thoughts, a common language, a shared destiny.

Second is the obverse: it is a clear sign that being uncircumcised is proof that a person is not a Jew. Maimonides evidently considered this important to note because of the frequent attempts in ancient and medieval history at infiltration into the Jewish community to uncover alleged "plots of the Jewish conspiracy." This was practiced in different eras by both the State and the Church. The numerous "debates" between leading rabbis and their inquisitors in the thirteenth and fourteenth centuries are ample evidence of those terrifying "religious" events.

It Symbolizes the Permanence of the God-Man Covenant

The irrevocability of the sign of circumcision prompted Rabbi Joseph Albo,[20] the medieval philosopher, to say that it is the primary symbol of the immutability of the relationship between Israel and God:

> So long as this covenant [the circumcision] lasts, it will be known definitely that we have the strength to live on, and through this relationship the nation will return to its former glory.

The fact that circumcision, once it was effected, could not be revoked was emblematic of the whole relationship between God and man, which could not be revoked under any circumstances.

This thought is amplified by two cognate ideas which illuminate the concept of irrevocability: the *"Covenant of the Fathers,"* b'rit avot, and the *"Merit of the Fathers,"* zekhut avot.

The "**Merit** of the Fathers" depends on people's behavior. When a Jew behaves morally, he is rewarded for his own actions and receives an additional reward for the deeds of the ancient Patriarchs whose values he perpetuates. If his actions are not in consonance with the tradition of his ancestors, embodied in the Halakhah, he does not acquire the merit of the Patriarchs, since he violates their heritage.

The "**Covenant** of the Fathers," on the other hand, does not depend directly on a person's behavior—although the whole covenant relationship serves to promote good conduct. The covenant is irreversible, never to be withdrawn by God even if the person violates it. Backsliding in religious behavior may cost a person the "Merit of the Fathers," but never the "Covenant of the Fathers."[21]

Not All Circumcision is Covenantal

One of the salient characteristics of the covenant is mutual agreement to abide by a set of rules. Both God and the Jews are covenanting parties; both are obliged to perform.

This idea, both simple and elegant, was, however, the subject of controversy between Jewish and Christian scholars. Prominent Christian scholars[22] maintain that man could not be conceived to be a covenanting party "equal" with Almighty God. The covenant, they maintain, is an unconditional *gift* of God.[23] The covenants with Noah and Abraham are God's generous contributions; subsequent "covenants" are nothing more than commands regarding the Sabbath and Priesthood.

Medieval Jewish scholars took strong exception. They maintained that the nature of man is such that he is specifically endowed by God with the freedom and ability to respond in a contractual sense, and it is that response which is demanded from him *every* day of his existence.[24] Man is indeed qualified to strike a covenant with God.

In light of this understanding, the relationship of man and God takes on new meaning for Jews. The covenant implies that man will commit himself to keep his side of the bargain. But, if he does *not* commit himself to that proposition, the circumcision is *not symbolic* of the covenant—it is just surgery.

This explains an apparent paradox in the biblical story of the Patriarchs. Abraham is commanded to circumcise himself and all members of his household. Both sons, Isaac and Ishmael, are circumcised. Isaac enters the covenant; Ishmael does not. But, does not circumcision trigger the covenant? If it does, why is Ishmael not included in the covenant?

The answer is that both sons needed to be circumcised, as all male children of Jewish parents require circumcision.

But, while both Isaac and Ishmael received ironclad promises of reward from God, only Isaac is required to keep the covenantal obligations—Ishmael is not asked to reciprocate and therefore needs no covenant. Isaac undergoes *b'rit milah*, the covenantal circumcision; Ishmael undergoes only *milah*, surgical circumcision.[25]

In the following generation, Esau is circumcised but he too does not enter the covenant. Jacob, his brother, is circumcised and also covenanted—he is expected to respond with appropriate duties that he takes upon himself as a party to the covenant. Maimonides says that Esau receives a *noncovenanting circumcision* because "he does not maintain his faith and the right path." Jacob pursues the right path and needs to reciprocate.

Most non-Jews undergo circumcision in the United States, but they do not enter the covenant. That is why there is a requirement of hatafat dam b'rit,[26] the drawing of a small drop of blood from a previously circumcised gentile who becomes a candidate for conversion. With that momentary touch of a pin, he moves from the realm of Ishmael to the realm of Isaac.

The Covenant is Uniquely Jewish

In no ritual so much as in circumcision for converts can one see the radical divergence of Christianity from Judaism. Paul realized that Christianity could not missionize the world if it insisted upon circumcision as a *sine qua non* of initiation into the faith. It was this very real confrontation with the possibility of failure to convert the pagans that impelled him to emphasize "faith" over "works" as the hallmark of Christianity and the basis for salvation. He says: "For I testify again to every man that is circumcised that he is a debtor to do the whole law . . . neither circumcision availeth anything nor uncircumcision, but faith worketh by love."[27] Christianity forcefully repudiated the "law" and claimed to possess not only a substitute for it, but a successor, "faith." The "good news" of the gospels is chiefly that the "chains of the law" have been lifted and superseded.[28]

In Judaism, the quintessence of goodness is the following of the Halakhah and the ethical and moral works it requires—doing deeds of kindness and righteousness. Jews have been mocked and denigrated and physically persecuted by the

Church since ancient times because of their tenacious observance of their "works."

Hostility Begat Heroism

As a consequence of its identification with the Jewish people and the tenacity with which it was kept, circumcision became the one major symbol which Jew-haters persistently targeted for eradication. They threatened the annihilation of the Jewish community and then literally wreaked death and destruction upon them because of their observance of this rite.

The dismal history of the hysteria over circumcision—which impelled kings and princes to declare death edicts if their subjects kept "this barbaric custom" and inflamed devout gentiles to tear Jewish children from their mothers' arms in order to "save" them—darkens the pages of western civilization.

The Syrian-Greek king, Antiochus Epiphanes (175-164 B.C.E.),[29] sought to convert the Jews by forbidding them to perform circumcision. The Talmud and the historian Josephus[30] describe the unbelievable viciousness with which gentile authorities treated the keepers of Jewish law. Mothers were led through the streets with infants in their arms, dragged to the top of the city's wall, then flung wildly to the streets below. King Antoninus enacted these death scenes in Rome, the supposed citadel of tolerance, where syncretism reigned and new religions were widely tolerated. Other persecutions scattered through early Jewish history are described in the Talmud[31] and they continued unabated throughout Jewish existence.

Is it believable that ordinary people could whip up so much hysteria and intolerance, so much viciousness, about a religious symbol performed on the most private part of the human being? How does one explain how this rite could trigger so much hatred and strife? In light of this reaction, it is not too shocking to observe that this powerful but benign sign of God's covenant in the flesh sends a grim but graphic subliminal message: religion has made circumcision a symbol of the covenant; history has made it the scar of the chosen people.

Persecution triggered remarkable Jewish acts of courage and martyrdom in stubborn defense of this covenant symbol. So often were these edicts enacted and so widespread was the hatred of this custom that a tradition developed among Jews in critical times of using code words to invite guests to the service and the reception that followed.[32] The Rabbis of the Talmud assured the people: "All mitzvot for which Jews offered their lives rather than obey royal edicts—such as the prohibition of worshiping idols and of performing circumcisions on newborn children—are still firmly with them."[33] The Rabbis declare in the Midrash that the "Jewish people was saved by God thanks to the merit of its observance of circumcision."[34]

Persecution for circumcision runs tandem to persecution for the conversion of children. An explicit illustration is embedded in two versions of the conversion protocol described in the Talmud of the first centuries of the common era. In the earlier version of the court's instructions to the convert,[35] the following cautionary paragraph is not found. By the time the later text appears, the persecutions must have become so nasty as to warrant this explicit warning of the Bet Din to converts:[36]

> What makes you want to become a proselyte? Do you not see how the people are humbled and afflicted among the nations of the world; how many ills and sufferings come upon them; how they bury their sons and grandsons; and *how they are put to death for circumcision, immersing in the mikveh* and all the other ordinances; and do not conduct their lives openly and freely like all the other peoples?[37]

Eight hundred years later, matters evidently had not improved. Maimonides, writing his great code of law in the thirteenth century, did not include the law on converts in a separate section. Instead he dispersed the laws, hiding them in subthemes. The laws on admission of proselytes he inserted into the prohibitions of intermarriage (*Hilkhot Issurei Bi'ah*); the requirement to love converts he placed in the chapters on interpersonal relationships (*De'ot*); the laws of circumcision for converts he placed with the chapters on circumcision for Jews (*Milah*).

The seesaw of history two centuries after that, in fifteenth-century Safed, enabled Rabbi Joseph Karo, author of the basic code of Jewish law, *Shulchan Arukh* (following his predecessor, the Tur), to include a chapter on converts, without any introduction to note the change. In the 1930's in Russia, an updated adaptation of the *Shulchan Arukh*[38] carries a chapter on conversion with the following subtitle:

> THE LAWS OF CONVERTS OF ANCIENT DAYS WHICH IN OUR LAND WE HAVE NO PERMISSION TO ACCEPT BECAUSE OF THE LAWS OF THE GOVERNMENT.

One generation later, the Russian Jewish author's son,[39] commenting on Genesis 36:12, begins his own writing on conversion with a strong qualification at the outset: "All the laws and subjects of conversion apply only to those times and places in which it was permitted by the host government." One can imagine the fear that gripped community leaders if such a warning label had to be affixed to an obscure academic treatment of the subject by rabbis who lived in our own century—let alone during the Crusades or the Inquisition.

The mitzvah of circumcision had the misfortune of causing the "observance" of another mitzvah—sacrificing one's life in martyrdom, *kiddush ha'Shem*.[40] Two words call out from within the circumcision ceremony. They form the only phrase recited by the reader and then repeated aloud by the participants: *B'damayikh chayi. B'damayikh chayi,* "Live in thy blood! Live in thy blood!"[41] In an irony both cruel and perverted, these words of the ceremony, which trumpeted the news that this child will live as a Jew by virtue of the covenant blood spilled in this ceremony of circumcision, became instead a sober reminder that he will live in the merit of the "life-blood" of martyrdom, spilled to keep the observance of his circumcision.[42]

Demanding, but Affirmed

Among Jews, circumcision has a surprising history. Many splinter sects arose during the millennia of Jewish history and they quarreled over virtually every tenet of Judaism. No principle was considered too sacred or too abstract to be above scholarly criticism or community controversy. But circumcision—the obligation which was to remain "for all future generations, as an everlasting covenant" (Genesis 17:7)—was the only ceremonial law accepted by Pharisees and Sadducees, Samaritans and Israelites, Karaites and Rabbanites alike.[43]

Even radical thinkers, such as the excommunicated seventeenth-century philosopher Baruch (Benedict) Spinoza, who could call into question even the belief in God, held that the practice of the circumcision rite by itself was sufficient to ensure the survival of the Jewish people.[44] Its influence on Jewish life was so strong that often its observance was a Jew's last vestige of Judaism and his only remaining affinity to the religion or the people. Its effect on the collective consciousness of Israel is incalculable.

The observance of circumcision lapsed during periods of assimilation, as during the reign of Jezebel, when lawlessness and corruption ruled,[45] and in the Hellenistic period when Jewish youths struggled to be accepted into Syrian-Greek society.[46] In the early, heady days of enlightenment at the birth of Reform Judaism,[47] a number of Reform rabbis at the conference in Frankfurt in 1843 sought to abolish it. That debate within the Jewish community in Germany lasted twenty years, but it caused rancor that endured for over a century. It is safe to say today that most Reform Jews have their children circumcised, albeit most often by physicians rather than by the mohalim that the tradition requires.

The ritual is demanding; the meaning abstract; the consequence of its observance was often persecution. But it remains tenaciously observed among Jews, the mark of unity in a world of assimilation and dispersal.

Le'Chayim!

How characteristic of this stiff-necked people, who because of their stubbornness survive to this day that, the more they were persecuted, the more strongly they held to their convictions. To the end of time, the Jews will remain *b'nai b'rit,* "children of the covenant." "Live in thy blood," the liturgy cries out. The Jewish people lived through and lives on—and the rite of circumcision is the symbol of that life. *Le'chayim!*

Notes to Chapter Nine

1. Ezekiel 32:21.
2. Ezekiel 44:1, 9. See also Jeremiah 6:10 and Rashi's commentary to Leviticus 19:23. A nicely developed explanation of circumcision prepared for high school teachers is to be found in the unpublished doctoral thesis of Dr. Howard Deitcher, "The Rites of Passage," Yeshiva University, New York, 1985.
3. The other commandment is the bringing of the Paschal sacrifice (Keritot 2a).
4. Rabbi Y. M. Epstein, *Arukh Ha-Shulchan,* Yoreh De'ah 265:5.
5. See the fine essay by Nachshoni on Parshat Lekh Lekha in *Hagut B'Parshiyot Ha'Torah,* p. 42. He refers to the wording of the circumcision blessing recited by the father, as does Rabbi Epstein, indicating that the word *le'hakhniso,* to "bring him into" the covenant of Abraham, implies

to bring him even by compulsion. According to Perisha (Yoreh De'ah 265), it is a blessing for all the obvious religious obligations of parents—circumcising, teaching Torah, redeeming children, and bringing the child finally to the marriage canopy.

6. The source for this appears to be Maimonides, *Guide for the Perplexed*, Part 3, ch. 49.

7. Yoreh De'ah 260:1, 2.

8. Rabbi Eugene J. Cohen, *Guide to Ritual Circumcision and Redemption of the First-Born*, Ktav Publishing House, Hoboken, New Jersey, 1984.

9. The general sources for the procedure derive from Tractate Shabbat, ch. 19; Tosefta, Shabbat 15; Orach Chayim 331; and Yoreh De'ah 260 ff. See *Biblical and Talmudic Medicine*, p. 242, by Julius Preuss, translated and edited by Fred Rosner, Sanhedrin Press, New York, 1978.

10. See *Torah Shelemah*, vol. XV, ed. Menachem M. Kasher (New York, 1949) on Exodus 18:13, note 82.

11. *Shiure Ha'Rav*, p. 51, published by *Ha'Mevaser*, Yeshiva University, New York.

12. See Ibn Ezra's commentary to Genesis 17:1.

13. Maimonides, *Guide for the Perplexed*, 3:7.

14. Yehudah Halevi, *The Kuzari*, 3:7.

15. In his commentary to Genesis 17:10.

16. Genesis Rabbah 11:6.

17. *Sefer Ha'Chinukh*, Mitzvah 2.

18. Tosefta, Nedarim 32a.

19. Maimonides, *Guide for the Perplexed*, Part 3, ch. 49.

20. Joseph Albo, *Sefer Ha-Ikkarim*, ma'amar IV, ch. 45.

21. See the views of Shmuel and Rav Yochanan in Shabbat 55a and Tosefot, "U'Shmuel Amar," who cites proof from the verse, "And I will remember My convenant with Jacob. . ." (Leviticus 26:42) even after the exile.

22. See the *Biblical Encyclopedia*, "Circumcision," by Perowne.

23. Since the terms *b'rit*, covenant, and *chesed*, kindness, are often linked, the one-sidedness of *chesed*—giving but not taking—would be characteristic also of *b'rit*.

24. See Abravanel *ad loc.*: *b'rit zo haskamah* (a covenant is an agreement). A one-way unconditional covenant does not need man's *haskamah*. Also see Ibn Ezra to *loc. cit.*

25. See Rosh to Shabbat 135a, and also Tosafot *ad loc.*

26. The halakhic requirement of hatafat dam b'rit has been discussed and debated throughout halakhic literature.

27. Acts, ch. 15.

28. See Appendix 3, "Christianity Rejected Circumcision and Accepted Immersion."

29. First Book of Maccabees 1:44, 48.

30. Second Book of Maccabees 6:10, Josephus, *Antiquities*, Book 12, ch. 5:4 and *Jewish Wars*, Book I, ch. 1:2.

31. Shabbat 130a; Me'ilah 17a.

32. The Talmud, Sanhedrin 32b, and Rashi *ad loc.* gives us one such code for an invitation to a circumcision: *Kol raichayim be'vorni: "shavu'a ha'ben*

shavu'a ha'ben"; or ha'ner bi'Verur Chayil: "mishte sham, mishte sham."
Paraphrasing the text with Rashi's comment, "If one hears the sound
of the mill [a play on the word *rechem*, womb] in the city of Borni,
it is as though someone announced "The week—the 8th day, of
circumcision—of a son, the week of a son"; if one saw bright candlelight
in the city of Berur Chayil, it is as though one announced, "A party
there, a party there"—a wedding is about to take place.

33. Shabbat 130a.

34. Yalkut Mishle, 964.

35. Yevamot 47b.

36. Gerim 1:1. Tractate Gerim is one of seven Minor Tractates, and its
    contents are gathered from early rabbinic sources in the Talmud. It is
    sort of a guide for converts (implying substantiation of sorts for those
    who say that the sages were intent upon missionary activities). In its
    extant form, the tractate probably dates from the Geonic period. The
    subject at the time of its redaction must have been of more than theoretical
    interest.

37. Gerim 1:1. See also the interesting and insightful article on the differences
    in the two accounts—in Gerim 1:1 and Yevamot 47a & b—in F. Gavin,
    The Jewish Antecedents of the Christian Sacraments, Ktav Publishing
    House, Hoboken, New Jersey, 1969.

38. *Arukh Ha'Shulchan,* by Rabbi Y.M. Epstein, Hilkhot Gerim.

39. Rabbi Baruch Epstein, author of *Torah Temimah*.

40. Nachshoni to Lekh Lekha in Genesis in *Hagut B'Parshiyot Ha'Torah,*
    vol. I, p. 45.

41. The Rabbis of the Midrash, Yalkut Shimoni to Va'etchanan 44:37, in
    the name of Sifre, make this striking comment: "The Torah says: 'For
    we are murdered all the day.' Rabbi Shimon, son of Menasia, asks: 'Is
    it then possible for a person to be murdered all day long?' Rather, say
    this refers to circumcision, for it is a life-long sacrifice for Jews—all of
    their days." Often in Jewish literature, as in *Pirke d'Rabbi Eliezer,* ch.
    29, circumcision is equated with the actual sacrifices brought in the ancient
    Temple.

    Rabbi Bachya ibn Pakuda, on Lekh Lekha 17:13, noting this terrible
    equation, takes the analogy further and concludes that circumcision is
    greater in religious significance than sacrifices, and is even considered
    equal with the *akedah,* the offering of Isaac on the ancient altar, the
    quintessential personal "sacrifice" of Jewish history. One rabbi, the Gaon
    of Pressburg, author of *Sha'are Simchah,* put it this way: "The Torah
    says, 'And I have made My convenant with you.' [The meaning is that]
    the Holy One, Blessed be He, said to Abraham: 'You already performed
    self-sacrifice for the sanctification of the Name in Ur of the Chaldees.
    Now circumcise your children, that they may know the meaning of offering
    to spill their own blood for the sanctification of the Name."

    A great Hasidic sage, Rabbi Joseph Meir of Spinka, author of *Imre
    Yosef,* adds that realizing what the gentile reaction to circumcision would
    be caused Abraham to decide on a curious response to God's mandate.
    Unlike his attitude to all other mitzvot, which the tradition maintains
    he understood and observed even before they were given at Sinai,

Abraham decided to wait for God's explicit instruction that he circumcise himself before he proceeded to do so. The Midrash explains as follows: "Abraham said: Before I was circumcised, the passersby always stopped to visit with me. Now that I have performed circumcision, no one comes" (Genesis Rabbah 41). Abraham hesitated to create a social barrier which might separate him from others, which his brilliant mind intuited would be the reaction to this mitzvah. The Divine word did not contradict his fear—it confirmed it, instructing him that he must do so even at that cost.

42. For more on the concept of covenant represented by the circumcision rite, see Appendix 2.
43. See the perceptive essay by Dr. Fred Rosner in Appendix 1 of *Biblical-Talmudic Medicine* by Julius Preuss, Sanhedrin Press, New York and London, 1978. (German edition published 1911).
44. *Tractatus Theologico-Politicus* 3:53, 1670.
45. I Kings 19:14.
46. Book of Jubilees 15:33-34.
47. *Frankfurt Journal*, July 15, 1843.

10

Immersion:

THE CHANNEL BETWEEN TWO ELEVATIONS

What physical act could a person perform in order to symbolize a radical change of heart, a total commitment? Is there a sign so dramatic, dynamic and all-encompassing that it could represent the radical change undergone by the convert to Judaism?

Jewish tradition prescribes a profound symbol. It instructs the conversion candidate to place himself or herself in a radically different physical environment—in water rather than air. This leaves the person floating—momentarily suspended without breathing—substituting the usual forward moving nature and purposeful stride that characterize his or her waking movements with an aimlessness, a weightlessness, a detachment from the former environment. The conversion candidate is at that moment what anthropologists[1] call "liminal man," a "threshold person," one in the "passageway" between two great phases of personal development. Individuality, passion, ego—all are submerged in the metamorphosis from the larval state of the present to a new existence.

IMMERSION AND MIKVEH: THE DEFINITIONS

Ritual immersion is the total submersion of the body in a pool of water. This pool and its water are precisely prescribed by Jewish law. The pool is called mikveh, a tiled reservoir, two square feet by six feet deep[2] containing a minimum of twenty-four cubic feet of water, 200 gallons, derived directly from natural sources, such as accumulated rain water or melted snow or ice.[3]

Immersion, *tevillah*, is the common core component of every Jewish conversion process, for male and female, adult and child, ignoramus and scholar. It is *sine qua non*, and a conversion ceremony without immersion is unacceptable to the traditional religious community and simply not Jewish in character. This requirement of immersion admits of no compromise, no matter where in the world one finds oneself. (While Conservative rabbis similarly require mikveh for conversion, Reform rabbis generally do not, although a tendency to more traditional symbols and a sense that a uniform conversion is desirable, are encouraging greater use of the immersion component even among the Reform.)

THE FUNCTIONS OF MIKVEH

Several religious functions are served by this powerful symbol of submerging in water. In the days of the ancient Temple in Jerusalem, the mikveh was used by all Jews who wanted to enter the precincts of the Sanctuary. The law required every person inside the Temple grounds to be in a spiritually pure state appropriate to the pristine spirituality of the Sanctuary itself.[4]

Throughout Jewish history, unmarried women have immersed in the mikveh prior to their wedding; married women immerse at the end of seven days of stain-less purity from the end of each monthly menstrual cycle, in preparation for the resumption of family relations in their most fertile days.

A major function of immersion in the mikveh is for conversion to Judaism. The Sages declare that a gentile who wishes to become a Jew must undergo the identical process by which Jewish ancestors converted. As Jews performed immersion at Mt. Sinai to complete the conversion process they had begun with circumcision as they left Egypt, so converts in every age must immerse in a mikveh.[5]

THE ENDURING NATURE OF MIKVEH

The mikveh is probably the most enduring religious structure of the Jewish people. It was required to be built in a new community *before* the synagogue or even the school. So critically important was mikveh that the Sages of the Talmud instructed even impoverished communities to go to the greatest lengths to build a mikveh. How else could family life resume? How else could Judaism accept proselytes? How else could Jews achieve purity? Thus, mikveh is a permanent fixture of Jewish private and communal life.

Masada in Israel is the site of the oldest known mikveh, built twenty centuries ago atop a barren mountain which housed the fortress palace of King Herod. After the Temple's destruction in 70 C.E., a small remnant community of Jews sought refuge there. Masada had sparse living conditions and little food—but it did have two *mikva'ot* (plural of mikveh). The two—one for men and one for women—were built to the exacting specifications of the Halakhah. The mikveh was used by the women on Masada, even during the fateful days preceding their community's mass martyrdom, to mark the end of their menstrual cycle and their availability for family life, according to the time-honored practice of their ancestors. Today, the institution of mikveh is so well developed that among the thousands of mikva'ot in Israel there is even one designed specifically for the disabled and injured, and paraplegics travel from great distances to avail themselves of this incomparable symbol of purification and spiritual cleansing. Mikva'ot were built in the Soviet Union even during years of oppression, and in the most impoverished and most wealthy Jewish communities from Kentucky to Beverly Hills.

DEEPER LEVELS OF MEANING

Submerging in a pool of water for the purpose not of using the water's physical cleansing properties, but expressly to symbolize a change-of-soul, is a statement at once deeply spiritual and immensely compelling. No other symbolic act can so totally embrace a person as being submerged in water, which must touch and cover every lesion, every strand of hair, every birthmark. No other religious act is so freighted with meaning as this one which touches every aspect of life and proclaims a total commitment to a new idea and a new way of life as it swallows up the old and gives birth to the new.

This powerful religious expression conceals layers of meaning beneath its surface. The mikveh, as we noted, has diverse uses. We must assume there is some common ingredient to all these instances of submerging in water. Probing deeper into the mitzvah will reveal new facets of the water mitzvah that sparkle like a jewel viewed under different lights.

Purifying the Past

The water of the mikveh is designed to ritually cleanse a person from deeds of the past. The convert is considered by Jewish law to be like a newborn child. By spiritually cleansing the convert, the mikveh water prepares him or her to confront God, life and people with a fresh spirit and new eyes—it washes away the past, leaving only the future. Of course, this does not deny that there were good and beautiful aspects of the past. But, in the strictest religious sense, that past was only prologue to a future life as a Jew.

In that sense, then, the common property of ritual immersion in all its uses is the setting aside of the past. For example, in its first usage, immersion was done in preparation for entering the sacred Temple. It was a purifying of the *tumah*, spiritual "uncleanness," that derived from having had contact with a cadaver, which the Torah says renders a person ritually "impure" (even though touching a cadaver in order to bury the unclaimed dead is one of Judaism's greatest mitzvot).[6] "But he who is unclean, and does not purify himself, that soul shall be cut off from the community if he defiles God's Sanctuary"

(Numbers 19:20). Entrance into the Sanctuary had to be un-encumbered by past associations with impurity.

Likewise, before marriage, a woman immerses in a mikveh to purify herself from the spiritual impurity of the menstrual cycles of her past. Men should also be advised to use the mikveh before the wedding. It also is a symbolic purification from pos-sible misdeeds of the past. This is also the reason why the day before a wedding ceremony is traditionally observed by groom and bride as a day of fasting, and of the recitation of the litany of sins from the prayerbook liturgy, as on Yom Kippur, the Day of Atonement.

Similarly, on the day before Yom Kippur, as at other critical moments in one's personal history, men and women traditionally went to the mikveh to purify themselves from sins committed during the past year. While this tradition was kept in the main only by pockets of Orthodox Jews, it remains a powerful declaration of the intent to make a fresh start.

The convert, in a similar sense, immerses in the water of the mikveh to purify herself spiritually from past associations with ideas, behaviors, and ceremonies unacceptable to the new faith.[7] Indeed, it is this purification which allows the newborn Jew, exactly as it does the born Jew, to enter the sacred precincts of Judaism's holiest ground, the ancient Temple. It is a symbolic act which separates her from all that has gone before and prepares her for starting a future with a *tabula rasa*, a clean religious slate.

In a real sense, the wiping away of the past is a miraculous technique, possible only in the world of the spirit and which cannot be duplicated in the physical world. In the physical world, one cannot possibly wipe out an action or event or even a thought which has already occurred. We can ask forgiveness for it; we can urge friends to forget it; we can ignore it. But it has happened, and it exists in our personal histories; the action has been engraved on the tablet of time and nothing can undo the engraving. "The moving finger writes, and having writ, moves on," laments Fitzgerald in *Omar Khayyam*.

Not so in the metaphysical world. In Judaism, God grants people the right, once they have changed direction and recanted their untoward actions, to erase the past. This is the basis for repentance and its startling power to enable people to start afresh. Immersion in the mikveh is the symbolic act that does this for the convert—it cleanses the soul and the convert starts life afresh.

Achieving New Status

There is a second layer of meaning to mikveh. It marks the beginning of the ascent to an elevated religious state. This function of mikveh goes beyond the basic purpose of purification. Anthropologists refer to this threshold of higher social status as "liminality." The person at this moment of transition is a "liminal" or "threshold" person. The liminal state is common to virtually all persons and societies, ancient and modern, and it marks a move to an altered status or to a life transition. Entering adulthood from adolescence, for example, requires a tunnel of time, a rite of passage, a liminal state which acknowledges by symbolic acts the stark changes taking place in one's self-identity, behavior and attitude.[8]

A ceremony such as the biblical consecration of Aaron and his sons for the Priesthood was symbolized by immersion in a mikveh. The Priests entered their new status by going down into the water and then emerging, fresh, into a new atmosphere.

Another example is the first time a woman uses mikveh before she is married. While this immersion begins the continuous process whereby women cap their menstrual cycles throughout their fruit-bearing years, the first immersion prior to marriage represents the liminal state—the elevation from physically unproductive status, legally and morally, to a childbearing status and to new relationships. In the process of her liminality, woman defines herself anew and may rearrange her goals and life-styles.

Still another example is provided by a Jewish custom not strictly formalized into a requirement of the Halakhah. This custom calls upon Jews who have strayed from the path of Torah and then have returned to it to immerse in the mikveh so as to symbolize formally their renewed commitment. The mikveh here, too, is the symbol *par excellence* of an upward religious movement, the ascent into the towering greatness of the life of Torah.

This marking of spiritual ascent is no place clearer than when it relates to a convert. The convert descends into the water of the mikveh and emerges "a newborn child." It represents the crossing of a threshold into the House of Israel, an elevation of religious status.

In a sense, it is nothing short of the spiritual drama of death and rebirth cast onto the canvas of the convert's soul. Submerging into waters over her head, she enters into an environment in which she cannot breathe and cannot live for more than moments. It is the death of all that has gone before.[9] As she emerges from the gagging waters into the clear air, she begins to breathe anew and live anew—as a baby struggling to be born.[10]

If we take this graphic metaphor a step further, we can sense that the mikveh is a spiritual womb. The human fetus is surrounded by water. It does not yet live. The water breaks in a split second and the child emerges into a new world. "As soon as the convert immerses and emerges, he is a Jew in every respect" (Yevamot 47b).[11]

Circumcision and Immersion: The Linkage, the Lesson

The two pivotal "performative" components of the act of conversion—circumcision and immersion—cannot serve as a complete conversion independently for a male convert. Although they constitute different religious symbols and occupy different spiritual moments in the conversion process, they are nonetheless intimately linked, both conceptually and halakhically.[12]

Conceptually, circumcision and immersion respectively represent the two aspects of "entering the covenant"[13] encompassed by the Sinaitic Covenant—the first immediately prior to the Exodus when the Jews were circumcised in preparation for leaving Egypt; the second at Sinai itself when all the Jews collectively were confronted by God. In both instances, the Jews united in a covenant. In Egypt, the Jews united for their self-defense, to protect each other and to come under the protection of God—their common *fate,* goral. At Sinai, they united in order to become a "Priest People," to accomplish together their God-given role and to achieve a common *destiny,* ye'ud. Exodus is a person-to-person covenant; Sinai a God-people covenant. When Jewish tradition refers to a convert "entering the covenant," it refers to accepting the double goal of the covenant—fate and destiny—of becoming a part of the people by wanting to share the Jewish fate as our ancestors did in Egypt, and of standing in the presence of God to share the Jewish destiny as our ancestors did at Sinai.

Circumcision represents the fate-sharing component of conversion. It returns the person to the soil of pre-Exodus Egypt before the Jews became a distinct people and recalls the beginning of the conversion of the whole people. It embodies the convert's full-hearted consent to be part of a united global people—its history and its future—and to be willing to suffer when any part of that people suffers, as the mind must cringe when the hand is cut.[14]

Immersion represents the desire to share in a collective relationship with God, to participate in the Jewish religious destiny as the chosen people of God.[15] Its origin recalls the desert foothills of Mt. Sinai where the Jews were told by Moses to wash in preparation for receiving the Torah. This was designed to be the climax of the conversion procedure. From that time forward, the ceremony of mikveh immersion, whether performed in Jerusalem, Warsaw or Los Angeles, was intimately linked with the moment at Sinai and the commitment to accept the precepts of Torah; it became for all time the ceremonial sign of sharing the destiny. It was the "religious" component, the standing in the presence of God, the leap of faith, the total commitment.[16]

As soon as immersion occurred, with its prerequisite acceptance of mitzvot, the two-phased process was completed. The gentile became a Jew—an integral, covenanted member and full participant in the fate and destiny of the Jewish people. Conversion was complete.

What was required for men—circumcision to recall the peoplehood covenant at Egypt, in addition to immersion required for all converts—was not required for women. Naturally, both men and women are equally and fully partners in the covenant. But women's acceptance of the religious destiny of the Jews is thought to embrace also acceptance of sharing in the communal fate of the Jews. The "Daughters of Israel," as Jewish women are fondly called in the literature, need no physical mark to remind them of their identity with the people; it is believed to be part of their souls, unlike men who need the reminder to be carved on the most intimate part of their bodies.

Though they represent two facets of conversion, circumcision and immersion are not to be bifurcated. The subject of the status of the convert who performed only one of these components engendered lively debate in halakhic writings throughout the centuries. Circumcision without immersion was a moot question—it could not possibly constitute a legitimate complete conversion. Immersion without circumcision similarly does not constitute valid conversion—but since it worked definitively for women, the possibility of it becoming so for men as well always inspired intellectual disagreements.

In age after age, notwithstanding these scholarly debates, both law and tradition confirmed that while everyone agrees to the need for the strictly religious commitment—symbolized by immersion—one could absolutely not become a Jew if one did not join the *community* of Jews as symbolized by circumcision.

Conversion is not a statement of theology. It is a declaration of existence.

Two Issues Which Trouble Immersion

THE ABSENCE OF MELODRAMA

Given the profound meaning and soul-transforming function of the immersion act, one would expect that the mikveh would be housed in a mansion, a temple at the peak of some historic mountain, a revered holy place in old Jerusalem. And one has every right to expect the conversion ceremony to comprise the drama of a procession of dignitaries, an awesome declaration by a synod of elders, the pomp and circumstance characteristic of such momentous events. Actually, however, this is not how immersion in a mikveh gets carried out, nor how it was ever accomplished in the long annals of Jewish history.

The immersion is genuinely a glorious event—a cataclysmic personal phenomenon. But "the entire glory of the princess is inward," as the Book of Proverbs characterizes the royalty of Jewish women. Inward is where the transformation actually occurs. Inward, in the sub-vaults of the soul, is where the new Jew is linked to old Jewish images—venerable mother Sarah of the Bible who first began to convert women; the wise Patriarch, Abraham, the "father" of all converts, who first converted men to believe in a God no one could see; Jews who used the mikveh atop the mountain fortress of Masada; the whole Jewish people as they stood transfixed at the foot of Sinai, accepting the obligations that every other people shunned as too difficult or too strange or too radical or just plain wild. Inward is where the convert's soul merges with the greatest people that ever lived and with the God who created the world. It is therefore an event that is all glory and beauty and spirit. But it is all inward.

In the actual world, this mikveh ritual is likely to be a prosaic affair. The mikveh is housed in a simple building (even in Beverly Hills and Manhattan), deliberately designed to be inconspicuous—not calling attention to itself precisely in order to protect the modesty of the women who use it monthly. Sometimes, for economic reasons, it remains located in a depressed neighborhood where Jews first settled before they became more affluent. (Read Roger Owen's article in Part One.)

The water the mikveh contains is not "holy" water; the ground is not sanctified earth; the pool is not a consecrated vessel; the mikveh is not "sacred." It is a simple, functional building that usually looks just like other nondescript buildings on the block with but one difference: inside buildings such as this the cherished terms of "Jew" and "family" and "God" have taken on new meaning for hundreds of generations of young people. This modest wood or stucco house is nothing less than the colorless cocoon that contains an emerging metamorphosis. All its glory is inward.

Not only the structure, but the process of this ceremony of inner conversion is as elegantly simple as its physical setting. But the human components of the ceremony may give the convert reason to pause. The convert is attended by an experienced person of the same sex. But that attendant may be a recent immigrant or one unrefined in the more courtly manner appropriate to religious ceremony, or may sound "all business" in preparing the convert for the immersion, or may be a person whose general demeanor is ungracious and abrupt. Such community functionaries likely were recruited from among a very small number of available people willing to undertake so sensitive and sometimes unrewarding a job, often for inconsequential reimbursement.

Even the three members of the Bet Din may appear matter-of-fact and uninspired in the face of the spiritually charged anticipating convert. In part, this is because the three are called upon to act as representatives of all Jewry and of God on high, and need to concentrate seriously on keeping the Halakhah in every detail. This for the very simple reason that what they are doing here—in effect, declaring a non-Jew to have become Jewish—is more halakhically decisive than virtually any other act any Jew will ever perform. This is not all pomp and ceremony and spirit and goodwill, but the fulfillment of the high legal standards of ancient and modern Sages. The hard facts of the conversion procedure, negligible as they sometimes may appear to the untrained eye, apply as a universal Jewish standard for all converts at all times, and these members of the Bet Din are the guardians of that cherished heritage.

In part, a lack of apparent enthusiasm may be because, in the back of their heads, they are worried that this conversion may not work out at all, and they are not only performing a meaningless function, but a counter-productive one. Maimonides himself was wary—and attributed one of the untoward statements of the Talmud about converts to that wariness—lest the convert not take Judaism seriously and one day revert to old ways thereby diminishing the Jewish people, a fact not easily undone.[17]

In addition, the jading effect that witnessing many conversions may have upon the Bet Din in a large city is that they no longer demonstrate their natural sensitivity. Of course, they realize the effect that the nature of this process has on most converts, and surely they appreciate the transforming significance that the entire act holds for the convert candidate. But they may not demonstrate that sentiment.

In truth, everyone agrees that this is a moving and beautiful and spiritual moment and that it should not be glossed over— even for understandable and legitimate reasons—and it surely should not be lost in the details of the Halakhah. Naturally, there is never an excuse for being ungracious, abrupt, or inconsiderate. But we are dealing with people—good, honest and well-intentioned—but, still, fragile people who may not measure up to the expectations of the moment. The old tautology remains essentially true—people are people.

IN SUM, REMEMBER THIS CAVEAT: THE CONVERT WOULD DO WELL TO PREPARE FOR A SPIRITUAL, MEANINGFUL, *INTERIOR* EXPERIENCE IN A SETTING THAT MAY BE LESS THAN INSPIRING.

"CLEAN" AND "UNCLEAN"

Of all the substances available to humanity, water, which cleans the body, is the obvious, intuitively correct medium to be used for cleansing the soul.[18] Yet, the reason for utilizing water, which appears to be edifying and harmless, for purpose of purification, has been grossly misconstrued and has consequently greatly diminished the use of mikveh. The image that the rite conveyed has proven a vulgar caricature of its profound symbolism—and nearly its undoing. The King James translation of the Bible refers to a woman in her menstrual state as "unclean" with only the water of the mikveh able to render her "clean"—thus requiring an arresting of sexual activity and a brief separation of the sexes. The word "unclean," a physical term meant to reflect the *spiritual* state of "impurity," implies that Judaism holds a woman in her natural God-given menstrual state to be *physically* or even *morally* "unclean." That is absurd. "Impure" implies the need for regeneration.

Another implication often drawn from the word "unclean" is that blood was somehow to be considered anathema. This unspoken implication was so widespread and so influential, though so far from truth, that it has wrought havoc upon the widespread observance of mikveh immersion in the twentieth century.

Just the reverse is true. Precisely because blood is the source of all life, it is held to be so precious that the Jew may never drink it and certainly never needlessly spill it, as in game hunting—let alone call it grime that needs to be scoured from the body. Precisely because a woman in her menstrual state is so much the gift of God to the human race, being the machinery of survival. She is never during these days to be subjected to physical or psychological pressure to cohabit; never to be harried, never to have this moment in her natural cycle violated. "Impure" conveys the need for caution and for prudent care on days which demand special sensitivity and delicacy and which abhor aggressiveness. The use of the aquatic term, "clean," for the spiritual concept of "pure" does a severe injustice to a delicate mitzvah.

The confusion of spiritually pure and physically clean is, in any case, more emotional than rational. First, a woman had to be physically clean before entering the mikveh, so that mikveh could not be used simply as a substitute for a bathtub. Second, men are considered continuously "unclean" since the destruction of the Temple, being that they were not required by the Torah to use the mikveh since then. Third, even though Judaism places a premium on physical cleanliness and even though westerners are fond of saying "Cleanliness is next to Godliness," it is absurd to believe that the Torah would raise this everyday value to the exalted level of the spiritual state of purity. Religion deals with the whole human being and Judaism emphasizes that the human body is a gift from God, but it stops well short of equating cleanliness with Godliness.

HALAKHIC REQUIREMENTS OF IMMERSION

The Mikveh

The mikveh must comply with a number of precise halakhic qualifications. If it does not, the best intentions and most pragmatic reasons will not effectuate the conversion as Jewish law requires it.

The mikveh must be built into the ground or the structure of the building. It must hold a minimum of twenty-four cubic feet of water—200 gallons. The depth must be such as to enable an average adult to stand upright and have the water reach at least eleven inches above the waist, so that immersion can be performed without backbreaking contortions.[19]

The water must originally have been transported to the mikveh in a manner resembling the natural flow of waters. The general practice is to build cement channels at the sides of the mikveh roof which will enable rainwater to flow directly into the mikveh. Done right the first time, with the required initial amount of water, other piped waters may be added later in whatever quantities and at any time and the mikveh will still retain its religious validity. Because of this need to be derived from natural sources, the mikveh cannot simply be another instrument of modern plumbing gadgetry. It may not be a portable pool or a tub or vat or spa or portable tank; the water may not be brought into the mikveh by human effort, such as drawn in pots and other vessels. Also, the waters must be stationary and not flow (not even the flow caused by a filter) while the mikveh is in use. The water, by all means, should be chlorinated to assure its meeting the highest standards of hygienic cleanliness. (While the chlorinated water may be somewhat discolored, it does have to retain natural water color.) It does not need reiterating here that the mikveh should be tastefully decorated and kept spotlessly clean at all times.

Water deriving from a natural spring is considered a valid mikveh if it complies with halakhic conditions (too abstruse for presentation here). Also quite proper is immersing in the ocean, where there is no mikveh available, given the satisfaction of certain halakhic conditions. Both these alternatives are subject to the qualification that they be totally and absolutely private. Because the Halakhah of these matters is complicated, rabbinic approval is necessary before these alternative sites are used.

The Conduct of the Ceremony

The rabbi will designate the three-man Bet Din and probably also the personal escort for converts. It is wise and altogether proper that the convert candidate take along a Jewish companion or the conversion teacher to alleviate the feeling of aloneness that often grips people at such occasions. Company is also desirable because, at critical times of great joy or great sadness, an experience shared with a friend multiplies the delight as well as divides the anxiety.

The ceremony must take place on a weekday and during daylight,[20] as do all other Jewish court procedures. In cases when a full circumcision has to be performed (unlike the touch of blood for previously circumcised males), enough time will have to elapse to be certain that the wound has healed completely. The time and day of the immersion will be determined by the availability of the members of the Bet Din and the escort, but also, in the case of a female convert, by the time of her menstrual cycle. Because of the laws of *niddah*, it must be timed to occur after the period itself, considered by Jewish law to last five days or until the disappearance of menstrual blood. Immediately after that, the immersion can take place and there is no need to wait an additional seven days.

Personal Preparations for the Immersion

The only assurance that the immersion will accord with halakhic requirements for a male convert is the presence of the rabbi at the mikveh; a female is to be accompanied by a person familiar with the practice, such as a rabbi's wife, the mikveh escort, or a very knowledgeable friend who herself uses the mikveh.

The body must be thoroughly cleansed immediately before the immersion. The convert should be careful that there are no adhesions such as bandages, Band-Aids, or ointment; that the hair is thoroughly brushed; the nails of hands and feet are pared; and that no traces of cosmetics or nail polish remain.[21]

The whole body must be immersed at one time, not sequentially, and the submerging must be total, without even a single hair remaining above the water.

The Order of the Service

NOTIFICATION OF THE MITZVOT: HODA'AT HA'MITZVOT

The Talmud makes very clear the requirement, not only of the convert's commitment to keep the mitzvot, but of the Bet Din's informing the candidate as to what Judaism requires of its adherents—as though the convert had not studied and read and experienced Judaism until this very moment. It is a compact replay of the total experience of the gentile coming to the Jewish community with the Bet Din representing the community and teaching him all that is important about Judaism, his accepting the obligations, and then formally immersing and becoming a Jew. This *hoda'at ha'mitzvot* by the Bet Din, actually for the second time, takes place after the convert enters the mikveh, but before submerging the head, the final act of immersion.

DECLARATION OF COMMITMENT: KABBALAT HA'MITZVOT

The members of the Bet Din will ask the convert several basic questions about the Jewish religion, its faith and its observance. This facet of the ceremony is the very essence of the whole admission procedure and it, more than any other part, must absolutely be presided over by a three-man Bet Din. The convert need have no fear of this aspect if he has made a credible effort to understand Judaism as it was taught him. The conversion instructor himself may very well be a member of the Bet Din, and he probably knows generally what kinds of questions its members will ask.

Even more important than the knowledge of Judaism is the commitment to keep it as a way of life. The convert is expected to have determined this already long before the immersion.

If the convert is not totally committed, he can still delay the immersion even at this late date.[22] If there is a possibility that the convert might wish to rescind his commitment, now is the time to do it. After the immersion, the person is considered a complete Jew in every way.

THE IMMERSION: TEVILLAH

The immersion is an act both of intimate privacy and of public declaration. The needs of both must be satisfied. The Rabbis have guarded the convert's modesty and also Judaism's halakhic requirement that the court procedure be accurate.

Privacy is assured, in the case of a woman, by the presence of a female escort, who assists the convert, and also serves to assure the Bet Din that all the immersion requirements are being met. In order to guarantee keeping the rules of modesty, some admission courts employ a large sheet which is spread across the mikveh waters with a small opening for the convert's head. The members of the Bet Din are seated immediately outside the mikveh room, with the door slightly ajar. When the attendant informs them that the candidate for conversion has been covered with the loose-fitting sheet, they enter the room in time to see the head submerged, and they immediately withdraw. In that way, the Bet Din can testify to the immersion, and also hear the declaration of commitment recited a second time before the immersion and the blessings afterward.

The Blessings

The blessing in the mikveh is as follows:

Barukh atah Ado-nai Elo-henu melekh ha'olam asher kideshanu b'mitzvotav v'tzivanu al ha'tevillah.

Blessed are You, O Lord, our God, King of the universe, who has sanctified us with His commandments and commanded us regarding the immersion.[23]

Blessings over the performance of mitzvot in Jewish life always take place *before* the action of the mitzvah. The reason for this is that it focuses the soul, raising the consciousness for the action to be undertaken, establishing the purpose of the mitzvah, and demonstrating that its origins are in God's command. Also, the blessing enhances the mitzvah by providing the reason for undertaking the symbolic action. Ritva notes that, since the blessing is a statement of the soul, it should precede the statement made by the physical action of the body.

There is one exception to this general practice of placing the blessing before the mitzvah—the immersion of a convert. The convert needs to recite the blessing *after* the immersion, not before. The reason is simple: one cannot declare "God commanded us," if one is not commanded by God because they are not Jewish. The convert becomes a Jew only after the immersion is completed.

There is much discussion in the literature as to the exact moment that one becomes a Jew. Generally, it was held that the conversion is not fully accomplished until the convert emerges from the water. Therefore, the blessing is recited *after* immersion and immediately prior to alighting from the mikveh. Tradition recognizes the convert's desire for achieving admission into Judaism and therefore it encourages the blessing to be recited as soon as possible after the convert raises the head from the water.

After the blessing, the convert immerses twice more and then leaves the mikveh. A seventeenth-century rabbi notes that this threefold immersion and the entire procedure underscores the sanctity of the act, and fulfills the mandate according to all rabbinic theories. There is weighty opinion that holds that the convert, unlike the menstruant, needs only one immersion, after which the blessing is recited and the convert emerges from the mikveh.

A second blessing is required by most, but not all, authorities. It is called *she'hecheyanu*, and with it a person thanks God that He has enabled him to live to experience the greatness of this moment. As one scholar said: "If the *she'hecheyanu* is recited after certain selected single mitzvot, it should surely be recited by one who is thankful that he, with this act, has been enabled to observe all the mitzvot of Judaism." The decision in this matter will be made by the leading rabbi of the Bet Din and, of course, it should be respected.

The procedure generally practiced in the Ashkenazic tradition is as follows:

1. The convert enters the mikveh, with loosely fitted sheet, submerging until the water reaches the neck.
2. The Bet Din notifies the convert of the important mitzvot.

3. The convert submerges completely.

4. The convert emerges and recites the blessing *al ha'tevillah.*

5. The convert then submerges twice more.

6. The convert now recites the second blessing, *she'heche-yanu.*

7. The convert emerges a full Jew.

The convert is then given a new name to accord with his new status. This will be discussed later. It is mentioned here because the naming takes place at the mikveh after the immersion service is complete.

Finally: Congratulations!

The Bet Din then extends its welcome in a personal manner. Some do so with the ancient formal greetings found in the Talmud which confirm for the convert that, even though the Bet Din tried to dissuade him from becoming a Jew, his choice of a God and a people is admirable and correct:

> When he has bathed and come up out of the water, they speak to him appropriate words of kindness and comfort:
>
> "Do you know to Whom you are adhering? Happy are you! You are adhering to Him who spoke and the world came into existence.
>
> The world was created only for the sake of Israel [Israel was the only nation to accept the Torah and, without the Torah, the world could not exist]. Only Israel are called 'sons of God' [Deuteronomy 14:1]. Only Israel is described as beloved of God [to wit: they were given the Torah].
>
> And all the things we have said to you [the words of discouragement in order to dissuade the lighthearted from undertaking conversion] we have said only so as to increase your reward [you will be keeping the faith courageously despite the downside of its experience in this society]."

There is, as we noted above, no formal festivity required by the law to celebrate this precious moment. However, it is a fine idea for friends to prepare a repast designed to honor the convert for his or her wisdom and heroism in undertaking this radical, yet magnificent step in life.

The new Jew should stop to contemplate her own soul and then mark in her mind the moment of finally achieving this milestone in life—one which will affect all future generations.

This is a time of truly ineffable joy. After all, the convert has just concluded an important covenant—he or she has joined in partnership with the greatest people of all ages: with Abraham and Sarah, Isaac and Rebecca, Jacob and Leah and Rachel, with Joseph and Moses and Aaron, with Ruth and King David, with prophets and Priests and builders of Temples, with Scribes and Rabbis and Sages of the Talmud and with the scholars of every age—all of whom are now family. This is the goal the convert was seeking and for which much was sacrificed. It is not just another day. The joy he or she derives in appreciating this should not vanish in the rush of daily life—it should fill this magnificent moment with a deep and exquisite contemplation of a grand and historic spiritual accomplishment.

Welcome.

Notes to Chapter Ten

1. Victor Turner, *The Ritual Process: Structure and Anti-Structure,* ch. 2, Cornell Paperbacks, Cornell University Press, Ithaca, New York, 1969.

2. The talmudic requirement is one *amah* by one *amah* by 3 *amot* deep. In the most stringent view, the *amah* is 2 feet.

3. See Moses Tendler, *Pardes Rimonim,* p. 40 (Judaica Press, New York, 1982), for a brief English condensation of the rabbinic requirements. See *Hedge of Roses,* by Norman Lamm, Feldheim Press, 1970, for its conceptual underpinning.

4. Maimonides, *Mishneh Torah, Tumat Ochlin* 16:8, and *Guide for the Perplexed,* 3:47. See also Rashi to Numbers 19:13 and Leviticus 17:16.

5. Laurence Schiffman, *Who Was a Jew?,* p. 26, Ktav Publishing House, Hoboken, New Jersey, 1985. One should note that, although this is not explicitly spelled out in the Bible, the Sages held that it is quite clearly what occurred at that time. The Rabbis, already in the early years of the first century, assumed the ancient requirement of tevillah in a kosher mikvah. This is also implied in the demand made of all Jews at Sinai before receiving the Ten Commandments to "wash their clothes"— surely their bodies, too. Also, it is evident by the simple deduction that, were it not for immersion, women would be provided no distinctive ceremony of admission into the Jewish Covenant. This is unthinkable in a religion which revels in "doing" mitzvot where only an action can symbolize a sentiment. It is a natural and reasonable assumption for the Rabbis, and it has never been contested throughout subsequent history—until recent times.

   This is not the place for a dissertation on this subject, but the "apparent paradox" of considering the burial of the unknown dead the greatest mitzvah for which all others are set aside, while considering handling a cadaver an essential source of ritual impurity, is only apparent, but not a paradox. One should note that this halakhic position drove the deepest wedge between the priesthood of the pagan religions—whose priests did virtually nothing other than pay attention to the dead and their entombment—and Judaism, whose priests, the *Kohanim*, were not permitted even to be under one roof with the dead. In its emphasis on the connectedness of life and religion, Judaism separated itself from all the world's religions, Christianity included. That is one reason why it is unthinkable that Jews should have a crucifix as their central symbol.

7. See Alon, Gedalyahu, *Jews, Judaism and the Classical World: Studies in Jewish History in the Times of the Second Temple and Talmud*, pp. 146-189 (Magnes Press, Jerusalem, 1977), who relates proselyte immersion to the general concept of the impurity of the gentiles. (This is difficult to understand, inasmuch as that impurity is of rabbinic origin, equating the *tumah* of the gentile with that of a *zav*, and requiring purification not in a mikveh, but in the *Ma'ayan*.) This purification, he says, is not unlike the ceremony gone through by *yefat to'ar*, the "beautiful captive" who could be converted and then married under certain conditions. Her immersion is a purification from her idolatrous past. So also the freed slave, who became a full Jew upon liberation, had to go to the mikveh to set aside the past.

8. See Victor Turner, *The Ritual Process: Structure and Anti-Structure*, ch. 2, *ibid.*

9. Rivash, quoted in responsa of Chatam Sofer to Yoreh De'ah 209, makes this point with the following insight: The waters of the mikveh must measure forty *se'ah*. But a person is traditionally considered to displace a volume of twenty *se'ah*. The total of forty thus legally nullifies the twenty of man, the waters of the mikveh nullifying man's existence while he is submerged. Samson Raphael Hirsch finds this idea in a turn of letters rather than a turn of numbers. He connects the word *rachatz*, washed in water, with *ra'atz*, breaking down [of one's ego]. It represents a temporary ego death no matter how you turn it. Both these comments are noted by Aryeh Kaplan in *Waters Of Eden*, p. 59, Union of Orthodox Jewish Congregations of America, New York, New York, 1976.
    See Appendix 4.

10. This concept is noted by the early Christian thinkers, and is recorded already in the *Didache*. Indeed,Lawrence Schiffman in *Who Was A Jew?* notes that the idea that mikveh was an *initiatory* rite, rather than a *purification* rite, smacks of Christian influence, and cannot be found in the Bible, Apocrypha, Philo, or Josephus. But this theory cannot hold up in any case if you take into consideration what other religions made of this rite—the sprinkling of "holy waters" on the initiate rather than a total submergence.
    Also, it should be noted that the waters of the mikveh are in no way possessive of sanctity so as to be called "holy" water. They are functional, a medium to sanctity, but not sanctity itself. It is not merely a facile transition from being a vehicle to being sanctity itself. The mikveh accomplishes any one of a number of religious goals: purification, increasing sanctity (as in conversion, the *Kohen* in the Temple, the

choosing of Levites, immersion of cooking utensils previously owned by
gentiles) and as a form of permission (such as permitting family relations
after menstruation).

11. See Appendix 4.

12. This portion of the chapter on immersion draws deeply on Rabbi Joseph
    B. Soloveitchik's profound and poetic essay, "Kol Dodi Dofek." To pursue
    the concepts of goral and ye'ud read the original essay in Hebrew. The
    essay has been reprinted in many journals, but is most easily accessible
    in his book of essays, *B'Sod Ha'Yachid Veha'Yachad* ("In Aloneness
    In Togetherness"), ed. by Pinchas H. Peli, Orot Publishers, Jerusalem,
    1976. A comprehensive analysis of the milah-tevillah conceptual axis is
    to be found in the essay by Rabbi Soloveitchik, p. 385, notes 21 and
    22.

13. *Becoming a Partner to the Covenant,* ch. 4, section III.

14. See Appendix 3 on Christianity's different attitude to circumcision and
    immersion.

15. This immersion relates solely to the giving of the Torah at Sinai—
    immersion for the sake of conversion may not even have been known
    in Egypt where, according to Maimonides, circumcision appears to have
    been sufficient for male conversion.

16. Together, circumcision and immersion, after the prerequisite acceptance
    of a life of mitzvot, represent the total ritual process of conversion. But
    they formalized two different aspects of that process. Circumcision served
    halakhically to remove from the convert candidate the status of the gentile.
    Halakhically, he was at this point not a non-Jew, having thrown his fate
    in with the Jews and having been circumcised. But he was still not a
    participant in the halakhic, religious destiny of the Jew and therefore
    not yet a part of the "Priest People" known as Jews.
        See Appendix 3.

17. See *Hilkhot Issurei Bi'as* 13:17.

18. *Sefer Ha'Chinukh,* ch. 175.

19. For an excellent presentation of these requirements and the whole subject
    of the Halakhah of the mikveh, one should read and study *Pardes Rimonim*
    by Dr. Moses Tendler.

20. Yevamot 46b; *Mishneh Torah,* Hilkhot Issurei Bi'ah 13:6; Yoreh De'ah
    268:3, 4.

21. Yoreh De'ah 268:2.

22. Yoreh De'ah 268:1.

23. Two variations on the blessing are discussed in the sources. One modifies
    it to read *al tevillat gerim,* analogous to the style of the blessing at the
    b'rit milah. This seems to be objectionable because, by the time the
    convert recites the blessing, he is instantly part of *klal Yisrael* and not
    especially to be singled out, unlike at the circumcision while he is still
    in the midst of the process, it not yet having been concluded by the
    immersion. See *Likute Meir,* p. 79.
        The other version sought to have it read *al mitzvat tevillah,* as with
    many other mitzvot, such as tefillin and *eruvin* etc. But all the decisors,
    without fail, cite the blessing as *al ha'tevillah,* without the addition of
    the word mitzvah.

11

The Convert's
Temple Offering

The least known aspect of conversion is the third of the three essentials the Torah lays down for admission of converts, one never practiced today. This third of the triad in the protocol of becoming a Jew is the bringing of an offering to God on the altar of the ancient Temple that was destroyed in the year 70 of the common era.

THE SOURCE OF THE LAW

The prototype for all conversions is the one which took place at Mt. Sinai when the whole Jewish people converted. At that covenant, the Bible records (Exodus 24:8) that "Moses took the blood [of the sacrifice] and sprinkled it over against the people and said: 'This is the blood of the covenant which the Lord has made with you in accordance with all these words.'" The Talmud establishes this as the model for conversion for all time[1]: "Rabbi says: 'As your fathers, so you' (Numbers 16:11-14). As your fathers did not enter into the covenant except through circumcision, immersion, and the sprinkling of the blood [of the sacrifice], so you will not enter into the covenant except through circumcision and immersion and the sprinkling of the blood." A conversion that took place as recently as yesterday must replicate the conditions that obtained at the covenant on Mt. Sinai.

But this is problematic: If the Torah stipulates that every conversion must be accompanied by a sacrifice, how can we perform conversions today with the Temple in ruins and no way to bring sacrifices? The Talmud records the answer of Rabbi Acha, son of Yaakov: "Scripture says in regard to converts who will live in your midst, that they shall be 'for all your generations'" (Numbers 15:14-17). The ideal of Jewish conversion must obtain for all times, even after the destruction of the Holy Temple, and cannot be rendered obsolete under any circumstances. This mandate of the perpetual availability of conversion overrides even the biblical sacrifice requirement and assures the continued practice of conversion for all time.

THE ANCIENT SACRIFICE TODAY

In order to keep the sacrifice requirement alive even when it was impossible to fulfill, the Rabbis devised an ingenious solution: the convert should remain indebted to bring a sacrifice to the altar when the Temple will be rebuilt, as the tradition requires![2] In fact, there are Sages of the Talmud[3] who held that a convert needs to set aside actual funds for the purchase of a sacrifice when the Temple ultimately will be rebuilt.

But the Halakha decided otherwise. Money should not be set aside for this purpose for a practical reason: Rabbi Simeon said that Rabbi Yochanan ben Zakkai, who witnessed the destruction of the Temple, did not permit setting aside funds for it because it would become a "stumbling block before the blind." The reason it would become a pitfall is that dedicated funds are not permitted to be diverted for other uses, even for sacred purposes. In this case, large numbers of converts spread through all generations and in every country of the civilized world would be designating funds for distribution at some undetermined future date. This would increase the likelihood of misusing dedicated funds. People would naturally be prompted to use money left untouched for so long, originally intended as a debt of some ancient convert ancestor,[4] which was reserved for use after the Messiah comes and the Temple is rebuilt. They might divert it for worthy causes—such as alleviating poverty or homelessness or helping the sick—but it would nonetheless constitute a misuse of the funds.

THE INNER OFFERING

But the historical impediments to performing so holy, soulful, and effective a symbol could not keep Jews from acting out the *inner value of the sacrifice*. The offering is a statement of gratitude to God for being able to come "under the wings of the Almighty." It is quite proper to express gratitude for being able to join the Jewish people and to share its destiny. "Judaism" derives from the name of Judah, one of the twelve sons of Jacob, so named by his mother, Leah, because it means gratitude. She thanked God for his birth and for his father's attentions. If Judah means "thanks," then "Judah-ism" is "thank-ism." In truth, the spiritual value of gratitude, *hakarat ha'tov*, for favors received, is one of Judaism's most characteristic moral values. Rav Saadiah Gaon, the leading light of early medieval Jewry, said that, even without referring to the existence of God, he could construct Torah on the basis of reason alone by starting with the idea of gratitude.

One way to express such gratitude might be to undertake a personal goal that will enable the convert to heighten his or her sensitivity to Torah and to our people's human needs; to observe more of the rich heritage than one thought practicable; to serve the Jewish community in its multifaceted goals and strivings; to make a contribution of time or funds to a worthwhile communal endeavor—a Jewish educational institution or synagogue, the enhancement of the community mikveh, support of Israel or any of its needy institutions, or to a medical institution or hospice for care or research. There is no dearth of needs in Jewish life and it would be proper to "bring the convert's offering" in that manner. The debt to the Third Temple remains, however!

THE OFFERING AS PASSPORT

But the offering has another significance today that does speak specifically to the convert. In Temple times, it served as a passport into the Sanctuary, the most sacred place of the Jewish religion, so that the convert could complete the

conversion and be accepted by the Jewish people. By implication, that passport—unconsciously perhaps, but quite forcefully—served as an identification mark that the convert had
been examined for admission by a Bet Din of the Jewish people
and had been accepted before God to enter the Temple's
precincts just as the most pious of Jews.

What other act could speak more eloquently to the Jewish
community about admitting this convert to their own inner
ranks than did this formal admission to the central Sanctuary?
It was almost as much a privilege as it was an obligation.

We have no equivalent symbol today, but the Jewish community should receive the convert into the inner sanctum of
its home and hearth, its community councils and its elite leadership. And the convert should look upon himself as meriting
to serve the Jewish world as once he would have done in the
center of the Jewish universe, the Holy Temple.

It is also entirely proper and very appropriate to demonstrate
one's admissibility into the Sanctum of the ancient Temple,
despite its state of ruin, by asserting admission to one's synagogue over and over again, making it the convert's own synagogue as surely as it is the synagogue of its most pious member.

We pray that the convert sacrifice—along with all the others—
will be offered again soon. Meanwhile, living as Jews before
God will increase the likelihood of our seeing the rebuilding
of the ancient Temple in our own day.

Notes to Chapter Eleven

1. Keritot 9:1. Indeed the source for the requirement of immersion, as we
   have noted above, is deduced from the obligation of the sprinkling of
   the blood of the sacrifice which always requires a prior immersion for
   purification.
2. Maimonides, *Mishneh Torah,* Hilkhot Issurei Bi'ah 13:5. Also see Tosafot,
   Kiddushin 62b in the name of Rabbi Netanel. Some commentators insist
   that this teaching that we derive from "all your generations," which would
   obviate the necessity of sacrifice, holds only for these times, but did
   not obviate the need for sacrifice in the times of the Temple. So that,
   if a convert in those days did not bring a sacrifice, her conversion would
   not be completed. See *Responsa Avne Nezer* to Yoreh De'ah *ad loc.*
3. Baraita, Keritot *ad loc.*
4. One should be careful to learn from this law only what it conveys. The

Rabbis never dismissed a biblical injunction because it didn't accord with their worldview, or with the needs of society. A cursory knowledge of the ways of the Talmud indicates that the talmudic sages did not deal cavalierly with biblical law, no matter the exigency, no matter the philosophy, no matter the seemingly "proper" way to do things. In the case under consideration, Rabbi Joseph Soloveitchik, one of the leading minds of this century, shows that even during Temple times, the bringing of the sacrifice did not constitute a *sine qua non* of entering the Jewish fold. One had to bring the sacrifice in order to be considered qualified as a Jew to bring an offering to the Temple at a later date. If one did not do this as part of the conversion process, one could become a convert, but not reap the full entitlements of the ordinary Jew. Today, the entitlement of entering the Temple is not available to any Jew, and therefore the Sages could have ruled that the conversion process could continue for all generations even without the offering until such time as all Jews, converts among them, will again be able to enter its holy precincts. See Rabbi J. B. Soloveitchik's Yahrzeit Shiur, 1981, available only on tape from Yeshiva University Rabbinic Alumni, 500 West 185th Street, New York, and also Rabbi Aron Soloveitchik's article "Be'Inyan Greut," in *Sefer Kevod Ha'Rav,* edited by Moshe D. Sherman, published by the Student Organization of Yeshiva University, New York, 1984. For the contrary view, see Zev Falk, "Megamot B'Dinei Gerut" in *Sh-naton Ha'Mishpat Ha'Ivri,* vol. I, 5734 (1974). The argument is elegant in its simplicity and persuasive in its apparent logic. It cannot be dismissed lightly, but due note should be taken of the view of both Rabbis Soloveitchik.

12

Newborn—New Name

"What's in a name?" Shakespeare asked rhetorically. Harvard psychologists report that people spend much of their lives living up to what they perceive to be the significance of their names. New parents expend much thinking and planning on selecting their child's name. It is, after all, the title of this child's life, the identification, the handle, the signature of his being, the sound to which he will instinctively respond until the last syllable of recorded time. During the ensuing years, we twist it, we shorten it or formalize it or personalize it or abbreviate it; we resent it or are proud of it. But we never ignore it.

THE SIGNIFICANCE OF NAMES

The Sages say that one of the virtues of the Jews in their exile in Egypt was that they did not alter their names. That would have signaled an altered worldview, the adoption of a new life-style, a quick and efficient scrapping of the past.

A change of name for the convert, following that logic, signals the embracing of a new philosophy, a new identification, a purposeful, mindful statement of intent for the long future. "A convert is as a newborn child," *k'tinok she'nolad*. A new person needs a new name. That is why the Rabbis instituted that converts should choose Hebrew names for their new Jewish lives.

An interesting offshoot of the significance of names in Jewish tradition arises as a curious but persistent custom. A name is added to the given name of a seriously ill person to give him a "new chance"—a desperate attempt to relieve his severe situation and appear before God as another person, as it were. The thinking is this: his pain and sickness undoubtedly must have motivated him to repent of whatever sins he might have committed, and now he is a "new" person, proved by the fact that he is given a "new" name, and therefore deserving of a "new" Divine judgment.

The name in Jewish tradition is important not only for what it signifies in the bearer's own perceptions. In the biblical era, it bespoke a special role, and it changed as that role widened or narrowed. The change was mandated by God and, in some cases, using the original name after it was changed was prohibited.

For example, Abram, the first Jew, had his name changed by God to "Abraham"—the addition of the Hebrew letter *hay*, one of the four letters of God's ineffable Hebrew name. Sarai's name was changed to "Sarah," again by the letter *hay*. Their names were altered to accord with their new roles as the Torah indicates—when they became "fathers" and "mothers" of a whole people, they were transformed from private persons to the leaders of a nation. The *hay* introduced a new spirit into the world—a trace of God was fetched from the heavens and became integrated into the lives of plain people (Genesis 17:16).

Jacob's name is changed to "Israel" after the struggle at the ford of Jabbok, when "Jacob strove with the Lord and with man and overcame (Genesis 32:28)." It signified a new role and a new meaning for Jacob's life. He went from "Jacob," named for the manner of his birth—holding onto the heel, *ekev*, of his twin brother Esau—to "Israel" which signified his triumph over the spirit of Esau.

The variety of names the Bible gives Jethro, the Priest of Midian, the father-in-law and counselor of Moses, has always been a source of confusion to commentators. What is clear is that his name was changed because of his conversion. According to the Midrash,[1] Jethro had seven names. The name prior to his conversion was "Yeter," and the new name given him was "Yitro." What appears as only a slight modification is a major addition of the letter *vav*, another letter of the four-lettered ineffable name of God. The addition of a letter from

God's name indicated, as strongly as anything could, the transformation in Jethro's service from that of cultic leader in Midian to the service of God and His people Israel.

Another commentator, Nachmanides,[2] believes that "Hovev" was the new name given to replace the original pre-conversion name, "Yitro." In ancient society, he says, a person's household servants took on the name of the master and a similar process was followed when a person entered the service of God.[3] The name of the Master, in this case, is one of the letters of God's name grafted onto the original name.

One rabbinic scholar[4] draws the penetrating insight that Yitro, the old idolatrous Midianite Priest, was never again mentioned in Scripture by "Yitro" or any other name after the sacrifice that capped his full admission to the Jewish people. He is referred to only as the anonymous "father-in-law of Moses"—one of the costs of having a famous, overshadowing son-in-law.

NAMES FOR THE CONVERT

Many rabbis hold, citing Yitro, that converts should not only add a Hebrew name but also modify the given name used in pre-conversion years. Other rabbis differ, pointing to Ruth, the most famous female convert to Judaism, who did not change her Moabite name at all.[5] There is a contrary tradition that the name Ruth is, in fact, the changed name given her at conversion, altered from the original "Golit." Indeed, the reputed descendant of her sister-in-law, Orpah, who did not accompany Ruth on her pilgrimage to the Holy Land, was none other than Goliath, "Goliat."

Still other rabbis hold that all converts should be named Abraham or Sarah,[6] the very names they were given when they "converted" to the service to God. Tradition imputes to them the constant activity of converting men and women to the worship of God.[7] But Jewish communities never followed that advice. After all, Yitro was not called "Abraham," and Ruth was never named "Sarah."

Following is a listing of some of the more famous converts whose names are recorded in Torah, Talmud and Jewish literature.

- Obadiah, the prophet, after whom a book of the Bible is named, was an Edomite convert.[8] The name recurs often and translates into "servant of God." (Its Islamic equivalent is the highly popular Abdullah.) It is also the name of the famous convert who corresponded with Maimonides and elicited from him a letter that is, to this day, one of the most eloquent Jewish tributes to the courage of converts.
- Queen Helena and her two sons, converted at the end of the Second Temple era.
- Shimon, son of Giyora, was a leader of the great Bar Kochba rebellion.
- Onkelos, son of Kalonymus, translated the Bible into Aramaic. Tradition actually requires his translation to be read every week in conjunction with the weekly Torah portion that will be read in the synagogue. Some identify him with the Roman senator, Flavius Clemens.
- Aquillas, "Aquilla of Pontius," translated the Bible into Greek.
- Antoninus was a close friend of Rabbi Judah, editor of the Mishnah.[9]
- Rabbi Yehudah, Hindaha, and his son Rabbi Samuel[10] were converts.

In the third to eighth centuries, there were numerous others, including kings of Yemen and of the Khazars, and names such as Hezekiah, Menasheh, Zebulun, Nasi, Aharon, Menachem, Binyamin, and Yosef appear consistently—without mention of an Abraham or Sarah.

Some rather strange names for converts surface in the times of the Talmud. One is "Son of Hay Hay," another is "Son of Bog Bog."[11] The theory offered is that these converts were in danger of reprisals for defecting to Judaism and, in order to hide their convert status, did not use their Hebrew names or their spiritual patronymic, "son of Abraham, our Father." Rather, they devised names that subtly conveyed their convert origins, as for example, "Son of Hay, Hay," which indicates that he is the spiritual heir of the two people who had the Hebrew letter *hay* added to their names, Abraham and Sarah. "Son of Bog Bog" did the same, only more secretively—the numerical total of the Hebrew letters *bet* and *gimel*, pronounced *bog*, is five, as is *hay*.

There was also a sprinkling of Abrahams and Sarahs as, for example:

- In 1264, "Abraham, son of Abraham," was burned at the stake in Augsburg.
- In 1270, Johannes, the ascetic named "Abraham, son of Abraham" was burned at the stake in France.
- In 1746, Graf Valentin Potocki, "Abraham, son of Abraham," was burned at the stake on the second day of Shavuot in Vilna.
- In 1911, the English Catholic priest, Count Charles Bucks, changed his name to "Abraham, son of Abraham," as did many other priests.

But this name pattern remained only a custom, never taking on the force of law. Indeed, as is obvious, the dominant tradition was to give converts other names. The choice is ultimately the convert's, and should be made with full knowledge of the scope of names available, not only in terms of pleasant-sounding words, but of their meanings.[12]

NAMES FOR THE PARENTS OF CONVERTS

What is *not* the choice of converts is the identity of the parents. In Jewish life, a person is formally called by their given name, and as the son or daughter of the parent. (Reference is generally made to the father—except in illness or in danger, when compassion needs to be elicited and the person is referred to as being the child of the mother. The very word for compassion in Hebrew, *rachamim*, derives from *rechem*, womb. Also, the mother who bore the child is a more positive natural identification of the person seeking God's attention.) While the convert's name is the convert's own choice, Judaism requires, in all formal documents, legal proceedings and religious functions such as being called to the Torah, an identification of parentage.

As the convert is technically considered to be a newborn child, reference to the parent must be of the spiritual parentage adopted by entering into the Covenant of Abraham. There must be a formal designation of the conversion that is plainly evident. That is why the convert is called "ben Avraham Avinu," "son of our Father, Abraham," or "bat Sarah Imenu," "daughter of our Mother, Sarah." In a Jewish marriage contract or divorce, it is not sufficient to write "child of Abraham," but of "Abraham, our Father," and "Sarah, our Mother," in order to avoid any possible duplicity which might lead some to believe that the father was actually Jewish and the person's name simply Abraham. Sometimes the word *ha'ger*, "the convert," is appended to the name.

This naming pattern was required only of the first generation of converts. All subsequent generations refer to their own father's Jewish name, without the convert appellation. *All Jews living derive from original converts* of previous generations, some going back to Sinai or to Abraham. Indeed, we are all children of converts who call ourselves by our own fathers' Jewish names. Thus, the second generation simply refers to the given name and the parents' adopted Hebrew name. Thus, in the listing above, as found in the Talmud, Rabbi Judah, Hindaha, is listed as a convert. His son is known as Rabbi Samuel, son of Rabbi Judah.[13]

The convert title appended to the name should be borne as a badge of spiritual courage and accomplished idealism.[14] But it should be noted that this title is required only on formal occasions and documents. It need not obtain in personal, familial and social life. It is evident from the letters included in Part One that converts generally resent being continually referred to as convert, and with good reason. It often serves to isolate them needlessly, or to deflect attention from their persons, and becomes a constant, sometimes irksome reminder in the Jewish community that they are not native Jews.

THE NAMING CEREMONY

The time of the naming ceremony was held by some to be the same as for a Jewish-born male—at the circumcision rite. However, as the convert is at this point still not fully converted—not having completed the immersion—and therefore not yet a Jew, the naming ceremony should preferably be delayed until immediately after the immersion.[15] It is generally recited at that time for both male and female converts.

The prayer recited is as follows (for males substitute the correct pronoun):

> Our God and God of our Fathers:

> Sustain this woman in the Almighty's Torah and in His commandments and may her name in Israel be _____, the daughter of Abraham, our Father. May she rejoice in the Torah, and exult in the commandments. Give thanks to God, for He is good and His kindness is to all eternity. May _____, the daughter of Abraham, our Father, grow to become great. So may she enter the Almighty's Torah, with His commandments and good deeds.[16]

At the conclusion of the entire ceremony, some versions add this prayer:[17]

> Our God and God of our Fathers:

> Enable this convert to succeed. Spread Your kindness over her. As You influenced her to find shelter under Your wings and to join Your people, so may You implant love and awe for You in her heart. Open her heart to Your teachings. Lead her in the way of Your mitzvot. May she merit to conduct herself in accordance with Your own attributes and may she always win favor in Your eyes.

Notes to Chapter Twelve

1. Exodus Rabbah 27:7, and Etz Yosef *ad loc.*
2. Commentary to Numbers 10:29.
3. Rabbi Moshe Ha'Levi Steinberg, *Chukkat Ha'Ger,* p. 109 (Reuven Mass Publishers, Jerusalem, 1971), indicates that this is the origin of changing the name. He notes Genesis Rabbah 43 in which Abraham's servants were called "Abraham." They were his converts.
4. *Meshekh Chokhmah* to Parshat Yitro.
5. See Bava Batra 14b, Maharsha *loc. cit.* and Rabbi Z. H. Chajes to Gittin llb.
6. *Or Ha-Chayim* to Genesis 28:5, cf. *Derekh Emet* of Rabbi Chayim Vital, who agrees.
7. Midrash Bereshit Rabbah 39.
8. Sanhedrin 39b; Rashi *loc. cit.* and Maharsha *loc. cit.;* Vayikra Rabbah to Metzora 18:2; Midrash Tanchuma to Tazria 8; and cf. Ibn Ezra's *Introduction to The Book of Obadiah.*

9. Shabbat 154a.
10. Yevamot 111b.
11. See Tosafot to Chagigah 9b, and the theory of Tosfot Yom Tov who cites Midrash Shmuel in Pirke Avot, who quotes Rashbam as the source of the names. But also see the question of Rabbi Gedaliah Felder, *Nachlat Zvi* 124, who notes that they lived in Hillel's times when the government was Jewish. Nonetheless, reprisals could have been threatened by individuals rather than by government.
12. There are many books of names; notable among them is *The New Name Dictionary: Modern English & Hebrew Names* by Rabbi Alfred J. Kolatch, Jonathan David Publishers, Middle Village, New York, 1989.
13. Yevamot 111b.
14. See Tosafot to Chagigah 9; Even Ha'Ezer 129:6; Mishpetei Uziel to Yoreh De'ah (Mahadura Tanyana), vol. I. ch. 58; Nachlat Shivah 12; *Kovetz Nidachim,* ch. 29, by Rav Hillel Ha'Posek, Tel Aviv, 1952/3.
15. Rabbi Moshe Feinstein decided to do just that. See *Iggerot Moshe,* Yoreh De'ah 127 responsum of Feinstein. He does make an exception in the case of an adopted child when the parent might be embarrassed if the naming is avoided in public. He stipulates that in such a case a phrase should be added which indicates that the whole procedure still lacks immersion, without which this child is still not a Jew.
16. See Rabbenu Gershom Ha'Gozer, *Zikhron Brit la'Rishonim,* vol. II, Jerusalem, 1970, Klale Ha'Milah, Hilkhot Gerim.
17. *Nahar Mitzrayim,* ch. 22, as quoted by Rabbi Gedaliah Felder, *Nachlat Zvi,* vol. 1, p. 46, Balshon Press, New York, 1959.

13

The Conversion of Minors

A minor is defined by Jewish law as a female under age twelve or a male under age thirteen. Such children, despite the fact that they cannot formally commit to the responsibility of performing mitzvot, may still be converted.[1] Such conversions occur primarily in the following circumstances:

1. Parents convert and want their child to be Jewish.

If the child is born before the parents' conversion, the child needs to undergo a separate procedure to convert. If the child is conceived after the conversion, there is no question that it is considered Jewish without any further action. In the case of a child conceived before the conversion, but born afterwards, the question is a subject of much debate. Most decisors hold that the child is, after all, born Jewish and nothing further need be done.[2]

2. A Jewish couple adopts a non-Jewish child.

The rate of infertility for Jewish couples in North America exceeded 20% as of 1990. Jewish babies given for adoption are very few, and those that become available present genealogy problems that are complex. Adoption of non-Jewish children presents a more reasonable possibility for success. But the question is whether we can effectuate a conversion for such an infant, and under what specific conditions.

UNDERSTANDING BASICS

Parents need to understand the following: a gentile child does not become Jewish simply as a result of a civil legal adoption. Nor is a child considered Jewish because he or she lives in a Jewish home or attends a Jewish school.

Roman law invests parents with ownership rights over their children. American civil courts have the power to confer or transfer these rights. But Jewish law endows no such ownership over children and confers no rights of transfer to the courts. A Jewish child belongs to no one—not the state, not the parent, not the religion—but to himself. However, it is true that, by their own actions, parents and children may assume obligations toward one another which may be enforced by the law. No action, therefore, whether by a civil court, an adoption agency or any other institution, can *create* Jewishness. This can be accomplished only by a proper religious conversion acceptable to the Jewish people.

But how can the conversion of a minor be acceptable to Jewish law when the very essence of the conversion procedure is an act of will—a conscious desire to enter the Covenant of Abraham—and such will is absent in the case of an infant? A change of faith should inspire a transformation of soul, a desire to be in God's presence, to bear the responsibility of His commandments, all of which require mature judgment. How can minors be expected to decide on such weighty matters?

And how can anyone make this life-decision on behalf of minors, even infants, without their consent? Further, circumcision and immersion do not automatically bring about admission to the Jewish covenant—circumcision requires conscious intent to enter the covenant; immersion must be associated directly with commitment to observe the tenets of the Torah. A child clearly is not capable of such decision-making.

The "Advantage" Principle

The answer is that the conversion of a minor rests on a fundamental principle of Jewish law: one may perform an act on behalf of another, even in his absence, if such action redounds to that person's advantage. For example, one may act as an absentee's agent to receive an unconditional gift on his behalf, even if that person is not aware he is going to receive it. It is considered beneficial, a *zekhut*, and the court makes the assumption that, were he to have known of the transaction, he would have desired that it be carried out.[3]

Hence, if the conversion of a gentile infant to Judaism is construed to be a distinct advantage to the child, then the process can go forward. The Court represents him and commits him to leading a Jewish life, just as he would have done for himself were he an adult. On the other hand, if the conversion is construed to work to his disadvantage, or there is no dominant factor that would enable the courts to say, "We are doing him a favor," then the conversion is problematic.

The question then is: Will converting this gentile child to Judaism work to his benefit or not?[4]

Words like "advantage" and "benefit," as the Hebrew *zehut*, are broad terms and leave some latitude for interpretation. Several contemporary schools of thought suggest views that are quite complicated. They are here abbreviated for the general reader.[5] Individual rabbinic scholars may take issue with one or another of the ideas and that is their prerogative.

One view[6] maintains that the sole litmus test of benefit to the child is the observance of mitzvot. If adoptive parents are not observant, it will place the child in the untenable position of being under a halakhic obligation to keep the mitzvot without a corresponding ability to do so. It is unfair, and distinctly not to his advantage.

Another view[7] notes that there may be another and different qualification for advantage—that is, if the conversion will enable the child to espouse the same religion as the adoptive parents. In this case, the test is not one of performance of specific mitzvot, but generally of being a Jew. This broadens considerably the scope of permissible adoptions.

Yet another view[8] is held by a contemporary Sage who wrote that children in a day school who had been improperly converted could receive legitimate conversion on the assumption that, although their parents' household may not maintain a high standard of observance, the school could be relied upon to teach them Torah and persuade them to live a life of mitzvot. This position, too, provides a leniency that could encourage adoption by Jews who are not strict observers.

It is the common view of all these scholars, however, that it is essential to urge adopting parents to provide the milieu for the growth of their children's religious observance by themselves keeping the tradition. A formal decision in these matters should be sought from knowledgeable rabbis, and not inferred from this brief popular presentation.

Can Strict Discipline Be of Benefit to a Child?

Conversion to Judaism is considered to be advantageous to the child, even though it imposes boundaries, ethical limitations and religious obligations. The following is an excerpt from the Talmud:

> What you might have supposed is that a gentile prefers an unbridled life. . . . Therefore [Rav Huna] informs us that this applies [only in the case] of an adult, who has already tasted sin, but, [in the case] of a minor, it is advantageous for him [to become a Jew even though it is limiting]. (Ketubot 11a).

Therefore, at the discretion of the court (and in the case of an adoption they act in place of the natural parents), an infant can be considered to have made a legitimate commitment to be a Jew even in the absence of his conscious will.

Does the Child Have a Right to Reject Judaism?

This idea that the Bet Din acts in the infant's behalf is reinforced by an important legal qualification introduced into this kind of conversion—that, upon maturity, the child has the right to reject the entire conversion retrospectively and thereupon revert to his non-Jewish status. But if, upon learning of his Jewishness as an adult, he nods his acceptance or even remains silent, he is considered to have accepted the court's action on his behalf and to be a full-fledged Jew from the moment of his original conversion. That is why leading rabbis today insist that the child be told of his genealogy and religious history *before* the age of twelve for girls and thirteen for boys. It is only on the basis of his right to protest the conversion as an adult that the courts perform the circumcision and immersion while he is an infant.

THE CEREMONY OF CONVERSION FOR MINORS

The ceremony for the conversion of minors entails one danger which often ensnares unsuspecting parents, rabbis and other community professionals. When the infant is adopted at birth, the circumcision for conversion is performed on the traditional day, the eighth day after birth. But, the immersion for an infant is usually delayed until months later, and by that time it tends to be neglected or conveniently avoided. The child then is not legally a Jew! At the end of the circumcision, therefore, a certificate is issued testifying to the proper performance of the circumcision that it was done for the purpose of conversion; but in no way is this to be considered a certificate of *conversion*. That cannot be issued until the immersion is completed. The document of circumcision is *not* a document of conversion, only of half-conversion, and Judaism does not recognize half-conversions. It will not accord to the child any of the rights of the Jewish people until the completion of immersion. Therefore, the mohel who performs the circumcision should do so for the specific purpose of conversion (not only as is done for children who are Jewish by birth). The certificate of circumcision should indicate that conversion is not complete.

Because of this concern, a contemporary scholar suggested that the name be given only after immersion.[9] If this is awkward in the eyes of the parents or the public, the rabbi or mohel should append to the closing reading after the circumcision a statement indicating plans for scheduling the immersion to effect final conversion. That is also the reason that the prayer *she'hecheyanu* is preferably delayed until after the immersion.

This is cumbersome at best and entails the bewildering possibility that inertia will prompt parents to leave well enough alone, and we will have a child who is neither circumcised nor immersed.

The ceremony of immersion is the same as for adults with the following exceptions: a member of the Bet Din should assist the young child to immerse properly. Often, it is safer for the mother or father to enter the mikveh itself, and this is quite proper. The child should recite the blessings. If the child is too young to speak, the Bet Din may follow a number of alternatives: the immersion may proceed without the blessing, or the blessing may be recited by the Bet Din after the immersion, or the Bet Din may recite the blessing before the immersion.[10]

Notes to Chapter Thirteen

1. Halakhic sources for this chapter are based on Ketubot 11a, Rav Huna; *Ba'ale ha'Nefesh l'Rabbenu Ha'Gadol Ha'Raavad,* cf. note 10 below, end Sha'ar Ha'Tevillah. Reference may be found in all the classic compendia plus in the following:

   Likute Meir, vol. I, by Dayan Meyer Steinberg (G. J. George & Co., London, 1970), Al Immutz Yeladim ve'Giyur Katan;

   Giyur Ke'Halakhah, by Dayan Meyer Steinberg, G. J. George & Co., London, 1970;

   Chukkat Ha'Ger, ch. 3 and others, by Moseh Ha'Levi Steinberg, Reuven Mass, Jerusalem, 1971;

   Nachlat Zvi, vol. I, by Rabbi Gedaliah Felder, Balshon Press, New York, 1959.

   Other sources, responsa and articles, are too numerous to mention here.

2. Some hold that the male child requires circumcision with the intent to convert, and that, if the eighth day falls on Shabbat, it must be postponed to the next day.

3. Ketubot 11a; Ritva on Ketubot 11a, "Amar Rav Nachman," and *Ketzot Ha'Choshen,* 263:7.

4. A concise and precise overview is to be found in *Encyclopedia Talmudit,* vol. 6, pp. 444-449 (Jerusalem, 1979), "Ger Katan."

5. This theme is nicely developed by Rabbi Jeffrey R. Woolf, Executive Chairman of the Orthodox Roundtable in a paper, "Adoption and Conversion: An Halakhic Perspective," Yeshiva University, New York, 1990.

   There is some movement among rabbis today to deal with this all-too-common situation. An article, which has been expanded to book length, has been written by Rabbi Jack Simcha Cohen, *Intermarriage and Conversion* (Ktav Publishing House, Hoboken, New Jersey, 1987), in an effort to validate conversions of such minors. The halakhic establishment generally has hesitated to accept his thesis, although I believe it does merit serious consideration. It proves worthwhile in at least this: that we need not be strait-jacketed about restrictive, monolithic decisions that admit of no other possibilities, and we should not shy away from solutions that may be more appropriate for our contemporary circumstances, if they fall within the acceptable boundaries of the Halakhah. Until such time as these matters are decided by leading authorities, the practice should be left to the local Bet Din.

6. Articulated by Rabbi Jacob Yehiel Weinberg in *Sridei Esh* II, #96, Mossad Ha'Rav Kook, Jerusalem, 1977.

7. Chatam Sofer in a responsum, Yoreh De'ah 153.
8. Rabbi Moshe Feinstein, *Iggerot Moshe,* Even Ha'Ezer IV, 26, par. 3.
9. See *Iggerot Moshe* and my comments in note #15 in Chapter 12.
10. Reciting no blessing at all is a view held by B'nai Yisaskhar, in his *Derekh Pikudekha;* that the Bet Din should recite the blessings *after* the immersion is held by Rabbi Joseph B. Soloveitchik; that the blessing be recited by the Bet Din *before* is held by Ra'avad, in his *Ba'ale Ha'Nefesh l'Rabbenu Ha'Gadol Ha'Ravad.*

14
The Jewish Mate:
BECOMING A JEW AGAIN

DEAR ABBY:

I am Jewish, thirty-three, was raised in the Jewish faith and had the Bar Mitzvah when I was thirteen. However, I do not attend services except on the High Holy Days once a year.

Last year, I fell in love with a wonderful gentile girl. Connie is twenty-nine and an atheist. I want to marry her and, out of respect to my parents, I want to be married in our synagogue by the rabbi who has been a family friend for many years. The problem is, the rabbi can't marry us unless Connie converts to Judaism.

She is willing, and even agrees to raise our children in the Jewish faith providing I become a practicing Jew! She says, if she takes the Jewish faith, she will follow it, but she's not going to be the only Jew in the family. This means attending services every Friday night and observing all the holidays.

What do you think?

DAVID

DEAR DAVID:

I think she's terrific. Grab her!

ABBY[1]

To undertake a protracted and anxiety-filled process of conversion, often for the sake of marriage, and then to become "the only Jew in the family" must be a frustration and a mockery. Without the Jewish partner's cooperation, the Christian's conversion is most often a failure. It starts the marriage on the basis of an implied deception or, at the very least, a moral compromise—a toying with very serious matters of the heart in a somewhat cavalier manner for the sake of an accommodation. The London Bet Din, as well as many others in the United States, Europe and Israel, therefore requires the Jewish partner to pledge to participate in the family's religious practice.

The born Jew, not of his own making, is sometimes a victim—of early childhood conflicts or parental authoritarianism, perhaps even of self-hatred as a Jew. Quite often he or she is a child who was raised with a total indifference to any faith, whose parents may have assimilated, and who is consequently alien to the both the spirit and the language of the Jewish religion. Frequently, the Jewish mate is totally ignorant of Judaism and may not even be particularly pleased at having been born a Jew.

What complicates matters for the convert is that often what the Jewish mate assumes is standard Jewish practice, one that he has observed in his youth, is nothing other than a fleeting brush with religion, a perception made on a child's intellectual level about the complexities of Judaism. It is often articulated with all the authority of those who have, in Francis Bacon's phrase, "a little knowledge . . . that tends to atheism." There is an unthinking assumption widely held that if you were born Jewish, you must have absorbed *in utero* everything one needs to know about how to live fully as a Jew. This is not true, of course. To assume that anyone knows all the answers when what he knows may be a smattering of a Yom Kippur service, a fond memory of Passover Seder or a touch of religious school, approaches the farcical.

It will be beneficial, therefore, in a practical as well as an ideal sense, for the Jewish partner to look once again into the traditions of his people as an adult. This may be purely utilitarian on the born Jew's part, but it will serve to secure the success of both the mate's conversion and the family's unity. Who knows but that he himself may undertake some form of a spiritual return? At the very least, he will become sensitized to both the demands and the distinctions of the Jewish faith.

Gentiles, before they convert, do not know what to make of the specific Jewish mix of impoverished religious knowledge and rich ethnic memories. Such selective behavior confounds even the most sophisticated born Jews—how can it be understood by people outside the faith? With unequivocal cooperation and sympathetic understanding—both by the born Jew for his mate who undergoes this transformation, and by the convert for a Jewish mate who might be disaffected or conflicted about keeping traditional observances— the conversion and also the marriage stand to be reinforced.

There is a full-blown return to Judaism in progress among Jews today in which people who have been completely estranged from the religion, while living sophisticated secular lives at the cutting edge of modern society, are finding their way back to their roots. This phenomenon, the *ba'al teshuvah* movement, has made a veritable army of teachers and guides available in virtually every major city in the United States. In addition, there are many books written in the contemporary vernacular that address the concerns of modern Jews in a clear and convincing manner.

The following is a letter from a young Jewish California woman, educated at a leading university, who has made the long trek home in the company of her convert husband, as a partner sharing the thrills of exploration and discovery and also the frustrations and disjunctures of abrupt change:

> When our daughter started Hebrew school, we joined an Orthodox community, and we thought it best for the unity of the family that my husband, Brian, "Boaz" in Hebrew, have an Orthodox conversion. He had already been through both the Reform and Conservative conversion processes. But I felt that, if he would not be accepted by all factions, the conversion was not complete yet.
>
> He began studying for Orthodox conversion. But after a few months, he started to balk. Not realizing the extent of the commitment he was pondering, I was not being really empathic. As a result, we went through the worst eight-month period in our (as of then) ten-year history together. There was much tension, little joy, and lots of lonely suffering by two people who had been best friends and confidants. For the first time in ten years, he was unwilling to make a com-

mitment for me. While I knew he had to do it for himself, I felt backed into a corner waiting for him. We were already keeping most of the customs, so what was the hang-up?

Then, one day, he came home from work and calmly asked if I would like to get married in a few weeks. I didn't know whether to laugh or cry. I had given up on him and was living my own existence, while looking and acting like part of the family. I didn't feel that he had much connection to me, or desire for me, so the question of marriage seemed quite silly. But he wasn't joking; he was finally ready. Incredibly, I found that I wasn't.

Because of my commitment to family unity, I allowed myself to be pulled through the ceremonial necessities—mikveh, wedding, etc. I had always liked the idea of having a "renewal of vows," but a wedding at a weekday afternoon minyan service, attended by a dozen men I didn't know, was not quite what I had in mind. That was to be the least of my complaints. I had "made my bed," nudging him into this conversion, and now I was going to "lie in it."

I had no idea that I also needed "converting." I thought being born Jewish qualified me as an acting Jew. Wrong. I needed an Orthodox education also. I didn't know about davening (praying), berakhot (blessings), or the details of the family purity laws. I had no idea how much of Boaz's time this new venture was going to take up, nor how observant he was to become. He was suddenly very interested in the "letter of the law."

What followed was a two-year game of "leapfrog"—he would want to adhere to a certain custom; I would feel put upon. I would check into the how's and why's, eventually agreeing to adopt this new custom. Then he would find another one to add to his observance list!

Two or three years later, the game changed from "leapfrog" to hurdle jumping. The difference was that we were jumping together. I could tell when he had learned more and wanted to do something new, and I was usually willing to "go with it." I eventually got excited about being observant and would often initiate the adoption of a new custom myself.

Four years later, we are in "sync" again, communicating abundantly. We feel spiritual needs almost simultaneously, and search for answers together.

A conversion is not something a person can be forced into. Even if one is "only" converting from non-observance to observance, the process needs to be gradual. Undergoing such a change is truly like being "born again." The convert needs to be treated as a newborn in terms of religion: taught gently, reinforced consistently, and nurtured lovingly throughout the growth period. The first year, the convert, as a newborn, is observing and filing all the information in the head. The second year sees imitation—copying others and acting out what was "filed." By the third year, the acting feels natural, and the convert now has confidence to live and to learn as a "grownup."

Any couple who can go through this process and emerge together is truly blessed.

Success in marriage, as in conversion, may well result from developing a community of values and a mutual respect that making such religious decisions requires. Also, as the couple negotiates its higher ideals in pursuit of spiritual goals, it finds that the subject itself elevates the level of discourse of the entire marriage enterprise. Indeed, from knowledge gained from a recent study of converts,[2] both partners are likely to have come from marginally religious backgrounds and this unexpected clash of ideals precipitates a new interest in the religious roots from which their families grow.

In addition, translating religious ideals into everyday living—such as educating and raising children, forming community alliances, deciding on synagogue affiliation, and determining which charities to support—requires husband and wife to discuss, plan, arrange, and decide on the family's ideals and priorities in a way they never had occasion to do before. The journey toward conversion not only explores religion—its ancillary benefits are that it bonds the couple to the community rabbi, the synagogue leadership, and others who often express their admiration for the courage to convert.

It is wise, therefore, to work as a team in the exploration of Judaism and to develop a new level of togetherness and self-consciousness, studying together as classmates rather than as teacher and student. For the convert, it will be discovering new ideas; for the born Jew, it may be not only that, but also unlearning old prejudices and discarding some of the old baggage which may never have been valuable or true.

There is a subtle wisdom to the recommendation introduced by some rabbis today that both partners, man and woman, should undergo separate immersions on the very same day for the sake of symbolizing a step up in religiosity for each—

in one case from gentile to Jew, in the other from lesser to greater practice. Immersion for the born Jew is an effective symbol of his own personal "newness" to his old religion. (Of course, the other aspects of conversion are not applicable to those born to Jewish parents.[3]) This requires headstrong courage and much determination—as this is not commonly done. But its symbolism is powerful, the experience unforgettable, and the message indelible. It should not be lost on those parents or rabbis who are stuck in old ways.

Notes to Chapter Fourteen

1. Los Angeles, Times, 1982.
2. See Steven Huberman's *New Jews: The Dynamics of Religious Conversion: A Summary Report of the Intermarriage and Conversion Project,* p. 89 (Union of American Hebrew Congregations, New York, 1979). "Based on the quantitative and qualitative data reviewed in this section, we conclude that converts come from marginally religious homes."
3. See above, ch. 10, Immersion, under "Achieving New Status." Also see the opinion of Radbaz, *Responsa,* vol. 3, responsum 415, where he argues for the halakhic advisability of ba'ale teshuvah undergoing tevillah, although not as a legal prerequisite.

Part Four

RESPONSA:
ANSWERING QUESTIONS
ON LIFE AND LAW

15
Questions on the Laws of Conversion I

Two types of questions are often asked by converts and of converts. The answers of Jewish law, Halakhah, are what Judaism terms "responsa."

The first type consists of questions relating to issues of the formal conversion process and related matters of personal status—primarily problems of marriage laws applicable specifically to Jews by choice. The second type relates to interpersonal relationships, problems arising from making the transition from faith to faith and family to family—the new Jew with his gentile family and the gentile family with a new concern for the Jewish religion—and questions that arise from each concerned about participating in the ceremonies of another faith. These latter concerns are more complicated because they deal with weighty issues which strain the fragile web of interconnectedness of the natural and adopted families. Often, these relationships are tried or disrupted by the conversion.

But, before beginning to determine what the Halakhah has to say on these matters, we need to understand how to ask a question of the Halakhah and what to expect of its response.

Halakhah is Not a Matter of "Common Sense"

In a religion like Judaism, so dedicated to law and discipline as the necessary instruments of survival, it is a grave error to decide matters of religious propriety by the canons of common sense or personal standards—"What sounds right?" or

"What seems nice to do?" or "What is better for the family?" or even "What appears to be better for Judaism?" In such matters, which replicate themselves in all generations, we are not concerned primarily with personal *sentiment* and right *feelings*, important as they are. We are dealing with the survival of the Jewish people and the Jewish religion, and with the wisdom our teachers and Sages have brought to these questions during our long past. For such determinations, we must follow the Halakhah which, after all, is the age-old, historically proven, and generationally accepted way of doing things. It concerns itself with the needs of the individual human being, yet it transcends each individual and community in its concern for the whole people and its relationship with the Almighty. It has a wonderful record of success in the most adverse circumstances and we, the Jewish people, are here to prove it.

Precisely the way the questions we put to the Halakhah are phrased, to whom they are addressed, and what solutions are expected from the responses may be the first test of the convert's understanding of the new faith. Will he or she submit these decisions to the recognized authority and forgo what the convert perceives to be "common sense"? Can he or she follow the new Jewish tradition even in a situation which causes psychological discomfort?

One of the more crucial lessons to learn in becoming a Jew, therefore, is to know how and whom to ask and to recognize that, when a doubt arises, the first question a convert must be willing to ask is: "Does the *Halakhah* have a point of view on this problem?"

Following are responses of the Halakhah to some of the questions that converts ask both before and after they convert.

THE CONVERSION PROTOCOL

The Marriage Motivation

IF IT WAS NOT FOR "HEAVEN'S SAKE"

Obviously, a convert's ideal motivation should be a pure one —Judaism for Judaism's sake, "for Heaven's sake." However, as we noted, such an unadulterated motive is not typical today. Decisions need to be made about converts who, while not coming to Judaism for its own sake, are nonetheless people of integrity who would not arbitrarily make Faustian deals when it involves a sensitive and important subject such as conversion.

The rabbis who wrote responsa were sharply divided on how to rule on this matter. They knew, without having to tally the number of those who convert for marriage, that "for Heaven's sake" is the ideal, but not the common cause for converting. While they insist that ultimate decisions in this matter must never be made without halakhic warrant, they do not agree as to exactly how the Halakhah should handle this personal crisis.[1]

Throughout the major periods of Jewish history, the Sages have disputed as to which conversion strategy best serves the Jewish people—insisting on purity of motive or accepting lesser, but nonetheless respectable grounds.[2] Reasoning on both sides has been cogent and forceful.

One side[3] argues that, even when the ostensible motive in a conversion is marriage, the social forces of the Jewish community that normally would affect this person would oblige him, willy-nilly, to comply with the generally high observance level of the rest of Jewish society.

The other side responds[4] that such an environment of observance does not exist in today's Jewish community. Indeed, the general absence of traditional observance actually works against conformity to a halakhically acceptable standard. Therefore, they argue, a hesitant or vacillating convert will have nowhere to turn for moral support or even for a good model of Jewish living.[5] One leading halakhic authority notes that a convert cannot be faulted entirely for his lack of commitment. Unfortunately, after he surveys the Jews' functional level of observance, he may well assume that the Jewish religion is nothing but a skein of charming folkways that are not at all compelling and do not bind Jews to observe what is commanded by the Torah or the Rabbis.

The first view responds that sincere and searching people can find practicing traditional Jews and abundant examples of the richness of Jewish tradition in most Jewish communities in America and opportunities for Jewish education in every major city in the civilized world.

Prominent cases can be found in recent responsa literature in which the marriage motivation was neither dismissed nor rejected lightly. For example,[6] a question arose about a Jewish male Holocaust survivor living with a gentile woman during the war whom he promised to marry if they both survived. They now live full Jewish lives and she wishes to convert specifically in order to formalize their marriage. The decision is to approve the conversion *ab initio*, because, in the final analysis, it would obviously be successful—though motivated by the desire to marry.[7] What is important is that the positive factor of anticipated success was considered weightier than the negative factor of the marriage motivation.

Indeed, many other factors do enter into the equation when judging these matters in our day.

One concerns the moral quality of society as it relates to marriage. When there was complete separation of sexes before marriage, sexual passion, which was otherwise unsatisfied or unrealizable without formal marriage, could be held to be a significant motive for converting. But in an age of "Living-Together Arrangements," the broad acceptability of civil marriage, and the virtually unlimited ability to satisfy one's sexual needs, the age-old fear of the Rabbis that the religion was being used to accomplish these less-than-exalted purposes is not quite applicable.[8]

On the contrary, because conversion for the sake of marriage today is driven more by desire to achieve legitimate moral goals—to raise a cohesive family, live peacefully with parents and in-laws, and avoid yet another possible source of friction in the whole series of difficult adjustments in lifelong relationships, the likelihood of "pure" conversion for other legitimate motives is now more credible. Few people feel that they need to convert in order to marry. It is no longer simply satisfying raw passion or blind romance—that often has a life span of three months—but a sincere, respectable ideal for which he or she is willing to invest body and soul. This is not distant from the elevated purpose of "for the sake of Heaven," and therefore ought not to be rejected out-of-hand.

A second factor is the effect that the rejection of the conversion candidacy might have on the Jewish partner to the prospective marriage.[9] If it is likely, or even only conceivable, to cause the Jewish partner to abandon Judaism, the matter is even more critical and must be dealt with very sensitively. Now, such threats cannot be allowed to hold the Halakhah hostage. Every halakhic decision affecting life-style has the potential of triggering severe adverse reactions or a threat of retaliation against the faith or the faithful. Surely, Judaism cannot afford to be molded by such concerns rather than by the truth. There is also the ancillary concern that mere knowledge of this "official" fear of Jews forsaking Judaism might instigate rash threats by fiercely loving or simply stubborn people who insist on having their way.

Nonetheless, it is true that Judaism does not take kindly to defection from its ranks and it is therefore important for those who deal with such issues, rabbis and lay people alike, to proceed cautiously and be extra careful with words and feelings.[10] They are, after all, dealing with the stuff of life, which "stands at the heights of the universe," and should give such fears due weight in making a determination.

The court itself should not reject a candidate unless it is certain that the ulterior motive is the dominant factor, the benefit of doubt most often going to the convert who affirms his sincerity.[11] The last word in this very complicated matter is the last word in almost all conversion questions—it must be left to the decision of halakhically competent authorities and the local Bet Din,[12] according to how they see it.[13]

THE ACCEPTANCE OF MITZVOT

The entire conversion process hinges on this one theme—committing one's life to keeping the tradition. That is why the acceptance of the mitzvot is both *prerequisite* to and the purpose of the process and thus needs to be expressed a second time, immediately prior to the conclusion of the process. Due process requires both the initial reportorial acceptance and the formal ceremonial acceptance. The formal acceptance is placed immediately before the immersion and always requires the presence of the Bet Din, which represents the full authority of the law and of the entire community.

If the Convert was Ignorant of Mitzvot

It should be evident to any serious thinking person that one who enters a new faith ignorant of its basic requirements is not sincere or authentic and will not be a credit to his people.

However, it should be noted that the talmudic requirement is that the convert study "a small portion of the major and minor mitzvot."[14] One is not expected to absorb the encyclopedic details of the law—which takes a lifetime—but only to know enough to practice the major observances and to have a sense of the scope of Judaism's universe and the range of commitment it demands.

A fine insight into the problem of this requirement is manifest in an interesting question posed by the Rabbis: How could the masses of Jews be converted at Sinai when all they knew were the Ten Commandments?[15] The answer given by Rabbi Joseph B. Soloveitchik is that just as a great oak is compacted in an ancient seed so are all the mitzvah requirements in the life of the Jew implied within the Ten Commandments. Theoretically, he argues, all the details of the mitzvot could be derived logically from the ten. Another answer was offered by a scholar of the last century.[16] While the Jews at Sinai could not possibly be familiar with all of the law, they did commit themselves unconditionally to be servants of God—ready to keep all of the law, even those elements which they did not yet understand.

Of course, it is necessary that converts learn as much as humanly possible, but the Rabbis did not require expert scholarship of them. They sought instead a full-hearted willingness to abide by what they had already learned and what they expected to learn in the future. This is similar to the initial commitment of bride and groom. Each makes a total life commitment to their mate despite the fact that they do not know that person thoroughly, in recognition both of what they already know of their partner's qualities, and of what they can expect to find out about them in the future. Thus, sometimes, even without comprehensive and lengthy instruction, if the convert conveys the sense that his ignorance of the law does not imply a lack of interest, the conversion is still acceptable, providing that all other aspects of the conversion are done properly.[17]

Converts should know that most rabbis who head a Bet Din understand that often what appears as an inability to answer questions may indicate not ignorance so much as a lapse of memory in a moment of tension—similar to the experience at examinations or on witness stands. In extenuating circumstances, the inability to answer frequently reflects not insincerity but its opposite—excessive concern. In such cases, a lack of knowledge in a person otherwise sincere and committed obviously does not invalidate the conversion.[18]

However, a lack of proper *commitment,* of kabbalat ha'mitzvot, unlike a lack of hard knowledge, renders the entire procedure meaningless and makes a mockery both of the faith and of those who practice it seriously. Without any intent to keep the faith, it is merely an elaborate charade for the sake of personal convenience.[19]

If the Convert Rejects a Mitzvah

While a smattering of *ignorance*, though objectionable, does not invalidate the conversion process, explicit *rejection* of even one of the commandments in a manner considered rebellious toward Rabbinic authority does. It is a red flag that signals only a conditional acceptance, a less-than-complete commitment in "the marriage of true minds."

It is, of course, the individual's option to observe or not to observe any given mitzvah. Every person, Judaism believes, has a God-given freedom of the will. But the Halakhah declares that it is not everyone's option to determine what the Halakhah is in any specific case, and whether it is valid or not. One may choose to observe or not to observe, but one may not decide what Jewish law demands to be observed.

The historic religious struggle for Jewish survival is analogous to a battlefield situation. Each soldier is responsible for carrying out his or her clearly defined mission. The best trained leaders have wider perspectives and see the larger picture so that they are best equipped to decide what needs to be done. Were every soldier to map his own battlefield strategy, the whole army would be thrown into disarray. Judaism does not hold to Protestantism's belief in the individual interpretation of the Bible. Following such a policy would have caused such a small community as Judaism to disappear from world history.

Therefore, if a convert candidate—before becoming a Jew—rejects the practice of a specific mitzvah as fundamentally not valid and therefore not to be observed (rather than because he simply does not have the capacity to keep it now), he disqualifies himself as a credible candidate for conversion. It is true that many Jews reject mitzvot, but such rejection *ab initio* constitutes a bar to a prospective convert's admission to the faith. (Too many born Jews have caused havoc already by such rejection throughout the ages—although Judaism never reads any Jew out of the faith.)[20]

The grounds for invalidating a conversion because of such rejection are limited to explicit purposeful denial of a mitzvah. Even more, they are restricted by some rabbis to a person who stipulates prior to the immersion that he be granted official permission as a Jew to disregard it. Only in such an instance would he be denied entrance to the Jewish people, because conversion brooks no exceptions: "There is no conversion by halves."

At first, it may seem highly unlikely that a convert would stipulate in advance that he rejects one specific commandment. But that problem does occur, and can cause great consternation, as in the following example. A Kohen who, as a descendant of the Priestly family, has both privileges and constraints, wishes to marry a convert. The gentile woman sincerely wishes to convert to Judaism, but only with the qualification that after conversion she will be permitted to marry the Kohen. According to the Halakhah, that would entail accepting the entire Halakhah with one exception—the Halakhah that Kohanim may not marry even properly converted women. (See the treatment of this subject in the chapter on marriage questions.) The rejection of this one mitzvah may invalidate the entire conversion.

THE BET DIN

Who Qualifies as a Judge?

While the lack of traditionally ordained expert scholars was not allowed to obstruct the admission of proselytes throughout history, it did serve to teach what were the optimum qualifications of members of the court: integrity, personal observance, scholarship. For example, it does not stand to reason that those who themselves reject fundamental halakhic principles should be allowed to determine the halakhic qualifications of prospective converts.[21] The litmus test for such judges is not textbook scholarship or ethical values alone, but traditional beliefs and religious practice. This provides an assurance that all aspects of the conversion are validly performed. For this reason, traditional Jews will not accept proselytes converted by those who themselves are not traditionally observant.

Also, no special sanctity adheres to anyone because he holds either a title or a specific nationality. Israelis are not specially endowed to witness conversions because they speak Hebrew, nor cantors because they know how to chant prayers, nor teachers because they dedicate their lives to Jewish children, nor relatives because they can conduct the family seder on Passover. They might be wonderful and deserve praise for being good at what they do. But that does not qualify them for this specific mission of conferring a new halakhic status on persons with Christian or Muslim backgrounds who wish to live as Jews. This is true also for professors of Bible or Jewish scholars, or rabbis who may not be competent in the highly specialized matters of the conversion protocol, even though they are pious and knowledgeable.

The ultimate tests for lay members of the Bet Din are religious conviction and observance of religious matters crucial to the Jewish faith and the Jewish people, and the knowledge required so that they may be relied upon to serve wisely as Judges for conversion. Besides these qualifications for members of the Bet Din, the Av Bet Din, its leader, must be one who is ordained and therefore authorized to decide such weighty matters.

All prospective converts should be forewarned on this requirement. This is not simply a matter of interdenominational politics or institutional jealousies. We often reduce even our most radical spiritual differences to political legerdemain and then institute major alterations of the Torah by political manipulation.

This also is not primarily a question of who is a naturalized citizen of the State of Israel today by virtue of its Law of Return, but whether the convert's descendants down the ages will be considered religiously validated by all Jews. The very nub of the public agony caused by the conflicting views on conversion is that it really is a matter of life-or-death for this religion. The whole of the Jewish people could split irremediably over such conflicts.

Does the Bet Din Require Three Expert Scholars?

Experts are called *mumchim*. Understandably, the preferred court is that of authoritative specialists in conversion law or those who sit as representatives of acknowledged institutional courts (as can be found in major cities in North America and Europe) and are very experienced in these matters. For so the Torah mandates (Deuteronomy 15:29): "One Torah and one judgment for the citizen and the stranger," indicating that just as three judges are required for judgments dealing with citizens, so three are required for the conversion of "strangers."[22] Theoretically, this would imply a requirement of three expert scholars who were fully ordained, with the chain of ordination reaching back from student to teacher up through the generations to Moses himself, who originally ordained the elders at Sinai. But history has cruelly severed that chain and the ordination of today is not really the old "ordination," but rather a rabbinate reconstituted for the purpose of avoiding the abuse of authority—fulfilling the Rabbinic edict that "a student may not issue halakhic decisions unless he has first been authorized to do so by his teachers."

As noted earlier, if the original chain were absolutely insisted upon, conversion would no longer have been possible. But the Rabbis considered conversions so important that the absence of this implied requirement was not permitted to undermine the whole religious institution of admission to Judaism. According to some authorities, indeed, the Torah could never have initially required *mumchim*, expert scholars, because there is a biblical requirement that conversion be "for your generations," and nothing could have been mandated which depended on the vagaries of human history and might in any way compromise the possibility of accepting converts.[23]

Because the ability to convert was so integral to the structure of the religion, the Rabbis decided that all knowledgeable and traditionally ordained rabbis should be considered *legally* to be the "messengers of the Sages" of old, permitted to render judgment in such cases.

The Halakhah today is that the minimum requirement for the Bet Din is three fully observant Jews, one of whom, at the very least, should be an ordained authority with expertise in conversion. The expert must oversee the halakhic compliance of the circumcision and immersion and, most important, assess the beliefs and commitment of conversion candidates, while also testing them on practical mitzvot.[24]

If Only Two Were Present at the Initial Acceptance

The initial pledge to observe the commandments, known as hoda'at ha'mitzvot, is too serious and formative a step to be done with less than a full complement of three judges. But, whereas the final acceptance stage leaves no room for leniency, this first stage, like circumcision, demands three judges, but, *ex post facto*, the absence of one or two will not be invalidating.[25]

If Three Judges Were Not Present at the Final Stage of Commitment

The conversion is not valid under any circumstances. The pledge of commitment to Torah is a legal act requiring binding legal judgment and due process. This requirement is deliberately positioned to coincide with the immersion, the climax of the conversion ceremony, to insure that the court of three will be present. For this reason also, it must be done during daylight as are all formal court procedures.[26]

The Rabbis considered that the absence of a full court at the initial pledge to observe, and at the circumcision itself, may be valid, *ex post facto*, under certain circumstances. They permitted no exception, however, to the requirement that three qualified judges be present at the final definitive commitment to mitzvot. After all, it is the Bet Din's judgment on the potential religious success of this conversion that will determine whether or not it takes place.

Their determination would not be so critical if they were merely grading an examination on mitzvot, rather than developing an insight into whether this gentile could be trusted to keep the Jewish faith and to pass it on intact to his Jewish descendants. While it appears like only a "pass-fail" question, the whole historic Jewish enterprise hangs in the balance. It will not do to depend on anything less than a full-fledged, duly constituted court to say, "Yes, that person is a Jew, with responsibilities and a destiny identical with ours."

THE CIRCUMCISION

Circumcised in Infancy, Does One Require the Symbolic Drawing of a Drop of Blood?

This depends on the specific intention of the mohel, for he is the messenger of the father in circumcising the child. There are three possible intentions:

1. Specifically to effect the conversion: This is the normative purpose. The circumcision remains a valid component of the protocol even if the remainder of the conversion process—the acceptance of mitzvot and the immersing—is done many years later,[27] and he does not require anything further.

2. Simply as a desirable surgery, without any intent to convert and without specific intent to fulfill a law of Torah: This procedure is considered exactly what it was intended to be, "surgery." It was not a conscious step of commitment to enter the Covenant of Abraham. Therefore, a new circumcising act will be required. Since, obviously, a person cannot be recircumcised, he requires a symbolic drawing of a drop of covenantal blood.[28]

3. To perform a general requirement of the Torah—to circumcise all males and not merely as a surgical procedure—yet not specifically for the sake of effecting a conversion.

For example, parents had an unacceptable conversion. The child was circumcised, but there was no intention to convert him by this circumcision because the parents were under the false impression the child was already Jewish. Nonetheless, the parents did intend honorably to keep a practice of the faith they believed they had adopted.

Or another example: A child of a mixed marriage—gentile mother and Jewish father—decides to practice Judaism. He does not know the original intention of the mohel at the time of his circumcision in infancy, but he does know that his parents wanted and tried their best to raise him as a Jew.

Or a situation in which the mohel did not know that the mother was not Jewish, and proceeded with the standard circumcision ritual with its general intent to fulfill the mitzvah.

Clearly, not having the specific intent to make the circumcision serve as the functional aspect of a conversion protocol is not ideal. The desired practice is that the mohel circumcise with the specific intent of converting the child—not only to effectuate the mitzvah to circumcise. But as this is now a *post facto* situation, the overwhelming majority of leading rabbis have decided that, so long as the intent was to satisfy the requirements of the law to circumcise, even though it lacked the specific intent to convert, the circumcision is acceptable as a step in conversion and does not require the drawing of the touch of blood.[29]

What If the Circumcision May Endanger Life?

The halakhic ruling on this question is based on the belief that Judaism never makes requirements that imperil a person's life. Conversion to Judaism is simply not more important than life itself. In addition, the Rabbis hold that jeopardizing a gentile's life for the sake of converting to Judaism is not only against Jewish law, it is also a desecration of the name of God, *chilul ha'Shem*, and may trigger a torrent of hatred to overwhelm the Jewish people.

On the other hand, the Rabbis were not given the right to set aside circumcision, a fundamental historic requirement of the Torah, regardless of circumstances. Therefore, this candidate may not be accepted.[30] If that person had already been circumcised, the symbolic drawing of blood generally would not endanger his life. If it does, the question remains as to whether the blood-spotting can be set aside, and that is a different question that the Bet Din will need to decide on a case-to-case basis.

May Anesthesia Be Used Before the Circumcision?

Anesthetics were already known during the time of the Talmud, but the Sages made no statement either encouraging or prohibiting their use to alleviate the pain of the surgical procedure. Their silence gave rise to a dispute among rabbis, especially of our generation which has made far-reaching medical advances in the field, as to whether or not anesthetics may be used in adult conversion procedures.

The answer hinges on the philosophy of mitzvah observance.[31] This is true especially of a mitzvah like circumcision, because the intent and effect of circumcision are crucial to the fulfillment of the mitzvah. The question can be formulated as follows: Is it necessary to *feel* the mitzvah itself in order to accomplish it in a religiously acceptable manner? If it is, then the convert, as Abraham himself, must endure the pain as part of the spiritual transformation the convert is undergoing. If what is required is to establish the *fact* of covenant, not the *experience* or the feel of it, then one should practice circumcision in the most comfortable circumstance possible— even to the extent of being circumcised in one's sleep. Surely, there dwells in this question a difference of religious outlook; at the very least, a difference in perspective on mitzvah observance.

Three conclusions are possible:

1. No anesthetic is permissible, because it would rob the individual of the proper frame of mind in the observance of this critical mitzvah—it was meant to be painful and could not be otherwise.

2. All anesthetics, under any circumstances, are permissible, so long as the foreskin is properly circumcised. There is no source that stipulates that this commandment needs to produce pain or that the pain which Abraham suffered was decreed for all generations.

3. There is a middle path: pain is not necessary to the mitzvah (although we can appreciate those who hold the opinion that it is), but being awake and mindful at such a significant event in life is very important.

In fact, this third approach is advocated by the late rabbinic authority, Rabbi Yaakov Yechiel Weinberg of Switzerland. He prohibits all *general* anesthesia because it induces sleep and one should maintain consciousness during the performance of a mitzvah, but he does permit *local* painkillers to be administered to avoid anguish in adult circumcisions.

Those who decide these matters know that this rite triggers very personal, very specific, and sometimes complicated and nonrational responses from different persons. No one can expect a convert to undertake such a procedure blithely, without long and agonizing forethought. Those who befriend or teach converts should be sensitive and compassionate when discussing adult circumcision. Also, each circumstance needs to be judged by a legitimate rabbinic authority who can make appropriate decisions that accord with the Halakhah and pay due regard to human frailty.

THE IMMERSION

How is the Immersion Witnessed by the Bet Din?

The Bet Din, in a sense, is in a logistical bind. In keeping with the canons of decency modesty must be protected. Yet, fulfillment of the halakhic requirement that the Bet Din witness the act of conversion dictates that the members of the court must witness the crucial event before approving it. To satisfy both needs, the female convert should wear loose-fitting garments which do not cleave to the body and into which the water can easily flow.[32] In this manner, modesty is protected during the witness of the Bet Din, and the endorsement of the court can be based on the proper testimony.

Some rabbis and many converts prefer a sheet to cover the entire surface of the mikveh water, with only a small hole through which the convert's head will protrude. The members of the Bet Din then can testify that the immersion is effected when the convert's head submerges. The determination in individual cases as to which is the preferable procedure to be used will be made by the presiding rabbi of the Bet Din. As such matters are highly personal, should the convert feel compromised in the slightest way, she should immediately inform the Bet Din. Such sensitivities are always appropriate and should be expressed rather than suppressed and carried as emotional baggage for years to come. In sum, the procedure should be done in a way that is least obtrusive while recognizing the need for proper witnessing.

AFTER THE CONVERSION

Questions Regarding the Convert and the Word "Fathers" During Prayers

How can converts refer to "forefathers" in the formal prayers? If, as the Halakhah insists, the convert is considered spiritually and also legally to be newly born, and therefore without legal relatives, how can he refer to "forefather"? And, since a convert is new to the faith, how should he read the text in the prayerbook, "God of our Fathers?" *Whose* fathers?

While the *actual* father is the natural father who is gentile, the *spiritual* father is the first Jew, Abraham, referred to by all Jews as "Abraham, *our* Father." As we noted in Chapter 13, it has become a custom, now firmly entrenched for centuries, that all converts are called sons and daughters of "Abraham, our Father." Therefore, in all official documents, such as in marriage and divorce papers, and upon being called to the Torah in a religious service, the convert is called by the Hebrew name, *ben Avraham Avinu,* which indicates both a distinguished and a distinguishing calling.

"Our Forefathers," in the prayerbook sense, however, is the same for all Jews—converts and born Jews alike. One who has accepted the Jewish faith has accepted not only its future but its past. The greatest of our teachers—such as Maimonides in his famous letter to Obadiah, the convert—have insisted upon not changing the words of prayers. Instead, they incorporated all Jews into the patrimony—born Jews and Jews by choice. Those who can choose to have Jewish descendants can choose to have Jewish forefathers as well.

Therefore, converts recite "God of our Fathers," in the Silent Devotion; "Who has chosen US from amongst all peoples," in the blessing over the Torah; and "the land which You have given to our Fathers to inherit," in the Grace After Meals.[33]

When Does Jewish Practice Begin?

The obligation to observe the mitzvot begins the instant one emerges from the mikveh at the end of the conversion process. The convert is immediately responsible to perform all the mitzvot as though he were a born Jew. That is why it is wise to have a reading knowledge of Hebrew before the actual conversion ceremony takes place. A Jew is obligated to pray and the obligation is triggered as soon as one emerges from the mikveh. Candidates for conversion therefore bring along the requirements for their first mitzvah: tefillin, or siddur, or other objects, if necessary, in order to perform with alacrity their first mitzvah upon becoming Jews.

This immediate assumption of Jewish duties hides a shy, but attractive idea. (It is often drowned in the tidal waves of feelings that overcome the convert in the wake of the sea change he or she has just effected—which is understandable, but unfortunate.) The idea is that, in an instant, the convert has inherited obligations and rights and is simply expected to go about his business as a Jew of ancient lineage. "If you are a Jew, where is your siddur?" "You are a Jew, are you not? It is getting late for performing the mitzvah at hand!"

The Jews' sense of equality was never more eloquently conveyed than in this requirement. It was very elegantly stated at first when Moses addressed the Jews as they prepared to leave Egypt: "There shall be one Torah for the citizen and for the 'stranger' [the religious convert] who lives among you."[34] No double standard was to be tolerated. Not two Torahs, but one.[35] The convert has the same Torah as the born Jew from the moment that he or she emerges from the mikveh.

The "One Torah" equality sends a strong, if also subtle, message: "One Torah" exclusively. Not two Torahs. Judaism is not an add-on, as some cultists would have it, and as the earliest Christians conceived of their new religion. There is only one Torah as there is only one God. Judaism should be practiced for Judaism's sake; accretions, dilutions and homemade modifications have no place in this long tradition, no matter how well-intentioned the modifiers. "Hyphenated Jews"—"Christian-Jews," or "Jewish-Christians"—are mutants undeserving of membership in an authentic historic faith.

The Rabbis went further in equalizing the native-born Jew and the convert. In order to insure that this equality would obtain for all time, they emphasized one verse at the ratification of the Sinaitic Covenant: "Neither with you only do I make this covenant and this oath; but with him that stands here with us this day before the Lord our God, and also with him that is not here this day" (Deuteronomy 29:13). This was to ensure that the Revelation includes converts of all later generations, whenever in the future they decide to commit their lives to the Jewish destiny.

Notes to Chapter Fifteen

1. For a well-argued case permitting *l'khatchilah* conversions for the sake of marriage in contemporary society, see article by Rabbi Yehudah Leib Kagan of Chicago's Bet Hamidrash la'Torah, written in 1946 in *Ha'Pardes*, vol. 20, #3, and vol. 20, #4. It concerns a response by Rabbi Kahane, the Av Bet Din of Kovno, to a responsum written by Rabbi Chaim Ozer Grodzinski in the third volume of his *Achiezer*. For a more contemporary survey of the subject taking a more cautious approach, see the brief, but fine insight into the *shakla ve'tarya* (the competing logic) on the question, although not on its final decision, in "Conversion in Jewish Law," by Rabbi Aaron Lubling, in *Journal of Halacha and Contemporary Society* IX, Rabbi Jacob Joseph School, Staten Island, New York, 1987.

2. See Yevamot 24b; Rambam, Hilkhot Issurei Bi'ah, ch. 13-17; and Yoreh De'ah, 268:12.

3. See *Nimuke Yosef* to Yevamot, ch. 2, *Ha'nitan,* in his third comment to the Mishnah *Ha'nitan:* If they converted for marriage, they are *gerim gemurim* and should not be separated.

4. See Rabbi Isaac Herzog, *Hekhal Yitzchak,* vol. 1, ch. 20-21.

5. This actually becomes a factor in the *heter* of sorts provided by Rabbi Moshe Feinstein in *Iggerot Moshe* to Yoreh De'ah, vol. 1, p. 160.

6. Responsa *Har Zvi*, to Yoreh De'ah, Hilkhot Milah 218, Rabbi Zvi Pesach Frank, Jerusalem, 1964.

7. *Har Zvi* quotes *Derishah ad loc.* and *Bet Yitzchak,* Yoreh De'ah, vol. 2, p. 86, end of part 4.

8. On this, see Rabbi Shlomo Kluger, *Tuv Ta'am Va'Da'at,* vol. 1, ch. 130, regarding the permissibility of accepting a convert who has cohabited with a prospective bride even once. See *Imre David* 124 where he says that the marriage motivation is detrimental only when there has been no prior cohabitation. See *Sridei Esh*, vol I, 3, ch. 50, and Melamed L'Ho'il, Even Ha'Ezer 10, regarding those who have married only by the authority of civil courts. Also see *Achiezer,* vol. 3, responsum #26 on this subject.

9. See *Iggerot Moshe*, Even Ha'Ezer, vol. 2, ch. 4.

10. There is sufficient authority on which to rely to avert such a situation. There is indeed a time for forsaking observance of a light precept to prevent the commission of a major transgression. In the words of the Rabbis, "It is preferable to eat the meat of a *trefah* than the meat of a *nevelah*." On this see *Teshurat Shai,* vol. 2; Yehuda Mintz, responsum 5; *Achiezer,* vol. 3, responsum 26.

11. *Achiezer,* vol. 3, responsum 24.

12. On this, see *Derisha* to Yoreh De'ah, ch. 268; and Shach, *ad loc.,* 23;

Pri Ha'Sadeh, vol. 2, ch. 3. This is a problem that has been confronted many times and, in almost all cases, has found only tentative solutions. On this subject, an insightful, if arguable, presentation was made by Rabbi Dr. Meir Simcha Feldblum, formerly professor at Yeshiva University's Bernard Revel Graduate School, in an address to the Rabbinic Alumni of Yeshiva University, March 1980. He develops the idea that *le'shem ishut,* conversion for the sake of marriage, in our day indicates a sympathy for, or at least an openness to, the possibility of sincere conversion since there is most often no longer any social pressure to convert in order to marry. This point has already been made by the greatest decisor of the age, Rabbi Moses Feinstein, in *Iggerot Moshe.* A second point Rabbi Feldblum makes, though as a pure academic he does not render halakhic decisions, is the possbility that if the convert undergoes the halakhic protocol meticulously—and believes in the oneness of God, rejects idol worship, and truly desires to be part of *klal Yisrael*—but believes that Judaism demands that he practice only what is being practiced by his Jewish peers, then rejection of such a conversion would have to be scrutinized very carefully. In this, too, he has been anticipated. In *Likutei Me'ir,* a recent volume of responsa, Rabbi Meir Ha'Levi Steinberg quotes the *Chemdat Shlomo* who decides an *ex post facto* situation leniently in such a case.

13. See Appendix 5.
14. Yevamot 46b: *miktzat mitzvot chamurot u'miktzat mitzvot kalot.*
15. The problem is treated with deftness, if also casuistry, by Rabbi Joshua Hoffman, in *Bain Kotlei Ha'Yeshivah,* vol. 4, available from Yeshiva University, New York.
16. *She'Elot U'Teshuvot Bais Ha'Levi,* end vol. II, *Derushim,* by Rabbi Joseph Baer Soloveitchik, Jerusalem, *Ha'Tenuah Le'Hafatzat Torah B'Yishuvim He'Chadashim,* 1967/8, 3 volumes.
17. Talmud, Shabbat 68a and Tosefot *ad loc.,* "*ger.*" Also see *Nimuke Yosef* to Yevamot ch. 4, "*Tanu rabbanan; Ger she'ba l'hitgayer*"; and also *Bet Yosef* to Yoreh De'ah 268, "*u'che-she'ba.*" See also Maimonides, *Mishneh Torah,* Hilkhot Issurei Bi'ah, 13:7.
18. See *Tuv Ta'am Va'Da'at,* vol. 3, Part 2, #111, by Rabbi Shlomo Kluger, in which he rules that one who underwent circumcision and immersion for the express purpose of conversion but without the formal acceptance of mitzvot required by biblical warrant is considered converted *d'rabanan* (by a ruling of the rabbis).
19. For the distinction between hoda'at ha'mitzvot and kabbalat ha'mitzvot, see responsa *Chemdat Shlomo* to Yoreh De'ah 29:22. The question was whether to equate the requirements for sitting on a Bet Din for gerut with *hoda'ot ve'halva'ot* or with *gezelot ve'chavalot.* A very insightful discussion of the theme of *shluchei mitzvah* was delivered by Rabbi Hershel Schachter in an address before Yeshiva University's Rabbinic Alumni on Parshat Yitro in February 1986.
20. See Talmud, Bekhorot 30b. Many decisors invalidate such a conversion even *post facto.* On this, see *Iggerot Moshe,* Yoreh De'ah, vol. I, responsum 124; Even Ha'Ezer, vol. II, responsum 4; *Achiezer,* vol. III, responsum 26.

21. This holds true for qualifications of any rabbinic court. He who may not testify because he does not keep mitzvot or believe in *Torah min ha'Shamayim* may not function on any rabbinic court. One who is not permitted to testify is not permitted to judge, and one who was considered a sinner could not testify.

22. The Talmud, Yevamot 47b, does mention *talmide chakhamim,* but Maimonides refers simply to three and there are no critical comments on that statement. Also note the distinction between Rashi and the Tosafists. For elucidation on this matter see *Iggerot Moshe* to Yoreh De'ah 159.

23. See Rabbenu Netanel, Tosafot to Kiddushin 62b, *"ger"*; also Rashba to Yevamot 46b, *"dilma"*; also *Kli Chemdah,* Massei, ch. 2, on the difference between the requirement of *korban* and *mumchin;* also see *Chiddushei Ha'Rim* to Choshen Mishpat I.

24. See on this *Choshen Mishpat,* Hilkhot Dayanim, 3:1 and Rama *ad loc.; Bet Ha'Bechirah* of Me'iri to Yevamot 46b, and *Iggerot Moshe,* to Yoreh De'ah 159; and *Chukkat Ha'Ger,* ch. 6, 1, Moshe Ha'Levi Steinberg, Jerusalem, 1971.

25. There is a distinction between hoda'at ha'mitzvot and kabbalat ha'mitzvot, as above, but also see Bach to Yoreh De'ah 268, who makes no such distinction, nor does Rabbi Joseph Karo, *Shulchan Arukh,* Yoreh De'ah 268:3. See also *Chukkat Ha'Ger, op. cit.,* p. 32, note 4.

26. See Talmud, Yevamot 46b.

27. Responsum of *Moznayim* I, 20.

28. No blessing is required, as the matter is disputable and therefore in the category of *safek berakhah.* See Yoreh De'ah 268:1.

29. On this, see *Tzofenat Pa'aneach,* Hilkhot Milah, ch. 3; *Melamed L'Ho'il,* Yoreh De'ah 82. In Responsa *Har Tzvi,* Yoreh De'ah 219, the response is addressed to Dayan Verner who, in his responsa, *Mishpetei Shmuel,* compiles an impresive list of lenient decisions—with one exception, Dayan Weiss in his *Minchat Yitzchak.* See also *Iggerot Moshe,* Yoreh De'ah, vol. 3, 105, where Rabbi Moshe Feinstein appears to accept three participating, observant Jews as a Bet Din for the circumcision, even though they were unaware that the purpose of it was conversion. Also see Tosafot to Yevamot 45b and Kiddushin 62b, *"K'ilu omdim sham dami."*

30. See *Sridei Esh,* vol. 2, ch. 102; *Melamed L'Ho'il,* Yoreh De'ah 86; and Responsa *Har Tzvi,* Yoreh De'ah 202.

31. The first major respondent to this question in our times in Maharsham, the Gaon of Brezin, in his responsa, vol. 6, ch. 95. He emphasizes the *fact,* not the *act,* of circumcision. See the dispute between Rabbi Tzirelson, in his *Ma'arkhe Lev,* and Rabbi Meir Arik, in his *Imre Yosher,* 140:3. More recently, see the difference between Rabbi Y. Weinberg, *Sridei Esh,* vol. 3, ch. 96, and Rabbi Ovadiah Yosef, in *Sefer Noam,* vol. 12, who says that the Bet Din of Jerusalem decided according to his judgment. Rabbi Felder in his *Nachlat Tzvi,* vol. 1, p. 5, wonders if pain were considered integral to the process, and asks how we could settle halakhically for hatafat dam b'rit for one who was circumcised, since this involves no pain.

No layman should attempt to decide this question for himself based on this scanty information. It is better left to scholars who understand all the ramifications, many of which are not mentioned here.

32. Loose-fitting garments do not form a *chatzitzah*. See Rabbi Ovadiah Yosef, *Yabi'a Omer* on Yoreh De'ah vol. I, 19; and Rabbi Steinberg, *Chukkat Ha'Ger*, pp. 47-8. See also Maharsham, *Responsa*, vol. III, 173.
33. *She'elot U'Teshuvot Ha'Rambam*, ch. 42, ed. Freiman, *Mishneh Torah*, Hilkhot Bikkurim 4:3; *Chiddushe Ramban*, Bava Batra 81; *Orach Chayim* 53:9 and *Turei Zahav* and *Magen Avraham ad loc.*
34. See Ibn Ezra to Exodus 12:49.
35. Mekhilta on *Masekhet d'Pischa*, Chapter 15; Maimonides, *Mishneh Torah*, Hilkhot Issurei Bi'ah 12:17.

16

Questions on the
Laws of Conversion II:

PERSONAL STATUS

THE CONVERT AND MARRIAGE

Privilege has its obligations. Although Jewish society emphasized the equality of God's creatures—even giving priority to an illegitimate Torah scholar over a High Priest ignoramus[1]—it did require and select whole groups of people to provide community leadership and serve in the Temple. Because they were "chosen," they were given both privileges and restrictions.

A good example of this is the Priest or Kohen. His privilege was the obligation to serve in the Temple and to teach. For this, he endured restrictions—such as not being permitted to marry a divorcée or a convert or to visit the cemetery—and received privileges—such as being called upon to bless the Jews during the service and always receiving the first call to read from the Torah.

Why a Kohen is Not Permitted to Marry a Convert

The Kohen was a descendant of the ancient House of Aaron, the first High Priest. The Bible (Leviticus 21:7) limited the Kohen's marriage options to those women who had never before married and, in fact, barred him from any sexual liaisons with those he was not permitted to marry. Throughout the history of the Priesthood, the sanctity and purity of the Kohen's office were preserved.[2] The Talmud[3] specifies which women were considered off-limits for the Kohen in marriage, and they included converts and many others.

A variety of reasons were offered by commentators for these restrictions, but the fundamental reason was a decree promulgated by the Prophet Ezekiel (chapter 44) and offered without explanation: "But they shall take *virgins* of the seed of the house of Israel."[4] Furthermore, Ezekiel mandates this as a *reward* for the loyalty of the "Priests, the Levites, the sons of Zadok, that kept the charge of my sanctuary when the children of Israel went astray from me. . . . "

This prophetic reward prompted Priests to insist upon the integrity of their lineage in accordance with Ezekiel's never-to-be-compromised ideal. This was not to be a resolution made by individual Priests, who could be zealous or not, depending on their private wishes, but an institutional *noblesse oblige*, which determined which woman a Kohen may bring into the family of the Priesthood to mother future Priests of the Jewish people.

It was with this in mind that Maimonides wrote in his code: "The tradition teaches that the appellation *zonah* (translated popularly as non-virgin, sometimes as the promiscuous one, sometimes as "one of unknown parentage") in the Torah refers to anyone at all who was not a born Jewess or who, as a native Jewess, had been involved in a prohibited union and therefore was not permitted to [the Kohen]."[5] The law was thus crystallized as a generic category which applied to all women in that *zonah* status, without exception—even to the logical extreme of applying it to a convert younger than the age of three. This ruling involved no value judgments, applied no moral criteria, related to no individual situations. It was not specifically applied, only categorically.

This *zonah* ruling should not be taken at its face value as a condemnation of the sexual mores of non-Jewish cultures, although, in fact, Judaism was born and grew for centuries in a milieu of just such conditions. In the enlightened, sexually liberated mores of our day, comparisons are not instructive and categories of moral superiority should not be assigned. But that, in any case, is the way the twig is bent in Jewish law. [The convert younger than three is proof of that.]

This view of Maimonides differs from that of Rashi, who does interpret the *zonah* prohibition as signifying a moral deficit which the Priesthood could not abide. He bases this on the assumption that the convert generally hails from a culture which allows a promiscuity that the Torah absolutely abhors. This was indeed the case in virtually every century of Jewish history.

Even Rashi's moral judgment was not issued on a personal level, but on a societal one—the female convert emerging as she does from surrounding tribes and nations whose moral bankruptcy was legend in biblical times and later. Nonetheless, she was never to be refused admission as a Jew.

Simply put: all converts from amoral or even immoral nations could enter the Jewish fold. But not one could enter the Kohen's genealogy—not even a child under age three whose conduct obviously is untainted.[6] If a Kohen married a convert in violation of the law, the marriage was dissolved.

But, if a Kohen married the *daughter* of converts (in violation of the stricture of Rabbinic, though not biblical, law) the Rabbis ruled that the marriage need *not* be dissolved after the fact.[7]

The genealogy of the Kohen is a sphere protected since ancient times, and it needs to be respected. It is looked upon today simply as an edict of the Jewish religion—uncomfortable perhaps, but unchallenged and unquestioned these many generations. Kohanim are expected to abide by this millennial decision.

Other Convert-Kohen Marriage Questions

In truth, this basic Halakhah is sometimes the cause of much consternation. A young Kohen falls in love with a non-Jewish woman; she, in turn, wishes to convert to Judaism and raise a Jewish family, without realizing the impediment that lies in their path.

Or, even more stressful, a Jew and a non-Jewish woman marry and raise a family. She then decides to convert to Judaism, only to find that Jewish law does not permit their continued marriage.

Each case has its individual merits and difficulties, and both the realities and the law have their complexities. No case should be decided flippantly or offhandedly. All such cases, even apparently open-and-shut ones, should be decided by competent rabbinic authority. There is much complex case law that stands behind this Halakhah, and it deserves the long and penetrating consideration of compassionate scholars.[8]

May a Jew Marry a Convert with Whom He Has Been Living?

A Jewish man is rumored to be sexually involved with a gentile woman. She decides to convert and the couple now wishes to be married. May they marry? The Talmud rules that he should not marry her, but that, if the marriage has already been performed, the marriage is valid and they need not be separated.[9] The authorities disagree in their interpretation of the Talmud's reasoning and therefore arrive at different conclusions in related questions, as follows:

Rashi says that the reason for not allowing the marriage is to avoid substantiating what was an ugly rumor. If he marries her, people will say that it proves that he was consorting with a gentile woman, and that would prove deleterious both to the individual and to the moral standards of the community. Nachmanides, however, holds that the reason is that everyone will say that she converted for the sole purpose of living with him, and the conversion will never be recognized as genuine even though it is accepted as valid and the marriage is valid.

The difference has practical consequences, as in the following situation.

A Jewish man and a gentile woman had been living together as husband and wife without benefit of marriage or were, perhaps, civilly married. She now converts. The question is: May they marry according to Jewish law?

Following the above reasoning according to the theory of Rashi, there is no question whether and what people will whisper, since the couple was publicly associated. Not being concerned with the validation or the effects of rumor, the courts could then approve their relationship, and she could then convert and be married. According to Nachmanides, they would not be permitted to marry *ab initio*, because her intent in conversion was simply for his sake.[10]

Leading authorities have decided to permit the conversion and the marriage in such a case. While such practices as Living-Together Arrangements or civil marriage without religious sanction cannot morally be condoned in Jewish law, they are brooked legally. One contemporary authority[11] notes trenchantly that, since the woman in this case could very well have remained an unconverted gentile, the conversion is no longer to be considered "for the purpose of marriage." The decision is left to the Bet Din as to whether, without this obstruction, she is otherwise worthy of being considered a convert to Judaism. Another rabbinic authority reasons[12] that, if we do not permit the marriage to take place, we risk the husband's abandonment of Judaism. The conversion, however, must be done with the express intention of observing the tenets of the faith in the future.

There is a further question about a Jew and non-Jew who were consorting with one another while one of them was married to a third partner. The non-Jewish partner now wishes to convert and they would then marry. The decision is complex and dependent upon factors too numerous for discussion in this volume.[13]

The Pregnant Convert

Is the fetus converted as well? Is there a waiting period required between conversion and Jewish marriage?

The children already born must be converted independently, because the parents' conversion is valid only for themselves. If the conversion candidate is pregnant, the child born after the ceremony is born Jewish.[14]

Most rabbis require no waiting period if, as is likely, pregnancy can be determined by medical, scientific or other means, or if there is other legitimate and convincing proof.[15]

A Gentile Couple Wishes to Convert

Do they convert together or separately? Can one speak for the other?

Both husband and wife need to undergo the full process of conversion, and each applicant must be considered separately by the Bet Din. According to Jewish law, their marriage does not exist in a Jewish framework. They need to be converted separately and then married in accordance with Jewish law.

A question arose recently of a case of only one partner to such a marriage who wished to convert, while the other desired to remain Christian. This, in effect, is creating a reverse intermarriage situation, which is of considerable interest, and which is unique in terms of the problematics of conversion. Such instances[16] raise unusual issues:

Will the Jewish partner be able to change the whole life-style of the couple when one partner remains loyal to the old faith? Will the prospective convert be able to carry out her religious expectations? Should, in fact, a Bet Din convert one whose chances of succeeding are not high?

On the other hand, those who wish to enter such an arrangement at mid-marriage must surely have given these matters weighty consideration and decided that the whole enterprise is achievable. But then the question is whether the convert could possibly know what to expect when everything in the marriage becomes dislocated, and even interpersonal relationships on the social level might very well be strained. This can only be left to the judgment of the Bet Din.

A husband and wife who converted together must separate from one another (abstain from living together) for a period of three months[17] in order to distinguish between seed sown in sanctity and seed not sown in sanctity.

Waiting Period Before Marriage

Jewish law expressly requires a waiting period of three months between the conversion of a woman and her marriage, the beginning of marital sexual life between convert and spouse. It is a law similar to that which obtains in other marital circumstances, such as remarriage after divorce and levirate marriages.[18]

The reasons for this delay derive both from domestic law and from the law governing genealogy. In the matter of domestic law, the Rabbis were very careful—intensely careful—that family life not be disrupted by extraneous causes, such as financial strains or domestic conflicts.

If a woman were to give birth seven months into her marriage, it would be an open question as to whether the child was fathered by a previous suitor or the previous husband after full term, or by this present husband after only seven months. While the husband may offhandedly dismiss this now in his ardor to be married, the court cannot be guaranteed that, after years of experiencing the marriage, he will not later refuse child support claiming that he is not the natural father after all. The Jewish court will not compel him to do something which cannot be clearly proven to be his responsibility.

The Sages therefore did not permit dispensing with the waiting period in any case where there might develop a reasonable doubt as to the extent of the father's responsibility. Thus, wherever there is even a remote possibility that some doubt may develop, the law takes the precaution—sometimes appearing to be strained and even unreasonable—of requiring a hiatus of ninety days—exclusive of the day of divorce from the first husband and the day of marriage to the second.

In dealing with Jewish marriage and divorce, this law of waiting holds, even if incontrovertible evidence can be marshaled that there could be no pregnancy. The Rabbis made a formal, statutory decision not to differentiate between one woman and another, for any reason, in these sensitive matters of genealogy. However, this principle of making no distinctions does not apply to the convert—which is clearly a unique case.

Therefore, in deciding the case for a convert, there need be no waiting period in the following circumstances: where there is no medical possibility of pregnancy, such as if the wife or husband is certifiably sterile; if there is incontrovertible physical evidence that the couple cannot have children (for example, if the woman had a hysterectomy or the man had an irreversible vasectomy, the latter procedure not permitted in Jewish law); in the event that it was not physically possible for them to have been together; if the woman is post-menopausal[19]; or if she is already pregnant.[20] If she menstruates immediately before conversion,[21] they are permitted to be married immediately, even without waiting the "seven pure days" after menstruation.[22]

If a Jewish woman lives with a gentile man who then converts and she wishes to marry him, they will need to delay the wedding for the ninety days, as they are both marrying as Jews.

Notes to Chapter Sixteen

1. Bemidbar Rabbah, ch. 6.
2. See Sefer Ha'Chinukh, Mitzvah 266.
3. Yevamot 61a.
4. On this, see Kiddushin 78a; Tosafot to Sanhedrin 82a, "Ve'iduch"; and Ritva to Yevamot 60.
5. Maimonides, Mishnah Torah, Hilkhot Issurei Bi'ah, 18:5.
6. See Rashi to Yevamot 61a; Tosafot and Rosh ad loc.
7. This is true if horata ve'ledatah bi'kedushah, both the conception and the birth occurred while the mother was Jewish. If, however, a child was conceived before conversion, even though born afterward, the marriage was to be dissolved.

8. An interesting and vigorous dispute among giants of the law developed
in the last generation between Rabbi Tzirelson, author of *Ma'arkhe Lev,*
and Rav Hillel Ha'Posek on the case of a Christian girl who converted
properly, but, directly before the wedding ceremony, the groom was
discovered to be a Kohen. A review of this case can be found in Rabbi
Gedaliah Felder's *Nachlat Zvi,* p. 105.

Also see the decision of Rabbi Dovid Zvi Hoffman, in his *Melamed
L'Ho'il,* Even Ha'Ezer, responsum 4, on the case of a Kohen who married
a gentile woman in a civil ceremony and she now wishes to convert.
This desire, honorable at first sight, actually appears to be a disqualifying
component, as it represents a rejection of a major halakhah that a convert
may not marry a Kohen, and rejecting one law is held to be sufficient
to invalidate a conversion.

Note there the leniencies utilized by Hoffman and also the condition
upon which he permitted her conversion—that she observe all the laws
of *taharat ha'mishpachah,* monthly sexual abstinence and immersion.
Then see the decision by Rabbi Moshe Feinstein, in his *Iggerot Moshe,*
Even Ha'Ezer, vol. 2, responsum 4, where he forcefully rejects Hoffman's
argument, but still provides certain leniencies to cover specific exigencies
under specific circumstances. Hoffman's decision is not upheld by most
authorities today—indeed, Chief Rabbi Isaac Herzog in his responsa,
Hekhal Yitzchak, asserts that he never heard of one Bet Din which
decided according to Rabbi Hoffman—but it does show the lengths to
which the rabbis went in order to solve human problems within the framework of the Halakhah.

The halakhic determination here discussed refers naturally to the
decision of a Kohen to marry the convert at some future date. If the
couple presents the court with a *fait accompli*—they have already gotten
married and are living together—the marriage is invalidated. The converted wife is technically a *chalalah,* literally "put outside," rendered by
her own action to be unfit for participating in the benefits of her husband's
Priesthood (not experienced in a practical sense today) and not considered
religiously valid for mothering Kohen children who, because of their
parents' actions, are themselves rendered *chalal,* unfit for the Priesthood.

A difference should be noted between a Kohen who is a chalal and
one who has a deficiency in his ability to perform the tasks of the Kehunah,
such as the *dukhan,* the priestly blessing at services. For example, one
who has a deformed hand cannot perform the service, but he retains
the integrity of his office. Whereas a chalal has a deficiency in status,
is considered "outside" the Kehunah, and may therefore marry one who
was prohibited to a Kohen.

In an ironic legal twist, though a very logical one, a chalal, a child
of a prohibited Kohen union—for example, one whose mother cohabited
with someone prohibited to her in marriage, such as a gentile, a chalal,
or mamzer—would be permitted to marry a convert—as could any self-
respecting Jew who was a non-Kohen. Thus, a Kohen, who is a child
of a mother who, even only once in her life, indulged in a dalliance with
a partner prohibited her in marriage, without even marrying, would be
a chalal, and under no more restriction than other Jews. He is "outside,"
the kehunah and thus does not share in its mission or its benefits, but

is also unencumbered by its restrictions. Such a decision was rendered by Rabbi Moshe Tendler, who agreed to be quoted in this regard.

9. Talmud, Yevamot 24b, the case of *nitan al ha'shifchah o al ha'akum.* See the dispute between Rashi and Ramban *ad loc.*

10. See Rabbi Shlomo Kluger, who rules against the validity of the marriage because that would be rewarding sin. It could be reasoned that giving public acknowledgment that it is all right to do this would cause a deterioration in the moral standards of the community.

11. *Achiezer,* vol. III, section 15.

12. *Divre Chayyim,* Even Ha'Ezer, vol. II, section 36.

13. See *Nachlat Zvi* by Rabbi Gedaliah Felder, p. 113-115, and the sources he quotes.

14. On this subject, see the dispute between *Noda Bi'Yehudah* and *Arukh Ha'Shulchan* as to whether the Bet Din is required to be told that she is pregnant.

15. The sources marshalled in behalf of both sides are impressive. Those who do not insist on it include *Maharsham,* vol. III, ch. 24; *Bait Yitzchak,* Even Ha'Ezer vol. I, sec. 24, ch. 5; and *Melamed L'Ho'il,* Even Ha'Ezer 11.

16. A number of such cases are recorded in the magazine *Sh'ma* (17/327, February 7, 1987).

17. Yevamot 42, Yoreh De'ah 269:9.

18. *Nachlat Zvi,* responsum 64, suggests that most authorities hold its origin to be rabbinic, and this holds for the *Bait Yitzchak,* Even Ha'Ezer, vol. I, sec. 29, ch. 5. There are, however, significant interpretations of Maimonides that say he holds it to be of biblical origin.

19. That is, she is technically considered to be a *zekenah.*

20. In *Sridei Esh,* there are two conflicting responsa on the issue of requiring *havchanah* when the truth can be determined scientifically. In the first, written before World War II, he decided stringently as a matter of *lo plug* to require waiting, regardless of determination. In a responsum written after the war, he cites many others who decide leniently that *lo plug* does not apply to converts. He relies on *Dagul Mi'Rvava* to Even Ha'Ezer. Rabbi Hershel Schachter advises that his father, Rabbi Melech Schachter, heard a similar decision from Rabbi Moses Feinstein to the effect that one could rely on pregnancy tests as to when we can determine with certainty whether or not she is pregnant. On the other side, the rabbis have characteristically refused to rely on a physician's "judgement" of no pregnancy, or even on the supposedly foolproof evidence of menstruation, as pregnant women sometimes do experience blood emission from the vaginal tract. For further elucidation, see Rabbi Schachter's article in the *Festschrift in Honor of Rabbi J. B. Soloveitchik,* Mossad Ha'Rav Kook and Yeshiva University, vol. I, January 1984, "Berurim B'Inyanei Yuchasin."

21. See *Maharsham,* vol. III, sec. 24.

22. Rabbi Moshe Feinstein, *Iggerot Moshe,* Even Ha'Ezer II, responsum 5.

17
Questions on Interpersonal Relationships I:
THE JEW IN GENTILE FAMILY CELEBRATIONS

CONSIDERATIONS OF INTERPERSONAL MATTERS

Personal Questions and the Halakhah

The problems of conversion are not solely or even primarily those that concern the conversion protocol. The most poignant problems, and often the most agonizing, deal with the human relationships recast by the decision to become a Jew. It changes attitudes, emotional investments, even the content of discourse among friends and relatives. The convert must learn to deal with the guilt, frustration and stupefaction of incredulous relatives who ask themselves how such a thing could possibly have happened.

Yet, in Judaism, such personal questions, just as those of the formal protocol, come under the scrutiny and judgment of the Halakhah. Judaism has known man's soul in the zenith of his achievements and in the nadir of his failures, and has never considered his inner being a province separate from his public activities, a sort of inner sanctum, private and untouchable even by religious tradition. The formal conversion merely enacts an internal transformation; both processes are the concern of Jewish tradition.

One needs to understand, moreover, that saying that Judaism is profoundly concerned with the person's anguish and satisfaction should not imply that Jewish tradition can be modified at will to suit personal sensitivities. Judaism has a long and venerable tradition of dealing with people's personal needs and that tradition must be respected.

We are concerned here with a number of such personal questions which Jews and converts have often asked and which the Halakhah has decided. But first, we need to understand the ground rules of the halakhic question (known in the vernacular as a *shailah*), especially in regard to conversion—not only of becoming a Jew, but of being one.

Jew and Non-Jew

The issue of interpersonal relationships between Jews and non-Jews involves both principle and history. The Bible says that the Jews are "a people that dwells alone." They dwell alone because, as a matter of principle, they want to protect their integrity and distinctiveness, and also because, historically, the surrounding peoples have not permitted them entrance into their own closed societies.

In order to become a kingdom of Priests and a light unto the nations, the Jews had to prevent at all costs the dilution of their mission and their people. Circumcision and kashrut are two prominent components of the structures the Jews designed for keeping themselves separate, even while they intermingled with their neighbors. The Jew in the diaspora always lived in two civilizations simultaneously, and the balance and adjustment were his perpetual concern. The existence of the outside world kept him always vigilant and self-conscious of his heritage.

"Do not walk in the ways of the nations" was the marching order of the Jews through history. It was not always because the ways of the nations were evil—other peoples developed ethical, philosophical, and religious systems, created advanced cultures, built cities and protected their citizenry. But they were not Jewish. The Jew was everywhere a minority, weak in the eyes of the nations, living by sufferance—even in his own homeland. His strength came from personal resolve; a stubbornness to continue his distinctive ways under all circumcstances; an awareness that his pattern of life was mandated by God. He was chosen, and he labored under that chosenness to deserve being chosen.

The problems of retaining one's singularity are enormous when the strange and exotic beckon to be tasted. But it needed to be done, and the Jew worked at his distinctiveness by intense study and singular behavior and by love of God and people. Now, distinguishing oneself from others does not imply dislike. Rather, it means emphasizing and concentrating on what is distinct in oneself. All people strive to preserve their integrity; the Jew makes of the effort a high art.

The new Jew must find this adjustment infinitely more difficult. His past beckons; his family entreats; his own will sometimes wavers. But distinctiveness is the way of this people; it must be maintained. All the more, therefore, are the questions of interfamilial relationships exacerbated by this radical change in pattern.

Caution: Judaism is Not for Today Only

In deciding on such interpersonal matters, we need to understand that decisions cannot take into account only concerns of today—our sentiments, our conflicts and problems and how they get resolved. The Jewish people exists not only in the present—it is part of a continuum spanning virtually all recorded history. To do justice to Judaism, we must not intersect that historical line and do what is appropriate only for our time. "If we are able to see the long past," Winston Churchill once said, "we will be able to see the long future—that is not a matter of philosophy; consult an oculist."

For example, in the past, the Jews were locked out of the larger society. As these barriers began to crumble after the French Revolution, some Jews became hell-bent on making up for lost time and rushed to integrate Judaism into the general culture. But at what cost? There is a risk/benefit ratio we need to balance. What if the benefits to us personally are outweighed by the risks to the people as a whole, as a corporate historical body? Will it still be worth serving our own comfort and that of our family?

We need to realize also that the Jewish religion, being a perpetual minority religion in constant real danger of being swallowed up by its more aggressive missionizing neighbors, had to build walls of protection around Jewish society and around the Torah itself. Lacking external enforcement capabilities throughout most of its history, the faith relied on moral suasion and religious law that the community took upon itself to observe.

One of the most powerful weapons in its arsenal was to prohibit participating in common celebrations, breaking bread and drinking wine together. Also severely frowned upon was visiting the religious services of other faiths. This was the arena in which Judaism faced its greatest danger—where its children were shamelessly missionized; where clerical and political hierarchies sought to crush stubborn Jewish nonconformance; where Judaism was theologically victimized and its people came under the threat of constant, unfounded accusations of blood-libels and poisoned wells, black plagues and child kidnapings.

Understandably, therefore, Judaism has the most profound reluctance to relax the social and religious restrictions on inter-mingling both celebrations and ideas—even though the prac-tices they designed to protect themselves tend to discomfit some well-adjusted western Jews. The larger picture, in virtually every generation, to a greater or lesser degree, has to predominate over the exceptional individual circumstance.

It can be argued, of course, that things are different today. In style and expression, of course they are. But, in essence are they? Is there no missionizing of Jews today? Are there no cults devising devious strategies to ensnare Jewish college students? No evangelical societies passionately interested in our "salvation"? And are there no "blood" libels today? And who will say, in our enlightened western society, that Judaism need have no fear for its future? Before we proceed blithely, therefore, we should remember the historical forces that have shaped, and do now shape, some of the Rabbinic mandates on interreligious relationships.

This historic insight, however, should not be construed as being a strictly negative judgment on our neighbors in the West. We have been fortunate to live in a predominantly pluralistic society, amongst understanding people, with religious freedom to a degree unknown in Jewish history. Some of our gentile neighbors have rescued little Jewish children from Hitler's ovens at mortal danger to their own families; others have given new meaning to the idea of personal sacrifice for the human good. There are truly righteous gentiles who have earned an exalted place in the world of sainthood.

The operative principle must take cognizance, therefore, not only of the immediate concerns of the convert in relation to his adoptive and natural families, but also of the history of such concerns which molded the general attitudes of the faith.

But Then There is the Individual

The Halakhah, while it is focused to protect the corporate, historic entity of the Jewish people, nonetheless does not overlook the individual. Because, despite the rightness or wrongness of a given proposition, the human being is never lost sight of in the Halakhah, and he remains the heart of Torah and of Rabbinic legislation. It would be cold comfort, indeed, to counsel the convert only in not attending a church funeral service for her father because of her newly adopted people, without at the same time encouraging her to express bereavement in the Jewish mourning customs and emotionally supportive behaviors that she adopted on entering her new faith. Striking a sensitive balance between the demands of the faith and the needs of the people is very complicated and requires decisions from very special, responsible people.

Following are some of the major considerations which enabled the rabbis in different ages to apply Halakhah to current problems. Please note that, as is characteristic of all Rabbinic literature, not all the rabbis were of one mind on any given question. There were stricter views and more lenient ones depending not so much on personal sympathies as on the interpretation of Jewish law and the nature of the reality.

But they all agreed on this: the decision to follow one or another track on any given problem is not left to the discretion of well-intentioned advisors, but of scholars of the law. Although the concepts are here outlined, the decision still remains the rabbi's.

THE BASIS OF THE CONVERT'S SPECIAL STATUS

The Convert is as a Newborn Child

Many of the complicated pastoral concerns arising from the new convert's interpersonal relationships stem from the radically changed status of the convert. In psychological terms, the action, if it is sincere and wholehearted, is a personal meta-morphosis. In religious terms, he or she is considered nothing less than newly born to this world. And more than being newborn, he or she is born to "spiritual" parentage, not bio-logical parents, which leaves the convert in a technical, legal sense, without family.

This concept appears again and again throughout the Talmud. To the question as to why proselytes seemed to be suffering unduly, one Rabbi answered that it was because, in pre-con-version days, they might not have kept the basic human mandates, called the Seven Noahide Laws. Rabbi Yose of the second century C.E. disagreed: "A newly converted proselyte is like a newborn child."[1] This concept of a convert being equated with a newborn child is mentioned in connection with the laws of inheritance. We also encounter it in response to a question as to whether the convert has fulfilled the law of "Be fruitful and multiply" if he had fathered children before the conversion. It is also referred to in connection with the proselyte who died without Jewish heirs; and also in regard to a convert testifying in a court of law.

To say that a convert is a newborn person is not just a nice idea or a lofty preachment or an honorable description. It is a law—nothing more, nothing less—and it is taken as seriously as any other law, with all the consequences attendant upon that status.

The Spiritual Dimension

It is a remarkable concept on three accounts.

First, the spiritual dimensions of the concept are towering. It means that, in consequence of this convert's profound personal decision, Almighty God miraculously erased from the convert's history all sin, guilt, and punishment associated with his pre-conversion life.[2] A Jew, by the force of religious law, is not permitted to remind the convert of his past by saying: "I remember when you. . . ." In effect, Jewish law declared to this newcomer: "You transformed your life to join our faith. Your past is now the history of another person. You have only the long future; make of it a glorious chapter in a new book."

The Historical Dimension

Second, the environment into which this idea was projected was the Greco-Roman paganism of the first centuries of the common era, in the early talmudic period. The pagan religions knew of no such thing as exclusivist conversions. A person converted to another faith simply by adding its rituals to his existing armamentarium of practices related to God. In classical Roman times, adopting a new religion did not demand a divestiture of all previous practices or a transformation of beliefs that recognized no prior commitments. People were syncretistic. They did not know of "jealous gods," of combative religious ideas. To the ancient Greek or Roman, the new Jewish religion was unforgivably intolerant—it was unwilling simply to add the majority's morality, religion, symbols and holy days to its monotheistic idea, and then take a new total and be done with it. Indeed, they expected the Jews to do as they themselves had done: admit the Jewish religion—despite the fact that it was alien and unreasonable[3]—into the pantheon of their own beliefs as an acceptable supplement.

The Legal Dimension

Third, the legal conception is equally remarkable. In one momentous act, upon arising from the immersion in the mikveh, the law crystallized into reality that which, only a minute before, was but a lofty spiritual idea. It created a reality, "a fact on the ground," out of that which had started as a germinating idea and had grown into a personal philosophy. The consequence of that act is that this adult human being is now a new person, with a new name and a new identity. That is as eloquent a substantiation of a person's ideas as one can ever find.

Now, the convert should note that this does not mean that all relation to the past should be obliterated. It simply is not possible to eradicate all traces of significant past events, whether that would be desirable or not. There is no indication that Judaism considers the past never to have existed. This is not only a psychological, but a spiritual truth.[4] Conversion is a radical change, a complete reversal of direction, but not actually a mutant creation of a totally new being. The caterpillar does not become a butterfly in a single act, but as a result of a gradual process. Within this natural process, there appear to be a series of jumps between distinct stages, and the convert is expected to do likewise. One small step for a single person can generate a leap for an entire family. The proselyte, whom the Halakhah regards as a newborn child, brings much good to his or her new life that he acquired in a previous existence; he is not required to eject everything good and courageous in order to begin anew. Great spiritual change does not necessitate a wholesale change of character, intellectual acumen, or spiritual sensitivity. Indeed, seeing the past clearly for what it was in the light of new-gained insights makes the conversion ever more valuable.

What Judaism does seek is that the convert bring with her or him valuable qualities of character and mind, but that they re-orient themselves toward the new goal. Only in this light is the past not to be counted in the new reckoning; as the Rabbis expressed it: "The first days shall fall away."

The decision by a gentile to convert, as the decision by a Jew to repent, does entail disconnecting from the past, in addition to plugging into a future, and this is a demanding process that moves from one of destruction to one of reconstruction. The Rabbis said that a person's sins undergo a metamorphosis when one corrects his behavior patterns: deliberate sins are transformed into unwitting ones, and they, in turn, are made into virtues. This change from the past to a new life requires that the person play a conscious role in the transmutation.

The Legal Problems in Being Newborn

If the convert is, in fact, held to be newborn, how are we to weigh their legal, and especially pastoral, relationships with the natural family of the "old" world?

A paradox lies hidden within this idea: Legally, the idea that a convert is as a newborn child would logically permit an incestuous relationship! If the convert is newborn, he has no relatives. His natural sister thus should not be considered "related" at all, and he should be permitted to marry her. But, of course, it is not conceivable that the Rabbis would have permitted that, considering that Judaism is a religion of the highest morality that sanctifies proper sexual partners and that makes public religious pronouncements of the stark prohibitions of incest and other illicit sexual acts on Yom Kippur, the holiest day of the year.

Despite this strange outcome of an elegant legal principle, the Rabbis refused to revise this concept which gives the convert a fresh start, and sanctifies his status in the religious code, and which demonstrates formally and forcefully the starting of a new life. But they did resolve it by resorting to a commonly accepted formula: to assume that the Torah is an immoral or unconcerned or lesser religion is patently absurd; and even though, on a legal technicality, this moral mutation could conceivably result, in reality incest obviously would never be condoned by Judaism, regardless of the niceties and technicalities of the law. They put the formula in unabashedly simple terms: Converts "should never be able to say 'We came from a greater holiness to a lesser holiness' "—from a higher morality to a lower morality. In that way, the Rabbis accomplished two goals—they avoided disturbing the magnificent *legal* expression of the *spiritual* creation of the new convert, and yet maintained and asserted Judaism's lofty morality.

This unprecedented conception created other legal problems: Since the Torah prohibits close relatives from bearing testimony about one another, may the convert testify in a court of law about his natural family? Does he inherit his natural relatives if he is, for all other intents and purposes, newborn? And what about the requirement to observe the fifth commandment to respect his natural parents, now that he is legally "unrelated"?

The Pastoral Concerns of the Newborn

The new legal status also triggers complicated *pastoral* questions regarding how the convert should manage interreligious and interpersonal relationships. There are many questions, asked more openly in the fluid society of today than ever before, about the Jewish tradition's posture regarding the newly converted Jew's involvement in non-Jewish festivities. This is of special concern when dealing with family religious events—the Jew in Christian celebrations, the Christian in Jewish celebrations.

For example, given that the new Jew (as any Jew) may not attend church services, may he or she participate in after-service collations at Christmas and Easter, providing the food is kosher?

May the convert speak at a parent's funeral service in a mortuary or funeral chapel, or in a private residence, as distinct from in the church?

May the convert be present at a Christian rite of passage—baptism or confirmation—when it does not take place in a church, and without participating in the service?

May a convert observe Jewish mourning rituals for gentile parents?

May the convert participate in dinners (kosher, naturally) which are national celebrations, such as Thanksgiving and July 4th?

Or consider the reverse situation: the convert's gentile family in Jewish celebrations. May the gentile family participate in the convert's family celebrations?

May they attend a grandchild's Bar Mitzvah services?

May the convert's gentile parents escort their now-Jewish converted child to the marriage canopy (*chuppah*)?

May they hold up the chuppah if it is a portable one? May they stand under it during the ceremony? May the gentile father deliver the wedding talk?

May gentile parents attend and participate in circumcision rites (b'rit)? May they be given the honor of handing the baby to the "godfather," called *kvater*?"

May they attend and participate in a Jewish funeral? If so, may they rend their clothing ritually, or fill the grave, or deliver the eulogy, or help carry the casket?

May they attend such celebrations as the Passover Seder? May they participate in the readings?

QUESTIONS OF RELIGIOUS PROPRIETY

Attending Non-Jewish Religious Services

Simply visiting with family and having dinner with them does not contravene the law, providing the food is prepared according to Jewish dietary requirements. Respect for parents is in order all the time, regardless of whether they approved of the conversion or not. The only caveat the Rabbis made was that a strong bond between the families be discouraged if it will cause the now-Jewish children to consider returning to the religion of the parents.

Knowing that little minds might be attracted by the beauty

of ceremony without the burden of faith—the Rabbis were profoundly concerned that exposing children to another faith might well diminish or even derail altogether the whole intent of the conversion. If there is a possibility that this familiarity will lead to backsliding or intermarriage, the leniencies of the Rabbis will have been a betrayal of their trust. This scenario was reason enough for some Rabbis to opt for a stricter inter- pretation.

Attendance at non-Jewish religious services, whether Christian, Muslim, Hare Krishna, or any religion or cult, is not permitted. It makes no difference whether these religious services take place in a church, mosque or ashram, or at home. There is some question about whether a dinner or collation at home that follows a religious celebration is to be considered "religious" or only social.

Participating in Gentile Celebrations

While Jewish law does not permit attendance at church services, may a Jew attend after-service collations at Christmas and Easter?

The Rabbis of the Talmud[5] were of the opinion that, if it is part of the celebration, it is not permitted. They based their attitude on the biblical statement, "Lest you make a covenant with the inhabitants of the land . . . and they call you, and you eat of their sacrifice" (Exodus 34, 15). All of the components of that relationship are to be avoided—the inviting, the eating, the [religious] rejoicing.[6]

In the writings of the later Rabbis, the subject of participation in these dinners revolves about the question of whether the meal is itself an integral part of the festival and therefore with religious significance (in which case attendance is surely prohibited and no leniencies may apply[7]) or whether it was feared that the familiarity of socially celebrating together would lead to a breakdown of barriers and possibly cause an intermarriage.

If it is the fear of familiarity, a whole new set of ideas comes into play. It is no longer a "religious" concern and there may be a mitigating aspect which should be considered under the halakhic rubric of "social breakdown," *aivah*. Specifically, avoiding gentile friends or business associates precisely during their periods of joy might trigger the old cannons of hatred, anger, and prejudice. So, in very specific circumstances, the Rabbis permitted some leniency to avoid that which might lead to catastrophe.[8]

Whether Christmas or Easter dinner is connected with the religious church services theologically, however, is less important than how that dinner is perceived by the public and by folklore. Attendance at such dinners by the Jewish convert, and especially the children, is inappropriate and counterproductive no matter how it is defended in theory. However, if the matter is likely to provoke some irremediable crisis, a rabbi should be consulted in order to weigh objectively all the competing claims on one's conduct.

The dinner is halakhically of one piece with exchanging holiday gifts and cooking special holiday foods. Suggestions by well-meaning people to finesse the problems by participating as "Jewish observers" to the holiday scene rarely works. The problems are often further exacerbated by unthinking relatives who may drop unkind, inappropriate, even caustic remarks. It is good to be prepared.[9]

Helping and Visiting Sick Parents

There is simply no question but that converts should visit and comfort their sick parents. This requires no documentation. Judaism strives to make its adherents more humane, not less. Did the parent not bring him into this world, raise him, suffer the pains of childhood with him?

The Prophet Isaiah (58:7) declares:

> Is it not to deal thy bread to the hungry? And that thou shalt bring the poor that are cast out to thy house? When thou seest the naked, that thou cover him? And that thou hidest not thyself from thine own flesh?

A person may not hide himself from his own flesh, whether that flesh be Jewish or gentile.[10] There is serious doubt that anyone can psychologically "hide from his flesh," although there are numerous people who make that attempt and cut themselves off from family—some without a flutter of regret. But this is not the Jewish way. It is distinctly not religiously desirable behavior.

A true and devout convert should go beyond words of comfort to words of prayer. It is not only permitted but proper to pray in behalf of a sick gentile to God who is the Healer of all mankind.

Did not God tell Avimelech, King of Gerar (Genesis 20: 7), that Abraham was a prophet who would pray for the king and that he would live? Did not the Prophet Elisha heal Na'aman, the Syrian general (II Kings 5:8 ff.), from his leprosy? Did not Mordecai (Esther 2:21) save King Ahasueros' life from Bigtan and Teresh?

Implicit in this decision is a concern larger than the interpersonal relations of parents and children. It is, in Jewish terms, nothing less than a matter of sanctifying the Name of God. The behavior of every Jew, especially of a convert whose actions are often scrutinized more than those of born Jews, should reflect favorably on God, who gave the Jews the Torah. The former Chief Sephardic Rabbi of Israel, Rabbi Ovadiah Yosef, considers it not merely good form or good advice, but obligatory upon the convert for this very reason.[11] Rabbi Kook, the first Chief Rabbi of modern Israel (then Palestine), vigorously maintains that, even though the convert is as a newborn child, he has a natural love for members of his family.[12] No one can or wishes to legislate that away. The concern of the Rabbis has always been the possibility of regression to the former, pre-Jewish condition. The "newborn" legislation of the Rabbis seeks to elevate the convert—not so much as to dismiss the past as to ennoble the future.

Attending Christian Rites of Passage in the Home

Jews are not permitted to attend a "religious" service—no matter where it is held. Although it may appear to be harmless because the setting is not a "religious" one, such cases have virtually no exceptions in Jewish law or tradition.

Attending Christian Funeral Services

May the convert deliver a eulogy at a parent's funeral service in a mortuary, funeral chapel, or in a home—as distinct from the church?

If the convert's portion is considered to be part of the "religious" ceremony, it is wrong for him to eulogize. If the participation is not formally "religious," but rather a personal, intimately expressed demonstration of respect of child for parent—especially if the convert is an important personage—the eulogy must be viewed from a different perspective. Maimonides[13] recognizes that, although legally and formally the convert is as a newborn child, the natural parents have and deserve a unique place in a child's life that no one should deny. While, in terms of Halakhah, this is not explicitly biblically mandated, it is required of the Jewish convert, both out of natural considerations[14] and for the self-evident reason that no one should ever come to say that he came "from a higher to a lower morality."[15]

An interesting biblical origin for the respect a Jew is required to pay his parents, aside from the Torah's mandate in the fifth of its Ten Commandments, is the Midrash on Abraham, the father of all converts.[16] The Rabbis note that immediately before the verse in which God commands Abram to separate from his father, Terah, the Bible already records the death of Terah who was the arch idolator of the era. The problem is that Terah continued to live for sixty-five years. The reason for this unusual juxtaposition, says Rabbi Yitzchak, is that Abraham was afraid, "Lest, when I leave the land, people will desecrate the name of God because of me, saying: 'He left his father in his old age.' Therefore, God said, 'I release you from the mitzvah of honoring father and mother, but I do not similarly release anyone else from this obligation. And not only that, in the Torah I will record his death before you leave.' Thus, the Torah records first 'And Terah died in Haran' and only then 'And God said to Abram: Get thee out. . . .'"

As superbly sensitive as is the Bible, according to the Rabbis of the Midrash, so must all people be to the relationship of converts with their natural parents.

Mourning for Gentile Relatives

The profound respect for Jewish parents which informs the entire Jewish tradition of mourning is not different from those feelings of love for gentile parents which informs their own bereavement practices. Beyond the commandment to honor parents, there is also the rational motive of gratitude which is compelling and which affects Jew and gentile alike. The Talmud abounds with examples of non-Jews devoted to their parents, as in the unforgettable story of Dama, son of Netina, who stood to lose a fortune because he refused to awaken his sleeping father.

One authority[17] writes that since parents, along with Almighty God, are partners in the creation of the child, a sin such as cursing parents is equivalent to the sin of cursing God.

Another scholar[18] wonders whether the essence of the commandment to honor parents is the vertical relationship between man and God—this is what God commanded, and this is therefore what one must do—or the horizontal one between man and man—since my parents brought me into this world and raised me, I owe them gratitude and should do good for them in turn. In Jewish law, the difference would emerge in a case where a child offended his parents and did not ask forgiveness of them before Yom Kippur. According to tradition, when man repents, Yom Kippur pardons all sins between man and God, but not sins committed against other people. Only the aggrieved party can forgive. If the parent did not forgive, can one be cleansed at the end of Yom Kippur?

All this demonstrates that the Jewish tradition is appreciative of the feeling of converts and expects them to continue to love their natural parents. And parents should be honored in life and also in death. Therefore, there is no doubt that converts should mourn their deceased gentile parents through Jewish rites and in a Jewish milieu.

It must be emphasized that the mourning practices should be Jewish observances and decidedly not those of the convert's former religion. Not only respect for parents is important, but also self-respect to express feelings in a way most appropriate to the mourner's life and philosophy.[19] The convert may perform all those mourning observances as do born Jews for their parents. They may serve as pallbearers, bury the dead at their cemetery, fill in their graves, and observe the seven-day (*shivah*) and thirty-day (*sheloshim*) mourning periods. Some authorities, however, say that the full observance of shivah and sheloshim and the full twelve-month period of mourning is not appropriate.[20]

As to the question of whether a Jewish mourner should recite the Kaddish[21] prayer for gentile parents, former Sephardic Chief Rabbi Ovadiah Yosef urges converts to do so. Whether, in fact, every other rabbi would rule in the same manner is questionable. But there is no doubt that, if the convert mourner wishes to recite the Kaddish, he should be encouraged to do so. Since his parents struggled to bring him into this world, should he not help them as they cross the threshold into the world-to-come? The Rabbis say that a child can reflect merit and "save" his parents from the effects of their own sins. Why should he not do so?

In many instances, prayers unrelated to the individual are recited for non-Jews. The likely basis of such prayers is the phrase in the Book of Esther, "May Charbonah [who spoke out against Haman's planned destruction] be remembered for good." It was his good deed that insured the survival of the Persian Jews.[22] The Rabbis were of the opinion that one should even pray for a renegade Jew if in some way he has helped the Jewish community or has performed virtuous deeds. And who has not accomplished some good in his life?

However, understandably, the Halakhah could not *require* the convert to respect his parents and formally practice the mourning rites. Only the relationship could determine the obligation. Psychological insights available today incline us to encourage the convert to express his mourning. It is a way of living and growing through a situation which, if not handled well, might be postponed for half a lifetime and affect virtually every experience of separation that may occur in the future.

Participation in National Holiday Festivities

American Jews participate in celebrations such as Thanksgiving and the Fourth of July as do all Americans. They are national and religious holidays. Often, however, Thanksgiving celebrations are held in churches and tied to religious forms. Indeed, properly conceived, Thanksgiving is the embodiment of religious values such as gratitude to God. The convert should not participate in the church service, but there is no violation of the Jewish spirit in a typical national Thanksgiving celebration and accordingly no concern exists for a diminution of Jewish values.[23] Eating kosher turkey seems a natural way for an American Jew to celebrate the Pilgrim holiday.

The same is true for the Fourth of July. Every country has a celebration of national independence. And, indeed, Jews are mandated by the Halakhah to follow the law of the land except when it conflicts with the religious or moral laws of the Torah. While the Halakhah does not require Jews to celebrate Independence Day, it certainly does not preclude such celebration. We should view this day as an opportunity for expressing Jewish appreciation for democracy and capitalism and for a system of government that has assured us peace and tranquillity and the freedom to practice our religion.

To review, in all these questions one concern predominates:

Will this encourage intermingling with the non-Jewish ways of the natural family which might ultimately lead to intermarriage or reversion to the previous faith? We need to be conscious of these concerns and take every reasonable precaution to prevent violating the spirit of the law. Genuine affection for family should not lead to assimilation. Loving is not succumbing.

Notes to Chapter Seventeen

1. Yevamot 48b.
2. See the dispute between the theologians Gavin and Strack-Billerbeck in F. Gavin, *The Jewish Antecedents of the Christian Sacraments* (Ktav Publishing House, Hoboken, New Jersey, 1969), on whether the newborn status according to Rabbi Yose means that the proselyte, by his conversion, becomes a regenerate man from the ethical viewpoint or whether it was purely legal legerdemain.
3. See the very perceptive essay by F. Gavin, "The Jewish Antecedents of the Christian Sacraments," Lecture II, op cit., for this point and those that follow shortly. (It strains the imagination, however, to believe even for a moment, as he avers, that circumcision is considered equal or analogous to the sacrament in Christianity.)
4. Adin Steinsaltz, *Teshuvah: A Guide for the Newly Observant Jew,* New York: Free Press, New York, 1987.
5. Avodah Zarah 8a.
6. See Rashi *ad loc.:* "It means that the fact of your being 'called' [invited] makes it equivalent to your eating on his altar."
7. See *Tzvi La'Tzaddik* to Yoreh De'ah 152:1, by Rabbi Zvi Hirsch Kalisher, who notes that Rashi suggests that the prohibition came into being because the worshippers were bringing sacrifices during the days of festivity. But that is patently not applicable today, so that, if the Jew were to attend, he would be able to eat his distinctive food—but, if he did *not,* his absence might trigger resentment. Under these circumstances, the decision is that he is permitted to attend.
8. The source for this is Yoreh De'ah 158:12: ". . . but in these times, they are not expert in the matter of idolatry, and therefore one is permitted to do business with them on the days of their holidays." To this statement, Shakh appends the comment of Perisha: ". . . there is another thing and that is the matter of *aivah,* anger, if we detach ourselves from them on their festival—and we live among them and need to deal with them all year. . . ." The Taz responds that he is stunned that such a great man as the Perisha could permit such a thing because of the fear of aivah, for that is the very point of the verse: that we not join in their festivity when we are invited, because it will lead to intermarriage. Aivah serves precisely this purpose. But Shach, in *Nekudot Ha'Kesef (ad loc.),* counters that aivah can indeed be used as a deciding factor in this situation,

as in similar situations. It is here that Zvi Hirsch Kalisher emphasizes the lenient view of Shach. Nonetheless, there were many who prohibited it even if the second reason applied, *viz.* the author of the *Darkei Teshuvah.* The Rabbi of Munkacz, Hungary, notes that in any case the festive meal is considered by gentiles to be part of the religious tradition, that therefore no leniency applies and aivah is irrelevant.

9. Linda Byard, "What Happens After Conversion?", *Jewish Digest,* pp. 26-30, May 1980, lists a series of verbal jabs to be prepared for.

10. On this, see Ketubot 52b.

11. The entire subject is covered in great detail by Rabbi Ovadiah Yosef, in *Yechaveh Da'at,* responsum 60.

12. See *Ishim Ve'Shitot,* pp. 258-9, by Rabbi Shlomo Zevin, author of the *Talmudic Encyclopedia,* who quotes Rav Kook, *Da'at Kohen,* ch. 147, who bases himself in turn on Ketubot lla and Sanhedrin 76b.

13. Hilkhot Mamrim 5; 11.

14. To wit, the prohibitions against striking or swearing at gentile parents, shaming or embarrassing them, etc., and the requirement of at least *miktzat kavod,* which probably refers to deep respect, but without the command and punishment for violating biblical law.

15. Therefore, Maimonides demands *lo yivazehu,* the child may not embarrass or shame the parent. Shaming a parent, even only with words, or only by hint, as in Yoreh De'ah 241:6, falls under the category of cursing the Almightly and the courts then consider whether to apply the penalty of flogging, *makat mardut,* or to punish in other ways according as they see fit. In Yoreh De'ah 241:9, we find this stricture in almost identical words as in Maimonides, without the inclusion of the requirement of miktzat kavod, which Rabbi Moshe Feinstein, in *Iggerot Moshe,* Yoreh De'ah, vol. II, reponsum 130, considers to be an unimportant distinction signifying no salient disagreement between the two decisors, i.e. the aspect of kavod is definitely not be be ignored.

16. On this see *Kiryat Melekh,* by Rabbi Chaim Konivski, to Maimonides, *Mishneh Torah,* Hilkhot Mamrim. His reference is to Bereshit Rabbah on Parshat Lekh Lekha, 39:7.

17. The author of *Nachal Eshkol,* Hilkhot Milah Ve'Gerim 39:1. Also *Yad Avraham* to Yoreh De'ah 241, and Malbim's *Commentary* to Deuteronomy 24:18.

18. The author of *Minchat Chinukh,* mitzvah 33.

19. See *Bet Yosef* to Yoreh De'ah 274, *"ger she'nitgayer."*

20. See Rabbi Hershel Schachter in a monograph on "Adoption in Jewish Law" in *Chavrusa,* p. 5 (Yeshiva University Press, New York, April 1982), and the many sources on the subject that are cited there.

21. See *Yechaveh Da'at,* responsum 60, p. 201, which says it is *raui ve'nakhon* to recite the Kaddish in such circumstances. The author marshals numerous sources, as is his custom, to come to this conclusion, in the face of a technical objection by the *Sefer Chassidim* that the legal status of newborns would preclude this.

22. On Charbonah, see *Jerusalem Talmud,* Megillah 3:7, the saying of Rabbi Yochanan. On child-parent relationship, see also *Chatam Sofer,* Even

Ha'Ezer, vol. 2, ch. 41, *ve'lulei;* also, Or Same'ach in *Meshekh Chokhmah* to Parshat Bo; also, Maharam Shik, *The 613 Mitzvot,* ch. 17. Also see further documentation on the relationship of the convert child to gentile parents in *Yechaveh Da'at, op. cit.*

23. Some, possibly including Rabbi Moses Feinstein, have wondered whether it is proper to celebrate a holiday which, in its origins, was a religious celebration, such as Thanksgiving, once celebrated by the Pilgrims in church. Others pay this no attention.

18

Questions on Interpersonal Relationships II:

THE GENTILE FAMILY IN JEWISH CELEBRATIONS

QUESTIONS OF RELIGIOUS PROPRIETY

The question of gentile parents participating in a Jewish event is informed by the same general principles as those that dealt with the Jewish convert in gentile celebrations: avoid backsliding to pre-conversion religious ways; honor to the fullest the integrity of Jewish law; love the natural family and do not cause them embarrassment; behave, within the precincts of Jewish tradition, in a manner that sanctifies God's name rather than brings opprobrium upon it; avoid provoking needless anger in non-Jewish friends; and always act to confirm that conversion is never "a descent from a higher to a lower morality."

Following are a series of relevant and complex questions, many of them never asked before this century.

Gentile Parents Escorting a Convert at a Wedding

This is a delicate matter and there is much discussion among leading rabbis as to the advisability of designing an elaborate ceremony that includes the full participation of both families. On one hand, there is some question as to whether the wedding *procession* is on a par with the wedding *service* itself. While there is much Jewish folklore regarding ushers and bridesmaids, there appear to be no halakhic restrictions, only customs, that apply. On the other hand, there is a question as to whether having non-Jews march down the aisle is not an implicit endorsement, a flattering, of non-Jews by publicly demonstrating that that which was seen universally by Jews as wholly improper is here being permitted.

It is in this framework that Rabbi Moshe Feinstein addresses the question of whether an *intermarried* couple—a Jew and gentile civilly married to one another—may walk in the procession, even though they are the parents of the bride or groom. He cites the concern for the appearance of "public flattery" that here is decidedly to be avoided. The wedding procession is not constituted simply of a well-coiffed couple marching elegantly along a fifty-foot aisle, every step choreographed by a social director. It is a statement of religious values. Intermarriage is a profound life-and-death concern to Jews, and prominently parading a couple living in violation of the Torah, no matter the niceties of etiquette emphasized at a wedding, is a flagrant violation of Jewish sensibilities. It is tantamount to "putting a stumbling block before the blind," as others watch what seems to be the legitimation of the intermarried status, and therefore Rabbi Feinstein decides against permitting this.[1]

While this applies to a couple that is intermarried—because providing them with high visibility creates the appearance of community endorsement—looking aside rather than looking askance—a gentile married couple could cause no such concern. They have violated no religious laws. The concern of implicit endorsement relates to the *Jewishly unlawful* situation of intermarriage, and not to the entirely commendable marriage of two gentiles to one another.

Indeed, there should be much consideration given to the convert's parents who have raised a child, agreed to see the child convert to Judaism, and who are willing to participate in the Jewish ceremony. Maimonides has said that the convert must show respect (miktzat kavod) to natural parents, and that one may not embarrass them. Therefore, if the parents desire to participate in this way, most rabbis (though not all) would permit them to do so, especially if the Jewish parents are to march down the aisle. Common human sensitivity suggests that if the non-Jewish parents are in fact not to march, it is less than proper that the Jewish parents do so.

Holding Aloft the Marriage Canopy

The wedding canopy (chuppah) is the symbol of the new home that encloses the bride and groom for the first precious moments of their marriage. The chuppah serves a distinct halakhic function in that sense. But there is no religious significance that attaches to holding up the canopy—whether it stands on its own base or is a prayer-shawl held aloft at its corners by four people.[2] It is an important social honor to participate in a wedding ceremony in any meaningful way and there appears to be no reason why a gentile relative should not be accorded such a tribute.

Delivering the Wedding Talk

It is not customary for any parent to speak at the Jewish wedding ceremony itself, unless that parent is a rabbi. And it is probably unnecessary to introduce this idea with a non-Jew at a Jewish religious wedding. The wedding is a very carefully designed halakhic event, which must be conducted or overseen by halakhically competent persons. Compromising this specific requirement of the Talmud and Codes is inappropriate. On the other hand, it is quite proper for both sets of parents or relatives to toast the new couple during the meal.

Participating in the Circumcision Ceremony

The circumcision ceremony is rich in pageantry and, accordingly, involves many close relatives and friends as honorees, participating in one way or another. It begins with a procession of couples, called kvater (f. kvaterin), a German-Yiddish term for "godfather," who ceremoniously take the infant from the mother and brings it to the father, who then places the child on the lap of the *sandek* to hold the baby during the ceremony. He then designates the mohel, who performs the circumcision in his behalf.

May gentile parents be honored to serve as the kvater couple to hand the infant to the father, or as subsidiary kvater, to receive the baby from the mother?

There is no doubt that gentile parents may and should *attend* this ceremony. While it is no mitzvah to persuade them to do so, they might well expect to be invited. However, much sensitive care must be taken in regard to the ceremony itself.

It is this very moment and this very act which Judaism endows with the sacred purpose of bringing the child into the Covenant of Abraham and it is this rite which distinguishes the child as a Jew forever. Because it bears this specific Divine purpose, it is not mere surgery; it is circumcision. And it is performed not by any upright, fine surgeon or urologist, but by a mohel, who, in addition to his expertise in the surgical procedure, is himself committed to the precepts of the religion. During the circumcision ceremony, many other "honors" are distributed—such as raising the baby, passing him, holding him during the circumcision, feeding him the drop of wine and holding him while the prayers are recited and during the naming and so on. The Rabbis held these honors in high esteem and referred to them as "subsidiary sandek." These honors have all been associated by tradition with the religious moment of the circumcision proper, as an elaboration of its significance and a heightening of its sanctity by increasing the drama and the participation of family and important personages.

The kvater role is just such an honor and it should be accorded only to those persons who are themselves members of the covenant which the child now enters. Some rabbis, however, believe that taking the child from its mother and giving it to the kvater is not, in and of itself, an essential element of the religious ceremony and, consequently, have permitted gentiles to assume that role. (If family members become emotionally upset because of this, the rabbi or mohel should arrange matters to accord with the value of "peace in the home," *shalom bayit*, on which the Sages place great emphasis.)

Converts' Parents Attending Bar or Bat Mitzvah

There is nothing wrong, and everything right, with the convert's gentile parents attending synagogue services and the reception. "For My House is a House of prayer for all peoples" suggests that the gentile can enter the synagogue today as his ancestor entered the precincts of the Holy Temple two thousand years ago. While it is the occasion that celebrates the child's becoming obligated to perform the precepts of Judaism and therefore a "religious" time, watching, being present and deriving satisfaction are surely not antithetical to the Halakhah. Denying that invitation, especially at the cost of a family quarrel, can shame the grandparents and is not encouraged.

Participating in Jewish Funeral Services

Should the non-Jewish family be invited to participate in or even attend a Jewish funeral? Should they be allowed to rend their clothing, deliver a eulogy, carry the casket, or act out any of the rituals of Jewish bereavement? The service at the chapel, and even more so at the cemetery, is religious in nature as it is the final rite of passage and it is therefore with care and sensitivity that one ought approach this subject.

Attendance at the service is unquestionably permitted and proper. Gentile relatives and friends also may express their grief in their distinctive manner, as they are accustomed to do. But they should not practice Christian or Muslim religious rites during the Jewish service. If they wish to make a tear in their clothing, as Jews do, they may of course do so. They should not serve as pallbearers nor deliver the eulogy at the chapel or cemetery, although they may do so at the home or at a memorial program at a later time.

Inviting Gentiles to the Seder and Holiday Meals

The Seder is the archetypical religious meal of the Jewish calendar, both because of its halakhic significance and its prominence as a public Jewish social occasion. It is often the last observance that assimilating Jews leave and the first to which they return.

Questions tend to focus on two areas: the kashrut aspect of holiday food preparations and also specific Seder concerns. Jewish law is anxious to protect the integrity both of the holiday regulations and of the liturgical retelling of the Exodus narrative, in the Haggadah, that is specific to the Passover Seder. In this framework, we need to consider the effect of this family-oriented holiday[3] upon both the converts and their non-Jewish relatives.

TWO KASHRUT PROBLEMS

One kashrut problem may arise regarding the special concern with wine and its ancient association with Christian and also cultic worship services, referred to as *yayin nesekh*. The Halakhah, in attempting to insulate the community from the invasive influences of its neighbors, prohibits Jews from drinking wine handled by non-Jews. This problem is easily circumvented by using precooked kosher wine which removes it from the category of natural, fermented wine that was used for cultic worship purposes. Most domestic kosher wines, but not all, are precooked.

A second kashrut problem has to do with preparing the meal. The law prohibits cooking on the Sabbath and holidays. However, this ruling was relaxed for holidays, but with certain restrictions. One is permitted to cook on the very day of Pesach, Shavuot or Sukkot, but only for that day itself and not for the next. Hence, one may not cook on a holiday, for example, for belatedly invited extra guests, nor even for the family itself if the food is to be eaten on the following day.

The reasoning is as follows: The holiday is not designed to be a "working" day—eating is fun, cooking is work—but one devoted to spiritual goals. The Rabbis enjoined Jewish people from extending invitations especially to non-Jews on the holiday itself on the likelihood that the Jewish hosts will want to impress their non-Jewish guests and be tempted to "cook up a storm" of gourmet foods and generous helpings, thereby violating the spirit of the day. Now, on the Sabbath, this presents no problems. The Rabbis did not need to institute any such enactment because, in any case, one may not cook on the Sabbath at all, and there will be no temptation to make more delicacies.

This is not a problem on the holiday *if* non-Jews are the cooks, such as at catered Seder dinners, because, even were they to cook additional foods, the Jewish hosts themselves will not be violating any biblical prohibitions. When the Seder is at home and Jewish hosts are doing the cooking, the crucial test must be the likelihood of being prompted to cook additional food on the holiday. Thus, for example, if it is just before serving the meal, but after completing the preparation, it is acceptable to invite more guests to share the meal.

These rulings relate to the proper observance of Sabbaths and holidays, not to the nature or quality of the guests. The enduring principle applied by the Sages in such a context is that Jews are obliged to maintain peaceful relations with their neighbors whenever possible *mi'pnei darkei shalom*, for the sake of peace. Acting "for the sake of peace" is not a form of compromise, but a noble gesture that here enables the invitation to be extended to private homes. This is bolstered by the opinion of a great medieval codifier that, if a non-Jew came to the house on the holiday, we should say "Welcome, join us for all the food that we have already prepared."

ONE SEDER PROBLEM

A Passover-specific question regarding gentiles at the Seder originates from the fact that the Seder is not merely food and drink, but primarily the "reliving" of the Exodus from Egypt by studying the Exodus narrative as rendered in the Haggadah and in its continuous amplification by rabbis, scholars, and lay-men over twenty-seven centuries. If the essence of the Seder is the "religious" act of studying Torah, is that an appropriate context for the admixture of Jews and gentiles? Such questions usually trigger an offhand "Why not?" But Jewish history as it relates to Jews and gentiles—especially at Passover time—is fairly complicated and provides an instructive moral. In addition, the question needs to be understood in the light of Jewish tradition as well as from the viewpoint of Jewish history.

In Jewish tradition, the Passover meal is meant to relive the scene of eating the Paschal sacrifice before leaving Egypt. The Paschal meal, which spelled the beginning of the Jewish peoplehood covenant, was one at which only members of the future Jewish people were to assemble, and in which none of the Egyptians could share. We jog our memories all through the Seder with symbols recalling the intimate shared meal of the Paschal lamb, the original Passover our ancestors celebrated.

In terms of history, we ought to remember that the Jewish community was time and again infiltrated by Christians who supposedly found out the "secrets" of the Jews, and waged public debates before kings and princes "proving the folly of the Jewish religion and its seditious nature." This exacerbated a centuries-old Jewish paranoia, quite legitimate nonetheless, that if the Jews did not assiduously protect every aspect of their religion, it might fall prey to the religious bestiary of the day. This had gone so far that Rabbi Akiva Eiger, a renowned nineteenth-century scholar, seriously questioned how much one was permitted to teach proselyte candidates while they were still gentiles. A cursory sampling of Jewish history would show the calamitously destructive effect that disenchanted converts have had on the Jewish community when they regressed to their former religion.

But, regardless of those dark chapters of Jewish history, Judaism did not respond to historic tragedy only instinctively. It calculated the moral and religious credits and debits of the response. If Judaism had precluded all teaching of Judaism to gentiles, how could sincere non-Jews become Jews? There are many examples of Torah being studied by non-Jews. In talmudic times, many gentiles, even during trying times of back-sliding proselytes, were learned in Jewish law; today, there are media broadcasts that feature rabbis teaching Torah to masses of people. How could anyone expect the Torah to remain the exclusive domain of the Jews? In any case, how could one avoid teaching Torah to non-Jews in this age of mass communications? The answer of contemporary authorities is that teaching Torah to Jews in the company of non-Jews has always been permitted.

A COMPELLING REASON TO INVITE GENTILE RELATIVES

While this halakhic response enables non-Jews to attend the Seder, there is an even more compelling human and philosophic response in terms of the convert and his gentile relatives today. Historically, Passover was a dread time for Jews. In medieval and modern Europe, Easter was the special holy moment for preaching that Jews killed the Christian Messiah. Numerous congregations in cities, towns and hamlets all over Europe were whipped into spiritual frenzy during church services, and sent out to wreak bloody vengeance on wholly innocent Jewish "neighbors" acting out the zeal fomented by their priests. Those days were also the chosen times for blood libels that created in graphic detail the fantastic fiction of how Jews drank Christian children's blood for their Passover wine.

It is with dramatic irony, therefore, that new Jews open to their gentile families the Passover Seder that for centuries was looked upon as closed, "mysterious," and secret. Under these conditions, converts can demonstrate how the Seder has always turned toward children with love; how it describes the monstrous, bloody persecution of the Jews; and how it responds to that persecution by courageously swinging open the door in the middle of the perilous black night to welcome the Prophet Elijah, the forerunner of the Messiah who will bring healing to the whole world.

ANOTHER REASON TO INVITE

Another aspect is that Passover is so joyous and festive a holiday that to refuse to welcome parents on this occasion is to invite rancor, resentment, and suspicion. This destroys relationships and may even cause the very convert Judaism wishes to embrace, to think fleetingly of withdrawing from a faith that comes between them and their parents, their children and their grandparents.

THE OBJECT OF AN INVITATION

The object of inviting gentile guests should not only be *mi'pnei darke shalom* (to keep peace in the family and with friends), but also kiddush ha'Shem, a sanctification of the name of God. When an act which is halakhically valid is shown to enhance the integrity of the Jewish people, kiddush ha'Shem is well served. It is therefore proper to encourage gentile parents to see how beautiful the religion truly is, how careful Jews are to train their children, how important good family life is to the Jews, and how rooted the Jewish people is to an ancient past as the central focus of contemporary religion.

It would appear, then, though some fine scholars may question it, that when non-Jewish parents wish to be invited to Jewish festive celebrations, we should open the doors to our faith and express sensitivity to their wholesome desire, and also to the needs of their children—our new Jews—who are the courageous people who gave up the family's religion, home, and hearth to join the Jewish people.

Notes to Chapter Eighteen

1. On this, see *Iggerot Moshe,* Yoreh De'ah, vol. 3, p. 349.
2. There are some rabbis who object to *any* person holding the canopy. They hold that it must constitute a separate enclosure and people do not form a mechitzah, separation, whereas poles do.
3. See Rabbi Grossnass in *Lev Aryeh*, responsum 23, p. 55.

Part Five

WHO ARE WE?

A CONVERT'S INTRODUCTION TO JUDAISM

19

A First Look at Judaism

What follows is a satellite view of the Jewish religion, viewed from a great distance so that what are visible are only the contours of Torah—grand outlines of the beliefs, laws, ethics and practices of Judaism. From this distance one can only sense, but not see, the detailed features of the terrain that needs to be studied: the winding biblical pathways, the elaborate network of the Halakhah, and especially the subtle turns of Jewish spirituality. What follow are signposts that point the way to these treasures. It is the reader's task to explore "on foot" the new world of Judaism.

Sir Francis Bacon's insight is appropriate in this regard: A little knowledge inclines a man's mind to atheism, but a depth of knowledge to religion. It will become self-evident that a closer and more intense examination of specific areas of Torah is absolutely essential. Resting content with just a passing acquaintance with Judaism will constitute a missed opportunity that will frustrate both Judaism and the convert. The new Jew must learn to do what every native Jew is obligated to do every day and every night: study.

AN OUTLINE OF THE CLASSIC CURRICULUM

The basic content of the convert's study of Judaism is presented in the Talmud, and a schematic on these lines is established by Maimonides. This is from the Talmud:[1]

> Our Rabbis taught: If, at the present time, a person desires to become a proselyte, he is to be addressed as follows: "What reason have you for desiring to become a proselyte; do you not know that Israel at the present time is persecuted and oppressed, despised, harassed and overcome by afflictions?" If he replies, "I know and yet am unworthy [of becoming a Jew]," he is accepted forthwith, and is given instruction in some of the minor and some of the major commandments. He is informed of the sin of neglecting the commandments of Gleanings, the Forgotten Sheaf, the Corner and the Poor Man's Tithe. He is also told of the punishment for the transgression of the commandments.
>
> Furthermore, he is addressed as follows: "Be it known to you that, before you came to this condition, if you had eaten suet [prohibited animal fat], you would not have been punishable with excision from the Jewish people; if you had profaned the Sabbath, you would not have been punishable with stoning. But now, were you to eat suet, you would be punished with excision; were you to profane the Sabbath, you would be punished with stoning."
>
> And, as he is informed of the punishment for the transgression of the commandments, so is he informed of the reward granted for their fulfillment. He is told, "Be it known to you that the world-to-come was made only for the righteous, and that Israel at the present time [seeing that they do not keep the laws] are unable to bear either too much prosperity or too much suffering." He is not, however, to be persuaded or dissuaded too much. If he is accepted, he is circumcised forthwith. In the case of a woman proselyte . . . [she immerses in water] . . . and given instruction in some of the minor commandments and some of the major ones.

Maimonides crystallizes the presentation to the convert[2] in these words:

> We speak to this convert on the following themes:
> - "Do you not know that the Jews in these times are oppressed . . . ?"
> - We inform them of the foundations of the religion—the oneness of God and the prohibition of idolatry. And we elaborate on this subject.
> - And we inform them of a few of the minor mitzvot and a few of the major mitzvot, but we do not elaborate on this.

- And we inform them of the punishment for [the violation of] the mitzvot . . . but we do not elaborate on it and we do not go into specifics.
- And as we inform them of the punishments, so we inform them of the rewards for [keeping] the mitzvot . . . and we elaborate on this in order to make them beloved [to the convert].

Based on these selections from the Talmud and Maimonides, the following is the skeletal classic structure of the teachings required to be learned by the convert, and upon which the following chapters elaborate:

1. The fundamentals of the Jewish conception of God. These should be taught at a level appropriate to the intellectual capacity of the convert, just as the book of Proverbs insists that one must teach a youngster "according to *his own* way." These teachings need to demonstrate the nature of the Jewish rejection of Jesus as a son of God, a prophet, a Messiah, and as an intermediary between God and man. The idea and personhood of Jesus are so universally ingrained in contemporary culture, let alone in specific Christian teachings, that their total repudiation by Judaism constitutes the one most difficult concept for converts to accept. There are Jews today who are fully observant, having converted twenty-five years earlier, who confide that they sometimes cannot forget that single aspect of their former religion.

2. The nature of idolatry and its prohibition. This places special emphasis on the differences between Judaism and the major religions and cults. Idolatry, in Jewish thought, is historically considered the primary moral and religious evil of the world; in Jewish literature, idolatrous rituals and practices are most often bracketed with orgiastic sexual practices, adultery and murder.

3. Reward and punishment in Judaism: the consequence of transgressing the laws for which the convert will now become liable—such as desecrating God's name—and the promised recompense for keeping them.

4. The obligation to give charity as it is defined, for example, in the laws of the farmer leaving the sheaves, the gleanings, and the corner of his field for the poor and strangers.

5. The major commandments, both positive and negative,

ethical and ritual—such as the study of Torah, prayer, the Sabbath and Holy Days, love of neighbor, acts of holiness, dietary laws, ritual family purity, interpersonal relationships, the symbols that mark the Jewish calendar and life passages, those that apply to one's home and community and even to one's clothing, and the bans on slander and prohibited sexual dalliance.

In this generation, we need to add to this sparse outline the following subjects which, although not explicitly suggested by the classic authorities, are vital in order to facilitate participating in Judaism today:

6. A reading knowledge of Hebrew, the language in which the Jew traditionally prays, which is necessary both for fluent prayer and as a key to the most important treasures of the Jews. No amount of persuasion will draw converts to the synagogue if they are not able to participate intelligently and equally. Acquiring a knowledge of key concepts, significant phrases, and familiarity with the prayerbook should also be stressed. The very first obligation to confront the convert, upon alighting from immersing in the mikveh and becoming a Jew, is prayer. How will the convert fulfill this very first obligation to pray?

7. The history of Jewish ideas and the life stories of the main teachers of the law are important to understanding the roots of Jewish belief and to give resonance to the faith.

8. Jewish history, its triumphs and defeats, in both Israel and the diaspora. This is the biography of our ancestors. It is appropriate, after all, for anyone interested in "joining the family" to study its genealogy.

9. Also vital to an understanding of the contemporary Jew, in addition to knowing its general history, is understanding and being sensitized to two of the most significant historical events of the last two millennia—the Nazi Holocaust and the rise of the independent State of Israel.

10. A knowledge of the Jewish community and its structure is recommended because the Sinaitic Covenant is not only the act ratified at Mt. Sinai which is the expression of the vertical relationship with God. It is also the horizontal connection with fellow Jews that stems from the earlier

thrust of the Sinaitic Covenant at the exodus from Egypt. Not only does the convert need community to embody and support personal religious practice, the Jewish community needs the periodic injection of vital and zestful newcomers to Judaism.

EXPERIENCE NEEDED

The most effective method of instruction in Judaism, as we have consistently maintained, is experiential. For several months prior to formal admission into the Jewish people, the prospective convert should try to live as an observant Jew: study personally and with a friend, attend adult lectures, pray at home and at synagogue, and celebrate the Sabbaths and Holy Days by keeping traditions such as lighting candles. Converts should make every effort to visit Jewish institutions— from the Jewish kitchen to the Jewish Federation—so as to better grasp the quality of Jewish living. That will be the beginning of a beginning.

Notes to Chapter Nineteen

1. Yevamot 47a, b.
2. Maimonides, *Mishneh Torah,* Hilkhot Issurei Bi'ah, ch. 14.

20
Who Are We?

Before proceeding to outline the ideals and practices of Judaism, it is well that we introduce ourselves. Who, after all, are the Jews?

We will tell you what we believe, who our God is, what He asks of us, how we respond to Him, what our goals and practices are, and why the Jews are chosen to be both the bearers of an everlasting mission and the objects of a perpetual prejudice.

We, the people of Israel, are the descendants of the Patriarchs—Abraham, Isaac and Jacob—and of the Matriarchs—Sarah, Rebecca, Rachel and Leah—whom God chose and with whom He struck His everlasting covenant. They who spoke with God and deeply believed in His Providence molded the future of the Jewish people. We are well over three thousand years old, but we have been promised by God an unlimited future, "the seed of eternity has He planted within us," and we strive to remain faithful to the faith of our ancestors.

After successive famines in the land of Canaan, at approximately 1500 B.C.E.—a land God promised to Abraham and his progeny in perpetuity—Jacob descended into Egypt where his son, Joseph, had become viceroy. Two centuries later, a Pharoah who "knew not Joseph" enslaved the Jews and drowned their first-born sons for fear they would grow and prosper and eventually overthrow the monarchy. God then redeemed the Jews from this slavery in exile and brought them out into the desert. There, at the foot of Mt. Sinai, God revealed

Himself in a mystic experience which changed the history of the world. Moses, the Jews' greatest prophet, was taught the Torah and its interpretation, and brought down the tablets on which were engraved the Ten Commandments. God had first struck His covenant with Abraham and now made a reciprocal, binding covenant, formally and publicly, with all the Jewish people at Mt. Sinai.

After the redemption from Egypt and the Revelation at Sinai, the Jews crossed the desert toward the Promised Land, but they could not cope with their newfound freedom, the sheer abundance of food, the clouds that guided and protected them by day and by night; and they pockmarked their march with recalcitrance and rebelliousness, with failures and futilities. Even after a number of miraculous interventions by God in their behalf, they yet doubted that He could lead them safely into Canaan and, for their lack of faith, were doomed to die in a forty-year, aimless meandering in the desert. The children of a new age arose and, with the help of God and the leadership of Joshua, conquered the land that they were promised. The People of Israel, the Torah of Israel and the Land of Israel, all elected by God, were now united.

Our ensuing history is the story of the alternating dismemberment and consolidation of this triad of God's elect—of the people keeping the Torah and prospering in the land, then forgetting the Torah, virtually self-destructing, being exiled from the land and then returning in spiritual triumph. It is a bewildering series of upward climbing to monumental heights and repeated stumbling into bottomless gorges of the spirit; of being exiled from the land and returning; being punished and being rewarded; of Temples built and destroyed and rebuilt and destroyed again; of awesome contributions to the ideals and hopes of civilization, and of awful sufferings which perpetually tugged at the Jew, urging him to give up the whole enterprise of the Abrahamic faith, the Mosaic Law, and the prophetic mission. It is a dynamic and creative march through the generations, of prophets and priests, scholars and scribes, rabbis and judges, of peddlers and financiers, over-achievers and common folk, of numerous students and a handful of warriors.

We lost masses of people during the long, dark centuries of wandering—especially during the 1,900-year exile since the annihilation of the Temple and Jerusalem in the year 70 C.E. But Judaism—the Torah, the Land of Israel, the chosen people—survived, redeemed always by the outstretched hand of God who gives and takes away—and gives back.

We Jews characteristically take pride in our heritage, though not always do we keep it faithfully. We believe ourselves to be heirs to a glorious tradition that we consider the most magnificent in the annals of mankind. In our bones is the marrow of prophets and philosophers. In our veins courses the blood of Sages like Hillel and Rabbi Akiva, of Rashi and Maimonides, of martyrs and saints, of teachers and thinkers, pioneers and heroes. In our hearts beats the rhythm of the hammers of the great builders of two Holy Temples, a Holy Land, an immortal culture, of synagogues and schools and institutions of philanthropy. It is not too difficult for most of us to believe that the people who chose God were chosen by God.

There are salient lessons to be learned from our history.

First, the Jews originate as a family which then grows into nationhood. This is important not only as a curious sociopolitical fact, but as a basis for the Jewish ethic. It undergirds the idea of *ahavat ha'rea*, the love of neighbor, of fellow Jews, of all upright people, as family members. As the love of family goes beyond the uniting factors of common backgrounds and shared goals, but is a meta-logical existential bonding, so we are to love others because they are created in the image of God, the Father. To this day this nation of Jews is called, the "House of Israel."

Second, this family grows not only by the natural increase of blood relatives but by those who "marry" into it and consider themselves part of the family—converts who espouse the idea of God and Torah and cleave to this people. They have enriched and increased the original family of Jews.

Third, unlike other peoples, the Jewish people became a nation at the moment it achieved freedom, before it had a land, when it bolted from Egypt two generations before conquering the Promised Land. The simple fact that the Jews were drawn together by ideas *before* they were land based may well be the engine that generated their ability to survive during centuries of homelessness *after* they left the land, when they possessed only a Torah in common.

Fourth, this family that grew into a nation, was chosen by God, as were its land and its Law, to serve as testimony to His moral law on earth and to bring to civilization the concepts of the brotherhood of man and the family of nations. By being chosen they bore the burden of peoplehood before they experienced the pleasures and security of nationhood.[1]

THE CHOSEN PEOPLE IDEA

It is important to understand the Jewish people from the point of view not only of God's description—"first among the nations"—but of their self-definition. The "Chosen" people is how the Jew has defined himself from the dawn of Jewish history. This emerged as a potent factor in the Jew's survival. In the Middle Ages, when he was reduced to labor as a lowly serf, he firmly believed that he, not the feudal lord, was elected by God. This gave him the inner strength to resist being subdued by more numerous and powerful conquerors. Jewish history is the only lasting record written from the viewpoint of the vanquished.

This notion of chosenness was recognized to be so formidable that it could not simply be dismissed or "fulfilled" by a protesting and revolutionary Christianity that sought to overtake it. The concept was therefore co-opted by the emerging faith which proceeded to teach that it had supplanted the "old" chosen people, the Jews, and that from then on it was the God's elect. It was this attitude more than anything else which divided, and continues to divide, the two faiths. The very idea that the confessors of Christianity claim to be "the true Israel of God"[2] implies the utter rejection of the Jews and the revocation of God's eternal covenant—and this is unthinkable, even absurd, and therefore anathema to the Jewish people.

That the "daughter" faith had to prove its own worth by negating the validity of the "mother" religion from which it derived virtually all of its spiritual DNA was extraordinary and tragic.[3] This stratagem might be understandable for the apostles in ancient times wishing to seek validity for a new order. What is unfortunate is that it remains *to this day* a major preachment of ministers everywhere. Judaism in the late twentieth century in the United States is still unblinkingly referred to as "the religion of death."[4]

This same pattern was used not only for the people but for Torah. The new religion needed to supersede Torah, which it did by a creating "new" covenant, or testament, which was said to replace the "old" testament. Indeed, to confirm the validity of a "new" testament, the "old" was said to have been given by God only in order to presage the "New Testament."

Steadfastly, however, whether from prison cells, flogging stocks, or cattle cars, Jews refused to succumb to any declaration that in any way hinted that the covenant God made with Abraham, Isaac and Jacob was not uniquely the Jewish covenant, that their Torah did not have eternal validity, and that "the true Israel of God" were not the Jews who assiduously worship the "true God of Israel." The fact of Judaism's endurance despite this continuous calumny; and the fact that despite persistent persecutions the Jews have contributed so mightily to the moral structures of civilization; and that despite a Holocaust that annihilated one third of the global Jewish population, they succeeded in returning to the Holy Land reinvigorated rather than exhausted, is deathless testimony to their election by an Almighty, All-Wise, and All-Powerful God.

THE JEWS—FEW, BUT FOREVER

One of the proofs adduced by the new religion that the Jews were no longer the chosen people is that they had no homeland and have been wandering since the beginnings of Christianity[5]— an assumption that has strained the imagination of the Christian theological establishment, especially since 1948 and the re-creation of the independent State of Israel.

In truth, history and demography do provide us with a striking profile of who we are and who we were as we wandered homelessly over the entire globe for centuries, and how we responded to the challenges we continually encountered in order to survive as a people. While there can be no doubt that many of our folk simply opted out of the family, a substantial majority of Jews clung tenaciously to God's bidding in the face of daunting penalties.

Forty centuries ago, Judaism began as a minority of one and, until today, it has virtually never achieved a numerical superiority. Even in modern day Israel, its majority status is constantly threatened by a burgeoning Arab population. Surely, there is no nation that has withstood such massive assaults and yet rebounded with such remarkable vitality—as though persecution were the very engine of its survival driving it ever more determinedly to attain greater heights. Today, the Jews number thirteen million out of a world population of five and one half billion, constituting only one quarter of one percent of humanity![6]

The threat that challenges the Jewish people comes not only from its small numbers, but from the conditions of its existence. While the Jews lived in their homeland, they clung precariously to a narrow strip of land along the eastern shore of the Mediterranean—valued because of its geography as the nexus of Europe, Asia and Africa, not for its resources.

The Jewish people lived in its homeland for only a small fraction of its history. The period from the conquest of Joshua until the destruction of the First Temple lasted six hundred years. The Second Commonwealth began by permitting Jews to return to Palestine. It ended with the destruction of the Second Temple by the Romans in the year 70 C.E.—another period of six hundred years. To this may be added a further one hundred and fifty years, during which Palestine continued to be the spiritual center of world Jewry, until it was eclipsed by Babylonia.

Jewish independence was even more short-lived. In the biblical era, Jewish independence lasted four centuries, from the days of Saul to the destruction of the First Temple in the post-biblical era, a little less than eighty years from the proclamation of Jewish independence by Simon the Maccabee in 142 B.C.E. until the seizure of Palestine by the Roman general Pompeii in 63 B.C.E. In total, the Jewish people lived in its homeland for less than one-third of its history, and enjoyed independence for less than one-eighth of its existence.[7]

The Jewish exile was equally remarkable: They preceded the very formation of the nations that constitute "the old world." There were Jews in Spain before there were Spaniards; in France centuries before the emergence of a French national group; in Germany for centuries before the creation of the German Empire. The Jews were aliens everywhere, but citizens nowhere, and their existence was by sufferance, not by right— at the whim of kings or the Church, as their presence seemed useful at any given time. When they outlived their material usefulness, as when they had successfully created a middle class for Charlemagne in France in the ninth century, they were unceremoniously expelled; thank you and goodbye.

BUT THE JEW SURVIVED

The self-recognition of the Jews as "Chosen" is not an elitist design to bolster Jewish pride, but the only device capable of translating Divine Revelation into human terms. This the Jewish people accomplished not by Crusades or Holy Wars, but imperceptibly by precept and example. All the while, however, they had to shoulder the burden of being suffering servants, bearing persecution with infinite patience. Anti-Semitism is the other side of chosenness. God chose the Jews for leading; haters chose the Jews for whipping.

Why hate the Jews? In whatever way thinkers may choose to rationalize it, at bottom, the battering of the Jews is a revolt against the God of the Jews. This was the common wisdom of all the generations until the modern age brought anti-Semitism new disguises couched in sophisticated concepts that obfuscate rather than reveal. For example, that it is a manifestation of xenophobia, that the world is in perpetual need of a scapegoat, or that it is simply old-fashioned racism.

Although such conjectures undoubtedly contain a modicum of truth, the predominant motivation for the hatred of Jews is—Judaism. The Talmud long ago noted: "It is a commonly known law: Esau hates Jacob." A simple, contemporary illustration: the breakup of Eastern European communism. After World War II, there were many Polish cities where not a single Jew remained from the masses who were gassed there during the Nazi Holocaust. In 1989, after freedom was miraculously achieved, anti-Semitism returned in all its virulent force. There were no Jews left at all, but somehow, in the "air," Judaism still lingered! How do such people express their hatred? Where there are no living Jews, the Jew-haters vandalize Jewish corpses. It is reminiscent of the amputated leg syndrome: even though the leg is removed, it continues to pain. The Rabbis linked the word Sinai, the mountain from which the Torah was given, with *sin'ah*, hatred—from the moment the Torah was brought down from Heaven upon Sinai, sin'ah descended upon the Jews.[8]

In this chapter we attempted to chisel a small window into the House of Israel to give the convert a quick glimpse into who we are. Naturally, there is no way at all even to scan Jewish theology, mysticism and history, the loves and fears of the people, their strengths and weaknesses, in one short chapter.

A convert once approached Hillel, the great Sage of the second century B.C.E. and asked to be taught all of Torah while standing on one foot. Hillel answered: " 'Love your neighbor as yourself'; all the rest is commentary. Go and learn."

Go and learn.

Notes to Chapter Twenty

1. See Herman Wouk, *This is My God* (a Touchstone Book, Simon & Schuster, Inc., New York, 1959), for a fuller description of these ideas.
2. Galatians 6:16.
3. Trude Weiss-Rosmarin, *Judaism and Christianity,* pp. 99 ff. (Jonathan David Publishers, Middle Village, New York, 1972), says: "By some strange hermeneutics, Paul 'proved' that the Jews are the descendants of Abraham's son by Hagar, the slave girl, while those who believe in Jesus are the true descendants of Isaac and the recipients of the blessings promised to him. The Christian dogma of the 'chosenness' of the church, in place of the 'chosen people' of the 'Old Covenant,' is central in Christianity; it consistently asserts that it is 'the true Israel of God' and that 'the natural Israel' has been superseded."
4. II Corinthians 3:6.
5. This view is that of 17th-century Cardinal Newman in his classic, *Grammar of Assent*.
6. See the Introduction to Robert Gordis' *Judaism in a Changing World* for a trenchant and encyclopedic overview of this aspect of Jewish history. His figure of the fraction of Jews in the world is erroneously stated as six-thousandths of one percent, four times lower than the actual figure, although he is not that far off, considering that he wrote the essay in the 1960s.
7. *Ibid.*
8. See Dennis Prager and Joseph Telushkin, *Why the Jews?* pp. 21-22 (Simon & Shuster, Inc., New York, 1983), for an excellent summary of this point.

21
Who Is Our God?

Judaism is based upon a set of beliefs which has become the possession of all mankind, not of Jews alone. Upon these beliefs, largely, is built the whole structure of western religion as we know it today. Each religion has introduced certain fundamental changes upon which it bases its uniqueness and from which it derives much of its energy. Generally speaking, in these religions, whether one does or does not hold one of the axioms to be true determines whether that person will be considered a member of the faithful. Beliefs associated with religion are commonly assumed to be dogmas—doctrinal tenets, the denial of which constitutes heresy.

Judaism, unlike other faiths, does not invest this degree of significance in "right beliefs." Judaism does not have dogmas in this conventional sense, as does Christianity. Its emphasis has been, and always will continue to be, on practice. It is not the condition of one's belief that renders a person a faithful Jew so much as the condition of one's practice.

But this does not mean that Judaism does not have fundamental principles which are axiomatic and considered critical to right belief. Surely it does, and this chapter outlines them. Naturally, the space available in such a volume, written primarily to elucidate the conversion protocol rather than the content of Judaism, is so limited that it must focus only on those principles which the Rabbis of the Talmud and the Codes have considered imperative for the convert to understand.

Following is the most important of the lists of such tenets. This formulation of the articles of faith is from Moses Maimonides (1135-1204) and is included in his commentary to the Mishnah.

THIRTEEN ARTICLES OF FAITH

1. Belief in the existence of God.
2. Belief in God's unity.
3. Belief in God's incorporeality.
4. Belief in God's eternity.
5. Belief that God alone is to be worshipped.
6. Belief in prophecy.
7. Belief in Moses as the greatest of the prophets.
8. Belief that the Torah was given by God to Moses.
9. Belief that the Torah is immutable.
10. Belief that God knows the thoughts and deeds of men.
11. Belief that God rewards and punishes.
12. Belief in the advent of the Messiah.
13. Belief in the resurrection of the dead.

At the end of this listing, Maimonides comments:

> When all these principles are in the safe keeping of man and his conviction of them is well established, he then enters "into the general body of Israel," and it is incumbent upon us to love him, to care for him, and to do for him all that God commanded us to do for one another in the way of affection and brotherly sympathy. And this, even though he were to be guilty of every transgression possible, by reason of the power of desire or the mastery of the base natural passions. He will receive punishment according to the measure of his perversity, but he will have a portion in the world-to-come, even though he be of the "transgressors in Israel." When, however, a man breaks away from any of these fundamental principles of belief, then of him it is said that "he has gone out of the general body of Israel," and "he denies the root truth of Judaism. . . ."

The principal belief in Judaism is, of course, the belief in God. But it is not God's existence primarily that is important, but what He does, what He expects from man, how He responds to man's actions.

THE JEWISH IDEA OF GOD

Before considering the obligations of Jewish practice, the non-Jew will want to take "first things first." To him or her, this will mean grappling with the Jewish conception of God.

In the Jewish world, this probably would not be the first thing to ponder. Jews, by and large, have followed the Bible in this. Standing at the foot of Mt. Sinai and being presented with the tablets of the Law, the people responded, "We will do and we will hear," placing action before comprehension. Although this runs counter to common wisdom that demands we understand something before we undertake to do it, a cardinal belief of the Jews is that since the Torah is God-given, *Torah min ha'Shamayim*, if God mandates an action, one had better do it first and comprehend afterward. Tradition repeatedly lauds this instinctive religious response and records that the Jews have been rewarded in many ways for this ancient declaration of priority by an appreciative God.

Now, while this might appear strange to non-Jews, the existence of God in biblical thought is virtually taken for granted and a belief in Him is not therefore a primary religious agenda item—it is the fundamental assumption underlying all other assumptions. Even today, there are few sermons preached about God, and there are fewer articles or books written by Jews about God than virtually any other religious subject. The first question Jews might ask, therefore, would be "What does God's existence mean to me?" or "Does He relate to me now?" or "What does this belief require of me in my daily life?"

Why many Jews maintain their belief in God as an unspoken assumption, or even hypothesis, without continually agonizing over the many philosophic and scientific dilemmas it poses, is that God has been a Jewish "possession," a sort of family heirloom, since Abraham. He has been the most prominent feature of the emotional, spiritual, and intellectual landscape from the very beginning under every regime and in every scholastic climate. The Jewish people introduced the idea of

God to the civilized world. They are often described as a God-intoxicated people. The common Jewish cry when facing personal trouble was *mammenyu*, Mother! then *tattenyu*, Father! and—when all else failed—*Gottenyu*, God!

It was therefore, for one thing, more "natural" for Jews to believe in God. Indeed, it is more difficult to claim, as does the atheist, that the complex universe is somehow the consequence of a fortuitous combination of atoms and molecules. If an unauthored, unplanned, unforeseen "big bang" could indeed have created the colossus of this physical universe, is it reasonable to believe that this chance occurrence could also have created the human mind? art? music? science itself? human self-sacrifice?

For another, in an atheist's *anschauung*, could life hold transcendent meaning? If it cannot, could life as we know it be lived—if it were meaningless in ultimate terms? And, if the human being cannot live without ultimate, transcendent meaning, is it reasonable to believe that the universe was created without a meaningful purpose? And can ethics and morality be justified in only earthly terms, without an anchor beyond humanity?

Naturally, intellectual problems always arise when a proposition cannot be proved conclusively by some mathematical formula or some irrefutable scientific evidence. Those who do not believe in God will have ready answers for the concerns just enumerated. But the most agonizing problems do not arise from theoretical ruminations. They come from existential crises. When a person faces unexpected and apparently unjust suffering and questions the justice of the God who Judaism taught the world is good and just, then Judaism must respond to that agony.

The history of Jewish literature shows only peripheral concern over the intellectual problems connected with the existence of God—but, since Job, laymen as well as scholars and students have agonized over the existential crises related to suffering. God's people apparently appeased themselves with the self-evident proposition that the world is unthinkable without Him, despite the fact that His works often elude our comprehension.

The philosophic and theological underpinnings of the Jewish conception of God will need to be studied in specific texts. What follows is the God-idea looked at from a *popularized, common-sense appreciation of the role of God in the Jewish mind-set*. These chapters are intended only to establish the framework of Jewish knowledge.

Because this book is directed to the convert candidate's non-Jewish orientation, it will consider the concept of God as the first of things. What follows, then, is an overview of these axioms, necessarily very brief and touching only on major themes.[1]

God is One

Monotheism, authentic and uncompromising, is a deeply in-grained, self-evident proposition to Jews. Indeed, the purity of Jewish monotheism is one of the hallmarks of the faith. Throughout history, Jews have resisted—often with their very lives—the dilution, diminution or modification of that exalted idea. While Christianity is considered a monotheistic faith, in Jewish eyes it does not adhere to the pure and undiluted monotheism of Judaism. Abraham Carmel, the former Catholic Priest who converted to Judaism in the 1950s, noted that it can take centuries for Christians to unlearn trinitarian ideas and appreciate the monotheism of the Jews.

The convert needs to understand the Jewish One God concept, especially as it differs from other religious conceptions of God. In the experience of many rabbis, the idea that Jesus is *not* the son of God or the Messiah or a prophet is the most difficult Jewish teaching to convey effectively to converts, especially those who had an intensive Christian upbringing. This idea fades slowly from the heart, and much time and effort must be expended in order to place it in proper perspective. It cannot be left as a problem area that ultimately will be solved by being dissolved in the experience of Jewish living.

God is the Creator

In Jewish teachings, God is not an abstraction residing comfortably above the clouds, but a vibrant, continuously involved God whose creative energy is constantly at work in the Universe, as Creator, Judge and Redeemer. "In the beginning, God created the heavens and the earth" (Genesis I:1). In words of matchless beauty and timeless grandeur, the Torah proclaims that the universe is not a product of chance, of an accidental collocation of atoms, but the purposeful handiwork of a Creator. This idea, with which the Bible opens, cuts through the murky haze of ancient mythology like a shaft of sunlight. When God reveals Himself, He reveals Himself as the Creator. "I am God, I make all things" (Isaiah 44:24).

God is the Judge

In addition to being the Creator, Judaism proclaims that He is Judge of the world He created, charging human beings to keep the laws of morality with the same tenacity with which they must, willy-nilly, keep His laws of nature. No sooner does man begin to understand God as the Creator than Abraham, the first Patriarch of the Jewish people and the teacher of the God-idea to the world, confronts God as the Judge of the universe He created: "Shall not the Judge of all the world do justice?" (Genesis 18:25). In this verse early in the Torah, there is already assumed the indomitable conviction that "the world is not ownerless" with no one to care or be concerned about what is happening to it. There is no event and no moment in human history over which God does not preside as Judge.

God is the Redeemer of Mankind

God is not only the Creator of the universe who judges it in accordance with His laws, He also intervenes in history and changes it when it needs to be redeemed. Thus God, with "outstretched hand," redeems His people from Egypt, without the people's effort and against inconceivable human odds. God's purpose in judging individuals and nations is not vindictive, but rather redemptive—to reclaim humanity from its distress for its own ultimate happiness and betterment.

He is a Personal God

Despite the Jewish insistence on the pure spirituality of God, He has been a living and vital reality to Jews throughout the ages. The Jew conceives Him as a *personal God*, but never as becoming a *person*.

An important, subtle distinction should not be lost here: belief in a *personal God* is based on the conviction that the Lord of the Universe, though unimaginably superior to man—his Creator and his Judge—is yet near and accessible to him. He is described in one verse as "the Lord of Hosts, the world is filled with His glory," implying that while God is Lord of the Hosts of Heaven, yet His glory manifests itself on the clay of earth. This belief obviates any need of transforming Him into a person, as Christianity has done, in order to communicate with Him. The Rabbis say that although God "is exalted above His world, still, when a man enters the House of Prayer, stands beside a pillar and prays in a whisper, the Holy One, Blessed be He, will hear his prayer . . . for God is as near to his creatures as the mouth to the ear."[2] When God introduces Himself in the Ten Commandments as "*thy* God," it is in order to teach that "He is the God of every man, woman and child."

Therefore, History is Meaningful

Because God continuously creates, judges and redeems people, and because He is a personal God, what people do in their lives holds significance—for themselves and for God. God reacts to reward or punish, redeem or abandon them. People are not feathers swept hither and thither by random winds; events are not the product of chaos or the interplay of blind forces. History is meaningful; it matters. Life is dynamic—a constant interplay between God and man, a drama that unfolds itself through people's actions and God's judgment.

One obvious implication of the idea of Divine purpose is to render fatalistic beliefs incompatible with the belief in God. God being in control of life, there are no random happenings in an uncontrolled process, indiscriminately dealing out haphazard fortunes to men. A throw of the dice, a black cat, a particular configuration of events or cluster of related deaths cause nothing to happen and are not predictive of God's decree.

The Human Being Counts

Judaism, from the very outset, has declared the human being to be a *shuttaf* (a partner), a co-worker with God, in the enterprise of creation endowed with a capacity to control, shape and direct things in his own life.

The Jewish contribution is best demonstrated by picturing a puppet show. The pagans viewed life as fatalistic—man is bound by fetters, a puppet totally controlled by the puppeteer's strings operated from above. The biblical revolution declared that man has freedom of the will and thereby severed the puppet strings—that is, there are indeed superior forces exerted by God above, but the human being is capable, to a large extent, of being the architect of his own destiny. The Kabbalah, Jewish mysticism, then introduced an even more radical understanding of the nature of the God-man relationship. The strings between puppeteer and puppet in fact are attached—but the puppet is pulling the strings![3] The human being, in this view, actually has it in his power to change cosmic reality.

The Sages taught that individuals should conceive of the fate of the world as hanging in the balance, so that each person's actions make the difference between failure and fulfillment on a global scale. Further, God is in constant search for man to fulfill the tasks God has set for him as His partner: to complete the world, to repair it, to utilize his free will so as to make the world a better place. Only as man bears testimony to God, Isaiah avers, is God truly God.

God is Unknowable, but . . .

Now, God is unique—absolutely unlike anything else that exists—and therefore *outside* the experience of human beings. His essence cannot be defined, because any definition would "limit" Him by using terms explicitly *within* human experience. Jewish thinkers teach that we may glimpse God's essence only through what we know in human terms He definitely is *not*. These are called negative attributes. From them, we have learned to deduce the nature of God: He is one, unique in all existence, the One and Only God, besides Whom there is no other; He is Incorporeal and Eternal; He is All-Powerful and All-Knowing.

The function of these philosophic concepts about God, however, is not primarily to achieve more wisdom but to modify practice. They affect people's view of their own lives and teach them what is reasonable to expect and not to expect of God, and how to act in accordance with His wishes as Creator, Judge and Redeemer.

Thus, His *eternity* is a guarantee that His purpose, however delayed, will in the end prevail; His *omnipotence* is a guarantee of the ultimate triumph of His eternal purpose; His *omniscience* is a guarantee that no thought, word or deed, can escape His judgment or circumvent the ultimate realization of His purpose; His *incorporeality* is absolute, else it would compromise His freedom to make physical changes in the universe as He determined they were needed.

The *unity of God* is positively "simple" and excludes such concepts as the Christian idea of the Trinity. It precludes, absolutely and unequivocally, the need for any intermediary between God and man, as that would compromise His uniqueness. God's voice resonates so loudly in Judaism because it does not get filtered through any other being. Any person can appeal directly to the Creator for his or her own needs.

Tracing God's Actions

Although God is essentially unknowable, except through deductions from His negative attributes, the person can detect what He is like by the acts we attribute to Him. The analogy is to one who cannot locate a person, but then decides to trace his footsteps in the sand, from which he learns the direction, the approximate weight and size of the person, and can then set out to find him.

These acts of God have been communicated in a special theophany to Moses in which God revealed Himself as a "merciful Being, gracious, slow to anger, abundant in loving-kindness and truth, keeping loving-kindness to a thousand generations, forgiving iniquity, transgression and sin, but who will by no means clear the guilty." (Exodus 34:7).

These qualities do not describe the Essence of God, but His dealings with man. They have been communicated as norms of conduct to man: "As He is merciful, so be thou merciful; as He is compassionate, so be thou compassionate; as He is abundant in loving-kindness, so be thou abundant in loving-kindness" (Shabbat 133b).

We are capable of knowing God because God intervenes in history, in the operation of His universe, and we can trace His footsteps, as it were, in the sands of our earth. One of the effects of this is to spur human beings "to walk in His ways," to comply with His moral demands. God's involvement in world history serves to reward good and punish evil.

REWARD AND PUNISHMENT

The belief in Divine Retribution—Reward and Punishment—is a cardinal belief of Judaism. The Rabbis of the Talmud incorporated this principle in the required studies for converts so that these new Jews would understand the consequences of their actions in advance of their commitment to keep the mitzvot.

An early reference to *punishment* is found in the Talmud:[4]

> Know that everything is according to reckoning, and let not your imagination give you hope that the grave will be the place of refuge for you, for perforce you were formed, and perforce you were born, and you live perforce, and you will die perforce, and perforce you will in the future have to give account and reckoning before the Supreme King of Kings, the Holy One, Blessed be He.

A description of spiritual *reward* comes from Maimonides in the thirteenth century:[5]

> Know that just as a blind man can form no idea of colors, nor a deaf man comprehend sounds . . . so the body cannot comprehend the delights of the soul. Even as fish do not know the element of fire because they exist always in its opposite, so the delights of the world of spirit are unknown in this world of flesh. Indeed, we have no pleasure in any way except what is bodily, and what the sense can comprehend of eating, drinking. . . . Whatever is outside these is non-existent to us. We do not discern it, neither do we grasp it at first thought, but only after deep penetration. And truly this must necessarily be the case. For we live in a material world and the only pleasure we can comprehend must be material. But the delights of the spirit are everlasting and uninterrupted, and there is no resemblance in any possible way between spiritual and bodily enjoyments.

Goodness for Goodness' Sake

Clearly, it is a major religious value to do the will of God "for the sake of Heaven," without needing to be compensated or penalized. "The reward of a mitzvah is a mitzvah, the punishment of a sin, sin" (Ethics of the Fathers 4:2). Nevertheless, throughout the Torah, God does instill a transcendent discipline of both admonition and inducement in the nature of rewards such as good health, many children, abundant harvest, and lasting peace, and also punishments such as disease, war, poverty, and slavery.

Of course, human beings are not capable of envisioning the incredibly complex calculus of the Divine system as a tidy scheme of retributions—else there would be no need for a *belief* in retribution. It would be folly to be wicked knowing that you will pay for it at once and, if it were possible mathematically to compute in advance the extent of the reward or punishment, life would simply be a moral double entry ledger.

Problems in the Belief in Retribution

Problems arise because God's response to man's deeds do not usually occur with immediacy, or in a one-to-one relationship. Not being God, we do not understand His method of retribution or His determination of proportionate justice. This concern is exacerbated by the obvious fact that there are righteous people who suffer while patently immoral ones seem to prosper. Also, on a theoretical basis, people cannot comprehend even the existence of evil created by an omniscient and good God. In addition, some have argued that a religion should not need to base itself on a system of Divine payments for behavior.

Judaism maintains that there is, indeed, a moral demand to do good and refrain from evil for its own sake. Yet, there remains a powerful need for rewarding good works and punishing evil deeds. But people may not apply this pattern automatically—no single person has the moral right to deduce that those who suffer must have done evil and those who prosper acted righteously. It is not possible to justify every disaster, nor to find reason for every good, as the ancient prophets were Divinely enabled to do.

When Bad Things Happen to Good People

How, then, are we to understand the old paradox of the suffering righteous and the prospering wicked? Many have attempted to answer this question, though a conclusive and satisfying answer has been out of reach these many centuries.[6] A response to the apparent injustice of reward and punishment must take into consideration, first, that life on earth is only one phase of man's cycle of existence. The "world-to-come" is spoken of only cryptically by the Torah, but the Sages refer constantly to that time as a settling of accounts, a balancing of the ledger. The very profound questions of theodicy—the justice of the reward and punishment system—compel a belief in the existence of such a world. If there were no next world, good and evil would hold no significance and it would remove a transcendent meaning to our days on this earth. Judaism holds that only our physical life comes to an end when we die; the soul continues to exist.

There is another insight into the apparent imbalance of reward and punishment. It is that some do suffer because of the evils perpetrated by others. While, at first look, this appears to be an immoral posture, it becomes more reasonable because, in fact, there is a human connectedness which no one can or should deny. The Rabbis say that "All Jews are guarantors for one another." The corollary is: "All Jews are liable for one another." This makes the individual responsible for the welfare of the entire community. Indeed, the biblical blessings and curses were issued to the community, not the individual. Ample rain or drought, good crops or bad, the possession of the land or exile, victory or defeat, the presence of the Divine *Shekhinah* or the destruction of the Temple are all matters promised the community and not the individual. Even for those special precepts whose reward the Bible describes expressly, such as length of days for keeping the precept to honor one's father and mother, the reward is linked up with the fate of the people as a whole. The demand made upon the human being is that, although he does not know whether an action will bring immediate reward, every person must strive to improve the condition of others.

While the idea of collective guilt and responsibility may be difficult for some to accept, we should have an even better grasp of this idea in our times when interconnectedness takes on new urgency and significance as communications and air travel have shrunk the world to a global village—Tienanmen Square in China was linked by fax machine to every major city in the world instantaneously. All people today are interlinked and interdependent economically, politically, and also morally. The kind of life we choose to lead is not without repercussions everywhere. It requires neither doctrinal narrowness nor unyielding dogma to understand this aspect of Divine retribution. One need not be a theologian to grasp this; consult any social scientist, attorney or environmentalist and they will demonstrate it.

THERE MAY BE A BETTER WAY OF HANDLING THIS THORNY PROBLEM

We need to understand that the grand, unanswerable questions of life are not logical, but existential, and therefore these problems can often be answered by metaphor and analogy, rather than by reason. In light of modern biological discovery, we should realize that we can satisfy our minds with the insight we derive from the right side of the brain, which deals in metaphor, symbol, pattern; rather than with the left side, which concerns itself with logic, precision, consistency.

This applies to our problem of the Theodicy. I know of no answer that *satisfies* our nagging need to justify God. But, *there is a metaphor, which, while it does not logically answer,* does go a long way in satisfying the mind's quest for insight.

Picture a tapestry hanging in the museum, with its face to the wall, and its reverse side in full view. It is a jumble of divergent threads, a riot of colors of all thicknesses and lengths; strings of every description shooting off in every direction; knots here and there, loose threads everywhere; making no pattern or sense. The viewers at the museum are horrified at this assault on their sensibilities. What can all this mean?

Now tell them that if we *looked at the tapestry from the other side, we would find the most magnificent masterpiece* of the greatest artist ever to have lived. The clutter, the disorder of the tangled mess, is precisely designed to produce, on its face, which we will never see, coherence, meaning, magnificence, glory.

That is how we need to picture the injustices we perceive of good and evil in the world. On the underside of the tapesstry we see the unadorned antinomies of good and evil, and the other persistent paradoxes of religious life, in a logical maelstrom, unreasonably arranged, defying all our senses. Given the Divine view man is incapable of ever understanding, everything would make sense.

This metaphor does not *answer* the question or solve the paradox. But it does give us a hint of an insight into our own limitations and the omniscience of Almighty God.

DEVIATIONS FROM THE JEWISH GOD-IDEA

The convert needs to have not only a Jewish understanding of God, but a clear idea of the differences between Jewish and Christian theology and the attitudes and practices that flow from those differences. This is of central importance to one seeking to convert from Christianity to Judaism and, for that reason, it is insufficient in this context to teach only the Jewish God-idea.[7]

Jesus is Not God

Coming from an environment in which an unspoken assumption is that Jesus is either God Himself, or at least a prophet, it is necessary to affirm that, to Judaism, Jesus is neither God nor a part of a Godhead, that he is not a prophet and emphatically not the Messiah. Some potential converts have cherished these beliefs long before they were consciously aware of the nature of these ideas or their implications.

Christianity formally adopted the belief that Jesus was God at the Council of Nicaea (325 C.E.) when it declared that Jesus, "the Son" was "begotten, not made" and "of one essence [*homoousios*] with the Father." In order to avoid the obvious deduction that this concept must preclude the belief in monotheism, Christianity responded with the trinity idea—that the three parts of God were really one, and one three.

Judaism declares that it is categorically impossible to comprehend a "three-that-are-one" doctrine, insisting that only God is God, and that He is not only one, but unique. Monotheism is strictly that: a belief in one, single God.

And Not His Prophet

A prophet is a messenger of God and, in that capacity, speaks only in behalf of Him who sent him, not on his own authority. The prophets characteristically begin their message with "Thus saith the Lord." Jesus occasionally refers to the Father who sent him, but more often he speaks on his own authority. At times (*e.g.*, Matthew 5:21 ff.) he contrasts what "you have been taught" with what "I say unto you," a contrast that the Jewish mind finds most problematic. The question that arises in the mind of the Jewish reader of the New Testament is: "Who are you?" In all of Judaism, it is God who teaches what is right and what is wrong; the prophets are only messengers and spokesmen. It is true that the Rabbis interpret the Written and Oral Law; they have the authority to legislate additions to the Law. But such additions are clearly recognized as Rabbinic enactments and cannot contradict God's law.

Two noted Jewish writers, Michael Wyschogrod and David Berger, give us succinct, but clear answers:

> Jesus lays down his own teachings, which he does not attribute to God but to himself. While this does not, by itself, signify that Jesus was considered God by the New Testament, it does mean that the New Testament attributes a very special status to Jesus beyond that of the prophets depicted in the Hebrew Bible.
>
> From the Jewish point of view, this belief is idolatrous. The prohibition against idolatry . . . is one of the most severe in Judaism. According to Jewish law, there are only three transgressions which are so severe that, when faced with a choice of transgressing or death, the Jew is commanded to sacrifice his life rather than transgress. One of these is idolatry. It is therefore important for Jews to know that a Jew who believes that Jesus was God in the sense asserted by the Nicene Creed commits idolatry as defined by Jewish law.[8]

Jesus is Not the Messiah

The Greek word *christos* means Messiah, and using either term as an adjective for Jesus is at once a confirmation of the central belief that lies at the heart of the Christian faith, and anathema to everything dear to Judaism.

Was Jesus the Messiah? How can we know whether or not he was? The question seems difficult to answer, but to believing Jews the test is at hand, and the resolution is there for all to see: Did Jesus perform as Judaism expects a Messiah to perform?

The Messiah, in Jewish tradition, is a king descended from the House of David, and is referred to as *Melekh ha'Mashiach*, the Messiah King—an inconceivably great leader of men anointed ("Messiah" means "anointed") to preside over an ideal world in an ideal, messianic age. Has the messianic age come? It is only in terms of this question that we can determine whether he has already arrived or is yet expected.

The Christian scholar, George Foote Moore, describes this age succinctly: "The recovery of independence and power, an era of peace and prosperity, of fidelity to God and his law, of justice and fair-dealing and brotherly love among men, and of personal rectitude and piety."[9]

Has Jesus fulfilled these grand expectations? Has suffering subsided? Have the killing fields been plowed under? Have ethnic hatreds been transformed into brotherly love? The Messiah was supposed to bring peace to the world, make the wolf live peacefully with the lamb, and see to it that "they learn war no more." In nineteen centuries after a supposed Messiah's coming have people yet learned to live in peace? And what happened to the Messiah himself? Now, it does not take great philosophic acumen to perceive this paradox; there were Christians in every century who have grappled with it. How did they decipher it?

> First of all, Jesus was said to have been resurrected. . . . Second, the Bible was examined with the purpose of finding what no one had ever seen there before—evidence that the Messiah would be killed without bringing peace to the world or redemption to Israel. . . . Third, there was the expectation of a second coming, at which time Jesus would carry out the task expected of the Messiah. . . . And, finally, there had to be an explanation for the first coming and its catastrophic end: the Messiah's goal, at least the first time around, was not the redemption of Israel (which had clearly not taken place), but the atonement for original sin, which was seen as a sort of inner redemption.
>
> Please don't misinterpret this as an argument which describes Jesus' disciples as cynical manipulators of religious beliefs. These are beliefs which resulted from powerful psychological and historical pressures and were surely sincere. But an understanding of the process that formed these beliefs should arouse some skepticism, not about the sincerity with which they were held, but about their truth.
>
> The Jewish people have refused to take the easy way out. If the Bible's description of the Messiah has not been fulfilled, *there is only one conclusion to be reached: he has not yet come.* To Jews, who were often subjected to mockery and contempt when asked where their Messiah was, this conclusion was painful, sometimes excruciatingly painful. But an honest facing of the facts made it—and still makes it— inescapable. In adversity and joy, through Holocaust and statehood, Jews faithful to the Torah and the Prophets can

only repeat the words of their forefathers: "I believe with complete faith in the coming of the Messiah and, though he may tarry, I shall wait for him every day, hoping that he will come."[10]

DEALING WITH DOUBT

After this brief survey of the theological principles that underlie the Jewish understanding of God, Reward and Punishment, the Messiah, and Judaism's attitude toward salient Christian dogmas, it would not be astonishing for the convert to close the chapter with a residue of doubt—perhaps a vague feeling of uneasiness with some of the concepts. Doctrinal statements often have a way of arousing as much doubt as they do faith. But honest doubt in those coming to Torah is healthy. It should be considered a challenge and an opportunity, rather than a setback which triggers feelings of resignation or self-criticism. It indicates authentic searching and, while it may prove to be frustrating, it is the inevitable pain of growth.

One could not say of Jewish thinkers, saints, or scholars that they have no unanswered questions or uncertainties. Spiritual and intellectual growth does not imply that we grow until we have no more questions, but that we grow until our questions are of a higher order, more universal in scope, deeper in perception. Great people are those who not only conceive great answers but generate great questions. Doubt is an element in the process of spiritual growth. Faith is not, as some people imagine, one single leap to end all leaps—and then, presto, heaven on earth.

Now, some nagging feelings do arise from self-doubt rather than from intellectual doubt: perhaps it is all built on sand, perhaps I'll never catch on, perhaps it is not important. These are emotions that cannot be disputed, only suffered. They are essentially irrational moods and should be allowed to pass, else they can immobilize our spirits and minds.

However, the convert should never hesitate to ask sincere questions; they are the only road to understanding. Now, not all questions can be answered, and surely not all Jewish people can answer these questions. Some questions may arise from ignorance, but others may be genuinely fundamental questions never considered by those who grew up in the faith and took certain natural assumptions as eternal verities. Some questions may be inherently unanswerable, such as the question of evil—a problem as old as Moses, Job, and Jeremiah.

Rabbi Adin Steinsaltz notes that there is much to be learned here from talmudic method.

> The study of the Oral Torah is largely a matter of posing questions, then answering them. While many are answered immediately, others remain "unresolved," "in need of further study," or "in need of much more study." The problem is that one cannot remain stuck forever on a complex issue; one must move on, setting that issue aside until later, when, as often happens, it may appear in a different light, turn out to be soluble in a different formulation, or cease to be an issue. . . . If people have questions, they deserve to be taken seriously and, if possible, to be answered, but the search for the perfect answer must not be carried to a debilitating extreme. Avoiding that extreme calls for inner clarity, forward momentum, and spiritual maturity."[11]

There are doubts, no doubt, in everyone's mind. Yet experience shows that numerous converts from other religions have found the Jewish doctrines of faith to be marvelously reasonable and easily acceptable, requiring little strain on the imagination. With all that, a "leap" is nonetheless required, and a commitment to the axioms of Torah is prerequisite to undertaking the entire conversion enterprise.

Notes to Chapter Twenty-one

1. A quick survey of these concepts can be found in Isidore Epstein, *The Jewish Way of Life,* ch. VII, published by Edward Goldston, London, 1947. Dr. Epstein was the former principal of Jews' College in London.
2. Jerusalem Talmud, Berakhot 13a.
3. See the brilliant exposition by Shalom Rosenberg in *Good and Evil in Jewish Thought,* ch. VII, Mod Books, Tel Aviv, Israel, 1989.
4. Ethics of the Fathers, IV, 29.
5. Maimonides' Commentary on the Mishnah, Introduction to Sanhedrin X. It is the eleventh of Maimonides' thirteen articles of faith.
6. Aron Barth, *The Modern Jew Faces Eternal Problems,* published by the Religious Section of the Youth and Hechalutz Department of the Zionist Organization, Jerusalem, Israel, 1956. Also see David Birnbaum,

God and Evil, Ktav Publishing House, Hoboken, New Jersey, 1989.

7. Much of what follows is distilled or excerpted from David Berger and Michael Wyschogrod, *Jews and Jewish Christianity,* Ktav Publishing House, Hoboken, New Jersey, 1978, sponsored by the American Jewish Committee.
8. See note 7.
9. G. F. Moore, *Judaism,* part II, p. 324.
10. Berger and Wyschogrod, *loc. cit.*
11. Some of the following thoughts are distilled or excerpted from Adin Steinsaltz, *Teshuvah: A Guide for the Newly Observant,* ch. 7, The Free Press, New York, 1987.

22
What Is Torah?

No word in the Jewish religion is so indefinable and yet so indispensable as the word *Torah.* Torah is the most comprehensive term for the substance of Judaism. Torah is Teaching. Torah is Law. No one can hope to achieve even a minimal appreciation of the Jewish religion without learning, and then reflecting on, the idea of Torah and its place in the life of the Jew. The word is defined in the Forewords and appears in a variety of contexts in every chapter of this book. Its significance is more fully explained in the following pages, but this must be still further expanded upon by gleaning from other sources.

Will Herberg describes the multifaceted brilliance of this crown jewel of world literature:

> It is a book, an idea, a quality of life. It is the Pentateuch; the Bible in all its parts; the Bible and the Rabbinical writings; all writings dealing with revelation; all reflection and tradition dealing with God, man and the world. It is represented as a bride, the "daughter" of God, as a crown, a jewel, a sword; as fire and water; as life, but to those who are unworthy, as poison and death. It is the pre-existent Wisdom or Word of God, present at creation and acting as the "architect" of the creative work. It preserves the world from destruction; without it, all creation would lapse into chaos; it is the harmony and law of the universe. It is all this and much more, for the exaltation of the Torah in Jewish tradition is a theme which no words can exhaust. Torah is the reason man was created. It is the equivalent of the Temple sacrifices.[1]

Torah has been for ages the sum and substance of Jewish scholarship. But it would be utterly wrong to conclude from this emphasis on study that Jewish spirituality runs dry in the sands of intellectualism.

In reality, the study of Torah is something very different. It is an authentic spiritual exercise, the Jewish equivalent of mystical communion with God. Indeed, it is more likely to run into mysticism than into intellectualism, although neither excess is intrinsic to it.

Photo archives from the Warsaw ghetto show a door of an inn that read, "Society of Wagon Drivers for the Study of Talmud in Warsaw." This referred to coachmen who seized a few moments from their work to gather in a group to "nosh" (grab a tasty morsel of) a page of Talmud, as was noted earlier. These were not intellectuals, concerned only with the intricacies of scholastic dialectics; they were deeply religious men thirsting for spiritual refreshment and they found it, as countless generations of Jews before them, in the study of Torah. "Oh, how I love Thy Torah; it is my meditation all day long" (Psalms 119:97). With Torah understood in its fullest sense, this may be taken as the authentic attitude of the believing Jew to Torah. Torah is law—but it is much, much more than law.

Question: What is Law Doing in a Religion?

But what, after all, is a system of law doing in the midst of a religion? Looked at through the eyes of western civilization, law should not function in the arena of faith. Law should be confined to the governance of society, relating to affairs of state; faith should apply to affairs of the soul, the domain of the individual. How then do these widely disparate elements coalesce in Judaism? What is the relation of "faith" to "deed"?

Answer: Man Cannot Live by Faith Alone

Judaism maintains, as a cardinal principle in its approach to religion and to all of life, that faith and deeds are inseparable. Modern man finds this difficult to understand because he has been schooled in a western frame of reference which looks at "religion" solely as a matter of the soul, residing in that which is inward. The emphasis of religion is attitude rather than obedience, belief over action. Judaism considers a person who lives by faith alone—not translated into deeds—to be living with vague, puffy spiritual generalities. To visualize the picture-perfect ideal of an earthly life achieved in the heavens, imagine Immanuel Kant, the German philosopher, walking down Wilhelmstrasse with his hands behind his back and his mind contemplating the firmament. In Christian terms, this setting might change—a monk meditating about the universal God in his tiny cell in a remote mountaintop monastery.

The picture of the Jew, on the other hand, is for all time inscribed on the tablet of his imagination by the narrative in Genesis which portrays Abraham searching for "a righteous man in the center of the city," *tzaddik b'tokh ha'ir*; Jacob building roads and public bathhouses to foster community hygiene in every city he visits; Moses leaving the isolation of Pharoah's palace to enter the fray on behalf of his enslaved people. In Judaism, there is no real question as to the superiority of right action or right intention; its only question is "What is right living?" Healing, helping, concrete betterment have their own intrinsic meaning regardless of the intentions that motivated them. Intention is important, of course, but it can be reflected only in tangible reality. Providing shelter for a homeless teenager has meaning that is independent of the intention behind the deed.

Judaism is averse to spiritual generalities, to looking for meaning in a life detached from doing, as if meaning existed as a separate entity. Its penchant is to convert ideas into deeds, to transform metaphysical principles into patterns for action, to endow the most sublime principles with bearing upon everyday conduct and, conversely, to sanctify the mundane.

But how do we know which deeds are called for? And how do we determine the difference between right and wrong if we are not guided by faith?

The answer is: Keeping the Law.

God's will is given as a gift to man encased in a body of commandments, "to do"s, what Jews call "mitzvot." They constitute the fixed religious standards of action that do not change with every impulse of society. The reasons for these commandments are not often self-evident and go beyond the reach of human beings, although they do depend on the stable understanding and steady interpretation of the teachers of every generation and on their application of these laws to daily realities. The ultimate obligation is not to *believe* in God, but to *do the will* of God.

MITZVAH: THE LEAP OF ACTION

Mitzvah is the irreducible, organic matter of the Jewish religion. In popular usage, it refers simply to "a good deed." But its significance and force stem from its original, formal, and correct usage: *commandment.* God, the issuer of the mitzvah, is the *metzaveh,* He who commands. The engine of Jewish law and observance is the keeping of the mitzvot, the commandments given by God.

By living as Jews, we act out our faith as Jews.

> The Jew is asked to take a leap of action rather than a leap of thought. . . . *Right living is a way to right thinking.*
>
> A mitzvah is an act which God and man have in common. We say: "Blessed art Thou, Lord our God, King of the universe, who has sanctified us with *His* mitzvot." They oblige Him as well as us. Their fulfillment is not valued as an act performed in spite of "the evil drive," but as an act of communion with Him. The spirit of mitzvah is togetherness. We know He is a partner to our act.
>
> The oldest form of piety is expressed in the Bible as walking with God. Only the egotist is confined to himself, a spiritual recluse. In carrying out a good deed, it is impossible to be or to feel alone. To fulfill a mitzvah is to be a partisan, to enter into fellowship with His Will. . . . Mitzvot are not ideals, spiritual entities forever suspended in eternity. They are commandments addressing every one of us . . .".[2]

Doing a mitzvah is not simply doing a "good deed"; it is, in fact, keeping God's law in its specific detail. The will of God is revealed in the mandates of Torah, primarily in the form of the Halakhah.

THE QUINTESSENCE OF JUDAISM: HALAKHAH

Halakhah, like "Torah" itself, is one of Judaism's most important and elusive terms and, without comprehending it, Judaism is not comprehensible. It is, more than any other single entity, the quintessence of Judaism. The candidate studying for conversion needs to appreciate the idea of Halakhah which has no parallel in Christian teaching.

The Torah provides for an oral interpretation that is dynamic and progressive and is absolutely necessary to understanding the written Torah. The Oral Law, is not only an interpretation of the law, but its application to the changing circumstances of reality by logical and traditional principles that the Torah itself establishes. The law is decided by learned rabbis in response to questions put to them by individuals and whole communities, which eventually get enacted and then written down as codes of law. The codes then get studied, interpreted and applied by the same system. These laws, in addition to a variety of regulations and decrees, form the body of the Oral Law.

> What we have then is a system of amendment originating with "the wise" and subject to ratification or annulment by the law-abiding community at large, in a quiet referendum that is continuous and effective. The question straightway arises: who are these "wise," and by what power are they ordained?

> They are the students who receive their *semikha*, ordination, from the heads of the great Yeshivot, the academies of Torah learning, who are not formally elected or officially appointed, but are simply acknowledged by the communities who keep the law. In a sense, then, the community of those who keep the law is the informal supreme court of Judaism. They decide who the religious authorities are. They do this by directing their religious questions to the few scholars in each generation, and by following or not following their rulings. But the Torah has lived on only in their lives and they have passed it on.[3]

FAITH AND LAW:
The Dispute Between Judaism and Christianity

The question of the relative values of law and faith was not and is not simply a matter of opinions. It is a life-and-death problem for both Judaism and Christianity, and the convert needs to understand the profound significance of both before making his or her choice.

In fact, the dispute that originally split Judaism from Christianity is nowhere more conspicuous than in the ideological clash over faith and the law. Judaism resolutely maintained that deed was paramount; that only action could express faith and attitudes. Christianity firmly held that faith was supreme; that deeds enacted as religious observances were inimical to right faith and served to divert man from his ordained goals.

The salient example and root cause of this clash was the persistent assertion by Judaism that a man could never become a Jew without circumcision, which is the mark of the covenant, the external sign of the inner transformation. The new Christians at the turn of the millennium could not expect to convert pagans if they were to insist upon circumcision as an absolute prerequisite. They then proceeded to declare it completely unnecessary, and even counterproductive to the religious life of a Christian, which demanded a man's soul not his practice.

Until this point in the life of the new religion, the Jewish Sages had regarded their views as untenable, absurd, even un-Jewish, but they explicitly considered these Jewish "christians" as sectarians, remaining within the fold of Judaism. Now, with the Christian annulment of the requirement of circumcision, they ruled that rejecting a Torah-required *practice* could not be countenanced and that the endorsers of this idea could no longer be considered within the ambit of the Jewish religion. No longer were they merely backsliding Jews; they were public betrayers who perverted the faith and then abandoned it.

The repudiation of the "Law" and the claim to possess a successor superior to it have been the contentions of Christians from the very beginning. The "good news" of the Apostles was chiefly that the chains of the "Law" had been lifted and superseded by faith.[4] Paul's attacks against the law in Judaism are fundamental to Christianity. The Halakhah (in this case, the law of circumcision) was the first impediment inherited from Judaism and it had to be jettisoned as obsolete and even harmful.[5]

Whereas Judaism holds that ethics and morality are preserved by the law, Christianity contends that they are bludgeoned by the law. The dispute continues to this very day; it is the reason for the canard, glibly repeated by unthinking multitudes of Christians, that the "Old Testament" emphasizes a God of revenge and the "new" one a God of love. That view will not withstand a moment's glance at the history of religious wars, which will quickly demonstrate whether it was law or faith that preserved the spirit of love.

The law, therefore, will forever be the strongest element of contention between Judaism and Christianity, for its existence spells the negation of Christianity and its abrogation the negation of Judaism.

In fact, far from being enslaved by the law, Jews were enamored of it. We cannot take our leave of the subject of Torah without expressing this most characteristic sentiment of Jewish literature—the love of Torah.

You may ask: can a people "love" a law? Yet, that is the exquisite paradox inherent in the concept of Torah—it is respected and studied and feared, while it is loved and embraced and kissed. All at once. There is no good in this world—no ideal, no blessing, no perfection, no glory—unless it is associated with the law. To Jews, the Torah is "light"[6]; it is the "glory of the sons of man"[7]; it is the energizing sap of life for "the dry bones" (Ezekiel 37:4)—which symbolize the "people in whom there is not the sap of the commandment."[8]

The law, so much criticized by its daughter faith as severe and unforgiving and identified with the "dead letter," is *mayim chayim*, refreshing, life-restoring, living waters to Jews; the sweetness of honey and milk, the joy and strength of wine, and the healing power of oil. It is an "elixir of life" that brings healing to all.

Notes to Chapter Twenty-two

1. Will Herberg, *Judaism and Modern Man,* Farrar, Straus and Young, New York, 1956.
2. This section contains a distillation of Professor Abraham Joshua Heschel's writing on the subject of mitzvot, especially his volume *God in Search of Man,* published by Meridian Books, Inc., New York, and the Jewish Publication Society of America, Philadelphia, 1956.
3. Herman Wouk, *This is My God,* Touchstone, Simon & Schuster, Inc., New York, 1959.
4. For a fuller treatment of this theme in a succinct form, see Trude Weiss-Rosemarin, *Judaism and Christianity,* Jonathan David Publishers, Middle Village, New York, 1972.

5. Galatians 2, 4.
6. Proverbs 6:23; Megillah 16b.
7. Derekh Eretz Zuta 75.
8. Sanhedrin 92b.

23
Jewish Time

YEARS, MONTHS, WEEKS AND DAYS IN THE JEWISH CALENDAR

The major ideas of the Jewish religion, even though they are intangible, are made accessible by being *embedded in time*—celebrated on specific days in a yearly cycle of feast and fast—and *anchored in space*—by palpable substances such as a hut or matzah or candles. Anything that can be done at anytime by anybody will be done at no time by nobody. Judaism preserves the exalted principles and the cataclysmic events of its history through a structured, well-defined, and specifically timed system of practices that it requires of its adherents. The religious calendar has therefore been referred to as the catechism of the Jew.

The Years

Ancient peoples started to count their calendar years anew with the reign of each new monarch. When Christianity rose to dominance in the western world, it began to date history from the birth of its own "king," later according to the Gregorian calendar. Hence, history was divided into B.C. and A.D., before the advent of the king's birth and in the "year of the Lord." Judaism could not consent to divide history along these lines; it did not divide universal history even to make a fulcrum of

Abraham's or Moses' birth. Therefore, the Jewish religious calendar was never oriented in this manner.

For many centuries, the Jews counted the years from one event—the formative event of its existence as a people—the Exodus from Egypt. After the destruction of the Temple in 70 C.E., that cataclysmic event for a while replaced the use of the Exodus as the inaugural date. But the sense of the Jew in this regard, which came to expression only after centuries, was that even an event of such magnitude was not critical enough to draw a line through time and to re-start counting world history.

Only one occurrence could serve as a beginning for history: the beginning *of* history. Judaism determined to count the years of the calendar on a universal scale—from the creation of the universe. But exactly how old is the earth? Even scientists with their most advanced and exacting instrumentation are sure of only one answer: there can be no precision in this matter. The only precise method for the Sages was to count the years according to the literal account of creation in the Bible itself. The year 1991, for example, is in fact the Hebrew year 5751, which is the actual number of years from Day One of God's creation of the universe, according to Genesis. These years were determined by calculating the lifespans of individuals in biblical genealogies and the reigns of kings, and also by counting the first seven "days" as actual days—not as stages or eons. Although this calculation obviously conflicts with accepted geological and archeological accounts, it should be remembered that the Torah demonstrates no interest in being a scientific or even historical treatise, but a moral document of humanity. Hence, what the Hebrew date 5751 implies is 5,751 years of God's sovereignty over the world according to the counting in Torah, and that is its timeless significance.

But this presented a problem: Jews everywhere were a minority and, while they could count time according to their view, they were living in an alien world where the overwhelming majority differed in this common legal practice. Jews, who reside over the face of the earth, could not ignore the way the world keeps time, the basis of a human being's daily life. While Judaism is not "of" this world—in the sense that it strives ideally to transcend it—it is very much "in" this world, and therefore, the Jewish community needed to accommodate its *secular* calendar to global usage.

As a result, it had to live its secular life according to "the nations" and to divide global history according to the exact dates of the Gregorian calendar. But it could not accomodate itself according to the Christocentric terms of the historical divide—B.C. and A.D.—and referred to them instead as B.C.E., before the common era, and C.E., the common era. In Jewish terms then, we are living in 1991 C.E., the ancient Temple was destroyed in 70 C.E., the Maccabees rebelled in 165 B.C.E.

The Jewish *religious* calendar, however, makes no recognition of this secular device, retains its universal format, and continues to count its years on a universal scale—from Creation, the beginning. Jews celebrate the religious New Year, Rosh Hashanah, on the day the Torah considers the day of creation, according to its literal reckoning, the first day of the Hebrew month of Tishre, which usually falls in late September.

The Months

Jews count the months by the moon; western civilization patterns its calendar after the sun. That presents a dilemma. The moon travels more slowly than the sun—by approximately forty-eight minutes a day. At the beginning of the lunar month, she sets in the west shortly after sunset, and each day forty to forty-five minutes later. She continues to lag further and further behind the sun (each lunar month being twenty-nine and a half days) until, at the end of twelve months, the year of the moon is eleven days shorter than the year of the sun, every three years losing a full month of time.

This introduces a special predicament for the religious calendar: Passover needs to be celebrated at the vernal equinox— springtime and harvest are its natural hallmarks, the resuscitation of nature coinciding with the redemption of the people. But, if the lunar calendar loses a month every three years, Passover would move further each year and fall successively in every season of the year. That is exactly what happens to the Muslim festival of Ramadan. The teachers of the Talmud made the adjustment by adding seven leap months (called "Second Adar") in the course of each nineteen year cycle, and thereby ingeniously devised a perpetual calendar that would keep the holidays in the approximate season for which they were originally conceived.

Celebrating the New Moon: Rosh Chodesh

The first day of the lunar month, called Rosh Chodesh, was originally proclaimed by the central court in Jerusalem after the new moon was visually sighted. After the destruction of Jerusalem, Rosh Chodesh was calculated by the astronomical calendar and it determined on which days the holidays fell. The Torah designates certain days of the month as beginning the holidays. As people cannot manage twenty-nine-and-one-half-day months, some months are twenty-nine and some are thirty days. The thirty-day months have two days of Rosh Chodesh, those of twenty-nine days have one day.

In a replaying of the ancient tradition of the court's proclamation of the New Moon, on the Sabbath prior to Rosh Chodesh the new month's arrival is now proclaimed during the synagogue service, replete with an announcement of the split second that Rosh Chodesh begins. Jews celebrate Rosh Chodesh primarily by prayers added to the service.

A marvelous Jewish tradition records that Rosh Chodesh, the renewal of the monthly cycle, celebrates womanhood. It is not only a toast to women and a reminder of gratitude due them, but is actually declared a holiday on which women should not work. This monthly tribute was initiated as a special reward because at Mt. Sinai, unlike the men, women refused to contribute their jewelry to the fashioning of a golden calf—the starkest demonstration by the recently freed slaves of their lack of faith in God and His servant, Moses. Unfortunately, the special significance of this Woman's Day has succumbed to general neglect. It is time for it to be renewed—just as the lunar month gets renewed.

The Week

Jews count the week from Sabbath to Sabbath. The Sabbath is the crown of the week; the crown of Jewish Holy Days; the crown of the Jewish spirit; the crown of the Jewish imagination.

The Sabbath is a Queen. It is a foretaste of the very world-to-come. The Day of Atonement, Yom Kippur, is the one day holier than the weekly Sabbath and its extraordinary sanctity gained it the appellation "Sabbath of Sabbaths." More than the Jews have kept the Sabbath, a great writer once said, the

Sabbath has kept the Jews. It is so rooted in the human condition that no matter how many societies have tried to uproot it, they could not. Some have simply moved the day: Christians to Sunday, Muslims to Friday. The Sabbath stamps its mark on the individual, on the nation, on the week.

All weekdays lead to the Sabbath. In fact, the days do not have names, only numbers, and these numbers all look to number seven, anticipating the arrival of the seventh day, the Sabbath, Shabbat. Thus, the daily service contains a special psalm that the Levites sang in the Temple for that particular day, so that on Wednesday, for example, we recite, "This is the fourth day toward Shabbat." The days from Sunday to Friday are viewed, psychologically as well as physically, as steps leading up to the Shabbat, the "palace in time." New clothes were worn first on the Shabbat; special foods were prepared for it; important guests were invited to join the family for it; meaningful discussions were delayed until the Shabbat.

Friday, because it of its proximity to the Shabbat, virtually lost its own identity; it was simply *erev shabbat*, the threshold of the Shabbat, on which even the most imporant scholars helped in the kitchen.

Following the analogy of weekdays as steps leading up to the holy day, at the close of the Shabbat, Jews experienced a precipitous drop of excitement—the Shabbat departed, and life on the lowest rung of the first day of the week had to begin the climb again.

The Day

The Jewish day does not begin and end at midnight as does the secular calendar day. Midnight is not a distinguishable astronomic event. In the era before the modern clock, a specific hour of the night could not be precisely known, whereas an hour of the day was easily determined by sighting the location of the sun. Thus, the day had to begin by precise, simple and universally recognized standards. This meant that the day had to be reckoned either from the beginning of night or the beginning of day.

In Jewish time, the day begins with the onset of night (the appearance of the stars) followed by the morning (which technically begins with the appearance of the North Star). (According to some Jewish teachers, night and morning begin with sunset and sunrise respectively.) For that is how the Torah describes it: "And there was evening and there was morning, the first day." The full-day day begins with night, especially so since the onset of night is more public and more pronounced than the dawn, and is therefore easier to observe as the starting period of the day.

For this reason, the Sabbath begins on Friday night and ends with the appearance of the stars on Saturday night. The same is true for the major holidays such as Passover, Sukkot, Shavuot, Rosh Hashanah and Yom Kippur, the fast day of Tisha B'Av, and Hanukkah and Purim.

Beginning the day with the night is, in a sense, a metaphor of life itself. Life begins in the darkness of the womb, then bursts into the brightness of the light and eventually settles into the darkness of the grave—which, in turn, is followed by a new dawn in the world-to-come.

It is a more hopeful metaphor than the popular one that says that the human being begins to die from the moment he sees the light of day. Life is not all descent. Life winds its way through the darkness until it reaches its zenith in the coming of the dawn. It is like a person walking. At first, he is upright. At each step, he breaks his balance and begins to fall, only to catch himself by putting his leg forward. He straightens up and then proceeds to fall again, only to catch himself and to straighten again. After falling and rising several times, he only needs to look back to see the progress he has made.

Life consists of light and dark: "And there was evening and there was morning." What we make of time is what counts.

24
Day-to-Day Judaism

God expects every Jew to be a full-time Jew, not a Jew for Sabbaths only. God created the Sabbath and made it holy. But He also created weekdays. On weekdays, man must make himself holy—in his morals and his thinking and his study and in his empathy and support of others. Tuesday is also Jewish. If a person is a believer on the Sabbath, he should be one every day. God does not believe in part-time believers.

The reverse is also true. Jews do not believe in a Sabbath God, or a Holy-Day God, or a Rites-of-Passage God. God is a part of life. He is all of life. He is everywhere or He is nowhere. His majesty cannot be contained within a synagogue ark, or squeezed into the stone walls of Jerusalem, or locked tight in the twenty-five hours of Yom Kippur. Torah study is every day, as surely as are food and thought and worry. Ethics are everywhere, in the kindergarten, the corporate office and the bedroom. The sacred in Judaism is not limited to the Inner Sanctum; it has battles to wage in the streets.

Now, people are not naturally mindful of the supernatural. Therefore, the Torah makes every effort at jogging the consciousness of human beings and it positions religious symbols as flashing beacons on all the pathways of life. After a while— subtly, subliminally, suddenly—the sense of God grows inside us and is everywhere. It is joy and meaning and hope and love.

There are special signals at the pivotal turns in life, at the major passages of our personal histories, and also at smaller cycles, when the wheel of time cranks its staccato rotations— the turn of the week, the month, the season, the year. God is everywhere, all the time, urging us to make ourselves holy.

This chapter is devoted to the daily acts of the Jew which, because they are the *constants of religious life,* most faithfully define the distinctiveness of Jewish existence.

KINDNESS, *CHESED*

What is quite clearly the most consistent and all-embracing act of faith is called chesed, which means kindness and implies the giving of oneself to helping another without regard to compensation. In a sense, the goal of the whole enterprise of Judaism is to develop human beings whose principal trait is chesed. The Rabbis of the Talmud (Yevamot 79a) considered kindness to be one of the three distinguishing marks of the Jew and, in a standard that converts must take to heart, they say: "Anyone who demonstrates these qualities deserves to be attached to this people." A favorite talmudic name for God is *Rakhmana,* "the Compassionate One." Every act of human chesed is an imitation of the benevolence of God. It appears on page after page of the Prayerbook, in chapter after chapter of the Psalms, and is implied in the legal and moral decisions on folio after folio of the Talmud. The Torah begins with an act of chesed as God clothes Adam and Eve, and ends with it as God buries Moses. The Halakhah formally begins with the Torah at Mt. Sinai, but chesed begins with Abraham, centuries earlier. The world could not have endured so long without chesed; it would have imploded.

Chesed is a daily requirement—which means it is a lifetime requirement—and it is most succinctly manifested in the act of giving. It implies attitudes integral to the person's character, inseparable from one's inner nature, and spans the whole gamut of virtues which operate in interpersonal relationships—charity and compassion, love and respect. This inner sensitivity is expressed in specific formal religious acts, which are mitzvot that have biblical or Rabbinic warrant. These mitzvot are not merely "nice," suggested behaviors, but *duties* mandated the Jew—

such as visiting the sick, providing a job for the unemployed, and such.

Three Primary Sources

THE FIRST

And thou shalt teach them the ordinances and the laws, and shalt show them the way in which they must walk, and the work that they must do (Exodus 18:20).

Rabbi Eleazar of Modi'im says: "And thou shalt show them," means show them how to live; "the way" refers to visiting the sick; "they must walk" refers to burying the dead; "in which" refers to bestowing kindness; "And the work" means the activities within the line of strict justice; "that they must do," beyond the line of strict justice.[1]

THE SECOND

After the Lord, your God, shall you walk (Deuteronomy 13:5).

Rabbi Chama, son of Rabbi Chanina, asks: Is it then possible for a human being to walk after the Shekhinah? For has it not been said, "For the Lord, thy God, is a devouring fire?" But, the meaning is to walk after the attributes of the Holy One, Blessed be He: As He clothes the naked . . . so you must clothe the naked; God visited the sick . . . so do you visit the sick; God comforted the mourners . . . so do you comfort mourners; God buried the dead . . . so do you bury the dead.[2]

Maimonides catalogues the mitzvot which are the chesed principles in action. They are paraphrased here:

It is a positive mitzvah of the Rabbis to visit the sick, to bring comfort to the mourners, to help remove the dead from the home, to help bring the bride to her wedding, to accompany guests into your house, to participate in all aspects of burial—to carry the casket, walk in honor before it, eulogize the dead, dig the grave and do the actual burial, to bring joy to a bride and groom and to provide them with all their needs. These are all *physical* acts of kindness and there are no limits to what one must do to fill these requirements.[3]

This inventory of virtues is only a short list derived from these specific verses. A longer list, the elements of which appear throughout the millennial Jewish literature, includes granting interest-free loans to the needy, feeding the hungry anonymously, giving shelter to the homeless, providing jobs for those in need of work, speaking kindly to the dejected, bringing enemies together in friendship, imparting hope to the depressed, giving extra care to widows and orphans, and so on. All of these Maimonides encompasses in the biblical law, "Thou shalt love they neighbor as thyself" (Leviticus 19).

THE THIRD

"This is my God and I shall glorify Him" (Exodus 16:2).

Rabbi Ishmael says: And is it then possible for a man of flesh and blood to add glory to His Creator? It simply means: I shall be beautiful before Him in observing the commandments. . . . Abba Saul says: O be like Him! Just as He is gracious and merciful, so be thou also gracious and merciful.[4]

Chesed here requires the integration into one's character of those qualities man venerates in God. It is the essence of the imitation of God, one of the fundamental philosophic bases for all human ethical conduct.

KINDNESS VS. CHARITY

To sharpen the focus on kindness, it is instructive to compare it with other important values. One of the great masters of the ages, Rabbi Judah Loew, known as the Maharal of Prague, contrasts acts of personal kindness, chesed, with acts of charity, tzedakah.[5]

The Talmud records the basic differences:

The Rabbis taught: In three ways is kindness greater than charity. Charity is done with money; kindness can be done either with one's person or one's money. Charity is done for the poor; kindness can be done for either the poor or the rich. Charity is for the living; kindness can be done for the living or the dead (Sukkah 49b).

Maharal expands upon the difference: Charity is sparked by the demands of compassion. One cannot bear to see a person in pain or starving, so his sense of sympathy compels him to help that person. If there were no pitiful situation, there would be no compassion necessary and no charity given. But kindness requires a broader, more sensitive heart that entails developing a chesed *persona*—integrating it into one's personality. In such an event, chesed will not be a value forthcoming only in response to sadness, but an ever-present quality which will anticipate needs, construct wholesome situations, and initiate acts of benevolence for needs undetected by others. Thus, charity is generally judged by the recipient—the magnitude of the pain suffered will determine the degree of assistance to relieve that pain. Kindness, on the other hand, is to be judged by the giver—the kind of caring that person is capable of will determine the nature and degree of the remedy.

The Maharal takes this distinction further: The only way that a person can be said to reach the exalted spiritual heights of imitating God is by doing an act of chesed voluntarily and naturally as it flows from his or her innards. On the other hand, observing a specific commandment *only* because God mandated it, laudatory and essential as that is, is not considered "walking in the ways of God," because it is actually responding to an external voice—even though it is God's—rather than an internal one. Thus, also, one who acts out of a sense of pity is performing a wonderful mitzvah, but that, too, is not considered "walking in the ways of God," because it is reacting to an external need rather than acting upon a truly visceral, internalized impetus.

Maharal makes a still more penetrating insight. Only kindness, chesed, as opposed to charity or Torah study or keeping the mitzvot, is unique to the *character* of the human being. And it is uniquely chesed which relates to the chesed attribute of God himself; unlike lawfulness, for example, which does not reflect the character of God that is to be imitated by man.

This is the sense of one the Talmud's most astonishing statements: "Rav Huna said: 'One who busies himself with Torah exclusively is equivalent to one who has no God'" (Avodah Zarah 17b). Maharal explains: Torah "exclusively" is what Rav Huna refers to, and that indicates an exercise in reason only, not a commitment to mitzvot. Therefore, when he is not studying Torah, he has no spirituality—and so he is equated with one who has no God. But one who practices chesed is not like that—because kindness is to be practiced every hour of every day, even without the needy demanding it, and it is directed to everybody in the world. It is an unlimited obligation, perpetual and pervasive and, because there can never be a respite from this mitzvah, one who does chesed "exclusively" can never be equated with one who has no God.

TORAH STUDY

One inevitable weakness in the chesed system is the human component which makes implementing kind deeds largely subjective. As reality changes, so does the nature of the kindness that deals with reality; as it confronts new variables, it becomes a variable. Without specific, objective guidelines, its application becomes nebulous. The splendor of chesed is that it is personal; the flaw, that it is subjective.

Halakhah or Jewish law, on the other hand, is explicit, pointedly demanding fulfillment at a precise time in a precise fashion, no matter the mood, the occasion, or the environment. Halakhah is the engine of Judaism, providing the direction and the driving power of Judaism.

Chesed has majesty and grandeur, but it needs Torah for its very survival. Chesed was indeed mandated to Abraham, earlier than the law was given, but it became operational only when it was received from God in a formal, legal context at the Revelation at Sinai. Chesed has to be learned in the laboratory of life; the ground of Torah needs to be intellectually plowed—penetrated, turned, sifted, analyzed and cultivated— with the total concentration of an alert mind, a *gemara kop* the Jews call it, a head for Talmud.

The Living Law

Torah must be studied day and night according to biblical prescription: "And you shall meditate on it by day and by night." This requires the Jew to set aside times for study every day, preferably with a partner. This day-to-day mitzvah of study— "learning" as the vernacular has it—made Torah the dominant feature of Jewish life, and it came to characterize the Jew throughout history. A compulsory system of education was in place in the first century of the common era, while cavemen still stalked the North American continent. The Jews became known as *am ha'sefer*, the People of the Book, a title given them by Mohammed. Their love of the book is legendary and, no matter how intellectual other societies had become, they never achieved this zeal for the book.

Jewish tradition treats books as though they are living scholars themselves. The Torah is treated as a living Torah, not merely in the metaphoric sense. Jews do not leave books open, as though abandoned. That would be insensitive to their "feelings." Closed books are left face up and a lesser text is not placed on top of a more important one. If a sacred book falls to the ground, Jewish people pick it up tenderly and kiss it, as though it were a bruised child. When the Torah is drawn from the Ark, everyone rises, as though in the presence of a great rabbi. As it passes by them, they kiss it, or throw it a kiss, in respect and affection. If it is accidentally dropped, the entire congregation present at the time fasts on a chosen day and gives charity. When the Torah scroll ages and its letters begin to crack, it is reverently buried.

The reverence that was rendered the Holy Scroll eventually filtered down to everyday volumes. When Bibles and other religious books become old and unusable they are, like the Torah itself, buried in a grave close to a scholar, or deposited in a vault or separate room, called *genizah*. Great authors were not called by their family name, but deferentially after the title of their books; they were more closely identified by their scholarship than by their families.

The Rabbis of the second century debated over which was greater—study or practice. They voted on the issue and decided that study was the greater—because inevitably it would lead to practice. Knowledge, they held, had to affect behavior. "The ignoramus is not a saint." Indeed, study—the process of learning itself—is the heart of Jewish religious practice.

Another debate in comparative religious values offers the choice of study or prayer. The Talmud makes short shrift of the subject. It records an incident of a Rabbi who chastised a colleague for spending time praying when he could more profitably be studying. Praying, he held, should be considered materialistic—natural to the temporal, material world, as one could pray for health, success, peace. But the study of Torah belongs to the eternal world, the world-to-come—it is a spirited exercise in God-wrestling at the highest level of spiritual life.

Torah study is not simply a matter of punctilious scholarship and academic excellence, although it is surely that, too. It accomplishes two purposes: one is the accumulation of knowledge; the other is worship—because the process itself is an act of prayer.

Study is the highest mode of worship. The act of praying is regarded as "permitted" by God—He agrees to listen to the pleading of His creatures. But study is "required" by biblical mandate. Torah study is crucial to the survival of the Jews, and it has earned Jews the reputation of being one of the most educated peoples in the history of the world.

Maimonides writes:

> Every man in Israel has an obligation to study the Torah— whether he is rich or poor, healthy or sick, young or old and without vigor. Even if he is poor and needs to beg from door to door, and even if he has a family to support, he is obligated to set aside time by day and by night to study Torah.

Learning as an Act of Love

More than a law, more than a prayer, learning is an act of love.

Many study in order to know; many more study in order to utilize what they know; others study for study's sake—they love to learn. When the Greeks called Pythagoras *sophos,* a "wise man," he answered that he was only *philo sophos,* a "lover of wisdom." There are scores of people in diverse cultures who are lovers of learning.

Among Jews, this is quite pronounced—the passion for learning being the heritage of generations and, the Torah for millennia being the cherished democratic possession of the common folk, the love of learning is natural. But Torah to Jews is different, qualitatively different. Not only are they in love with learning; learning is itself love. It is the language of adoration, the music of celestial spheres. It is the means and the goal. *Torah is both the arrow and the heart of Judaism.*

More telling than the commandment to study and the importuning of the Rabbis is the description of how the study of Torah was integrated into the life-style of the Jews in the cities and shtetls of the diaspora. Abraham Joshua Heschel describes the place of Torah in shtetl life:

> There were many who lived in appalling poverty, many who were pinched by never-ending worries, and there were plenty of taverns with strong spirits, but drunkards were rarely seen

among Jews. When night came and a man wanted to pass away time, he did not hasten to a tavern to take a drink, but went to pore over a book or joined a group which—either with or without a teacher—indulged in the enjoyment of studying revered books. Physically worn out by their day's toil, they sat over open volumes, playing the austere music of the Talmud's groping for truth or the sweet melodies of exemplified piety of ancient Sages.

"Once I noticed," writes a Christian scholar, who visited the city of Warsaw during the First World War, "a great many coaches on a parking place, but with no drivers in sight. In my own country, I would have known where to look for them. A young Jewish boy showed me the way: in a courtyard, on the second floor, was the *shtibl* of the Jewish drivers. It consisted of two rooms: one filled with Talmud volumes, the other a room for prayer. All the drivers were engaged in fervent study and religious discussion. . . . It was then that I found out and became convinced that all professions, the bakers, the butchers, the shoemakers, etc., have their own *shtibl* in the Jewish district; and every free moment which can be taken off from their work is given to the study of the Torah. And when they get together in intimate groups, one urges the other: "*Zog mir a shtickl Torah*—Tell me a little Torah."[6]

An old book saved from the countless libraries recently burned in Europe, now at the YIVO Library in New York, bears the stamp, "The Society of Wood-Choppers for the Study of Mishnah in Berditchev."

THE PRAYER EXPERIENCE

Prayer is subordinate to study, but taken together, Jewish prayer and Torah study are the yin and yang of religious life. The Prayerbook, the siddur, did not compete with study for the Jewish soul; rather, it reinforced Torah study. It was designed to incorporate excerpts from Torah, Mishnah and Talmud, in order to fulfill the Jew's minimum daily requirement of "learning." The Siddur championed the person's prayer to God for a sharp mind and an understanding heart, elevating it to first place of all the nineteen petitions Jews include in their Silent Devotion three times every day.

But the unique Jewish experience of prayer does not come as easily as studying Torah. Praying is a flow and a sway; it evokes a sentiment, a way of relating to God, a priority of concerns, an expression, a mood that is embedded in the soul of the Jew. However, praying cannot be confined to moments of inspiration or desperation—praying only when one is moved by events and "feels like" praying. Anyone who waits for the mood to strike—a visit to the Grand Canyon, a magnificent twilight, the baby-freshness of a rosy-fingered dawn—is not a praying person, and probably will not be able to pray authentically even when the mood arrives. One needs to domesticate the stimulus—to make prayer a natural, comfortable event, a day-to-day happening.

Jewish prayer is designed to become second nature, a part of a person, a daily diet. In that way, one comes to be on comfortable speaking terms with God, who, in turn, becomes accessible, almost a conversation partner. Not only is an intermediary between man and God undesirable, it is unnecessary. And God can be found at home as readily as in the synagogue. As the founder of Hasidism once said, "He can be found wherever one lets Him in."

We simply cannot force God to come before people; people need to intrude themselves before God. The Yiddish word for prayer, *davenen*, derives from the French *devant* "before," as in "Know *before* Whom you stand." Even if we could feel the desire to pray surging regularly from the soul, what prayer would come forth if there were no book of prayers written by great souls, the Siddur? Perhaps only improvised stammering, well-intentioned simplistic words that last one minute. Improvised prayer is acclaimed today for its spontaneity and subjectivity, but the fixed liturgy of the ages is the foundation of the religious life, and provides the tools with which one may build one's own prayers.

Prayer is an art, yet it can be learned. It requires the mechanical skill of reading (though the words may not be understood) and the spiritual attitude of a willing heart, a sympathetic mind, and an authentic desire to succeed. If pursued with diligence, the result will be well worth the effort invested. Just as a person must practice a learned language to gain and retain fluency; just as an athlete and musician must rehearse daily, rigorously to perform smoothly, so must a Jew pray regularly in order to do so effectively.

The daily diet of prayer consists of morning and evening prayers, *Shacharit* in the morning, *Minchah* and *Ma'ariv*, in late afternoon and evening. On the Sabbath, there is an additional service, *Mussaf*, added on to the morning. One prayer is central to every worship service, morning and night, weekday, Shabbat, and holiday: the *Amidah* (the "Standing" Prayer or *Shmoneh Esrai*, the "eighteen" blessings or Silent Devotion). All prayer speaks *of* God; the Shmoneh Esrai speaks *to* God. It is the peak experience of the prayer service, emphasized by taking three steps backward to withdraw symbolically from your surroundings and three steps forward to symbolically enter the presence of Almighty God. It is recited silently, standing, and occasionally bowing. In all morning and evening prayers— Shacharit and Ma'ariv—it is preceded by the most well-known verse in the Bible or Siddur: *Sh'ma Yisrael, Ha'Shem Elokenu Ha'Shem Echad,* "Hear, O Israel, the Lord, our God, the Lord is One." It is referred to affectionately as the *Sh'ma.* Surrounding these two key prayers are clusters from the classics of Jewish literature: the Torah, the Prophets, the Psalms, and the Talmud.

As a child learns to walk by walking, so we learn to pray by praying. Regularly.

Herman Wouk graphically describes a person first entering a synagogue—an episode any convert might experience:

> He [the newcomer to the synagogue] is handed a prayerbook that strikes him as a jumble, with English translations that, for long stretches, make little sense. He is apt to observe preoccupied and inattentive worshippers reeling off Hebrew with few external symptoms of devotion, or whispering together while a reader chants a long singsong. Now and then, everybody stands, he cannot say why, and there is a mass chant, he cannot say what; or, if he dimly recalls it from childhood, he cannot find it in the prayerbook. The time comes when the Holy Scroll is taken from the Ark for a parade to the reading desk, the bells tinkling on its silver crown. The reading in a strange Oriental mode seems endless, and he observes that it seems endless to some other worshippers too, who slump in an unfocused torpor, or chat, or even sleep. . . . The skeptic leaves—early, if he can— well satisfied that his views are sound, that his religious fancy was a temporary touch of melancholia, and that, if the Jewish God exists, there is no reaching him through the synagogue. . . .
>
> The newcomer in a synagogue will, of course, feel strange and ill at ease; he will be put off by the matter-of-fact manner

of many of the worshippers; he will find the process hard to follow, and he will be an exceptional person not to feel discouragement at first. But persevering attendance, especially linked with any kind of elementary Hebrew training, will in a short time give him back the key to the storehouse of Jewish prayer. Then, when he wants to, he will pray in the measured and fine words of the tradition; at the synagogue if he can go there, at home if he cannot. . . .

The fact is, prayer is never easy. True prayer is as demanding—at least as demanding—as the carrying on of a business conversation or the writing of a letter. It purports to be a communication with a Listener. The child and the newcomer struggle with their unfamiliarity. Devout worshippers struggle with their overfamiliarity. All men of any training or any faith are put to the greatest mental effort, I imagine, to get at any real sense of talking to God.[7]

CHARITY, *TZEDAKAH*

Charity is traditionally thought of as relating solely to helping fellow man, to relieving the burden of neighbors in trouble. But it is not so: charity is considered by the Rabbis to be more than aid and assistance. It is, in every sense, *a religious act*, a way of relating to God, by whose "charity" we survive. Giving charity fulfills one of God's commandments. Giving is not an extraordinary event, but a common one expected of every Jew.

There was no truly Jewish home without its charity box, the *pushka*. The pushka became a depository not only of moneys, large and small, but of the family's prayers that ride on every coin as it is dropped in—before the Sabbath, after hearing good news, during important events—for the sake of family peace, for an aunt's recovery, Israel's safety, Ethiopian Jews, even good grades and good business. The Yom Kippur prayerbook positions charity alongside repentance and prayer in a vigorous declaration—the combined power of these three acts can overcome evil edicts; it can "save" us from a meaningless death; it can bring the redemption.

And redemption indeed it brought. If kindness is one of the distinguishing marks of the Jew, charity—although less difficult to execute—is globally and historically reputed to be the chief characteristic of Jewish communities. In the twentieth century alone, the Jewish people have literally redeemed millions of homeless and persecuted brothers and sisters. In this regard, they are indeed the paragons of giving in the modern world.

The Three Poverty Laws

The charity responsibility obligatory upon every Jew was explicitly and formally required of converts before being received into the Jewish people:

> And we inform [the convert] of the sin for violating the laws of the "Gleanings", the "Forgotten Sheaf", the "Corner of the Field", and the "Tithing" for the poor.[8]

Now, this is a strange condition. There are no other distinct mitzvot enumerated in the Talmud or in Maimonides' short list except for these laws which are hardly known to the Jewish public at all. Further, there is no popular literature that deals specifically with this subject in any detail. Yet, they have steadfastly remained in the traditional curriculum for converts. While candidates for conversion will not derive much practical guidance from these regulations, designed originally for an agricultural society, they will be able to glean a sense of the significance of charity and its imperative nature. In any case, examining them is a valuable exercise in Torah study.

These three laws constitute the fundamental poverty legislation of the Jews:

A. GLEANINGS AND THE CORNER OF THE FIELD

> And when you reap the harvest of your land, you shall not reap all the way to the edges of your field, or gather the gleanings of your harvest; you shall leave them for the poor and the stranger: I, the Lord, am your God (Leviticus 23:22).

Rashi, the classic biblical commentator, comments that the law of the corner of the field is placed between two sections dealing with the holidays of Passover and Pentecost on the one side and the holidays of New Year, the Day of Atonement and Tabernacles on the other. On all of these holidays, sacrifices were brought to the Temple. "This is to teach that one who obeys the laws for the relief of the poor is regarded as though he had built the Temple and offered sacrifices there."[9]

B. FORGOTTEN SHEAF

When you reap the harvest in your field and overlook a sheaf in the field, do not turn back to get it; it shall go to the stranger, the fatherless and the widow in order that the Lord, your God, may bless you in all your undertakings. When you shake the fruit from your olive trees, do not go over them again; that which is left shall go to the stranger, the fatherless, and the widow. When you gather the grapes of your vineyard, do not pick it over again; that which is left shall go to the stranger, the fatherless, and the widow. Always remember that you were a slave in the land of Egypt; therefore do I enjoin you to observe this commandment (Deuteronomy 24:19-22).

Rashi: Even though the forgotten sheaf is an unintentional charitable act, the owner will receive God's blessing; how much more so if one helps the needy intentionally. [One Rabbi made a feast when he forgot the sheaf. Said he: "This is the only mitzvah I could perform by forgetting. Thank God He gave me the chance."]

C. TITHE FOR THE POOR

Every third year, you shall bring out the full tithe of your yield of that year, but leave it within your settlements. Then the Levite, who has no hereditary portion as you have, and the stranger, the fatherless, and the widow in your settlements shall come and eat their fill, so that the Lord, your God, may bless you in all the enterprises you undertake (Deuteronomy 14:28,29).

Rashi: The portion given them must be sufficient to satisfy them. This served as a basis for the Rabbinic law that not less than half a *kab* of wheat or barley should be given to the poor. [Giving is not enough; satisfying is enough.]

Why must the convert especially learn these laws? Because the Sages were insistent that the prospective convert know the cost before making the purchase. Before entering the fold, a convert should know all the hidden charges—in terms, perhaps, of the enmity he might trigger, the time and effort he will need to expend for the performance of the mitzvot, "the heaviness of the yoke" of keeping Torah, and the punishment every violation might cause, as well as the reward for the observance of mitzvot.

But it is also very important that the convert understand

the cost in terms of hard cash that it will take to be an observant Jew, who will now be obligated to provide (in a capitalist economy) the equivalent of the gleanings, the forgotten sheaf, the corner of the field, and tithing.

Caritas vs. Tzedakah

As the convert will come to understand, support for the disadvantaged in Judaism is not altruism. It is "justice." The Latin term for charity, caritas, implies an act of giving by the "haves" to the "have-nots"—out of the goodness of their hearts. The "have-nots" may not be strictly deserving of the support because they didn't earn it, but the "haves" want to be merciful and so they share their wealth. Contrariwise, in Judaism, the term for charity is tzedakah, which derives from *tzedek*, which means justice. God gave limited resources to people. Some garner a greater share, some a lesser share. But since all are created equally in the image of God, there is a *duty* that devolves upon the "haves" to give of their substance to the "have-nots" in order to effect justice and to enable the have-nots to survive, as they themselves do.[10]

To these insights into the Jewish concept of charity, we should add another. The Halakhah does not require learning other laws of charity—even of tithing for Priests and Levites—only these three, harvest-type laws. Why? Because, says a commentary[11] to Maimonides, in these cases the owners exercise no control over which poor receive the produce of their fields, the product of their beneficence! Generally one designates the recipient of one's charity: "A poor man who is a relative, comes before all others," etc.[12] A specific Priest or Levite may be chosen for receiving the tithe and the farmer, though it costs him, nonetheless could thereby derive some benefit—their gratitude. But in these three cases, the owners have absolutely no rights of selection. "The poor come into the field and take *their due* from the owners"—by right!

Although we do not live in an agricultural society, these laws translate into our economy. The knowledge that Jews are obligated to give these kinds of funds and to operate under such a definition of charity might deter some converts, Rashi explains, so it is necessary to inform them of this in advance. Otherwise the "sale" (the representation of obligations) of the Covenant of Abraham is morally fraudulent.

Such is the obligation and such the glory of the Jewish religion.

That Jews are known for their charitable ways is no aberration of history. Giving is indigenous to this people and it echoes through the long corridors of Jewish history, from the brittle voices of ancient ancestors to the tzedakah songs of kindergartners in today's Hebrew day schools.

CLOTHING SYMBOLS

Judaism weaves commitment throughout the entire fabric of life, placing symbols in everything—even in the clothes we wear. There are special articles of dress, some associated with prayer, others worn for specific occasions, and still others commonly worn all day that are the man-made skin by which we choose to be identified.

We are not here considering the different modes of dress of the global Jewish population—for example, the caftan and fur hat of Hasidism, or the wearing of black. Those are traditional styles, usually co-opted from neighboring peoples at stages in history frozen by individual sects, but having little to do with the actual demands of the Halakhah.

Tallit and Tsitsit

During morning prayers, men wear a shawl called a *tallit* that has eight-stringed tassels on its four corners. The Torah requires all four-cornered garments to bear these fringes, or *tsitsit*: "That you may see them, and remember all the commands of God, and do them, and not turn aside after your hearts and your eyes." Of course, this is a tall order for these short strings to fulfill, but that is characteristic of Judaism. We need to be mindful of our obligations; mindlessness is the way of most people, most of the time. Wrapped in a cloak the Torah designed to remind us of God makes it a bit more difficult to turn aside after our eyes.

A four-cornered garment was conventional in ancient Israel, and the prod to be mindful was effective. Now that dress has changed, we would lose this biblical cue, except at services. Pious Jews, therefore, put on a special, small, four-cornered shawl with *tsitsit* under their shirts every day to preserve the commandment in its given form. Enveloped by this *tallit*, we should be less prone to let our minds wander.

Tefillin

It is not fair to ask a person to get out of bed and pray without providing a conducive setting to encourage a burst of piety. The Torah designed such an environment of prayer: a person puts on a tallit. But that, by itself, was not adequate. The primary articles of prayer are the phylacteries, called *tefillin*. These consist of a pair of black leather boxes which are gently tied with leather straps around the forehead and left arm. These boxes contain small parchment scrolls on which are inscribed the Sh'ma ("Hear, O Israel, the Lord, our God, the Lord is One") and other Bible verses. While this symbol is not known outside Judaism, the source is quite clearly written in the Bible for all the world to see: "Bind these words as a symbol on your arms, and let them be emblems between your eyes." The Oral Torah fills in the details of the writing, the dimensions, and the times for wearing the tefillin.

Here again, the Torah uses concrete everyday objects to remind us of our religious and moral obligations, to establish a mood, to keep our hearts from going astray, to express gratitude, to prod us in the right direction. The tefillin provide Jews with a convention that directs man's brain and hands to useful and creative endeavors. There is no more definitive symbol of Jewish identity than donning the tefillin. Often, a young man began to put on tefillin at Bar Mitzvah (it was the symbol of passage to adulthood, *par excellence*) and wore them every weekday for years, until suddenly one morning he gave it up—when he entered military service, or on his first day at college, or when he moved from his parent's home. That day is explicitly recalled as a sea change in his religious life, the first moment of compromise with the secular world. Frequently, years later, when he is thirty or forty or even eighty years old, he is offered the tefillin again—perhaps upon returning to the synagogue after a parent's death—and he resumes this very pious act. All the complex reasoning and well-constructed theories could not have kept prayer alive or Torah entrenched as effectively as did these seemingly curious, alien-looking objects.

Kippah

Covering the head is a sign of respect in the east as much as uncovering it is a sign of respect in the west. Wearing a hat in a restaurant or library or at a corporate board meeting is a sign of bad manners. Not wearing one at religious services is a sign of bad faith. Jewish men have had the custom of covering the hair for at least two thousand years, especially during study and prayer; married Jewish women since biblical times.

The Talmud records that a man should not walk more than seven feet ("four ells") bareheaded. One rabbi noted that wearing a *kippah*, or skullcap, does not make a man religious, but *not* wearing one calls his religion into question. Praying bareheaded is rarely seen today, although, in some Reform temples, it still lingers as a matter of principle to insist that the kippah be discarded along with the tallit and tefillin. This policy is rarely enforced upon visitors to a temple today. (On the contrary, recent surveys of Reform congregational practice suggest a resurgence in the use of such traditional gear.)

There is no halakhically prescribed form of head covering. The actual style of the kippah is a matter of taste, and also identity. In the United States and Israel, traditional Jews wear simple monochromatic kippot—the mainline Centrist and Zionistic types wear a knitted cap clipped (or even Velcro'ed!) in place; right-wing yeshiva students wear larger black velvet ones; newly returned Jews often wear brightly colored large kippot; Hasidim wear black kippot with hats over them; day school children wear them in all bright shades. In earlier times, kippot were worn only indoors and regular hats outdoors. With the growth of freedom and especially with Israeli independence, new courage was found and the kippah began to be worn in the streets as a staple of traditional Jewish garb, acceptable in businesses and offices. There are some today, however, who are traditionally observant although they go bareheaded in places of business or at public gatherings not religious in nature, covering their heads only as they make the blessing over food, while at home and in places of worship.

Sha'atnez

There is a biblical injunction against the mixing of linen and wool in the making and wearing of clothing. Essentially, sha'atnez is one of those laws for which we can divine no reason. Many brilliant teachers throughout thirty-five centuries have tried their hand at making practical sense of it. For example, Maimonides refers to the urgent biblical crusade to uproot the pagan practice of sympathetic magic—the idolatrous priests wore clothes mixed of these two materials as a sign of power over the vegetable and animal kingdoms. Others hold that it is part and parcel of the Torah's universal insistence on avoiding blending diverse materials—such as grafting two tress of different genres, plowing with an ox and mule, eating meat and milk. Judaism makes a determined effort to retain the integrity of animals, vegetables and other materials.

In the final analysis: God has His reasons.

HOME SYMBOLS

As the Torah's mark is impressed on clothing, so it is placed on the houses we call home, in the symbol called *mezuzah*. Literally, this refers to a passage of Torah placed on a doorpost as a sign posted at the coming and going of the residents and their visitors. It transforms a prosaic, mindless motion of every day—goings and comings—into a fleeting encounter with God and with Jewishness. It is no wonder that Jews are called "God-intoxicated"—God and His Torah are designed by Judaism to be ubiquitous in the Jews' existence.

Mezuzah

Jews affix onto their doorways—of homes, rooms, offices, playrooms—a small case containing Torah passages which are hand-inscribed on parchment. This is called mezuzah, actually the Hebrew word for an entire doorpost. It is a sign that a Jewish family occupies the home or apartment. It derives from the time that God instructed the people, during the virulent plagues in ancient Egypt, to place a smattering of animal blood on the doorpost as a mark of their identity; God noted the mark and passed over their homes. The word *Shaddai* is inscribed on the mezuzah case, as an acronym for "[God], the Watcher over the doors of Israel."

The mezuzah is placed two-thirds of the way up the doorpost, on the right side, and at a tilt, with the top leaning toward the inside of the house or room. The case without the parchment is of no use. A parchment that is machine-made is also of no use. Also, the use of a little mezuzah as a pendant on people's necks is of no religious value. It is a custom of young Americans, probably for self-identification, and, to the extent that the wearers are proud of their Jewishness, is it valuable. A kosher parchment wrapped in transparent tape is acceptable; the case serves only to protect the parchment and is itself without significance.

THE KOSHER LAWS

The Meaning of "Kosher"

In the same manner that Judaism reminds the Jew of his duties by fixing its seal on a person's home and on his clothing, so it places its distinctive imprint on the most ubiquitous practice of all—the eating experience—in what are known as the kosher laws. The effectiveness of these laws is legendary. What was said about the Sabbath—that more than the Jews kept it, it kept the Jews—can equally be said of the dietary laws.

"Kosher" is a Hebrew word now found in standard English dictionaries. It implies being acceptable, passing the grade. In Jewish law, *kasher* means "fit," "proper," "prepared according to religious requirements." While the word "kosher" does not appear in the Bible, it is universally the word most identified with standard Jewish religious observance. In the American vernacular, "He's kosher," means "He's O.K."

While "kosher" laws do insure a great degree of cleanliness, all kosher food is not necessarily hygienically pure, just as hygienic food is not necessarily kosher. Herman Wouk describes it humorously: "A hog could be raised in an incubator on antibiotics, bathed daily, slaughtered in a hospital operating room, and its carcass sterilized by ultra-violet rays, without rendering kosher the pork chops that it yields."

"Unclean" is a *levitical* term denoting food that was not prepared in accordance with the laws of *religious* purity. That is why the Torah defines lions and rabbits as "unclean," but goats and chickens—of all things—as "clean." It is to be expected that laws promulgated by a good God are not harmful, and indeed promote the welfare of the human being, but that is the ancillary, not the primary purpose of the law.

Thus, there is a prohibition against eating the flesh of an animal that dies of natural causes or of disease, or that is torn to death by carnivores, or that meets any other violent death— what in Hebrew is termed *nevelah*. Surely this law, especially in earlier times, has clear hygienic value, but that is not its intent.

There are many halakhic rules which determine how a kosher animal is to be selected, how it is to be processed in accordance with religious, humane, and hygienic standards, and finally which parts of even a kosher animal may not be ingested.

Which Foods are Kosher?

All vegetables and fruits that grow naturally from the ground are kosher.

Among animals, there are specific natural signs that qualify an animal as kosher. There are two such marks: split hooves and cud-chewing. In effect, this excludes all beasts of prey, rodents, reptiles, domestic animals such as swine and horses, and permits only those which eat grass and vegetables.

Among fish, the kosher signs are fins and scales. This rule quickly eliminates shellfish and the carnivorous mammals of the sea, plus some beloved delicacies of the American palate.

Kosher birds are not determined by signs, but by actually being designated by the Torah. Generally, the excluded ones include birds of prey or carrion eaters.

All insects are forbidden, no matter how they are prepared.

How Must Kosher Food Be Prepared?

The very first commandment God gave man occurs at the dawn of civilization and is a dietary law: Do not eat of the fruit of the tree of knowledge. While this law does not address contemporary Jews, who, after all, are not living in Paradise, all subsequent rules of the diet apply today.

Fish, fruit and vegetables require no special method of handling. In order to eat meat, however, the animal's life must be terminated in only one acceptable way: a single instantaneous severance of the carotid arteries in the neck. The blood supply to the brain is cut off and the animal is rendered unconscious. The animal is oblivious to the remainder of the process, much the same as is a person in a coma. This is the law that comes from Moses on Mt. Sinai. Biological evidence demonstrates that it is a merciful death, as kind as most alternatives that well-intentioned people have devised, and far more merciful than hunting. An animal, even one with proper kosher signs, that is not prepared in this manner is considered "torn," in Hebrew *trefah*, or in the common vernacular, *traif*. (This word, as it is used today, actually covers the whole range of forbidden foods.)

Following are other rules that apply to the kosher preparation of food:

1.   The Torah prohibits, absolutely and for all people, not only Jews, the tearing off of a limb from a living animal. This is one of the Seven Noahide Laws, and is a universal, moral, fundamental law of diet.

2.   It forbids the drinking of blood, because blood is considered the essence of life. It also excludes meat which has a residue of circulatory blood. This does not mean that kosher beef needs to be dry and flat. Enough juice remains in the tissues to make wonderful gourmet servings. Overcooked meats are characteristic of an old style in the old country, not of the laws of kashrut.

3.   A more ancient, but more meaningfully symbolic rule is the exclusion from the kosher diet of the animal's hindquarter sciatic nerve. The Torah describes Jacob's wrestling with a mysterious stranger, an angel in the night considered by the tradition to be the image of Esau, the enraged brother whom Jacob was to encounter the next morning. Jacob emerged victorious, but lame, his thigh crippled. In honor of this valiant struggle God changed his name from Jacob to Israel ["God-wrestler"], because he "contended with God and with men and prevailed" and, in memory of that confrontation, the children of Israel do not ever eat the nerve of the thigh.

4.   Jews may not combine meat and dairy foods. This prohibition is repeated three times in the Torah: "You shall not boil a kid in its mother's milk." Meat and milk, and any products containing them, are not to be cooked in the same utensil or eaten at the same time, nor may such an admixture benefit its owner monetarily or personally. Fish and vegetables are neither meat nor dairy. (This "neutral" state is called *parve* and parve items may be eaten with all other kosher food.) In traditional homes, separate sets of dishes and utensils are maintained for meat and dairy meals.

5. The Torah forbids consumption of the hard fat formed below the diaphragm, reserving it for the Temple altar. The regulations separating this fat from other fat which is edible are many and complicated.

The kosher laws sound more complex than, in fact, they are. Today, they are easier to keep than ever before. The *New York Times* in 1990 surveyed the kosher foods available and noted that companies manufacturing them form a vast industry, that literally thousands of kosher food products are available in markets across America, and that all the major companies have investments in these foods. Surprisingly, a large number of non-Jews eat these items, obviously for reasons other than complying with Moses' laws.

Today, there are available delicacies, gourmet foods, and staples from popular brands—from baked goods to meats— that satisfy the standards established by Torah and the Rabbis for the past thirty-five centuries. There are certifications of a product's kashrut on the packaging. Most appear with a circled U, which stands for the approval of the Union of Orthodox Jewish Congregations of America, others have a circled K. The letter K by itself, without design, is unprotected by copyright law and too general to be authoritative, although the product may be kosher.

Information on how to *kasher* [make kosher] utensils and what makes them *traif* should be known to the convert, although all technical decisions on the kashrut of questionable products should be made by a rabbi. The convert needs to understand at least the outline of these laws. Unfamiliarity with them is a sure sign of unfamiliarity with the entire religion.

Finally: Why?

After all is said and done, what is the primary aim of these laws? Over the years, many learned people have stretched and shrunk the laws of logic in order to fit the mold of the kosher laws so as to provide rationales for this unconventional observance—among them, the promotion of health and the avoidance of pagan practice. But none ever really fit this multidimensional practice. One realization becomes clear: for whatever reason God chose to give the Jews these limitations on food, the functional goal they serve is to render the people distinct, thus helping prevent them from assimilating into indigenous populations and faith groups. They also serve as constant cues, especially while travelling, that a distinct God requires a distinct diet. *Vive la différence.*

Notes to Chapter Twenty-four

1. *Mekhilta,* vol. II, Masikhta d'Amalek, Yitro, ch. 2, edited by J. Z. Lauterbach.
2. Sotah 14a.
3. Hilkhot Avel 14:1.
4. *Mekhilta,* Masikhta d'Shirata, 3.
5. Maharal, *Netivot Olam,* Netiv Gemillut Chasadim, ch. 2, 3, 4.
6. Abraham Joshua Heschel, *The Earth is the Lord's,* Harper Torchbooks, Harper & Row, New York, 1966.
7. Herman Wouk, *This is My God.*
8. The reading in *Mishneh Torah* is *ma'aser sheni,* but it is a scribal error and should read *ma'aser ani,* as is the reading in Yevamot, *loc. cit.,* and in the *Kitve Yad Teman,* Hilkhot Matnat Aniyim, ch. 7, Halakhah 4.
9. *Ad. loc.*
10. I am indebted to my brother, Dr. Norman Lamm, for this insight.
11. Rabbi Aryeh Karlin in *Commentary to Maimonides, loc. cit.,* Mossad Ha'Rav Kook, Jerusalem, 1954.
12. Maimonides, *Mishneh Torah,* Hilkhot Matnat Aniyim 7:13.

25
The Jewish Week

THE SABBATH: *SHABBAT*

There is no day which characterizes the Jew more than the Sabbath, *Shabbat*. It is the most important institution in the Jewish religion. It is the only ritual observance listed in the Ten Commandments; it appears more often in the Torah than any other mitzvah; the Talmud devotes two major tractates to it; the *Code of the Law* devotes over 190 chapters to it. (Henceforth, we will refer to Shabbat, rather than Sabbath. Please refer to Fore Words.)

The Shabbat is a separate covenant that God struck with the Jews, an everlasting sign between Him and the people Israel. The correct observance by all Jews of two successive Shabbats will bring the Messiah. It is regarded as a foretaste of the world-to-come in this life; the most cherished future bliss is described as *yom she'kulo Shabbat*, a Day which is all Shabbat. It is not so much an eternal sign, a rabbi once said, as a sign of eternity.

Shabbat is the central celebration of the Jews and it establishes the pattern of all the major holidays; it sets the tone of Jewish time; it characterizes the style of Jewish living. Whether a person is a traditional Jew is not determined by institutional affiliations, but by whether or not that person keeps the Shabbat: Is he or she a *shomer Shabbat?*

Not a Day Off; A Day On

The Shabbat is not a workday. But it is also not a day of rest—if, by rest, you mean going to the ball game. It is not a vacant day after a full week. It is by no means a breather that enables you to be ready to rush around for another six days.

It is a day of renouncing mastery over your private world, of not carrying with you the keys that unlock your material possessions, of a respite from designing your next conquest.

It is a day of thinking and growing, of talking to people because they are people, of singing with the family at the table, of praying with neighbors, of lifting the spirit and elevating ideals, of getting an intimation of truth and beauty, of growing closer to God by inserting yourself again into the environment of His Torah. It is a day for going to the synagogue, for study, for concentrating on the larger questions of life. It is also a day of special food and rest and slowed pace—all with the purpose of designing a new ecology in this sacred island of time.

There is good and substantial reason why Jews "love" the Shabbat. But its charms can have little effect upon you unless you are serious about loving it, and unless you commit yourself to love it for itself and keep it as it wants to be kept. There is no other way of understanding and appreciating it than by "making Shabbat" and "doing Shabbat" and doing it faithfully. From a quick reading of the laws of Shabbat, observing it might appear too difficult to undertake. But living the Shabbat, especially in the company of other *shomrei Shabbat* may well give you a glimpse of eternity.

The concept of Shabbat has too vast a scope, its halakhic dimension spans too large a universe, its practical implications cover too wide a literature to do anything here other than give the convert a fleeting glimpse of it.

The Holiness of Shabbat: A Palace in Time

Judaism is primarily concerned with the dimension of time and its sanctification, rather than with the dimension of space. According to Dr. A. J. Heschel:

> Unlike the space-minded man to whom time is unvaried, iterative, homogeneous, to whom all hours are alike, qualitiless, empty shells, the Bible senses the diversified character of time. There are no two hours alike. Every hour is unique

and the only one given at the moment, exclusive and endlessly precious.

Judaism teaches us to be attached to *holiness in time*, to be attached to sacred events, to learn how to consecrate sanctuaries that emerge from the magnificent stream of a year. Shabbats are our great cathedrals, and our Holy of Holies is a shrine that neither the Romans nor the Germans were able to burn, a shrine that even apostasy cannot easily obliterate: the Day of Atonement. According to the ancient Rabbis, it is not the observance of the Day of Atonement, but the Day itself, the "essence of the Day," which, with man's repentance, atones for the sins of man."[1]

The Halakhah Defines Work: *Melakhah*

We cannot climb the spiritual ladder to the heights of Shabbat without grounding it in a Halakhah that secures it. The Halakhah molds the spirit into actions—performed in a prescribed manner at a precise time, by all practicing Jews in the same way. The laws of Shabbat appear complex, but, once they are lived, they become, like the complexity of the human body, taken for granted, rarely protruding into consciousness. The practice of Shabbat needs to become second nature for it to be truly enjoyed. What follows is a halakhic overview of Shabbat. Do not be overwhelmed. Millions are doing it this very week.

The primary means by which the Halakhah can ensure that Shabbat will be experienced as God intended it to be is by emphasizing the Torah's insistence that we refrain from doing any manner of work. This is the flesh and bones of Shabbat law. The very name *Shabbat* implies rest.

The Torah's word for work is *melakhah*. This is by no means related to physical strain or exertion. This is demonstrated by the curious fact that one does not violate the Shabbat by carrying a very heavy sack of clothes inside the house, but carrying even a handkerchief from the house out to the street is a transgression. For this reason, it is preferable not to use the misleading word "work," but the original word, melakhah. Indeed, it is similar to the case of the dietary laws where it is better to say "kosher" than "fit," which implies "clean."

When the Torah says: "You shall do no manner of work" it means "work" in a ceremonious sense, not an actual one. That is the concept of melakhah which the Torah defines when it prohibits all work on the construction of the desert Tabernacle

on Shabbat. All the categories of work involved in that construction are called, "father works," *av melakhah* [plural: *avot
melakhah*]. From these generic categories, the Halakhah
derives detailed, specific classes of work which are not permitted
to be done on the Shabbat. Following is a short list of examples
of Tabernacle work to be avoided on Shabbat. Included are
activities derived from the generic categories and also their
Rabbinic extensions, which are added prohibitions designed
to avoid the unwitting violation of the biblical laws.[2]

> PLOUGHING—includes digging, leveling the ground;
> safeguards include sweeping earthen floors with a hard broom.
> WEAVING—includes knitting, crocheting, basketwork;
> safeguards include plaiting hair.
> WRITING—includes drawing, painting, making letters or
> figures; safeguards include doing any activity that normally
> triggers writing, such as concluding a sale, marriage, divorce,
> judicial proceedings.
> KINDLING A FIRE—includes fire production by any means,
> regulating a flame by turning it up or down, smoking a ciga-
> rette, starting or driving a car, switching on an electric mecha-
> nism; safeguards include traveling in a bus or car, even if
> driven by a non-Jew, moving a lighted lamp or candle.

If we examine the whole list of thirty-nine prohibited activities,
we discover that they are a representation of all the main types
of creative, constructive human activity. On Shabbat, we
abdicate our purposeful control of nature, every act of human
physical creativity, in order to make a declaration: God is the
Creator of the Universe. Thus, any act, no matter how apparently insignificant, which demonstrates human control or
manipulation of nature in a purposive, useful way is performing
a melakhah.

The entire halakhic enterprise proclaims one common slogan
beyond all others: Actions speak louder than words. What in
daily life constitutes a mindless, trivial effort—switching on the
light, for example—on Shabbat, its rejection constitutes a
declaration of the most profound religious import.

Celebrating the Day: The Idea of Rest, *Menukhah*

The celebration of Shabbat requires, first of all, that we understand the positive spiritual component of rest and learn how
to use it.

The laws of melakhah define the fundamental principle of

Shabbat. All week long, we believe that, to a large degree, we are the masters of our little world; on Shabbat, we declare rest, and realize that in fact we are—the biggest and the best of us—in God's hands.

Terminating work is not sufficient. On Shabbat, God ceased creating, except for one thing: on Shabbat, He created rest, *menukhah*. We can realize our potential only if we can rest creatively—allowing elevated thoughts, deeper values to fill the vacuum, spending the hours studying, playing with the children, speaking and walking in a peaceful, unhurried manner.

Sheer Joy: *Oneg*

The Jewish tradition did not require the human being to rejoice spiritually while denying himself physically. *Oneg Shabbat* means the "Delight of the Shabbat," not, as one might suspect, spiritual delights, but common earthly delights: eating well—meat, wine, fish and pastries; and often—three meals a day; and in a bright atmosphere—where there is abundant light. That is what the Rabbis mean by oneg. And not only eating, but sleeping—the afternoon nap on Shabbat afternoon— is also sheer delight. And why not? Lighting candles—bringing actual brightness into the Shabbat home, not only for atmosphere, but to avoid accidents—is oneg as surely as is spiritual light. That is why the Shabbat meal must be eaten only in the place where the *kiddush*, sanctification over the wine, is made, and where the candles have been lit.

Oneg with menukhah plus the avoidance of melakhah—no work plus joy and rest—is the formula that gives the Shabbat not only character, but personality; it enriches the beauty, attractiveness and the sheer magnetism of the day. Is it any wonder that the Jews fell in love with Shabbat? Is it any wonder that they begin to count the days from Sunday impatiently each and every week until they get to Shabbat? T.G.I.S., they say—"Thank God It's Shabbat!"

Greeting the Queen

Celebration of Shabbat requires, also, sensitizing ourselves to one of the most striking metaphors in all Jewish literature— enthroning the Shabbat as Queen. The Jewish people, for most of history, was without its own government, let alone a king or queen or prince. So they borrowed a crown from the realm of space, transferred it to the realm of time, and placed it on a day. The Jews made Shabbat into their own very real royalty—and the Queen still makes her faithful weekly visits. If, indeed, the Shabbat is Queen, her subjects, the Jews, must know how to greet her in a courtly fashion and how to bid a fitting farewell to the visiting monarch when she leaves on Saturday night.

How do you get into the soul of Shabbat? By keeping *Erev Shabbat*.

The concept of *Erev Shabbat* is vital to appreciating Shabbat. *Erev* means "eve of," or more properly, "the day before" the Shabbat. Too many people, especially working people, "slide" into the Shabbat. The mind conjures the image of a baseball player who hits a triple and tries to stretch it into a home run. He rounds third base and scampers home, diving headlong into home plate a second before the catcher gets the ball. He makes it sliding into home—covered with dust, scratched from hitting the ground, and on all fours. Acting like this on *Erev Shabbat* is to obliterate the *erev*—the preparation, the mood-setting—and it bids fair to shattering the feeling of the whole Shabbat.

Shabbat begins precisely eighteen minutes before sunset; that is the last possible moment for candlelighting. Please remember: Shabbat does not begin when dinner is served, when Dad comes home from work, when guests arrive, or at the beginning of a late Friday service. The exact time can be found in Jewish calendars—sunset is different for different cities and parts of the country—or, if there is no such calendar, find sunset time in the local newspaper and subtract eighteen minutes.

If Shabbat begins at 5:42 PM, try not to "slide into home base" one minute before—out of breath, muddied, scratched, panting, and virtually on all fours. Shabbat is a Queen. Everything needs to be in place for her arrival.

WELCOMING THE SHABBAT

"Greeting Shabbat" encompasses candlelighting, the prayer service called Welcoming Shabbat, the dinner-table singing of Shalom Aleichem, and kiddush, the sanctifying of the day.

CANDLELIGHTING

Lighting the candles is the privilege of the lady of the house. If she cannot perform the mitzvah, a man may do it. But the house requires candles to be lit within it. She lights the candles at least eighteen minutes prior to sunset in the room in which dinner will be served. The candles symbolize *sh'lom bayit*, "peace at home," basically because it provides enough light to enable the family to avoid accidents. On a higher level, more appropriate to today's metaphor, sh'lom bayit, "peace at home," is a vivid reminder that not only do we rest from work, we should rest also from quarreling.

The blessing for candlelighting should ordinarily be made, as every other mitzvah blessing is made, *before* the lighting. Yet, if the woman makes the blessing first, she ushers in the Shabbat when one is not permitted to kindle a flame, and how then will she light the candles? Therefore, a woman first kindles the candles, then covers her eyes, recites the blessing, and, as she opens her eyes after the recitation, she sees the flames. It is only then that Shabbat formally begins for her. Some women light one candle for each child. That is a matter of personal decision, so long as the minimum two are lit. It is a silent applause for the family to surround her at this beautiful moment.

THE WELCOMING SHABBAT SERVICE

The prayers welcoming the Shabbat are called *Kabbalat Shabbat*, and they consist of joyous psalms, the *Lekha Dodi* song welcoming the Shabbat, and the official Shabbat Psalm which was always sung at the Temple in Jerusalem. This is followed by Ma'ariv, the short evening service.

SHALOM ALEIKHEM

"Shalom Aleikhem" is the first song at the Shabbat table after completing the service. This is followed by the singing or recitation of the last chapter of Proverbs, "The Woman Of Valor." If this song that husband and children sing is appropriate at any time, it is now—the moment to pay tribute to a woman who, after all, is the primary person responsible for welcoming the Shabbat Queen.

KIDDUSH

Kiddush, the declaration that sanctifies the Shabbat, is recited—often by all present at once—over a full glass of wine. We do this in fulfillment of the biblical mandate to "*remember the Sabbath day*." If one cannot drink wine, kiddush could be made over diluted wine, grape juice, or even the two twisted loaves (*challot*). A second, more abbreviated kiddush is made on Saturday afternoon before the meal.

Farewell to the Queen: *Havdalah*

The end of Shabbat is sweet sorrow. It is delayed for about an hour beyond the twenty-four-hour day to demonstrate our regret at its departure. Also, it is delayed in order to avoid accidentally ending it too early, thereby short-changing the sanctity of Shabbat. The fading glory of the day comes through in the melancholy tunes of the "Third Meal," *Se'udah Shlishit*, which are slow and hesitant, unlike the vibrant songs, the *zemirot*, of the Shabbat afternoon meal.

Havdalah is a short, delightful, richly symbolic home ceremony that marks the boundary between the sacred and profane, the light and dark, the seventh day and the six days of work. Havdalah, literally meaning "division," is made up of blessings and colorful symbols that make the transition from Shabbat to weekday.

It begins with a declaration of trust in God, especially appropriate after the Shabbat has removed her protective royal shield from the people, and before the tense busy world of the next week lays its burdens on our shoulders.

It then proceeds to three blessings. The first is over wine, which, in addition to being the drink of sanctification, represents rich flavor, bouquet, head-spinning and heart-lifting bountifulness, and, with them, hope and optimism as we look from the darkness of week's end to the future. The second is over sweet smelling spices, such as cloves and cinnamon, as if to compensate for the fragrance of that lovely Shabbat which is now evaporating before our eyes. The third is a blessing over the gift of fire, which symbolizes the productive world from which we have been absent for twenty-five hours, and to which we now return for six days.

Some Jews make family and community "Escorting the Queen" parties, called *melaveh malkah*, because even after Shabbat has gone and it is already the night of the first weekday, there is a glimmer of radiance in the wake of the royal departure, and whatever is left of her presence is celebrated.

Preparing for the Day: *Kevod Shabbat*

"MAKING SHABBAT": *EREV SHABBAT*

No matter how we celebrate the day itself, it will not be the same—in holiness, in meaning, in satisfaction—if we do not prepare for it and put our hearts into enhancing it.

SOME HALAKHIC HINTS

Set the table for Shabbat as would befit a reception for a queen—complete with fine china, silverware and tablecloth—no matter how many guests are coming to dinner, and even if you are eating alone. Place on it the two challot symbolizing the breads brought at the Temple—your table is an altar—and cover them with a special cover. Some interpret fancifully that the two challahs represent the twofold amount of manna that fell in the desert on Friday for both Friday and Shabbat, and the cover represents the dew that covered them in the morning.

When returning from synagogue, or after praying at home, greet the family with a jubilant "Shabbat Shalom" or "Good Shabbos." Many greet the Shabbat even if no one is at home to greet them!

After singing "Shalom Aleikhem" and "Woman of Valor" and reciting Kiddush, as described above, everyone should line up before the sink to ceremoniously wash hands, recite the appropriate blessing, and remain silent until the challah is dipped in salt and the blessing over bread recited. At the end of the meal, we recite Grace, called *Bentching*.

Make the second Shabbat meal—which we eat at midday—as much of a banquet as the Friday night meal. The meal is called *Se'udah*.

Because we wish to make Shabbat not only a spiritual feast but a physical celebration we are bidden to make a light third meal, *Se'udah Shlishit*, before Shabbat is over—usually in late afternoon.

SOME PRACTICAL HINTS

Following are some suggestions for preparing for Shabbat:

During the week, if you are a woman, memorize the blessing for candle lighting; if you are a man, memorize the Friday night

Kiddush; both should do the same for the "motzi" over the challah. It is preferable to work from the Hebrew you've just learned, even if it slow going. If not, learn it from the transliteration.

For Erev Shabbat, develop a weekly routine of cleaning and straightening up the house so that it is neat and special for Shabbat. Buy challot and other special Shabbat foods, and preferably also flowers. On Friday the food needs to be cooked *before* the Shabbat—try making a kugel, or *cholent* or other favorite food. The stove should be set—one burner on low, with a metal sheet (a *blech*) over it so that the food will be kept warm, but will not cook. You may not use electricity, so the lights must be set—some left on all day Shabbat, some regulated by a timer. The table has to be set, the candlesticks polished and set up.

Immediately prior to the onset of Shabbat, one should dress in fresh Shabbat clothes; even if only staying at home, we dress for the occasion and not only the company. If new clothes were bought during the week, they should be worn for the first time on Shabbat. On Friday, it is good not to eat too much, so that when Shabbat finally arrives, in addition to being exhausted and prepared for Shabbat rest, you are also sufficiently hungry to truly enjoy and appreciate the Shabbat meal.

The mind should also be prepared for the Shabbat—emptying it of all weekday plans and schemes; slowing the pace and striving to be at ease with ourselves and with others; setting aside money for *tzedakah*, charity; if possible, reviewing the Torah portion to be read on Shabbat morning.

Stopping for Shabbat: A Personal Digression, by Herman Wouk

All that was said of the Shabbat in this chapter comes together in this wonderful insight into the mind and will of one of America's great writers, Herman Wouk. Stopping work for the Shabbat in many instances is very difficult, but rewarding nontheless:

> The Sabbath has cut most sharply athwart my own life when one of my plays has been in rehearsal or in tryout. The crisis atmosphere of an attempt at Broadway is a legend of our time, and a true one; I have felt under less pressure going

into battle at sea. Friday afternoon, during these rehearsals, the inevitable seems to come when the project is tottering on the edge of ruin. I have sometimes felt guilty of treason, holding to the Sabbath in such a desperate situation. But then, experience has taught me that a theater enterprise almost always is in such a case. Sometimes it does totter to ruin, and sometimes it totters to great prosperity, but tottering is its normal gait, and cries of anguish are its normal tone of voice. So I have reluctantly taken leave of my colleagues on Friday afternoon, and rejoined them on Saturday night. The play has never yet collapsed in the meantime. When I return, I find it tottering as before, and the anguished cries as normally despairing as ever. My plays have encountered in the end both success and failure, but I cannot honestly ascribe either result to my observing the Sabbath.

Leaving the gloomy theater, the littered coffee cups, the jumbled scarred-up scripts, the haggard actors, the shouting stagehands, the bedeviled director, the knuckle-gnawing producer, the clattering typewriter, and the dense tobacco smoke and backstage dust, I have come home. It has been a startling change, very like a brief return from the wars. My wife and my boys, whose existence I have almost forgotten in the anxious shoring up of the tottering ruin, are waiting for me, gay, dressed in holiday clothes, and looking to me marvelously attractive. We have sat down to a splendid dinner, at a table graced with flowers and the old Sabbath symbols: the burning candles, the twisted loaves, the stuffed fish, and my grandfather's silver goblet brimming with wine. I have blessed my boys with the ancient blessing; we have sung the pleasantly syncopated Sabbath table hymns. The talk has had little to do with tottering ruins. My wife and I have caught up with our week's conversation. The boys, knowing that the Sabbath is the occasion for asking questions, have asked them. The Bible, the encyclopedia, the atlas, have piled up on the table. We talk of Judaism, and there are the usual impossible boys' queries about God, which my wife and I field clumsily, but as well as we can. For me, it is a retreat into restorative magic.

Saturday has passed in much the same manner. The boys are at home in the synagogue, and they like it. They like even more the assured presence of their parents. In the weekday press of schooling, household chores, and work—and especially in a play-producing time—it often happens that they see little of us. On the Sabbath, we are always there, and they know it. They know, too, that I am not working, and that my wife is at her ease. It is their day.

It is my day, too. The telephone is silent. I can think, read, study, walk, or do nothing. It is an oasis of quiet. When night falls, I go back to the wonderful nerve-racking Broadway game. Often, I make my best contribution of the week then and there to the grisly literary surgery that goes on and on until opening night. My producer one Saturday night said to me, "I don't envy you your religion, but I envy you your Sabbath."[3]

Friday night has come and the Queen has arrived. A feeling has blown away the market place; a prayer has swept in a new joy; a bow of the will has welcomed the royal guest. The day flies by and children and friends and Torah and food and sleep have filled twenty-five hours with a touch of the world-to-come. Farewell, sweet day. The light and spice and wine soften your parting. We await your return.

Notes to Chapter Twenty-five

1. Abraham Joshua Heschel, *The Sabbath, Its Meaning for Modern Man*, p. 8 ff., Harper Torchbooks, Harper & Row, New York, 1966.
2. Isidor Grunfeld, *The Sabbath*, Feldheim, Jerusalem, 1959.
3. Herman Wouk,*This is My God*, p. 59, op. cit.

26

The Celebration of the Jewish Year I:

ROSH HASHANAH TO PURIM

NEW YEAR: ROSH HASHANAH

Standing at the head of the Jewish year is a solemn yet festive two-day New Year that differs in purpose, quality, and intensity from other New Years.[1]

Rosh Hashanah celebrates the creation of the universe, and the Divine judgment on the human beings who occupy that universe. These are awesome days that call for a period of introspection and self-criticism, and for a resolve to alter the spiritual and ethical blunders and the negativity of the previous year. It is no small order—but, if there is to be no change, can there be a *new* year? It is a solemn undertaking indeed.

The great theme of the ten days which begin with Rosh Hashanah and reach their climax on Yom Kippur, is standing trial in a court of law with Almighty God as the Judge, deciding on life or death, comfort or penury, health or disease, for every living person, indeed for all creatures. The testimony is in everyone's own handwriting, as the High Holiday Prayerbook puts it, and there is no hiding the truth from the eyes of the court, for they are the "eyes" of the All-Wise God who sees all.[2] Awe is the only spiritual attitude that can define the temper of the day.

For all the solemnity of Rosh Hashanah, however, there is a bright string of optimism that runs through the liturgy and the ceremonies. It is born of the confidence that, although personally we may be undeserving, our plea for forgiveness and pledge of improvement will elicit God's compassion and He will clear our slates, accept our resolve and renew our years. If we rejoice, it is with the conviction that life—despite its frustrations and distress—is genuinely worth living, and that this day is but the first in a year that holds out a promise of better things.

Rosh Hashanah, because it is in the nature of a trial, is also an occasion when, in the words of the Holy Day prayerbook (called *machzor*), there comes before God, "the remembrance of every creature—man's deeds and destiny, his works and ways, his thoughts and designs, and the workings of his imagination." This "Day of Remembrance" is not only a recollection of monumental events of the dim past, but of the journey we ourselves have made since the year began—its destinations and its detours, the false steps we may have taken and the temptations to which we may have mindlessly yielded. As we glance backward, we need to view positive accomplishments as well, not as "proof" of our right to continue to live or to live well, but to enable us to assess ourselves truthfully. Also, it enables us to recall with gratitude the times we have been delivered from mishap and pain by the unseen hand of the Almighty.

Rosh Hashanah is not only a celebration of the birth of the world, a trial day, a day of remembrance, and a beginning of change in ethical and religious behavior—it is a Coronation Day. In a very real and spiritually meaningful manner, we enthrone God anew at the start of every year. Beginning with the New Year and for ten days concluding with the Day of Atonement, the liturgy changes the way we refer to God— it substitutes the word *Melekh*, which means King, for the standard term *El*, which means God. On these Days of Awe, we relate to God as a Sovereign—He is the King of Kings, and we are His subjects. He is a King who passes judgment; a King who sits on His throne on High with the books of life and death open before Him; a King who dispenses mercy; a King who administers reward and punishment and has the power to compel the world to do His bidding.

If the central theme of New Year is a day of judgment, it

is fitting that the central feature should be a summoning to judgment. That is accomplished by the *shofar,* an ancient instrument, a ram's horn, whose sound is unlike any other heard all year. It is alternately wailing, pleading, angry—a shrill alarm that calls one back to ancient roots. This instrument is designed to trumpet the forthcoming solemn season, and to awaken Jewry to the need for repentance. Its call serves also to associate those historical events heralded by the shofar which made Israel a people, whether at Mt. Sinai or upon its entrance into Israel, or on the occasion of the proclamation of the Jubilee year. In biblical times, the shofar was used to announce every important national event. Thus, the Jubilee was launched at the end of forty-nine years by sounding the shofar; the Revelation on Mt. Sinai commenced with its sound; its call was a trigger to war and it proclaimed the advent of peace; it warned of imminent danger, and it was blown to begin a fast as Jews solemnly pleaded with God for respite from woe.

The blowing of the shofar occupies the central place in the arrangement of the Synagogue service. Although, originally, the shofar was blown during the morning Shacharit prayer, the ceremony was later transferred to the early afternoon Mussaf service, and is now blown at both times. The reason for this time shift is instructive. Persian government officials thought the shofar blast was a real call to arms instead of a symbolic call to hearts, and believed it to signal, at dawn, the beginning of an insurrection, and therefore prohibited its use. It was then moved to the later service. When the threat subsided, it was moved back to the early service, but many were reluctant to remove it from the later service, and so blew it twice.

The shofar's notes give fitting expression to the feelings aroused by the festival. Three notes are emphasized in the strains of the shofar: the *tekiah,* a firm, unwavering note; the *shevarim,* a combination of three broken notes; and the *teruah,* a staccato succession of nine short blasts.

The tekiah expresses power, demonstrating confidence in its uncompromising trumpeting; the shevarim represents a moaning presence, and the teruah bespeaks sobbing—a more passionate and intense weeping than the shevarim. These wailing notes were modeled, according to some commentators, after the crying of the mother of Sisera as she was looking through the lattice waiting for her son to return from battle. But Sisera, the hated Syrian general who fought against the Jews, was slain and never returned. A mother's tears strike sadness in the mind, no matter for whom she is crying. They are clearly an expression of a contrite or broken heart. Each set of shofar blasts begins and ends with the tekiah so as to bracket the sadness with optimism.

The shofar served uniquely to express the different levels of meaning of Rosh Hashanah. According to the ninth-century scholar, Saadiah Gaon, it symbolizes the coronation of God, the King. In another sense, it bespeaks our appearance in the Court on Judgment Day, not filled with arrogance, but with contrition and also a touch of hope, the tekiah of confidence that the Good God will deal kindly with us.

Most well known of all, and probably the shofar's most apparent purpose, is a call to be mindful of the importance of repenting. Maimonides summed up the significance of the shofar in the following words:

> Although the blowing of the shofar is a commandment of the law, there is this further meaning in it: "Awake you slumberers, from your sleep and rouse you from your lethargy. Search your deeds and turn in repentance. Remember your Creator, you who forget truth in the trifles of the hour, who go astray all your years after vain illusions which can neither profit nor save. Look to your souls and mend your ways and your actions; let every one of you leave his evil path and his unworthy purpose. Seek the way of God."

On this day, then, we confirm that, for Jews, God is Creator, King and Judge. For all those august titles, God is also Father—who grants our wishes and who looks upon us as erring children and not only as wayward servants. There is no thought that there might be a contradiction in these terms—Jews are equally at home with a King and a Father at one and the same time, with God who is both immanent and transcendent, loved and feared. Thus, immediately after each set of shofar blasts, we recite a prayer:

> This day, the world was called into being; this day, all the creatures of the universe stand in judgment before Thee, as children or as servants. If as children, have pity upon us as a father pities his children; and if as servants, we call upon Thee to be gracious unto us and merciful in judgment of us, O revered and holy God.

Customs of the Festival

A Festival so awesome and so filled with significance had to become rich in folk customs and symbols.

The most well-known is the Rosh Hashanah greeting. Abbreviated, the wish is expressed in Hebrew words it is well for the convert to learn: *Shanah tovah,* "Have a good year." It is abbreviated from *L'shanah tovah tikatevu ve'tekhatemu,* "May you be inscribed and sealed (in the Book of Life) for a good year." Following a talmudic thought, one gives expression herein to the hope that all friends may be granted a year of life and happiness. So popular is this custom that letters written during the entire preceding Hebrew month, Elul, begin or end with this wish.

The holiday table, too, reflects this all-pervasive greeting and gives expression to the character of the festival. In the words of the great Sage, Abaye, in the Talmud, "Signs are significant," which means to say that on this day of judgment when we must be especially careful of the details of our behavior, every gesture has special gravity—every word and action is freighted with significance. If people want a sweet life, they should eat sweet foods. And so, after reciting kiddush when returning from the evening service, they dip the challah into honey rather than into the usual salt. Later, they dip an apple into honey and wish for a *shanah tovah u'metukah* "a good and sweet year," as not all good things are sweet, and not all sweet things are necessarily good. Some make a habit of eating fish, denoting the wish that good deeds should proliferate all year as fish do, or beets or dates or whatever sweet item is local custom, and whatever the significance attributed to the sign.

The day following Rosh Hashanah is the Fast of Gedaliah, observed on the third day of Tishre. It commemorates the assassination of Gedaliah, who was appointed Governor of the Jews by Nebuchadnezzar. His death marked the final blow in the destruction of the First Commonwealth.

PAY TO PRAY?

An old strategy of synagogues in large cities in the Jewish community should be noted here lest it offend converts who are confronted by it without warning. That is the custom of buying tickets for reserved seats at High Holy Day services.

It appears to smack of commercialism and theatrical perform-ance and to be not only devoid of spirituality, but contradictory to it.

Jewish congregations cannot raise revenues by an offering plate at a weekly service, as do most churches. In synagogues, Jews pay an annual membership fee and are thereby entitled to all membership benefits, including tickets for Rosh Hashanah and Yom Kippur services. Not all Jews wish to, or can afford to, take memberships, although they may want to come for services on the High Holy Days. The ticket is a way of insuring that support for the synagogue is democratically spread among all the community members, and not only a burden on the faithful. Also, many congregations thereby assure their mem-bers that they will have first call on a seat for the synagogue service. Accordingly, while synagogues are open to anyone who wishes to pray at every other time of the year, Rosh Hashanah and Yom Kippur services are often restricted to "ticket holders only." Converts, especially in the first year, should make their presence known to synagogue leaders to avoid embarrassment. Be assured, however, that no one may be turned away because they cannot afford a seat. Tickets are often necessary, un-fortunately, but they serve only to insure that the Jewish com-munity is fiscally capable of functioning throughout the entire year.

THE TEN DAYS OF REPENTANCE, OR RETURN TO GOD: ASERET YEMAI TESHUVAH

The ten days from Rosh Hashanah through Yom Kippur are known as the "Ten Days of *Teshuvah*," or, literally, "Re-turn." The first thing that strikes one about *ten* days is that teshuvah is not an overnight accomplishment; one cannot simply affirm a belief in God and consider the matter done. Judaism considered teshuvah a process of growth and reali-zation and therefore gave its adherents ten intense days to achieve this task in a credible manner. And it designed many symbols, ritual practices and prayers to help actualize this teshuvah: as on Rosh Hashanah, the compelling graphic pray-ers, the astonishing shriek of the *shofar*, the awesome "feel" of the day, impel serious soul-searching. Indeed, even this ten-day period proved to be too short, and it prompted the Rabbis to design the month of Elul preceding Rosh Hashanah as a month of preparation for the arduous task of self-examination, rather than to jump-start so demanding a challenge on Rosh Hashanah itself. Further, to encourage serious teshuvah, the Sages activated a daily alarm by instituting shofar blowing every morning to awaken the soul to rehearse for Rosh Hashanah.

A true "returning" is no easy matter. It necessitates, nay demands, honest self-searching. Teshuvah is fundamental to Judaism. Understanding it in depth is no simple matter, let alone accomplishing it, and the candidate for conversion needs to read more on the subject and to think about it very seriously.

The foundations of teshuvah are three:

1. Deep and sincere regret at the wrong committed and then confessing it;
2. Uncompromisingly terminating the sinful behavior; and
3. Resolving never to pursue that course again, once and for all.

Anything short of this prescription is not valid repentance. To regret an action while continuing it, is patently absurd; to end it, yet not be sure that it is over, is not to have changed but to have modified. Maimonides refers to one who sincerely does teshuvah as a new person—"It is not I who have sinned, but some other."

These ten days reserved for teshuvah were considered by the Sages as the most "acceptable time" to God—when God is most accessible to Jews because of their heightened sensitivity to good and evil and their increased prayers (called *Selichot*), and when God, as it were, is Himself more sensitive to people's intercessions on their own behalves. These days should be spent in increased ardor, in earnest self-examination, and in a serious effort to turn over a new leaf in the Book of Life. Indeed, could there be a more sublime way of celebrating the beginning of the year than by dedicating its first ten days to an inventory review of our spiritual assets and liabilities?

DAY OF ATONEMENT: YOM KIPPUR

The climax of the entire spiritual enterprise of the year is Yom Kippur. The Sages held that not only does a person's repentance gain him or her forgiveness, but the day of Yom Kippur itself is so sacred, that the very day itself has a forgiving quality.

> On the tenth day of this seventh month is the Day of Atonement; there shall be a holy convocation unto you, and ye shall afflict your souls (by fasting). It shall be unto you a Shabbat of solemn rest, and ye shall afflict your soul, in the ninth day of the month at even, from even unto even (Leviticus 23:27).

This Holy Day is observed by abstaining from all food and water. The Oral Torah teaches that, in addition to prohibiting eating and drinking, the phrase "to afflict your souls" implies a prohibition against all physical pleasures—washing and bathing, moisturizing one's skin, wearing leather shoes, and even having sexual relations.

The washing that is prohibited is that which is done for pleasure—for feeling comfortable and refreshed. Washing for cleansing or upon arising or after taking care of one's toilet needs is permitted. The Yom Kippur fast may be broken only for reasons of critical illness—the sick person's expressed wish or the opinion of physicians may be the determining factors in permitting it. A rabbi's decision in any such case must be sought. To fast and to abstain from all bodily nourishment and pleasure for a space of about twenty-five hours is a profound personal expression of complete submission to the realm of the spirit.

At the Entrance to Yom Kippur

FORGIVENESS FROM FRIENDS
BEFORE FORGIVENESS FROM GOD

Yom Kippur atones for sins committed against God but unequivocally provides no forgiveness for sins committed against one's fellow man unless the aggrieved party has been pacified first and has agreed to forgive the wrongdoer. Yom Kippur should serve as a yearly deadline for reconciliation, for expressing regrets and asking forgiveness, and also for forgiving and forgetting the sins of others.

Judaism makes a bold statement with this fundamental aspect of its holiest day: living well under God is not sufficient for the religious person. A Jew must first live well with neighbors, who are, after all, God's creatures, before he can begin to approach God for himself and his family. The actual name for Yom Kippur is Yom Kippurim, the plural "Day Of Atonements"—atonement for sins against people and atonement for sins against God.

The custom developed, therefore, that Jews greet one another during the Ten Days of Repentance with: "Please forgive me if I have offended you." Of course, if there are specific disagreements between people, these should be handled in a special manner, not offhandedly as a greeting.

CHARITY

Charity funds should be set aside and brought to the synagogue prior to the evening services—preferably at the brief afternoon Minchah service before Yom Kippur when the first confessional prayers are recited—for distribution to the poor and the homeless and to religious, educational and social welfare institutions. The Rabbis say that "Charity saves one from death," by which they mean not that one could buy his way to eternal life, but that a good deed could delay God's final decree. On Yom Kippur, when life and death hangs in the balance, we work every angle to build up our virtues before the onset of the trial.

FEAST OF FORGIVENESS

The meal in the late afternoon prior to the fast should be a festive meal—although one should not overeat or eat anything that might cause thirst and make fasting more difficult.

But this meal was not eaten only as a needed preparation—stopping at a filling station before a long stretch of wilderness—as Shabbat is not a day of rest just to prepare for six working days. The meal itself had special significance, and the Rabbis said that eating this meal before Yom Kippur was virtually equal to fasting on Yom Kippur itself. To explain this, the Hasidic Rabbi of Sassov pointed out that it is really more difficult to eat in the quest for forgiveness than to fast for forgiveness! Human beings understand self-denial as a means of achieving spirituality. Judaism insists that enjoying the goods God has given is also a means to achieving closeness to God. So on Shabbat we enjoy *oneg* (delight) and *menukhah* (rest) in the pursuit of obeying God's wishes.

Purity and a Rehearsal For Death: The Kittel

The *kittel* is a white robe customarily worn on Yom Kippur, especially by those whose families hail from Eastern Europe. It has deep symbolic importance. It represents the ideal of purity and the unsoiled confidence of the Jew that God's forgiveness will come. The wearing of white accoutrements on Yom Kippur—white tallit, white kittel, white skullcap—symbolizes the prophetic promise: "Though your sins be as scarlet, they shall be as white as snow" (Isaiah 1:18). The repenting worshipper is likened on this day to the ministering angels whose sinless record is as white as snow.

But there is a deeper resonance of the Yom Kippur ritual that the kittel and the wearing of white confirm. In addition to all the spiritual meanings of the day, Yom Kippur is also a rehearsal for death: fasting is a deprivation of the sustenance of life; the lack of washing is symbolic of decay; abstaining from sexual relations is removing oneself from the source of life; not wearing leather shoes is a requirement made of mourners; sheathing oneself in a white kittel and tallit in the evening, is a dramatic embodiment of being wrapped in the white shrouds in which the dead are buried.

This enactment of a death scene is not done out of morbid fascination with the end of days. It is a very real means of traumatizing by symbol in order to awaken religious sensitivities on this Holy Day. Repent one day before you die, the Rabbis counseled in the Talmud and, since we do not know when that day is, we must repent every day. The confrontation with death sets our priorities in order: terrible annoyances become insignificant, our great victories but minor achievements, and our sins with their short-lived gains become absurd profits that we mindlessly barter for eternal life.

A by-product, by no means insignificant, is that Jewish people were thereby connected to a part of life from which most people struggle to separate. They literally rehearse for an eventuality that terrorizes people, causing panic and creating taboos that paralyze the mind. Death is a night that lies between two days, the day of life on earth and the day of eternal life with God. Yom Kippur is in a very real sense a domestication of the diabolic in the sub-vaults of our consciousness.

Yet, for all that, Yom Kippur is certainly not a "Black Fast"; there is nothing black or gloomy about a day on which we approach the throne of the Heavenly Father to seek atonement and pardon for sins. It is, on the contrary, a very bright festival, a *Yom Tov* assuring the sinner of pardon and forgiveness if the change of heart is sincere and the resolve to leave the wrong path unconditional.

It is told of the great Hasidic Rabbi, Levi Yitzchak of Berditchev, that when he entered the synagogue on Kol Nidre night, the eve of Yom Kippur, he sensed sadness, pessimism, an anticipation of doom. He turned to the congregation: "Why are you so melancholy? Do you think you are appearing in trial before some petty tyrant? No, not tonight. Tonight, we appear before the merciful God, the Master of the Universe."

This confidence was in no way better expressed than by the gala festivities held immediately after the Yom Kippur fast at which singles met and subsequently married. They met after the most intensive day of soul-searching and pledging to do what is right in the future.

BLESSING THE CHILDREN

The custom is for parents to bless their children before leaving the house for the synagogue on the night of Yom Kippur. This is an awesome day, and the seriousness of the Yom Kippur teshuvah undertaking is conveyed to children subliminally via this special blessing. Parents implore God, in that blessing, that their offspring may be sealed in the Book of Life for good health, personal fulfillment and spiritual growth.

The Liturgy

KOL NIDRE

The impressive opening service of the day is the Kol Nidre service, on the eve of Yom Kippur. With its plaintive and stirring melody, the Kol Nidre prayer infuses worshippers with feelings of joy and fear and a sense of anticipation.

The text of the Kol Nidre prayer belies the pathos of its compelling strain. It is a simple legal formula abolishing vows and pledges that have not been fulfilled. In a way, however, it is the very text as it has been corrupted and construed by Israel's enemies that has provoked the sadness of its tune.

The abolition of vows, of course, addresses only vows made to God, not to fellow men. If atonement is given on Yom Kippur only for sins against God, but never for sins against fellow man, surely pledges and promises made to others could not be dissolved by Yom Kippur. Nonetheless, this was not to be understood by our many detractors. The text was transformed into pretext.

In Jewish history, Kol Nidre was often the cause of wanton and malevolent accusations against Jews. Jew-haters used this prayer to prove to their ignorant followers, that since a Jew can annul his promises through this prayer on his holiest day, he cannot be trusted. Thus, on June 24, 1240, Rabbi Yechiel of Paris had to disprove the challenge made by Bishop Nicolaus Dunin in the presence of King Louis IX and the Queen Mother Blanche, and to show, by quoting evidence from the Talmud, that the Kol Nidre does not absolve the Jew from keeping a promise made to his fellow.

In 1656, Manasseh ben Israel had a similar experience in his negotiations with Cromwell for the readmission of Jews into England (from which they had been expelled in 1290 by Edward I). Even as late as the eighteenth and nineteenth centuries, after repeated representations to the Russian authorities from unfriendly quarters, the authorities issued an order on October twenty-fifth, 1857, prescribing a special introduction to the Kol Nidre prayer. This reaffirmed explicitly that it applied only to such vows as involve the person making them and no other.

PRAYERS OF CONFESSION

A special characteristic of the Yom Kippur services are the confessional prayers recited at five distinct times during the day. The two prayers of confession, *Ashamnu*, and *Al chet*, are arranged in alphabetical order and recited in the plural, "We have sinned . . . ". Each sin is accompanied by a slight beating of the breast to indicate a truly broken heart.

Now, of course, each person has private sins he or she committed, but these are the business solely of the person and God and should not be recited aloud to be heard by anyone else. That is why the confessions are formulaic and alphabetical. Also, it is also more appropriate to join in a plural prayer rather than in a personal confession of wrongdoing. These prayers are recited by the whole community collectively, even by those who have not themselves committed any sins. The thought in their recital is that they, too, confess, and regret their inability to prevent others from committing transgressions. Also, it is not sufficient to *feel sorry*; one needs to express the profound regret. Confession was thus considered an essential for atonement and a necessary step to perfect repentance.

THE SACRIFICES

The liturgy of Yom Kippur is largely modelled on the proceedings in Temple Days. Therefore, apart from a number of important prayers which are the same as those recited on Rosh Hashanah, the central place in the afternoon Mussaf service is reserved for the *Avodah*, prayers that simulate the service of the High Priest in the Temple on Yom Kippur. The Avodah service is a graphic representation of the ancient Temple scapegoat and atonement service.

An emotional peak of the service refers to another kind of sacrifice—the narrative that describes the ten Rabbinic martyrs killed by the Romans for doing nothing other than studying Torah.

NE'ILAH

The concluding service of Yom Kippur, is called *Ne'ilah*, or Closing. This closing refers not so much to the concluding service of Yom Kippur, as to the metaphoric closing of the gates of Heaven at dusk that marks the finale of Yom Kippur. It is particularly outstanding for the pathos of its prayers, pleading in the most bold and graphic terms for God's mercy on us all before the gates of mercy are locked. Recited as the sun begins to set and night draws near, it gives expression to the penitent's confidence in God's forgiveness, as he or she asks to be not only "written," but "sealed" in the Book of Life.

The service ends in a rising crescendo, proclaimed responsively, with the cantor first crying out *Shma Yisrael*, "Hear,

O Israel, the Lord, our God, the Lord is One"; then, followed
immediately, three times, by a cry of *Barukh Shem Kevod*,
"Blessed be the Name of His glorious Kingdom for ever and
ever"; then, in a burst of exhilaration, seven times, louder and
louder, *Ha'Shem hu ha'Elokim*, "The Lord, He is God!" At
this point, there is sudden quiet; the shofar is removed from
the Reader's table, and one very long blast, *teki'ah gedolah*,
is sounded. At that climactic moment, all break into a triumphant cheer, *Le'shanah ha'baah bi'Yerushalayim*, "Next year in
Jerusalem!"

AT THE END OF YOM KIPPUR

The Fast is finally over. It is time to eat and rejoice. Our
day in court is won. The effect is stunning. Rabbi Simeon Ben
Gamliel says, "There were no happier days for Israel than the
fifteenth of Av and the Day of Atonement."

THREE PILGRIM FESTIVALS

"Three times in the year shalt thou keep a feast unto Me."
During these three holidays—Pesach (Passover), Shavuot
(Pentecost) and Sukkot (Tabernacles)—the Jews made pilgrim-
ages to the Temple in Jerusalem. These Festivals were occasions for much personal and communal joy and spiritual
elation as large numbers of pilgrims from all parts of the Holy
Land and beyond journeyed to Jerusalem. These holidays then
became known as the three Pilgrim Festivals, *Shalosh Regalim*.

These three festivals not only commemorate vital national
events in our history, but are also agricultural landmarks. Thus
Passover records the early harvest, Shavuot the second harvest
and Sukkot the ingathering of the fruit. During the Passover
and Sukkot festivals, there are intermediate Days between the
beginning and ending celebrations. These are known as *Chol
Ha'Moed*, literally the weekdays of the holiday.

The first of these festivals to occur in the Jewish calendar
year is the holiday of Sukkot, the Feast of Huts, or Tabernacles.

FEAST OF HUTS: SUKKOT

Sukkot is a festival that follows naturally on the heels of Yom Kippur. Rosh Hashanah and Yom Kippur do not grow out of natural or historical occurrences. They are formal, awesome, soulful, intense and abstract; they are solemnized by spartan observances and they deal with the major, ponderous themes of the faith such as creation and death, justice, sin and redemption. Judaism, which is so fine-tuned to balance the emotions of normal life, needs to follow those heavy holidays with a burst of energy, exuberance, enthusiasm.

Now comes Sukkot, built on a bounty of history and a cornucopia of nature. It is not abstract, but earthy. And it is a natural complement of Rosh Hashanah and Yom Kippur. Those who think of Judaism as comprising only these two High Holy Days see only a distortion of Judaism. They need to experience the celebration of harvest, the ceremony of the water, the affirmation of pleasure and success, the buoyant festival of frail huts that symbolize trust in God, and the triumphant dance of the Torah at the crowning end of Sukkot.

The festival of Sukkot, or Tabernacles, is known by three names—the Sukkot Festival, the Harvest Festival, and *The Festival*—and has both a national and historical, as well as an agricultural, background.

The Sukkot Festival

As *Chag ha'Sukkot*, the Feast of Huts (or Tabernacles), the Festival is a physical reminder of the dawn of Jewish history, when our ancestors wandered for decades in the endless, dusty and terrible wilderness on their way to freedom and independent nationhood. The Bible instructs expressly:

> The fifteenth day of this seventh month shall be the Feast of Tabernacles for seven days unto the Lord. . . . Ye shall dwell in booths seven days; that your generations may know that I made the children of Israel to dwell in booths, when I brought them out of the land of Egypt (Leviticus 23:39).

There is an important lesson implicit in the idea of sukkah which the Sages taught: The sukkah is a demonstration of the Jews' faith in God's ability and willingness to perform miracles on their behalf. Our ancestors, to be sure, could never have survived that long journey in the wilderness but for their indomitable faith in that Divine providence. The transient tents, feebly constructed, could never have provided safety in the savage desert, but for God's protective shade. Implied in this teaching is that, if our ancestors could have survived and built a nation in these tents, their descendants, living in more secure circumstances, ought to be impregnable to the onslaughts of their enemies.

But there is an ongoing teaching that addresses Jews not from history, but from the keeping of the sukkah mitzvot in the present. We observe an annual routine at Sukkot when we leave our luxurious homes and take up residence in a fragile lean-to, which may not be higher than thirty-six feet nor lower than forty inches. The message is clear: Do not revel in the glory of your possessions; do not depend on them—learn to live even in a hut if need be; understand that the festival of joy, as the Bible refers to Sukkot, can be celebrated even in penury and homelessness.

The roof covering of the sukkah, called s'khakh, is very precisely detailed in the law. Too much covering provides too much protection and negates the message of fragility; too little is not to take recognition of God's protection at all. The s'khakh may be made only with detached branches of trees or with leaves which must be placed thinly enough for the stars to be visible through them, yet thickly enough so that the shade on the floor of the tent exceeds the rays of the sun. The walls of the sukkah must be able to withstand ordinary gusts of wind, and they can be made of three sides, if necessary.

Two Rabbis debated the exact nature of the sukkah symbol. One held that it represented the actual hut that the Jews lived in during the harvest and when they wandered in the desert. Another Rabbi said they represent the clouds of glory that guided the Jews thorough their forty-year trek in the desert. Whether heavenly or earthly, the sukkah is one of the most treasured symbols of the year.

There is a special mitzvah to adorn the sukkah, and the greatest of scholars spent time crafting colorful birds out of eggshell and cardboard. This hut away from home was considered a family's palace to which they invited many guests, and also special "guests"—the most notable heroes of history, Abraham, Isaac, Jacob, Joseph, Moses, Aaron and David—

one per night, formally introduced before the evening meal in the sukkah. They consider it an honor to sit with a Jewish family huddled in the autumn cool, under a ceiling of straw, hanging apples, bananas, and craft-paper birds, and a door made of draperies.

The celebration of Sukkot, and the actual building of sukkot according to halakhic standards, is enjoying a great revival in our day, even among the non-observant. It is a beautiful, colorful, fun-filled, children-oriented holiday. Naturally, then, "it is an everlasting statute for all your generations."

The Halakhah requires that we eat all meals in the sukkah for the entire holiday. In case of rain or extreme cold, or if one is ill or even believes he is catching a cold, he is excused from the sukkah. On entering the sukkah, we recite two benedictions, found in the prayerbook. The blessing over the mitzvah of sukkah deserves a hearty recital—as Rabbi Elijah, the Gaon of Vilna, noted, only the mitzvot of sukkah and mikveh, and the mitzvah of settling Israel, can entirely surround the Jew— and that is as close as one can get to a Heavenly embrace.

Harvest Festival

The second name by which Sukkot is known is *Chag he'Assif*, the Feast of the Ingathering, reflecting the harvest motif of the early fall season. The crops of the fields having been gathered in, the people rejoiced in gratitude for God's blessings. This nature component gives an unusual tone to the character of this festival. It is expressed symbolically through the use of the "four species," a bouquet of assorted plants very specifically designed for the meaning it needed to convey. This is the central liturgical expression of Sukkot.

The four consist of an *etrog*, a citron; a *lulav*, a branch of palm; three *hadassim*, myrtle branches; and two *aravot*, willow twigs. Three of these are bound together and held in the right hand—the palm, the three myrtles, and the two willows—and the citron is held in the left hand, and then both are brought together, the fruit hugging closely, and a blessing over them is recited every holiday and weekday morning of Sukkot (but not on Shabbat).

This luxurious, natural symbol became the subject of a thousand interpretations. For example, the *etrog* is a heart; the *lulav* is a backbone; the *hadas* leaf is a mouth; the *aravah* leaf an eye: all our faculties should be used in the service of God. Or, another example: A Jew should have a good heart, a strong backbone, an eye that sees good in others, and an educated and soft-spoken mouth.

And it became the object of Jews' affections for centuries. The attention lavished on these four prosaic plants was sheer poetry in the world of the humdrum. The etrog had to be free of spots; not round, but rather tapered; not smooth like a lemon, but grooved; at the end opposite the stem, there is a button-shaped growth called the *pitom*, which may not be broken off. The lulav should taper to a point; the haddasim should be thick enough to cover the stem; the aravot should be smooth-edged, preferably a bit red. The bouquet should retain its freshness—withered plants will not win our affections. (And, for these thousands of years, we still have not learned how to keep them really fresh for eight days!)

In the synagogue, those who have the four-species bouquet make a "circuit" with the lulav and etrog around the synagogue. The custom is at least as old as the time of the Maccabees, and the Book of Jubilees traces it back to the days of Abraham. The Mishnah relates that, in the Temple, they used to circle the altar with these bouquets singing the Hallel and Hoshanah prayers.

The Festival, Par Excellence

The third name given to this Festival is *Chag*—simply, "Feast"—*the* Festival, *par excellence*. This was the most luxurious and festive festival. Unlike Passover, when the pilgrims had to return home after the first day to begin reaping the early harvest, on Sukkot the people had already harvested the crop, and it afforded them the time to celebrate all seven days in Jerusalem, rejoicing with family and friends in the environs of the Temple.

Sukkot also boasted a unique and powerful universal message. This was demonstrated daily in the sacrifice of seventy oxen offered for the well-being of the "seventy nations" of the known civilized world. This act was a public expression of Israel's solidarity with all mankind at a time when universal peace and the brotherhood of man were dim images appearing on the furthest horizons of humanity. Sukkot thus embodies a messianic ideal which it broadcast to the whole world: Let us pray and work for each other's welfare—we are one. The

Prophet Zechariah invited all the nations of the world to "go up (to Jerusalem) from year to year to worship the King, the Lord of hosts, and to keep the Festival of Sukkot!" (Zechariah 14:16).

THE GREAT HOSHANAH DAY

The seventh day of Sukkot is called *Hoshanah Rabbah,* for the special Hoshanah prayers recited on this day. It was observed with an exotic, but exquisite, ceremony in the Temple. The Priests, holding willow branches, circled the altar seven times in procession, singing *Hoshanah*, which pleads, "Save us," for sustenance through the winter months in years of mediocre harvests. They then struck the willows on the ground at the side of the altar. The custom in synagogues today is to make a procession of seven circuits with lulav and etrog singing Hoshanah. At the end of the service, we strike the leaves from the willow. In post-talmudic times, Hoshanah Rabbah, takes on a touch of the character of Yom Kippur, even down to the wearing of a white kittel by the cantor.

In Israel, Sukkot is observed by one day at the beginning, and also one day at the end which incorporates two celebrations observed separately in the diaspora, Shmini Atzeret and Simchat Torah.

SHMINI ATZERET *AND* SIMCHAT TORAH

Sukkot, the holiday of rejoicing, is over. Sadness, anti-climax, back-to-worry thoughts should begin to set in. *Not yet.* The Torah insisted on one more holiday—a special one. It is connected to Sukkot; it caps the High Holy Day season; but it is neither of these. It is a gift—a holiday of pure joy.

Throughout the Sukkot days of heightened sensitivity and dependence on the Almighty, we have reconnected spiritually to our source, God. Now we are saddened to leave His presence. Might it not also be said that God has reconnected to His people who look to Him and praise Him, and that He, too, is saddened to see us leave? The talmudic Sages described the reason for Shmini Atzeret by relating the following parable: God is like a king who invites all his children to a feast to last for just so many days. When time comes for the children to leave, he says: "My children, I have a request to make of you. Stay another day; your departure is difficult for me." This is the spirit of Shmini Atzeret. We have been with God from the beginning of the year. We must leave. To God and to man, it is holy regret.

Although it is commonly regarded as the final day of Sukkot, Shmini Atzeret is distinct and has its own integrity and requires none of the special observances related to Sukkot. What is left after the many symbols and rituals of seventeen special days have been filtered through the soul of the people is a distillation of crystal-clear joy.

One special event does occur on this day. The year-long cycle of Shabbat Torah readings comes to its close on this day. Characteristic of this People of the Book, it begins once again on this same day! The holiday is therefore also called *Simchat Torah*, the Rejoicing of the Torah. In the diaspora, where Jews observe two days of holiday (unlike in Israel when only one day is observed) the Simchat Torah portion gets its own day—the last day, the crown of all the holidays. It is marked by seven processions around the synagogue with all the scrolls of the Torah. The day is characterized by everyone's receiving an *aliyah*, being called to the Torah. All young children stand together around the open scroll under a wedding canopy, a *chuppah*, to recite the blessing in unison; the last person to receive an Aliyah concludes the cycle of the year as he stands under the canopy, and is called "Groom of the Torah;" the first person called to begin the new cycle takes his place under the *chuppah* and is called "Groom of Genesis." It is a day of singing and dancing, of children with hats and flags marching in a Torah procession, of melodies and laughter, and of childish pranks like tying the tallit to chairs, to other people, to solemn bearded teachers.

It is a hearty goodbye to days of exaltation and exultation.

HANUKKAH

Hanukkah may be twentieth-century Judaism's most popular holiday—surely it is the best known amongst gentiles. Of all the holidays in the entire Jewish calendar, it is the last holiday of the ancient world; it is the only one not based on a biblical narrative; the only one that celebrates a military conquest; the only holiday based on a miracle not instituted by a prophet; the only one not celebrated by a synagogue special service, or by a scroll, or by biblical reference. But, as the Hanukkah lights are increased by one each for eight nights, the power, the significance and the popularity of Hanukkah and its message grow ever brighter—from day to day and year to year.

What is Hanukkah?

After the death of Alexander of Macedonia in 323 B.C.E. and the collapse of his empire, his Seleucid Greek successors in Palestine, led by Antiochus Epiphanes in 168 B.C.E., set out to "domesticate" the Jews and assimilate them to Syrian-Greek culture by outlawing, at the pain of death, the teaching of Torah to youngsters, the observance of circumcision, the Shabbat, and kashrut. He subjected the population to degenerate behaviors, among them sexual assaults upon women. As if that were not oppressive enough he introduced an idol into the Temple in Jerusalem and had apostate Jewish Priests slaughter pigs as sacrifices to Greek gods in cities and villages across the Holy Land.

This caused too much pain. Life to many Jews was simply not worth living under these circumstances. But no one was moved by his anger until an old Priest in Modin, Mattathias of the Hasmonean family, refused to sacrifice the swine and killed a Priest who wanted to replace him. His five sons rescued him from the oppressors and, in the process, touched off a three-year guerrilla war which was to end with a stunning upset victory that drove the Greeks from all Judea. On the twenty-fifth of Kislev in 165 B.C.E. (exactly three years after the first defilement of the Sanctuary), the Jews burst triumphantly into the Temple, rededicated it to the service of God and restored it to its former glory.

The Macabeean War was launched by one passionately

idealistic old man against unbelievable odds which he never calculated in advance. It was a revolutionary war, essentially anti-colonial, against the oppressive occupying force of the Syrian Greeks. It was also a civil war, against the sycophantic, assimilating, Hellenized Jews who licked their masters' Spartan boots and assumed that the day of the Jews was over.

If there were no Mattathias would there have been a Temple? If there were no war, would there today be a Jewish state? If there were no Hanukkah, could there have been a Christmas?

It might seem strange that Hanukkah is referred to in the Talmud almost in an offhand manner. The Rabbis allude to Hanukkah in an aside, in the midst of a discussion on Shabbat in the Talmud, in response to the question "What is Hanukkah?" only three centuries after the event. It appears to be the process of Jewish history to transform military victory into historical memory of spiritual triumph.

Celebration: Light or Sword?

It would appear that since the Hasmonean War was a military victory—a consequence of passion and wisdom and arms and strategy—it should be celebrated with gusto, by star-spangled songs and military symbols. But early Jewish history did not view the Macabeean revolt as a battlefield triumph. The odds against successful combat were impossible—the Jewish "army" consisted of a collection of ragtag, untrained civilians who were outnumbered, outgunned, and outmaneuvered by a professional, battle-hardened, military force. The ultimate triumph was a conspicuous religious victory achieved not only by the confluence of superior dedication in the cause of a noble ideal by men of monumental courage, but by the protective interdiction of God—and that is the nub of the central prayer of Hanukkah:

> You, in Your great mercy stood up for them in the time of their travail. . . . You delivered the strong into the hands of the weak, the many into the hands of the few, the impure into the hands of the pure, the wicked into the hands of the righteous, and the wanton into the diligent students of Your Torah. . . .[3]

The Rabbis of the Jerusalem Talmud kindled the lights in jugs fastened to the tops of their swords, celebrating a battlefield victory. The Rabbis of the Babylonian Talmud decided that the holiday would be observed, not primarily for the victory on the battlefield, but for the victory in the Temple. They record the miracle that occurred there at the climax of the three-year struggle:

> When the Hasmoneans prevailed against the Greeks, they made search in the Temple and found only one cruse of oil which lay there untouched and undefiled, intact with the seal of the High Priest. This cruse contained sufficient oil for one day's lighting only; but a miracle was wrought therein, and they lit the lamp with it for eight days. The following year, these days were appointed a festival with the recital of Hallel and thanksgiving (Shabbat 21b).

The celebration of Hanukkah, the Festival of the Dedication of the Temple, is expressed in a spiritual mode by the addition to the service of psalms of praise, the Hallel; thanksgiving for the miracles, *Al Ha'Nissim*, introduced into the Silent Devotion and the Grace after Meals. The character of the celebration is unlike the Shabbat and major holidays, on which one does no manner of work. Primarily, Hanukkah is celebrated by the kindling of little tapers that burn for half an hour each night for eight nights of Hanukkah in honor of that miraculous one-day jug of oil.

Kindling the Lights

One should kindle the lights near a window or door, in order "to proclaim the miracle." If that is not possible, care should be taken not to light them in a place where candles are lit the whole year, in order to distinguish the Hanukkah lights from all others. The time of lighting begins immediately with the appearance of the stars. If at all possible, the time should not be delayed, and the candles or the oil, either of which may be used, should burn for at least half an hour.

The order of lighting is as follows: One begins on the first night by placing the light at the right end of the *menorah*—all Jewish honors start at the right, such as when approaching the reading table when receiving a Torah honor. On the second night, a candle is placed on the right again and an additional light is added to the left of it, and so forth on each consecutive night. The new candle is always the first to be kindled. The light from one candle should not serve to light another. An extra light, called the *shamash*, a utility candle, is used specifically for the purpose of kindling the other lights. It is preferable for every individual to light a separate set, but it is sufficient for one set to be lit for every household.

Hanukkah candles are different from Shabbat candles in that those lit for Shabbat are purely functional—to prevent accidents in the dark and to be conducive to domestic peace. Hanukkah candles, on the other hand, are kindled solely as symbols, and are not permitted to be functional. Therefore, one should not read by the light of those candles—as the paragraph recited after the lighting reminds the kindler. The shamash is placed near the eight so that anything done near the menorah may be derived from its light, in addition to its function of lighting the other candles.

Festival of Hope

Hanukkah is remembered not only for the miracle of the lights that burned in the Temple, but for the miracle of bringing light to a darkened world. The days of December on which Hanukkah usually falls are the shortest in daylight and the longest in night of the entire year. On the twenty-fifth night of Kislev, the moon begins to shrink from sight altogether, and at the winter solstice, the sun begins to weaken and sheds least of its warmth on the cold earth. It is a time of year when a little light must go a long way. Running counter to the natural process of diminishing light, the ceremonial candles grow in number, shedding more light with each successive night.

But it is as a symbol that light serves on Hanukkah. The Jewish people were in the throes of their darkest hour during the Maccabean days—needing to wage both a Revolutionary War and a Civil War at the same moment in order to remain alive. The small flask of oil is a symbol of the exhaustion of the Jewish people—beset by powerful enemies without and within, racked with self-doubt about its future, and about its self-worth being only a minuscule presence in the center of immensities and in the conflux of eternities.

At the same time, the fact that, despite the decimation of the people, the annihilation of the land, and the destruction of the Temple, one pure, unadulterated jug of oil could still be found, must have been exhilarating. And then the discovery that that exhausted pittance could survive and grow and become a source of energy and a torch of liberty and they themselves a "light unto the nations," must have been a thrilling confirmation of the Almighty's intent for the future of the Jewish people.

As a source of hope for the future, the little light was more instructive and inspiring than the recitation of battlefield heroics. The celebration of the spirit rather than the might stood the test of time and served the Jewish people in every year of its exile. To the Jew in the old narrow dark ghettos, the candle had a gratifying message that brightened his heart; the sword in such instances would have been a figment of nostalgia, but mockingly fantastic and close to absurd in the middle of the night of exile. This is the message the Rabbis encased in the Haftorah, the prophetic portion read after the Torah reading, on Hanukkah. It calls on the world, even today, to remember the eternal message of the Prophet Zechariah: "Not by might, nor by power, but by My spirit, saith the Lord of Hosts."

A convert needs to know what Hanukkah means to convey, and that is that it is not just a national celebration of religious freedom, but a statement of personal sacrifice for Jewish observance and identity, and a declaration of hope in Jewish survival. It is important for the newcomer to Judaism to know, therefore, that Hanukkah is not simply the Jewish counterpart to secular winter festivals or Christian celebrations, that there is a profound distinction between light and light, and between joy and joy.

For the Convert: A Season of Crisis

On a practical level for the convert, this season highlights the conflicts between past and present, one family and the other, and they are daunting. Here is how Lydia Kukoff describes it:

> I remember my first Hanukkah after my conversion. Sure, I lit the candles, but I really didn't feel I knew enough about Hanukkah to make it meaningful. I didn't know the context. My husband didn't get too excited about Hanukkah either, and that didn't help. It was a big disappointment. Then came Christmas. On Christmas eve, I turned on the radio and there were Christmas carols playing. I just dissolved in tears. It was only then that I realized what I was missing. It wasn't the gifts and it wasn't the tree. I was missing the sense of family. I was missing Mother, and the smells in the house, and the music. The problem was that my husband didn't think of Hanukkah in those terms at all. He bought me a

Christmas tree! I was furious. Now I know better. Hanukkah can be just as much a family holiday as Christmas used to be in my life. And the meaning of Hanukkah is so much a part of me now that it's hard to believe that my first Hanukkah and my first Christmas after my conversion were so painful.

It is important for you to realize that Hanukkah is not a Jewish Christmas. It should not become a compensation for the loss of Christmas in your own life. It is not about buying silver and blue wrapping paper instead of red and green, or Hanukkah decorations instead of Christmas wreaths. It is a completely different holiday, and you must learn about it so that you can celebrate it on its own terms. Hanukkah has important values to teach. . . .[4]

There is a distinctiveness to Judaism that belies all attempts to make it just another route to God. These attempts are made most vocally and forcefully at this winter season of celebrations. And it is at no time of the year more painfully evident that a superficial understanding of Hanukkah, as of Judaism generally, does it grave injustice.

The very use of light in Judaism is just one small, but surprising example. In ancient times windows had no glass; they were wide within, to let in as much light as possible, and narrow without, to keep out the dust. According to the Rabbis, the ancient Temple windows, over against where the candelabra stood, were turned in the opposite direction—they were narrow on the inside and wide as they extended outward. Why? Because God does not need light—He is the source of illumination. The world needs light. The light of the menorah shines outward to brighten and irradiate the world. The Hanukkah candles are placed in a window to proclaim to the world the miracle of the light and the light of the miracle.

TU BI'SHEVAT

Tu bi'Shevat, the fifteenth day of Shevat, is a midwinter New Year for fruit trees, usually falling in February. The year is reckoned from this date in matters relating to the tax of one-tenth, or tithing, of the fruit. The tithing was taken for the sake of the Priests and Levites (who were not permitted to own property) and for the indigent. It was considered the formal end of one fruit-crop year and the beginning of another. This day was celebrated as a minor holiday: there were no work stoppages or lengthy prayers or colorful rituals. The only custom associated with this day is that of eating a fruit that is grown in large quantities in Israel, the fruit of the carob tree (St. John's Bread, or *bokser*), which is mentioned as the mainstay of the food eaten by Rabbi Simon bar Yochai during the years of his hiding in a cave to escape the wrath of the Roman Army. Those who find bokser impossibly hard to chew can eat other fruit indiginous to the Holy Land, such as olives, dates, grapes, and figs. Children often make this day one of field trips and plantings.

Historically the Jew has scowled at the pagan worship of trees; indeed, the Jew was bidden not to harm precious fruit trees even in wartime. *Tu bi'Shevat* should be a time for becoming sensitive to the beauty of nature that God has given so freely for human enjoyment.

Notes to Chapter Twenty-six

1. There are several valuable books on the subject of holidays. One is Herman Wouk's *This is My God,* cited often in these pages; *To Be a Jew,* by Hayim Halevy Donin, Basic Books, New York, 1972; *The Cycle of the Jewish Year* by Yaacov Vainstein, World Zionist Organization, Department for Torah Education and Culture in the Diaspora, Jerusalem, 1953; Irving Greenberg's *The Jewish Way;* and others found in every Judaica bookstore in the country.
2. This theme is emphasized most graphically and sensitively by Irving Greenberg, *The Jewish Way,* p. 186, Summit Books, New York, 1988.
3. From the prayer, *Al ha'Nissim,* recited during the Hanukkah Amidah.
4. Lydia Kukoff, *Choosing Judaism,* ch. 6, pp. 68-70, Hippocrene Books, New York, 1981.

27

The Celebration of the Jewish Year II:

PURIM TO ROSH HASHANAH

PURIM

Purim is carnival time in the Jewish year. Just as there is a distinct quality to the Jew's fasting and praying, so there is a special flavor to his rejoicing. This annual holiday is a holiday of merrymaking that is an outcropping of one of Jewish history's nastiest conditions.

It celebrates the turning of the tables against as powerful and as malicious an anti-Semite as the ancient world had ever seen. It is with a historical sigh of relief that the *pur*, the lots Haman cynically drew for choosing the day of our destruction, proved to be the very day of his downfall. The day, the four-teenth day of Adar, is an intertwining of blessed relief, a touch of revenge, a twinge of fear, and a vague disbelief that days of anticipated mourning could actually be transformed before our eyes into heady days of rejoicing. "And it was reversed," the Bible says.

This reversal is expressed every year by the rapid alternation of fasting and feasting on the thirteenth and fourteenth of Adar, the Fast of Esther and the Feast of Purim. The eve of Purim is observed as a fast day, albeit a minor one observed from sunup to sundown, called *Ta'anit Ester*, the Fast of Esther. This was the day, the Book of Esther records, that Haman, the Persian Prime Minister, had designated for the slaughter of all the Jews in the Persian Kingdom of King Ahasuerosh. Queen Esther called upon all her fellow Jews to fast with her, and thus averted the evil decree. (An additional reason might be that, on this day, the Jews were preparing a counter attack and proclaimed a fast to pray for success.) The Feast of Purim was the day on which the Jews turned the tables on Haman and had him hanged and his cohorts destroyed. Purim's celebration is defined by the observance of four special mitzvot.

The Four Mitzvot of Purim

THE MEGILLAH

While Hanukkah is referred to only in passing in the Talmud, Purim has a full talmudic tractate, Megillah, devoted to it—in which are detailed the mitzvot of this day, primarily the requirement of reading the *Megillah*.

On Purim Eve and at the morning service on the day following, the "Megillah [or scroll] of Esther," or as the Talmud and all Jews refer to it, "*The* Megillah," is read to the chanting of a special expansive and lighthearted tune appropriate to the narration of the Purim story.

The Megillah is unrolled completely and then folded to give it the form of a letter, like that sent by Mordecai to the Jewish communities with the first break in the news of Purim.

The Megillah is usually read in packed synagogues, but with a touch of concern. There is a need to draw a fine balance between the competing claims of the Halakhah and the crowds. The law's requirement is that every single word of the Megillah be heard; the crowd's equally demanding requirement is the keeping of the custom that every mention of Haman be drowned out by *groggers*, noisemakers—or by foot stomping, catcalls, an occasional, smuggled-in trumpet, police whistle or base drum. The reading of the Megillah is a happening—its success is judged by the community by decibels of noise, the impatience of old men with the tricks of other people's grandchildren, the internalized fits that rabbis mask in their smiles as they try to keep the Halakhah's requirements by keeping a lid on the bedlam of a congregation of Haman survivors gone berserk.

THE FEAST

Since Purim is a holiday of joy, one is expected to eat, drink and be merry on it, reliving the incredulous release of tension our ancestors must have experienced, for which reason they declared it "a day of feasting and gladness." A special se'udah, or "festive meal," is held in the late afternoon, candles are lit and the whole family sits down to a fun dinner, recalling the royal banquet at which Esther procured the annulment of Haman's evil decree and featuring a three-cornered pastry filled with prunes or poppy seeds that symbolize Haman's hat. (It is the closest thing to having his head!) It was customary, as early as the days of the Mishnah, to make a special communal appeal for the poor on Purim, so that they might have a proper Purim Se'udah.

The Talmud quotes instances of extraordinary jubilation by the Sages themselves on Purim. In some talmudic colleges or *yeshivot* the students elect a special Purim Rabbi and indulge in the controlled chaos of lampooning their teachers good-naturedly in limericks and song, while yet retaining a modicum of respect; of costuming themselves, yet retaining a shred of dignity; of presenting "Purim Torah," mock dissertations their rabbis might give, which yet demonstrate a depth of learning. In its finest expression, it is indeed unique artistic humor.

SHALACH MANOT

Each person must send "portions" to a friend. The "portions" consist of gifts of food or drink. The minimum gift should consist of two items of baked or cooked food, usually including haman-taschen, plus a smattering of candy or drink. Although the minimum obligation is fulfilled by sending such a gift to only one person, it is customary to send *Shalach Manot* to all close friends and assorted rabbis, and to have the children serve as delivery persons.

GIFTS TO THE NEEDY

Each person needs to give charity to at least two poor people or needy causes. If one is in a place where there are no poor people or is otherwise unable to distribute the funds on that day, the money should be set aside for later distribution. Even a poor person who is himself a recipient of charity must give to others.

Perhaps the gift to the needy—demonstrated especially by the poor man's gift to the poor—is the way in which a brilliant tradition declares that, while fun and games are healthy, even at the expense of revered teachers and straight-laced grandfathers, the serious business of helping others takes no vacation, even to celebrate the dethroning of tyranny and the opportunity to breathe freely once again.

PASSOVER: PESACH

In the spring, a new world is born—the greening earth, the shy bud, the sprig of grass. That is the announcement of nature. In the spring, a new nation is born. That is the proclamation of Passover.

For Jews, nature and history coalesce to celebrate new beginnings. But neither history nor nature can begin without experiencing the agony in emerging from the womb of the past. The seed breaks through the winter crust of the ground, with the sun and the rain working their culinary magic, and bursts its shell to flower in the garden of earth. A nation, leashed to Egyptian overlords by the chains of slavery, shatters its iron collar and flees into the desert. It struggles to be born. The waters of the sea break and Israel emerges into the sunlight of history.

Passover narrates the travail of the Exodus and the birthing of the Jewish people; it sings of God's strong hand that delivered it; it sheathes in timeless ritual the grand ideas of subjection and emancipation. The narration is encased in the Haggadah, a book read only on the first two nights of Passover; the songs and rituals are embedded in the Seder, the decorous ceremony that is celebrated at home on those nights.

Historically, Passover commemorates the deliverance of the Israelites from two centuries of Egyptian bondage 3300 years ago. The story of Israel's oppressive servitude, the Divine mission entrusted to Moses and his brother Aaron, the hard-hearted rejection of the Pharaoh, the Divinely ordained catastrophes that caused Pharaoh's temporary change of heart, and the Israelites' escape into the desert are told in the Book of Exodus, chapters 1-15.

The Exodus became the focus of Jewish history; redemption the theme of Jewish theology. So important are the concepts of this festival, that the first of the Ten Commandments opens with a reference to it —"I am the Lord, thy God, who brought thee out of the Land of Egypt, out of the house of bondage." One of the most important of the biblical mandates of Passover is "telling the story" of the Exodus from Egypt. The energy of these ideas of exodus and redemption has vitalized the French and American revolutions and is the driving idea behind most independence movements, let alone the struggle for emigration of Jews from the Soviet Union and the creation of the modern State of Israel. These are the subjects that are symbolized and sung on Passover.

Passover's Names

The Torah calls Passover by several names signifying a number of intertwined themes of the day. One is the Festival of Spring, *Chag He'Aviv,* the season when all creation and vegetation come to life again. This conveys an enduring message of nature's renewal, one that addresses oppressed and unfortunate people in their despair of seeing freedom and a full life again: pain can result in the birthing of a new world.

A second, more familiar title is the Festival of *Matzot,* the observance with which the holiday is most distinctly identified. This speaks of the hurry of the Jews in preparing to abandon the country and who, having no time to wait for the yeast to rise, grabbed unbaked bread— *matzah*—and fled into the wilderness. It speaks of the people's participation in the liberation process.

A third is Festival of Pesach, the most commonly used name. Pesach is a reference to the Paschal offering brought on the eve of the festival, which commemorates God's promise to exempt Jewish families from the plague of death for the first-born: "I shall *pass over* you, and there shall be no plague upon you to destroy you" (Exodus 12:13). This theme addresses God's benevolence and His redemption of the Jews from slavery. From this point on, we will refer to Passover as Pesach.

A great Hasidic rabbi once remarked that this expresses the reciprocal love of God and Israel: Jews pay homage to God, and call the holiday Pesach for His generosity, while God pays tribute to the Jews for their willingness to follow Him into the terrifying desert by calling it the Festival of Matzot.

The Omer

Beyond the Exodus theme, there is an agricultural aspect of this spring festival. When the Israelites settled in the Holy Land, they brought an offering of winter barley harvest on the second day of Pesach which, by that time, had usually just ripened. Barley is the quickest ripening grain, and therefore the quintessence of fruitfulness of the earth. This offering was known as the *Omer* and had to be brought before the people were permitted to eat the new corn.

In recollection of this beautiful ceremony, we now count the Omer from the reaping of the barley harvest for forty nine days—from the second night of Pesach until Shavuot when the wheat harvest was ready. These days and weeks are times of tension, the entire economy of the land and the fortunes of individuals depended on these harvests, and the day-by-day counting is a result of either communal anxiety or communal gratitude—probably both at the same time. The practice today is that we count the days and weeks each night after dark, first reciting a blessing and then reciting the number of day and week—for example: This is the twenty-eighth day, which is four weeks of the Omer.

Both nature and history are celebrated on the three pilgrim festivals. The people kept the holiday of Pesach not only as a harvest festival, but as a celebration of the Exodus, and they celebrated Shavuot not as a harvest festival only, but as a celebration of Revelation, the giving of the Torah on Mt. Sinai. The forty-nine days between the two harvests represented the anxiety and hope for the economy. The forty-nine days between the Exodus and the Revelation represent the spiritual thirst of the people, anxiously ticking off the days in anticipation of receiving the Torah as they came closer and closer to Shavuot.

Chametz and Matzah

The two terms on which the entire celebration revolves are *chametz*, normal yeast bread, and *matzah*, flat bread made without any yeast whatsoever. The Torah, both the written Torah and very extensively the Oral Torah, goes to great lengths to make absolutely sure that chametz not be eaten or profited from or even seen or found in Jewish homes or businesses during the entire eight days of Pesach. It also insists in absolute terms that matzah be eaten, at least at the Seder each of the first two nights, unless the consumption of this unleavened bread proves physically harmful. These precepts were among the first conveyed to the Jews by Moses immediately prior to their departure from Egypt:

> "For whoever eats leaven from the first day until the seventh day, that person shall be cut off from Israel" (Exodus 12:15).

> "Seven days shall there be no leaven found in your houses; for whoever eats what is leavened, that person shall be cut off from the congregation, whether he be a ger, a stranger, or a citizen" (Exodus 12:19).

What is Chametz?

Chametz consists of any one of the five major grains—wheat, rye, barley, oats and spelt—that has come into contact with water for the time it takes to sour and rise, beginning the leavening process—at least eighteen minutes. Chametz also is any food or drink that contains even minute traces of these leavened grains. Examples of chametz are not only bread, but cereal, whiskey, cakes, and most other food, unless specifically supervised for conformity to the chametz restrictions.

Interestingly, only those five grains are acceptable ingredients for baking matzah, providing they have *not* been allowed to leaven through eighteen or more minutes of contact with water. It is a clear indication that, as in most acts of immorality, it is not nature that is impugned, but what people make of it. The right process makes it the *desirable* food for performing the mitzvah; consuming a product of the wrong one brings total excision from the Jewish people.

The strict avoidance of all contact with chametz extends to every food or utensil associated with it. The use of dishes and utensils in which even minute traces of chametz have been absorbed is not permitted during Pesach. Ovens and ranges used throughout the year for chametz must first be cleansed in accordance with the prescribed koshering procedure before using them for Pesach. The regulations governing the prohibition of chametz on Pesach are stricter than those concerning dietary restrictions. During Pesach, even a particle of chametz of *any* quantity makes *all* the food forbidden for consumption.

The following foods are not chametz, and may be eaten, but like all other Pesach food, should not be prepared in contact with chametz:

Meat, fowl, fish.

All fruits.

All vegetables (except corn, rice, and peas, and look-alike grains, among German-originated Ashkenazic Jewry).

All spices.

Dairy products.

To assure that industrially processed foods contain no ingredients that would cause them to be prohibited for Pesach, one should purchase only such canned, bottled or packaged foods as have been certified by rabbinic authorities who supervise the company's compliance with Pesach's unique kosher laws. Fresh or raw foods in the categories above need no special endorsement. Dairy products do.

WHAT IS MATZAH?

Most matzah today is baked by machine, although there are still some people who prefer to use hand-baked matzah. The development of modern machinery to mix and bake the dough has guaranteed greater speed in the process, thereby reducing the danger of leavening. It does not matter if matzah is round or square; there is no special significance to shape.

Pious Jews eat a specially cared for matzah for the Seder nights, called *matzah shmurah,* which means watched or guarded matzah. This matzah is followed closely from the time of the harvest throughout the baking process to make absolutely sure it has had no contact with anything that might cause it to leaven.

AT WHICH TIMES?

The Torah prohibition against chametz goes into effect at noon on the fourteenth day of Nisan, although the festival itself does not actually begin until that evening. To prevent the inadvertent violation of the biblically proscribed period, the Rabbis required that chametz disposal be completed two hours earlier, to approximately 9:30 A.M. depending on the length of the day. In countries outside Israel, the chametz laws are extended along with the holiday for an extra day for a total of eight days of Pesach.

Preparing for Pesach

A thorough housecleaning is usually undertaken in preparation for the Pesach festival. Shopping for the week is a special undertaking as it involves scrupulous care that the food products have been duly certified by rabbinic authorities. A good rule of thumb is: When in doubt, don't.

Ovens and burners on cooking ranges must be kashered for Pesach use well before the onset of the holiday—in no case later than the morning before the holiday begins. Refrigerators, counter tops, sinks and other kitchen items require special attention to avoid the contact of embedded chametz with the fresh Pesach food. There is much literature on the subject available before Pesach. Knowledgeable rabbis will be happy to assist you. It is a new and invigorating, but also difficult experience—but it is easier today than ever before.

THE CEREMONY OF THE CHAMETZ SEARCH

On the night before Pesach, the family launches a formal, ceremonious, but nonetheless deadly serious, inspection of the household. It is the annual search for chametz. The house is darkened, except for a single lighted candle; the head of the house recites the blessing over searching for chametz; and, with the entire family following, he gropes from room to room in detective-like investigation to find the chametz culprits, armed with a feather (or similar item) for gathering all the crumbs and a wooden spoon (or any receptacle) to hold them. It is a dramatic teaching medium for preparing children for the rigors of Pesach.

Since it is unlikely that crumbs or other chametz will be found in a household which has already been well cleaned (creating a situation where a blessing is recited in vain), it became customary for a responsible member of the family to place, prior to the beginning of the formal search, small pieces of bread in various places throughout the house so as to make certain that *some* chametz is found. One should not, however, do so indiscriminately, but should know exactly how many pieces were thus placed so as to be sure that they have all been found.

The chametz found during the search, together with the receptacle used to collect it, should then be wrapped and put safely aside for burning the next morning.

Conducting the Seder

The Seder is the religious service and grand festive meal of the first two nights of Pesach. The word "seder" means order of service, and is so called because of its orderly integration of the elaborate symbolism in food, prayer, narrative, and ritual. It is a meticulous and mysterious blend of exuberance and melancholy—the heady wine to celebrate the sudden release from tyranny and the achievement of freedom—and the bitter herbs to commemorate the immense suffering and the agonizing cries of the innocent that rose unto the very throne of God in Heaven.

Aside from the food served for the dinner, the following items are necessary to conduct the ceremonial part of the meal:

A Haggadah: The book that narrates the Exodus and presents the order of the Seder—the blessings, symbols, prayers, and primarily the Rabbinic exposition of the biblical story of the servitude and emancipation of the Israelites. The same Haggadah text should be available to everyone, preferably one with color and commentary, so that everyone can share in learning and experiencing the moment of redemption.

Wine: There should be sufficient wine to fill each person's cup four times and the Cup of Elijah once.

Matzah: Three matzot are covered and placed at the head of the table before the leader of the Seder.

A vegetable: Some use celery; others use parsley or boiled potatoes for *karpas*.

Maror, bitter herbs: Some use freshly grated horseradish, others use romaine lettuce.

Charoset: A thick mixture of ground apples and walnuts with wine. (Sephardic Jews, those of Mediterranean and Near Eastern extraction, often make charoset with dates.)

A dish of salt water.

One roasted shankbone: This is a symbol only and should not be eaten.

The vegetable, maror, and charoset, should be provided for everyone at the table.

One roasted egg: Hard-boiled eggs served one per person at the table. It is a widespread custom, though not a requirement.

A ceremonial plate, of any size or shape, should be arranged as follows:

egg   **shankbone**

bitter herbs

vegetable   **charoset**

Pesach issues an eternal call of hope not only to Israel, but to all mankind. Throughout the generations, Jews have celebrated this festival with special ardor and zeal wherever they found themselves. In Siberia, a Russian refusenik could not find maror, the bitter herb, for the Seder, but he said that life in the Gulag was bitter enough not to need a symbol for it. In the free world today, Jews celebrate Pesach with intense gratitude, realizing that it is the first generation to have achieved a free and independent State of Israel, the fulfillment of a cen-turies-old dream—short of the coming of Messiah—and the consummation of the climactic song that each year concludes the Seder, *L'shanah ha'baah bi'Yerushalayim,* "Next Year in Jerusalem."

We are there. It is ours. We await God's final redemption.

LAG B'OMER

History dealt a severe blow to the traditional joy of the harvest celebration and the spiritual elation of Exodus and Revelation. The days between Pesach and Shavuot became days of mourning for a series of communal tragedies, but primarily for thousands of Rabbi Akiva's students decimated in this season by a deadly plague in the second century. These days were transformed over the years from happiness to humiliation and became, as they are today, days of semi-mourning—a time for avoiding weddings, music, dancing, haircutting and partying.

Lag b'Omer, the thirty-third day of the forty-nine-day Omer count, or Sefirah, was the one exception and it became a field day for the world Jewish community. On this day, the plague terminated and, every year, traditional Jews experience a communal sigh of relief. It is therefore observed as a semi-holiday, when weddings *are* permitted, and other forms of partial mourning are suspended. Because of its identification with Rabbi Akiva and his disciples, the day has become known as the Scholars' Festival. Tradition has lifted the corner of the black drape of catastrophe and exposed the green of the old harvest, and it swung open the gates of schools and homes for an exuberant day in the fields.

HOLOCAUST DAY: YOM HA'SHOAH

The reason for commemorating the Holocaust perpetrated by the Nazis and their infamous allies in Europe is self-evident. The annihilation of one-third of all the Jewish people—only because they were Jews—is a genocide unlike any other crime in history. It is unlike previous pogroms and inquisitions and crusades and massacres in terms of sheer numbers—the magnitude of the quantity of killings transforms the very quality of the catastrophe—and it can therefore not be subsumed into other fast days or left unrecognized as just another in the sordid series of persecutions of Jews in history.

Absent basic knowledge of the Nazi era and a clear insight into the character of the Holocaust, the convert will not be able to understand today's Jewish community nor sense the nature of Jewish history, the love for Israel and Jerusalem, the unrelieved drive for survival and identity, the horrible fear of loss of Jews through assimilation, intermarriage or infertility, and the whole tenor of Jewish peoplehood throughout the ages. For a beginning reading of the Holocaust literature, read any of Elie Wiesel's books; for academic study of it, see the works of Lucy Dawidowicz; for viewing it in its graphic detail, see Herman Wouk's television movies "Winds of War" and "War and Remembrance" or the Simon Wiesenthal Institute's film, "Genocide."

INDEPENDENCE DAY: YOM HA'ATZMAUT

The Jews live in a country with two geographies—one, a visible landscape of prosperity; the other, a metaphysical atlas that lies embedded in memory. One is the ancient country renewed by greenery and industry and laced with new roads and high-rises—the Land of Israel. The other is the spirit of Israel, the indwelling of the presence of God over centuries, deposited in the imagination of that same land, beneath the sand. As the Jew takes pride in the second and will not and cannot relinquish it, so he is tied forever to that visible geography. They are both part of his soul—one, a remembrance of the past, the other, the hope of the future.

Yom Ha'Atzmaut, the Day of Independence on the fifth day of Iyar, marks the reestablishment of the State of Israel in 1948, the renewal of the collective Jewish aspiration. The Chief Rabbis of Israel have declared this day a holiday and therefore a one-day release from the partial mourning of the Omer. They established the propriety of reciting the Psalms reserved for holidays, collectively known as Hallel, and special prayers, in addition to the communal celebrations that usually mark the day. The specific religious forms of the Israel Independence observance are still evolving.

The new Jew must come to understand the unique place that Israel holds in the Jewish religion and in contemporary Jewish thought and feeling. These matters were briefly touched upon earlier.

JERUSALEM DAY: YOM YERUSHALAYIM

The twenty-eighth day of Iyar, usually falling in the middle of May, commemorates the reunification of Jerusalem and the return of the ancient part of the city with its Western Wall and Temple Mount to Jewish sovereignty for the first time since 70 C.E. This singular event has touched the heart of Jews everywhere and reflects Divine miraculous elements that are clearly of religious significance. The exact nature of its religious observance has yet to evolve. Those who seek to become Jews would do well to visit Israel or, in any event, should seek ways of feeling, and not only understanding, the profound significance of Israel and the city of Jerusalem, and the two events that occurred in 1948 and 1967. Without doing so, one can hardly appreciate the quality and concerns of the contemporary Jewish community.

FEAST OF WEEKS: SHAVUOT

Being one of the three Pilgrim Festivals, Shavuot commemorates both a natural and an historical event. The bi-polar character of the pilgrim holidays, as well as the forty-nine-day bridge between Shavuot and Pesach, have been touched upon earlier, but need deeper probing.

Shavuot is celebrated on the sixth and seventh of Sivan. In biblical times, the holiday celebrated exclusively the cornucopia of nature—the wheat harvest and the ceremonious bringing of the First Fruits—in the name of gratitude to the Almighty. The Bible calls it *Chag Ha'Shavuot*, "the Feast of Weeks," on account of its celebration of the climax of the seven weeks from the time of the offering of the Omer at the barley harvest on Pesach. The term "Pentecost," by which this festival is often referred to, is the Greek word for "fiftieth," signifying that it is the feast celebrated on the fiftieth day, the day after the seven weeks.

The Day God Gave the Torah

In fact, however, Shavuot has a historic significance that goes far beyond the nature component. It commemorates the auspicious moment when the Torah was given to the Jews at Mt. Sinai.

The Rabbis—in a reasoned argument based on a number of passages in the Bible dealing with Israel's journey through the wilderness and their arrival at Sinai—prove that the Revelation on Sinai must have taken place on the sixth of Sivan, which is the first day of Shavuot. The exact manner of this communication between God and man is not known and has always been the subject of varying opinions of the great teachers.

Whatever the exact moment and however it was communicated, the giving of the Torah was clearly a unique historic and theological event in the annals of humankind and one that is of awesome proportions. It was an ecstatic spiritual experience which indelibly engraved itself upon the Jewish soul, endowing the Jews with their unique character, their faith, and their destiny. The giving of the Torah marked the end of Israel's infancy and its entrance into religious and national maturity. At the moment it formally entered the covenant with God, agreed to observe His commandments and the laws of justice, truth and loving-kindness and proclaimed the unity of God, the Jewish people secured for itself a permanent and eternal existence.

That is the quality and character of the day as it is referred to in the prayerbook: "The season of the *giving* of our Torah." But this poses a dilemma: This epochal, inconceivable, extra-ordinary event is not recorded in the Bible as the basis of Shavuot. Could the birthday of Torah have eluded the Torah itself? Is it possible that the wheat harvest was of greater importance to Torah than the giving of the Torah itself? On Pesach, the Torah refers to both the natural component, the harvest, and the historical, the Exodus. The same is true for Sukkot. Why did this pattern not hold for Shavuot, the third of the holiday triad?

The answer that appears most plausible is that one could mark a day to commemorate a great event, even an awesome event, such as the Exodus, or the sacking of the Temple, or repentance before God. But no twenty-four-hour period could be said to contain the magnitude of the whole Torah, the whole knowledge of God, the whole moral code, the whole religion, the whole Revelation of Ten Commandments engraved on stone by Almighty God. That is too much to ask of any day, any symbol. It is much like the creation of the universe which, while it is celebrated on Rosh Hashanah, is only referred to as a minor theme, subordinate to returning to God. It is too massive for the limited capacity of the human imagination.

On the other hand, to ignore this monumental phenomenon was not conceivable—the religious personality, which celebrates important, but lesser events, plainly could not allow the moment to slip by. Thus, while God's Torah does not pay attention to it, man's prayerbook insists on doing so, despite the difficulty of expressing it or articulating a reaction to it.

The significance of this idea is subtly implied in a sharp answer to another Shavuot question on the same theme: Why is this festival not called "the season of the *receiving* of Torah," instead of "the season of the *giving* of Torah, *mattan Torah*"? The answer offered is that, while the *giving* has taken place at one time and that singular occasion can be commemorated, the *receiving* of the Torah must continuously take place—every day and everywhere by everyone. Shavuot celebrates the giving; 365 days a year celebrate the receiving, which cannot be encompassed on a single day in Sivan.

Who Received the Torah?

While the Jews who were present at Sinai affirmed their covenant with God, the Torah emphasizes that:

> Neither with you only, but with him that standeth here with us and also with him that is not here with us this day [do I make this covenant]" (Deuteronomy 29:13-14).

The Talmud interprets the latter part of the verse as a clear reference to future generations of Jews and to future converts who will accept the faith in ensuing generations (Shavuot 39a).

Appropriately, therefore, the Book of Ruth is read on Shavuot. Ruth is the most popular convert in Jewish history and, appropriately, the setting of the story of how Ruth received the Torah and embraced the Jewish religion is the grain-harvest in ancient Israel, which is celebrated on Shavuot. As the Jews on this day, in different epochs, experienced the harvest and received the Torah, so did the Moabite princess Ruth. Indeed, there is also a tradition mentioned in the Talmud that King David was born and died on Shavuot. Since David the King is the descendant of Ruth and progenitor of the Messiah, the reading of this book, which is climaxed by the recording of the birth of David, is most fitting for the festival.

Customs of the Festival

There are no halakhic requirements specific to this holiday beyond those general ones which apply to all three pilgrim festivals, but there have accumulated over the centuries a number of customs that give a special flavor to the festival. Thus, reminiscent of its harvest character, synagogues and homes are decorated with a variety of leaves, herbs, and flowers—in some countries, the floor of the synagogue is strewn with fresh grass; in others, the walls are festooned with large plants.

In honor of the giving of Torah, an excellent custom arose which is both elevating and meaningful. On the first night of Shavuot, men and women, boys and girls, stay awake all night studying Torah at the synagogue or some other congenial location. Where there is no rabbi or teacher, or the community is not sufficiently learned, or if an individual cannot follow the studies, there is an old custom of reading pre-selected portions from Torah and Talmud, incorporated in a special text. Then, at first light, they pray the morning service and return home.

There arose a custom of eating dairy foods and honey on Shavuot. One source is the passage, "honey and milk shall be under your tongue," which implies the hope that the words of the Torah may be as pleasant and acceptable to the ears and heart as are milk and honey to the tongue.

The subtext of the festival of Shavuot is one of the foremost lessons of Jewish living—the release from bondage and the winning of political freedom of a Pesach does not constitute complete freedom for the individual unless it is consummated in the spiritual restraints and duties inherent in the receiving of Torah.

TISHAH B'AV

The blackest date of the Jewish calendar is the ninth day of the Hebrew month of Av, *Tishah b'Av*, which usually falls at the end of July. It is not only that immense disasters have been mysteriously magnetized to this ominous date. Primarily, it is that the destruction of the two Temples fell in close proximity to this ninth day and are commemorated on it, and that they have brought in their train all subsequent calamities, including exile from the Holy Land.

The Mishnah records the following lamentable events that occurred on this day:

> The decree that Israel should wander through the wilderness for forty years; the destruction of the First Temple by Nebuchadnezzar (in 586 B.C.E.); the destruction of the Second Temple by Titus (in the year 70 C.E.); the fall of the fortress of Betar; the subsequent fall of Bar Kokhba and the massacre of his men; and the ploughing-up of Jerusalem by Hadrian (in 135 C.E.)" (Ta'anit 26b).

Jewish history is extravagant with hanging other calamities on the Ninth of Av. To list only two among them: on this day in 1290, King Edward I signed the edict expelling his Jewish subjects from England, and, on the same date in Spain in 1492, following Torquemada's appalling Inquisition, 300,000 Jews were expelled from Spain by Ferdinand and Isabella. The weight of history made its way into common folk wisdom: it is not a good date, the Rabbis suggested, to go to court against a gentile adversary.

None of the misfortunes has had so monstrous and debilitating an effect as did the destruction of the Second Temple and the nineteen hundred years of exile which followed. The Sages instructed Jews to mourn this cataclysm by abstaining from all food and drink. The Talmud declares in the name of Rabbi Gamaliel that "if a man eats or drinks on the Ninth of Av . . . it is as though he ate on Yom Kippur itself." Rabbi Akiba said, "He who works on the Ninth of Av will see no blessing from it." A Yiddish proverb sums it up: "On Yom Kippur, who *wants* to eat? On Tishah b'Av, who *can* eat?"

The value of fasting lies not only in remembering the past and applying its lessons to the present, but also in recognizing the pathology of purposeless hatred which the Rabbis saw as the root cause of the destruction, and the overriding value of solidarity as a key to Jewish continuity.

Lamentations

The biblical reading most appropriate to such a day is the Book of Lamentations, in which the Prophet Jeremiah, who witnessed the destruction of the First Temple, records, with a pathos unequalled in the annals of literature, the calamity of orphaned children and ravaged women, and of proud Jerusalem now bereft: "How she sits alone, the city once filled with people . . .".

Echah, "How!," the pleading and mournful lament is repeated throughout this scroll and serves as its title. In five chapters, the prophet gives heart-breaking expression to his lament over the desolation that was the glory of Jerusalem. Grief-stricken, he mourns the anguish of its citizens who were forced into exile, and assigns the cause of the tragedy to the sinfulness of the people and their leaders. Although he chastises them severely for ignoring God's Torah, he pleads fervently for the Almighty's compassion upon His children and their reestablishment in the homeland.

This book, one of the five biblical scrolls, is read in the evening, usually by the dim light of candles, with the worshippers sitting on the floor or on overturned benches. As a sign of deep mourning, the tallit and tefillin are not worn during the morning Shacharit service, but are delayed until the afternoon Minchah service.

Immediately after the Book of Lamentations, a series of liturgical dirges, called *Kinot*, composed by Jewish poets of different ages, are chanted. The Kinot are an accumulation of elegies for an assortment of tragedies glued by blood to the annihilation of Jerusalem.

A profound insight into Jewish survival lies hidden in this precious morsel of Jewish tradition: "On the ninth of Av, the Messiah will have been born." Tragedy often bears the seed of its own resolution.

TWO FAST DAYS

There are two "minor" public fast days that relate to the destruction of the Temple and which, unlike Tishah b'Av, are observed only from dawn to nightfall. They are the Tenth of Tevet, which marks the beginning of the Babylonian siege of Jerusalem, and the Seventeenth of Tammuz, three weeks before Tishah b'Av, which marks the first breach in the walls of Jerusalem during the Babylonian siege. Halakhah is somewhat flexible for those who find fasting particularly onerous on these days.

28
Rites of Passage

The transition from stage to stage in a person's life is celebrated by Judaism for a number of reasons: One, to express gratitude to God for enabling us and our kinsmen to evolve normally and to experience progress in our own lives; two, to ease the pain which is a common factor of personal growth by containing and solidifying the flux of human development within the permanence of age-old ceremonies.

A third, and very important reason, is to mark the hours—to stop the mindless flow of days, the tick-tock monotony of time, in order to enhance significant moments in life by endowing them with special meaning and making them memorable. Man is a celebrating animal, *homo festivus*, always seeking to enrich his days and to add color to a life too quantified by civilization.

BIRTH

WELCOMING A NEW BABY: SHALOM ZAKHAR

The first such festivity is the custom of "*Shalom Zakhar*," a celebration that welcomes a newborn boy into the world. This takes place between birth and the eighth day, the day of circumcision. It is held on a Friday night, usually at the home of parents or grandparents. The fare traditionally consists of light refreshments—plus garbanzo beans (of all things). There is no known origin for this party, and no ritual formula that defines it. But it is fun. The plain fact is that, as birthdays should be, it is a celebration of the mother who has endured months of hardship to develop this child, except that it focuses on the product, rather than the producer.

SHALOM BAT

There should also be a welcome for baby girls. Traditionally, a boy born into a family meant, in addition to all the reasons of the heart, another hand to work in the family business or farm, and, of course, another potential Torah scholar. Also, a boy was considered easier to raise than a girl. A girl, while she helped with chores in the house in pre-modern days, was not gainfully productive because she could not enter the work force. Also, some of the Sages noted, she triggered anxiety in her parents at every stage of life—in order to protect her from aggressive males when young, encourage eligible bachelors to seek her in marriage when she matured, and pray that she be fertile and that she raise a new generation properly when she herself becomes a parent. Today, many people celebrate the birth of a girl with a party called *Shalom Bat*, welcoming a daughter.

Both welcoming events are equally amorphous and need not be structured. If one feels the need for programming, there should be a word of Torah, *D'var Torah*, relevant to the occasion, selected songs for Shabbat, and the recitation of Proverbs 31, the much-quoted tribute to womanhood in the Bible.

Especially in our day, when the Jewish community is at its least fertile stage in history and we do not replace even our own selves, there should be greater emphasis on celebrating births. Every effort needs to be made to encourage raising the next generation and changing the prevalent attitude of our age which brought us contraception and abortion, but not an equal emphasis on the glories of parenthood.

BABY NAMING FOR A GIRL

Baby girls are traditionally named at the Torah Scroll during Shabbat services in the synagogue. The sexton will need to know the mother's and maternal grandmother's Hebrew names in order to recite a prayer for the mother's normal recovery.

Also, he will need to know the baby's Hebrew name and her father's, to recite a prayer for her at the Torah—the first ever. In the case of a convert, the name to be used is discussed in the chapter on names. If the Jewish member does not remember the Hebrew name, the English one should be used. In attendance should be the parents and members of the family. The naming is usually held on the first Saturday morning after the birth, or at the first holiday service. If the mother can attend only a week later, the naming may be delayed.

CIRCUMCISION, *B'RIT MILAH*

The reason for the circumcision, its significance and the laws pertaining to it, are discussed at length in a separate chapter. The naming of a boy takes place at the circumcision ceremony.[1]

BAR MITZVAH, BAT MITZVAH

Bar/Bat Mitzvah is, first of all, a state of being—the time of religious maturity, from age thirteen for a boy and twelve for a girl—and whether one celebrates the occasion or not, he or she is responsible for religious observances after the *age* of Bar/Bat Mitzvah. Second, it is the celebration—at the synagogue or at home—of the beginning of that state of religious responsibility.

The nature of religious responsibility in Jewish life is determined by the boy or girl's ability to observe the commandments, the *mitzvot*, intelligently. Maturity, as a product of intelligence and emotions, is quite nebulous and anything but uniform in the early teens. Despite this, a date simply had to be established for the law to be able to operate, to know when this youngster may be counted for a religious quorum, *minyan*, for the wearing of tefillin and other commandments. The Rabbis say that the establishment of this date derives from an oral tradition given to Moses at Sinai.[2]

Bar Mitzvah is celebrated by boys by receiving the honor

of being called to the Torah and reciting the blessings before and after the reading. Different countries and ethnic subgroups have different customs, as the tradition provides no specific requirement for the celebration. Some have the child recite the blessings over the Torah, others add the actual reading of the Torah, others the reading of the prophetic reading called Haftorah, still others have the child conduct the entire worship service. In most communities, the Bar Mitzvah takes place at the Torah reading on Shabbat. In some, it is held on weekdays of Torah reading, such as Monday and Thursday mornings.

Girls become Bat Mitzvah at an earlier date because of their presumed earlier maturation. The celebration takes on a different note from the boys in the Orthodox tradition. Girls often have home celebrations; in some communities, the celebration follows services on Saturday or Sunday and involves an address by the young lady on a Torah subject. The different movements within Judaism have developed their own practices and styles. An old custom had worshipers in the synagogue throw small bags of candy at the youngster immediately after the "coming out."

The educational preparation for the tasks undertaken at the Bar/Bat Mitzvah is usually exhaustive, the duration of which depends on the Jewish education of the child and the degree of participation in the service.

"The ignorant cannot be pious" is a popular statement of the Rabbis. Unfortunately, too often the preparation for Bar Mitzvah is mechanical, the celebration routine, and the purpose of the entire ceremony is the *leaving* of the synagogue—a sort of graduation. This is a travesty of religious responsibility, not a fulfillment of it. Preparation should be a natural element of the broad study of Torah. The leading of the services is not a "performance," but a spiritual experience. The celebration afterwards should not be an excuse for parents' friends to gather nor should it be in the nature of a gala party, but a serious festivity celebrating the passage from childhood to religious maturity. In all cases, the test of the proper celebration is how it accords with the Halakhah and with the spiritual nature of the occasion.

LOVE AND MARRIAGE

The State of Marriage Today[3]

The institution of marriage stands serene and firm amidst the buffeting winds of change. The greatest pleasure of which the human being is capable is best attained within the boundaries of monogamous marriage, not in a world of unbridled sensuality and multiple lovers. Rooted in loyalty and integrity, nurtured by true love, and immortalized by children, marriage has been the locus of love and beauty and happiness for too many centuries to be written off because of periodic historic malaise.

What other human institution can provide so much warmth and intimacy? What other setting allows one generation to bestow the care needed to raise the next? Where else can one find such readiness for self-sacrifice? Where else can pain be so effectively divided and contentment so magnificently multiplied? Is there another harbor as welcoming and protective in the storms of daily life as marriage? No other relationship can so surely guarantee the survival of the human species and perpetuate morality. And where else but in marriage can we find the mystery, the dignity, and the sacredness of life?

The conjugal act is the only physical act in Jewish law that may evoke dire biblical penalties or elevate the soul to a glorious partnership with God in the creation of a new human being. The deciding factor is the identity of the partners: adultery is considered the most heinous misuse of sex, while sex within marriage is most honorable. The prostitute is *kedeshah*, set aside, apart from the moral community; but the newly married couple enters *kedushah*, set above, elevated beyond their former status. Prohibited partners can produce the mamzer, the illegitimate offspring of incest or adultery; preferred partners can produce the light of future generations.

Jewish matrimonial law is divided into two categories: the prohibitions of forbidden acts and the preferred positive laws of marriage. The prohibitions are clearly defined, proclaimed as absolutes, and read aloud to the congregation on the holiest day of the year, Yom Kippur. The positive laws, which deal with the obligations and conduct of marriage, are primarily inferred from the violations, loosely constructed in biblical sources, but painstakingly formulated by the Rabbis in the Oral Law.

This apparent imbalance is instructive. The Torah wanted to provide the widest possible latitude for the boundaries of permissible marriage in order to encompass the full legitimate variety of human passions and combinations. But the restrictive boundaries had to be carefully observed to ensure that the integrity and purity of the Jewish family would be preserved. Thus, the law of endogamy—a Jew must marry a Jew—marks a line beyond which marriage is prohibited, encircling the furthest limit of the nation. The prohibition against incest draws a circle within which marriage is proscribed, enclosing the nearest limit of the family.

Qualities of the Ideal Mate

The first prayer in the Bible is uttered by Eliezer, Abraham's servant, as he sets out to seek the ideal wife for Isaac. He is the first person of whom it is expressly recorded that he prayed for Divine guidance at a critical moment in his life; not a formal prayer, but a "prayer of the heart," uttered spontaneously. He did not pray for Divine intervention, but that his criteria for selecting the ideal mate be in accordance with God's will. The confident assurance of Abraham that Eliezer will succeed in this venture are the last words Scripture records of the Patriarch: "He will send His angel before you, and you shall take a wife for my son from there" (Genesis 24:7).

The image of an ideal wife (Genesis 24:12 ff.) projected by the servant is fascinating. He notes Rebecca's beauty and he stresses her chastity, but the dominant criterion that emerges is that she is generous, hospitable to strangers, and kind to animals. These qualities of compassion in the Jewish character remained the most important of all virtues throughout the millennial history of the Jewish people.

Compassion is one of the three qualities considered the hallmark of all Jewish women, indeed, of all Jews. If a person does not exhibit at least one of these three qualities—modesty, compassion, and kindness—one should investigate further.

Planning the Wedding

The style of the wedding celebration is a reflection of the

personal values of the couple and their families, and of their perception of communal standards.

The tradition calls for dignity, simplicity, and integrity. Coarseness, loudness, exhibitionist display, and revelry are not the hallmarks of a people who were taught the ways of modesty. A religion that considers the quality of licentiousness despicable, and whose highest encomium is reserved for those who are modest and humble, cannot abide the grossness and vulgarity of weddings designed for show rather than for genuine rejoicing.

The Wedding

The wedding celebration is composed of two distinct and successive ceremonies: betrothal (*kiddushin*) and nuptials (*nissuin*). The kiddushin includes the betrothal blessings, the proposal, and the giving of the ring before two witnesses. This is followed by a transition stage—the public reading of the marriage contract. Afterwards, the nissuin begins. This consists of the seven blessings, followed by the breaking of the glass, and finally by *yichud*, several minutes of seclusion after leaving the chuppah.

THE BRIDAL CANOPY

The chuppah is a tapestry attached to the tops of four poles. The word chuppah means "covering" or "protection," and is intended as a roof or covering for the bride and groom at their wedding.

The chuppah ceremony is not merely a charming folk custom, a ceremonial object carried over from a primitive past. It serves a definite, though complicated, legal purpose: It is the decisive act that formally permits the couple's new status of marriage to be actualized, and it is the legal conclusion of the marriage process that began with betrothal. Together, these two *kinyanim* (acts of acquisition) are called *chuppah ve'kiddushin*.

Chuppah symbolizes the groom's home, and the bride's new domain. More specifically, the chuppah symbolizes the bridal chamber, where the marital act was consummated in ancient times.

THE PROCESSION

The groom must arrive under the chuppah before the bride. After all, it is his symbolic home and legally he has leased it for the bridal chamber. The bride's transition from her parents' home to her husband's is demonstrated by this procession, and the chuppah affords the opportunity for that expression.

THE RING

Before the groom places the ring on his bride's index finger, he recites the following marriage proposal in both Hebrew and English, because it must be understood by both bride and groom:

> *Harei at mekudeshet li be'tabaat zo ke'dat Mosheh ve'Yisrael.*
>
> Behold, thou art betrothed unto me, with this ring, in accordance with the Law of Moses and Israel.

1. The ring should be of plain metal, preferably gold, and with no precious stones. The reason for this is the avoidance of possible misrepresentation on the part of the groom.
2. The ring should be placed by the groom on the bride's index finger, not her "ring finger." Because it is the most active finger, it may serve as a symbol that the ring is not accepted as just another gift, but as an act sealing the most important transaction in life.

The procedure is as follows:

(1) The groom, or best man, gives the rabbi the ring;

(2) The groom specifies the witnesses;

(3) The rabbi shows the ring to the witnesses to ascertain minimal value;

(4) The rabbi asks the groom if the ring belongs to him and if it is of the minimal required value;

(5) The bride lifts her veil, if it covers her eyes;

(6) The groom takes the ring and recites the proposal;

(7) He then places the ring on her index finger in the presence of the witnesses (she may place it on her ring finger after the ceremony); and

(8) The bride replaces the veil.

THE KETUBAH

The reading of the entire Aramaic marriage contract is an honored tradition. It serves as a separation between the two distinct ceremonies of betrothal and nuptials.

The *ketubah* is written in the language of the Talmud. The reading is difficult and unfamiliar to most people, and probably only rabbis and scholars will be able to read it creditably.

After it is read, the document is given to the groom for him to hand to his bride and for her to hold in her safekeeping for all the days of their marriage.

BREAKING THE GLASS

The end of the public wedding ceremony is marked by the breaking of a glass, usually a thin glass wrapped in a napkin to contain the fragments. It is smashed under foot by the groom after the seven benedictions, or after the rabbi's address, if it follows the benedictions.

Ancient custom designated that one of the wine cups be broken, although there was a difference of opinion as to which of the two wine cups. Maharil held that it was the nuptials cups, because the breaking immediately followed the nuptial blessings. Rema and most others held that it was the betrothal cup, and for good reason: Breaking the nuptials cup, over which the seven benedictions were recited, is a gross symbol when great concern at this moment is for making the marriage, not breaking it. However, once the nuptials are recited the betrothal has been accomplished, and the breaking of that cup signifies that the nuptials have been satisfactorily completed. The author of *Mateh Mosheh* held that it may be any glass at all. Originally, the blessing was recited over a glass cup which was then smashed. But when silver cups began to be used, any other glass was used for breaking. One commentator held that smashing either of the wine glasses was not an auspicious sign and that another glass should be used.

The general custom that prevails today at traditional weddings is the use of a prepared glass or bulb. However, this robs the ceremony of its historic beauty and significance. Therefore, it is preferable to use a glass goblet for the betrothals and a silver kiddush cup for the nuptials. Immediately after the seven benedictions, the rabbi can pour the remaining wine from the glass into a prepared bowl, wrap it in a cloth napkin and have the groom place it on the floor and crush it.

THE CELEBRATION OF PRIVACY

The symbolic consummation of the wedding takes place in a private room after the ceremony. This is not custom, but a firm requirement of the law that must be attested to by witnesses. It is the final act of chuppah that seals the marriage. When the couple emerges from yichud, they are man and wife.

Family Purity

An appreciation of the concept of family purity is fundamental to a deeper understanding of Jewish marriage. Because it offers new and fresh insights into the sexual aspects of marriage, it is important to consider it before one enters into marriage. The law, indeed, requires that a bride begin the practice of family purity within four days before the wedding, as she stands at the threshold of creating her family.

A superbly written account of the concepts of "family purity" appears in the book *A Hedge of Roses* by Dr. Norman Lamm.

THE CONCEPT

Jewish law forbids a husband to approach his wife during the time of her menses, generally from five to seven days, and extends the prohibition of any physical contact beyond this period for another seven days, known as the "seven pure days." (That is why one finds, in observant Jewish homes of young couples, two beds for husband and wife, not a double bed.) During this time, husband and wife are expected to act towards each other with respect and affection but without any physical expression of love—excellent training for that time, later in their lives, when husband and wife need to discover coupling modes, in addition to the sexual bond, to tie them one to another. At the end of this twelve- to fourteen-day period (depending upon the individual woman), the menstruant (known as *niddah*) must immerse herself in the body of water known as a mikveh and recite a special blessing in which she praises God for sanctifying us with His commandments and commanding us concerning immersion (tevillah).

By thus preparing for their wedding and afterwards for their monthly marital reunion—separating from each other and then, before joining each other, the wife immersing in the mikveh, and reciting thereupon the blessing thanking the Almighty for sanctifying us through this institution—husband and wife acknowledge, in the most profound symbolic manner, that their relationship is sanctified and blessed, that it is pure and not vulgar, sacred and not salacious. Family purity has a magnificent cleansing effect upon the psyche. It purifies and ennobles the outlook of man and woman upon each other and their relationships to each other.

STAYING MARRIED

That Judaism's view on these most intimate aspects of married life is worthy of consideration by modern young couples is indicated by the striking record of domestic happiness characteristic of Orthodox Jewish homes even in the midst of an environment where the breakdown of family life becomes more shocking with each year.

This typical Jewish family cohesion is surely not the result of any indigenous ethnic or racial virtue of the Jewish people. Nor does it derive from some general, well-intentioned, but amorphous "concern for religious tradition." It is, most certainly, the product of the specific "Orthodox" tradition—the Halakhah or Jewish "way of life." It is this codified tradition, this obligatory law, that has bestowed the gift of stability upon the Jewish family.

The family purity laws are also crucial in protecting the marital bond from one of the most universal and perilous enemies which comes to the fore soon after the newness of married life has worn off: the tendency for sex to become routinized.

It is easy enough to get married. It is quite another thing to stay married.

REMARRIAGE

Judaism recognizes the pain of solitude. It seeks to encourage those who are alone to seek meaningful and richer lives. *Tav le'metav tan du mi-le'metav armelo*, Better to remain coupled than a widow (single). Hence, whenever possible, it urges remarriage.

There is a positive value to the suggestion that divorced couples remarry one another. The Torah, however, forbids a man from remarrying a former wife who had married another man in the meantime.

RELIGIOUS DIVORCE

Judaism discourages loneliness, but it also realizes that a bad marriage can be far worse than being alone. Thus, a Jewish divorce, *get*, when necessary, is condoned.

People familiar with civil court procedures in divorce matters are not aware of the simplicity, ease and relatively low cost of a Jewish religious divorce.

The prerequisites for a Jewish divorce are the consent of both parties and the husband's authorization for the writing and transmission of the divorce to his wife.

The divorce is written in the presence of a Bet Din according to specified regulations.

The husband may deliver the divorce personally to his wife or through an agent. The wife must receive the divorce in her hands. Until this is done, Jewish divorce is not consummated.

Jewish religious law does not make it necessary for both parties to be in the same city. The husband in his community may authorize the writing and witnessing of the writ of divorce. A Jewish divorce may be sent to any Jewish community of any country. It is valid everywhere when prepared and delivered by recognized, ordained rabbis. It permits either party to remarry in accordance with Jewish law. The actual divorce proceedings are normally completed in about an hour and a half. Compliance with this simple procedure will go a long way in alleviating future problems.

DEATH AND MOURNING

The convert here confronts the crisis of a parent's death and simultaneously confronts once again her personal decision to convert. The feelings for a parent antedate every other sentiment. The adopted religion represents her most mature decision. The two appear to conflict with one another—how to commemorate a parent's death with ceremonies just brought into the family.

Lydia Kukoff, in her *Choosing Judaism*, describes her own dilemma:

> Perhaps the single most difficult moment of my Jewish life occurred when my father died. The death of a parent is always painful, and serves as a catalyst for the release of deep and powerful emotions. This I knew. But I was totally unprepared for the range of feelings I experienced, and the confusion that suddenly engulfed me eight years after my conversion, long after I thought I had become quite comfortable with my Jewish identity.
>
> I had come cross-country from my Passover seder to my Christian father's funeral. Surroundings once so familiar seemed somehow strange. I helped arrange a funeral service whose ritual was completely at variance with my own Jewish beliefs. I reentered the church in which I was raised, so well known to me, yet so removed from me. During this pre-Easter week, I listened to my family's minister speak of my father and of the resurrection, and the better place to which he had gone. These were comforting words to many, but not to me. And, even as the service ended, with the choir singing his favorite hymn which I had always sung to him as a little girl, I realized that I could find no comfortable way in which to mourn my own father.
>
> In the home of my childhood alone, with none of my Jewish friends and community around me, I could not sit shivah or recite Kaddish. I felt that I had gone back in time and space. Indeed, to this very day, I still have not resolved the situation to my own satisfaction. . . . God willing, our parents will enjoy long, happy, and productive lives. But when the end comes, as it must for all of us, all that anyone can ask or expect is that we will do our best. In the midst of our own grief, we will try to be true to them and to do what they believed. Beyond that, nothing can be asked. Beyond that, nothing can be promised.[4]

The conflict is sometimes more apparent than real. The love for mother or father or sibling is proper and should be expressed with full vehemence. But the form of the expression must comport with the mourner's own ideas and temperament. It is important, therefore, that the convert learn the Jewish concepts that underlie the mourning practices and the religious expression, via symbol and ceremony and liturgy, of the deepest sentiments known to humankind.

THE JEWISH WAY OF DEATH[5]

Death is the crisis of life. How a man handles death indicates a great deal about how he approaches life. As there is a Jewish way of life, there is a Jewish way of death.

As the Jewish way of life implies a distinctive outlook and a unique life-style based on very specific views of God and the place of man in society and the universe, so does the Jewish way of death imply singular attitudes toward God and nature, and toward the problem of good and evil; and it proffers a distinctive way of demonstrating specific Jewish qualities of reverence for man and respect for the dead.

For example, the prohibition of both cremation (the unnaturally speedy disposal of the dead) and embalming (the unnatural preservation of the dead), bespeaks a philosophy of man and his relationship to God and nature. Repugnance for the mutilation of a body expresses a reverence for man, because he was created in God's image. The ban on necromancy is founded on very precise theological concepts of creature and Creator. Likewise, the commandment to bury the dead without delay draws a very fine, but clear line between reverence for the dead and worship of the dead. The profound psychological insights implicit in the highly structured Jewish mourning observances speak eloquently of Judaism's concern for the psychological integrity of the human personality.

PREPARATION OF THE REMAINS: *TAHARAH*

"As he came, so shall he go," says Ecclesiastes. Just as a newborn child is immediately washed and enters this world clean and pure, so he who departs this world must be cleansed and made pure through the religious ritual called *taharah*, purification.

The taharah is performed by the *Chevra Kadisha* (the Holy Society, i.e. the Burial Society), consisting of Jews who are knowledgeable in the area of traditional duties, and can display proper respect for the deceased. In addition to the physical cleansing and preparation of the body for burial, they also recite the required prayers asking Almighty God for forgiveness for any sins the deceased may have committed, and praying that the All-Merciful may guard him and grant him eternal peace.

Jewish tradition recognizes the democracy of death. It therefore demands that all Jews be buried in the same type of garment, shrouds that are called *takhrikhim*. Wealthy or poor, all are equal before God, and that which determines their reward is not what they wear, but what they are. Nineteen hundred years ago, Rabbi Gamaliel instituted this practice so that the poor would not be shamed and the wealthy would not vie with each other in displaying the costliness of their burial clothes.

The clothes to be worn should be appropriate for one who is shortly to stand in judgment before God Almighty, Master of the universe and Creator of man. Therefore, they should be simple, handmade, perfectly clean, and white. These shrouds symbolize purity, simplicity, and dignity.

THE CASKET

"For dust thou art, and unto dust shalt thou return" (Genesis 3:19) is the guiding principle in regard to the selection of caskets. . . . The coffin must be made completely of wood. The Bible tells us that Adam and Eve hid among the trees in the Garden of Eden when they heard the Divine judgment for committing the first sin. Said Rabbi Levi: "This was a sign for their descendants that, when they die and are prepared to receive their reward, they should be placed in coffins made of wood."

FLOWERS

In ancient days, the Talmud informs us, fragrant flowers and spices were used at the funeral to offset the odor of the decaying body. Today, this is no longer essential and they should *not* be used at Jewish funerals at all. In our days, they are used primarily at Christian funerals, and are considered to be a non-Jewish ritual custom which should be discouraged. It is much better to honor the deceased by making a contribution to a synagogue or hospital, or to a medical research association for the disease which afflicted the deceased. This method of tribute is more lasting and meaningful.

TIMING THE FUNERAL SERVICE

The Bible, in its mature wisdom, required burial to take place as soon as possible following death.

The religious concept underlying this law is that man, made in the image of God, should be accorded the deepest respect. It is considered a matter of great shame and discourtesy to leave the deceased unburied—his soul has returned to God, but his body is left to linger in the land of the living.

THE NIGHT BEFORE THE FUNERAL SERVICE

The "wake" is definitely alien to Jewish custom, and its spirit does violence to Jewish sensitivity and tradition. The custom of visiting the funeral parlor on the night before interment to comfort the mourners and to view the remains is clearly a Christian religious practice, and not merely an American folkway. If the convert finds that not visiting the night before will be an affront, he or she should make a token appearance. Nonetheless, the convert should realize that, in Judaism, the place for offering condolences is at home, during the seven special days of mourning called *shivah*.

RENDING THE GARMENT: *KERI'AH*

The most striking Jewish expression of grief is the rending of outer garments by the mourner prior to the funeral service.

WHO MUST REND THE CLOTHING?

1. Seven relatives are obligated to perform this command: son, daughter; father, mother; brother, sister; and spouse.
2. They must be adults, above the age of thirteen. Minors, who are in fact capable of understanding the situation, and appreciating the loss, should have other relatives or friends make the tear for them.
3. Divorced mates may cut their clothing, but they are not *obligated* to do so.

THE FUNERAL SERVICE

The funeral service is a brief and simple service designed primarily . . . for the honor and dignity of the deceased.

The service consists of a selection from the Psalms appropriate to the life of the deceased, a panegyric of his finer qualities which his survivors should seek to implant in their own lives, and a Memorial Prayer asking that God shelter his soul "on the wings of His Divine presence."

THE INTERMENT

Jewish law is unequivocal in establishing absolutely, and uncompromisingly, that the dead must be buried in the earth. Man's body returns to the earth as it was. The soul rises to God, but the physical shelter, the chemical elements that clothed the soul, sink into the vast reservoir of nature.

CREMATION

Cremation is never permitted. The deceased must be interred, bodily, in the earth. It is forbidden—in every and any circumstance—to reduce the dead to ash in a crematorium. It is an offensive act, for it does violence to the spirit and letter of Jewish law, which never, in the long past, sanctioned the ancient pagan practice of burning on the pyre. The Jewish abhorrence of cremation has already been noted by Tacitus, the ancient historian, who remarked upon what appeared to be a distinguishing characteristic that Jews buried, rather than burned, their dead.

THE MOURNING PATTERN

There is no legal obligation upon a person who had converted to Judaism to mourn his non-Jewish parents in the prescribed Jewish manner, but it is expected that the convert will show utmost respect for his natural parents. The grief that the convert expresses, although technically not required by Jewish law, should possess a markedly Jewish character. Therefore, it is important to know these mitzvot.

Judaism, with its long history of dealing with the soul of man, its intimate knowledge of man's achievements and foibles, his grandeur and his weakness, has wisely devised graduated periods during which the mourner may express his grief, and release with calculated regularity the built-up tensions caused by bereavement. The Jewish religion provides a beautifully structured approach to mourning. . . .

Five Stages of Mourning

The first period is that between death and burial (*aninut*), during which time despair is most intense. At this time, not only the social amenities, but even major positive religious requirements, were canceled in recognition of the mourner's troubled mind.

The second stage consists of the first three days following burial, days devoted to weeping and lamentation. During this time, the mourner does not even respond to greetings, and remains in his home (except under certain special circumstances). It is a time when even visiting the mourner is usually somewhat discouraged, for it is too early to comfort the mourners when the wound is so fresh.

Third, is the period of *shivah*, the seven days following burial. (This longer period includes the first three days.) During this time, the mourner emerges from the stage of intense grief to a new state of mind in which he is prepared to talk about his loss and to accept comfort from friends and neighbors. The world now enlarges for the mourner. While he remains within the house, expressing his grief through the observances of *avelut*—the wearing of the rent garment, the sitting on the low stool, the wearing of slippers, the refraining from shaving and grooming, the recital of the Kaddish—his acquaintances come to his home to express sympathy in his distress. The inner freezing that came with the death of his relative now begins to thaw. The isolation from the world of people and the retreat inward now relaxes somewhat, and normalcy begins to return.

Fourth is the stage of *sheloshim*, the thirty days following burial (which includes the shivah). The mourner is encouraged to leave the house after shivah and to slowly rejoin society, always recognizing that enough time has not yet elapsed to assume full, normal social relations. Shaving and haircutting for mourners is still generally prohibited, as is cutting the nails, and washing the body all at once for delight (as opposed to washing for cleanliness which is required).

The fifth and last stage is the twelve-month period (which includes the sheloshim) during which things return to normal, and business once again becomes routine, but the inner feelings of the mourner are still wounded by the rupture of his relationship with a parent. The pursuit of entertainment and amusement is curtailed. At the close of this last stage, the twelve-month period, the bereaved is not expected to continue his mourning, except for brief moments when *yizkor* or *yahrzeit* is observed. In fact, our tradition rebukes a man for mourning more than this prescribed period.

The effect of shivah and sheloshim is on a biological, prerational level. The mourner generally has not yet physically dissociated from the deceased; mourning is all sentiment and therefore the religious practices deal with skin and water, nails and hair. Emerging from the sheloshim, properly observed, is to emerge from the maelstrom of emotions brought on by the death.

The year-long observances, however, are on a strictly rational plane—the avoidance of joyous situations is a formal rejection of fun for fun's sake in recognition of the loss, and the recitation of Kaddish is a strictly community-oriented declaration in the form of a prose-poem, mystically-based, but intellectually articulated.

In this magnificently conceived, graduated process of mourning, an ancient faith raises up the mourner from the abyss of despair to the undulating hills and valleys of normal daily life.

WHO IS THE MOURNER AND WHO THE MOURNED?

Who is a mourner? Jewish law formally considers the bereaved to be those who have lost any one of the seven close relatives listed in Leviticus 21:1-3: father, mother, wife (or husband), son, daughter, (married or unmarried), brother, and sister (or half-brother and half-sister).

COMFORTING THE BEREAVED

A sacred obligation devolves upon every Jew to comfort the mourners, whether he is related to them or not, and whether he was a close friend or a passing acquaintance. In Judaism, exercising compassion by paying a condolence call is a mitzvah, considered by some of our greatest scholars to be biblically ordained. . . . It is a person's duty to imitate God: as God comforts the bereaved, so man must do likewise. . . .

The fundamental purpose of the condolence call during shivah is to relieve the mourner of the intolerable burden of intense loneliness. At no other time is a human being more in need of such comradeship. Avelut means withdrawal, the personal and physical retreat from social commerce and the concern for others. It is the loss that he alone has suffered.

KADDISH: WHEN IS IT SAID?

The Kaddish is recited at every service, morning and evening, Shabbat and holiday, on days of fasting and rejoicing.

The period that the mourner recites the Kaddish for parents is, theoretically, a full calendar year. The deceased is considered to be under Divine judgment for that period. Some communities, therefore, adhere to the custom that Kaddish be recited for twelve months in all cases. However, because the full year is considered to be the duration of judgment for the wicked, and we presume that our parents do not fall into that category, the practice in most communities is to recite the Kaddish for only eleven months—even on leap years, which last thirteen months, the Kaddish is recited for only eleven months. We subtract one day, so that we terminate the Kaddish in time to allow a full thirty days before the end of the twelve-month period.

The Kaddish is to be recited only in the presence of a duly-constituted quorum which consists of ten males (including mourners) above the age of Bar Mitzvah. If there are only nine adults and one minor present, it is still not considered a quorum for a minyan.

JOYOUS OCCASIONS DURING MOURNING

The observance that most affects the daily life of the mourner during the twelve-month period is the complete abstention from parties and festivities, both public and private. Participation in these gatherings is simply not consonant with the depression and contrition that the mourner experiences. It borders on the absurd for the mourner to dance gleefully while his parent lies dead in a fresh grave. Thus, the Sages decreed that, while complete physical withdrawal from normal activities of society lasts only one week, withdrawal from joyous, social occasions lasts thirty days in mourning for other relatives, and one year (twelve Hebrew months) in mourning for one's parents. Joy, in terms of the mourning tradition, is associated largely with public, social events rather than with personal satisfactions.

THE UNVEILING

The service of commemoration, or unveiling, is a formal dedication of the cemetery monument. It is customary to hold the unveiling within the first year after death. It should be held at anytime between the end of shivah and the first yahrzeit.

YIZKOR: RECALLING THE DEAD

Recalling the deceased during a synagogue service is not merely a convenient form of emotional release, but an act of solemn piety and an expression of profound respect. The yizkor memorial service was instituted so that the Jew may pay homage to his forebears and recall the good life and traditional goals.

This memorial service is founded on a vital principle of Jewish life, one that motivates and animates the Kaddish recitation. It is based on the firm belief that the living, by acts of piety and goodness, can redeem the dead. The son can bring honor to the father. The "merit of the children" can reflect the value of the parents. This merit is achieved, primarily, by living on a high ethical and moral plane, by being responsive to the demands of God and sensitive to the needs of one's fellow man. The formal expression of this merit is accomplished by prayer to God and by contributions to charity.

YAHRZEIT: MEMORIAL ANNIVERSARY

Despite the Germanic origin of the word yahrzeit, the designation of a special day and special observances to commemorate the anniversary of the death of parents was already discussed in the Talmud. This religious commemoration is recorded not as a fiat, but as a description of an instinctive sentiment of sadness, an annual rehearsing of tragedy, which impels one to avoid eating meat and drinking wine—symbols of festivity and joy, the very stuff of life.

Yahrzeit may be observed for any relative or friend, but it is meant primarily for parents.

Notes to Chapter Twenty-eight

1. See chapter 9 of this book for a fuller understanding of this rite.
2. See Rosh, *Responsa,* ch. 17.
3. For a fuller treatment of this subject, read Maurice Lamm, *The Jewish Way in Love and Marriage,* published by Jonathan David Publishers, Middle Village, New York, 1989, from which book paragraphs in this section were excerpted.
4. Lydia Kukoff, *Choosing Judaism,* ch. 7, pp. 82-4.
5. Paragraphs in this section have been excerpted from Maurice Lamm, *The Jewish Way in Death and Mourning,* Jonathan David Publishers, Middle Village, New York, 1969.

Part Six

WELCOME HOME

29
WELCOME HOME:
WE ARE KEEPING THE LIGHTS ON

We stood together—you and we—in the morning cool of that ancient day when God gave the Torah to the Israelites in the Sinai desert. It was given, so Moses said, to those who were standing then at the foot of the mountain and to those not yet born—embracing the descendants of the very families that heard the actual "voice" of God thundering from the mountain top, but then got lost in the mists of time. Millennia later, these children hear that clear voice resonating in the chambers of their new hearts and they turn around and come home to the old family.[1]

The Torah could justly have proclaimed that the tired throng of slaves that had been freed only three months earlier included only those who already were Jewish. After all, the Jews had just come through the lengthy process of conversion after generations of living on Egyptian soil—circumcision was performed at the Exodus from Egypt; immersion was performed at Sinai; the acceptance of mitzvot would be enthusiastically embraced at the giving of the Torah. Only they and those who spring from their loins are the chosen people of God, the Jews. No one else need apply.

But the Torah insisted otherwise. Converts, in whichever generation of the forever future, in whatever city of the world, were not "new" Jews but "old" Jews; actually present at the birth of the religion when the Torah was given, having shared in the most sacred and significant event in all of human history. They are as native Jews—no more, no less. By enacting this bold declaration into the law of daily life, the Jewish teachers renewed the command that Jews must love the convert, even as they are charged to love their neighbors.

The difference today, therefore, between born Jews and Jews by choice, is that born Jews are children of ancestors who had converted centuries ago; Jews by choice converted only yesterday. Years from now, this new Jew's grandchildren will look all the way back to the old ancestors who converted to Judaism. If we are not converts, we are the children of converts who have committed to a life of Jewishness, of loving God, fellow Jews and fellow man. "Those who stood at Sinai" is a phrase that comprises those who are born to Jewish ancestors, all of whom originally converted at Sinai, those whose ancestors heroically converted since that time, and those who will convert today and tomorrow.

When the Lord thundered His Revelation on that sixth day of the Hebrew month of Sivan in the parched desert, there were some who did not want to stand anyplace near that mountain; others disappeared in the "mixed multitude." In troubled times since that day, many of the progeny of the old families split company to find easier living, an unthreatened existence, better livelihoods, more appealing universal customs, assimilation into the great undifferentiated human mass in which to hide under the protective cover of anonymity.

Now you, their descendants, have returned. Welcome back. We knew you would come home.

The Beginning of the Return

The narrative of your return began centuries ago—it is recounted in Deuteronomy 29—when Moses, on the day before his death, assembled all the people and initiated them into the covenant with God:[2]

> 9. You are standing this day, all of you before the Lord, your God—your heads, your tribes, your elders, and your officers, even all the men of Israel. . . .
>
> 11. That thou shouldest enter into the covenant of the Lord, thy God, and into His oath, which the Lord, thy God, maketh with thee this day. . . .

13.   Neither with you only do I make this covenant and this oath—but with him that standeth here with us this day before the Lord our God, and *also with him that is not here with us this day. . . .*

In an enigmatic, mystical digression in the Talmud, the rabbis ask a pertinent question about whether this includes those who were living at that time, but were not present at Sinai—idolators, for example. The Rabbis answer metaphorically:

Why are idolators lustful? Because they did not appear at Sinai. For when the serpent came upon Eve, he injected her with lustfulness. Now, as for the Israelites who stood at Mt. Sinai—their lustfulness departed (because it was counteracted by the sanctity of Revelation); but the idolators, who did not stand at Mt. Sinai—their lustfulness did not depart.[3]

The healing power of God's Revelation neutralized the primordial serpent's poison. Keeping the mitzvot commanded at the Revelation continuously counteracts the serpent's toxic libido. The Talmud notes, "The Holy One created evil passions—but also the Torah as their antidote."[4] In this sense, the Torah negated the influence of that primal sin.[5] Those who did not stand at Sinai remain under the influence of the serpent!

The Convert "Mazal"

But it is to the next question, as to whether the Revelation also includes proselytes, that the Talmud directs a subtle and very important point—for converts and for all Jews:

Rabbi Acha, son of Raba, asked Rav Ashi: What about proselytes? [Rav Ashi answered:] Though they were not physically present, their *mazal* was present! As it is written: "Neither with you only will I make this covenant and this oath—but with him that standeth here with us before the Lord our God and also with him that is not here with us this day."

The Talmud concludes therefore that converts, just as born Jews, will not suffer the serpent's poison—because they were at Sinai in their *mazal*! They experienced the marvelous effects of the Revelation; they absorbed the antidote of Torah.

But what is the *mazal* of the proselytes that was present at Sinai? According to the leading interpreters, *mazal* here refers to the "spirit" of the converts. The Sages hold that all creations that God made in His image have an abiding mystical spirit that hovers above them and is their true essence.[6]

The Talmud, in a courageous and ingenious way, thus finds every convert to have been at Sinai by his "spirit's" attendance, and thereby includes under the same biblical rubric of "those who are not here with us this day" all proselytes along with all future Jewish-born descendants. The ancestors of proselytes may not have come to the foot of Sinai in those days, or they may have departed from its teachings at some point in Jewish history. Today, the convert has come full circle; he rejoins the people of Sinai.

This is not just facile homiletic legerdemain, some inventive Rabbinic playfulness. It is fundamental to an understanding of Judaism's unflagging welcome of proselytes; its insistence on keeping doors open regardless of the forces that have always sought to shut them tight. This is the reason that the primary talmudic source on conversion introduces the entire subject of converting gentiles in remarkable terms. It says:[7] *Ger she'ba l'hitgayer ba'zeman ha'zeh*, "A convert who comes to be converted in these days. . . . " The former Chief Rabbi Ovadiah Yosef notes that it should have said, "A **gentile** who comes to convert. . . . " Obviously, a "convert" does not need to come to be converted! What is implied, he says, is that the gentile's ancestors have departed from the ways of the true God and His covenant, and now he is *returning*. He thus comes to the Jewish people already in a sense of "belonging there." He just realizes his potential: he is a "convert" who comes to be converted.

The Return

This understanding of the tradition also explains why Maimonides, who was precise and spare in his use of words, writes about converts in a similarly remarkable manner.[8] He speaks of converts whom the Bet Din, after investigation, judges to have *"returned"* out of love for Torah who are therefore welcomed. Time and again, he describes converts as those who have *"returned* from idolatry."

The convert has indeed returned. The Jews have waited patiently for many centuries and now welcome the lost sheep back into the family, old Abraham's family.

In an analogous sense, the term for a born Jew who has defected and then returned is a *ba'al teshuvah,* "one who has

come back" or *chozer bi'teshuvah,* "one who has *returned.*"
A former Dominican priest, Richard Kajut, now living as an
Orthodox Jew in Memphis, Tennessee, told me that, from his
viewpoint, there is no difference—"A *ba'al teshuvah* comes
back after nineteen years or so. I returned after 1900 years.
We are both *chozer bi'teshuvah.*"

RETURN TO WHAT?

But returned to what? The *ba'al teshuvah* may never have
observed a single commandment of the Torah, yet he is
generally no more removed than three or four generations from
people who did keep the faith. But the convert—from what
practice or belief did he or she depart to which he or she
is now "returning"? How can the tradition postulate that a
person could return to something he has never experienced?

Conjecture allows several options. The departure may reflect
the original departure from the truth of monotheism that Abraham first discovered. That would presuppose that the belief
in one universal God was the original belief of mankind and
that paganism is a later corruption. (The common understanding is that polytheism was a tentative, preliminary mode of
belief that preceded monotheism in the evolution of the God
idea.) Maimonides begins his treatise on the early history of
idolatry in this manner: "In the earliest days, in the age of
Enosh, grandson of Adam and Eve, people, including Enosh,
made the original pagan error. They began to worship the
creations of the Creator, believing that this was the desire of
God Himself, and the whole skein of idolatrous practices grew
from that cardinal error. The idea of one God went through
successive stages that witnessed substitutions for the Deity
and perversions, the subsequent diminution and shrinkage of
the idea of one God, and then its rediscovery by Abraham."[9]
The present convert's "return" is then a return to the original
pristine idea of One God, before it was corrupted.

Perhaps the departure and subsequent "return" represent
a breaking away from the truth which Isaiah envisions will come
full circle when all right-believing people will *return* to the
mountain of God. Perhaps the dynamics of truth-seeking are
such that all search for truth is an uncovering of the original
veracity, as the Latin term *educare* means a "bringing out of,"
implying that education is not an implanting, but rather an

extracting of ideas already buried deep within human beings. Thus, Isaiah portrays a people receiving the truth on a mountain and, after losing it and searching the world for it, returning to the mountain to find it again.

This thread weaves through the intellectual odyssey of many converts. Richard Kajut writes:

> If I were to serve the One God of Moses and the Prophets in the manner I was drawn to Him, I could only do it as a Jew. Like Avraham Avinu [Abraham, our Father], by rational inquiry, I had come full circle to the doorstep of the *Ribbono shel Olam* [the Master of the Universe].

More likely closer to fact than to homily, *chozer*, which implies returning after departing, is a mending of the original split in the religious community that existed at the beginning of the common era. The community that developed around the man from Nazareth and/or his legend was split between those Palestinian Jews who believed in the Christian Messiah, while still adhering to the norms of the Jewish religion, and those non-Palestinians who were converted to Christianity without ever having had a Jewish base: one was Jewish Christian, the other, gentile Christian.

The Judaism of the Second Temple did not sever the growing Christian community from its roots, but tolerated it as just another sect, albeit with unacceptable and erroneous principles and strange customs. The break came when Paul, who never personally knew Jesus, made every effort to split the new community from its Jewish roots. When the Temple was destroyed and the gentile Christians moved their center to Syrian Aleppo, Jewish influence on the new Christian movement waned, and the observance of even the most fundamental laws that the Nazarene kept, lapsed. Eventually, it was that branch of the new Christianity which won the day.

What caused the break was something Judaism would never tolerate—the emasculation of the process of conversion—the elimination of the rite of circumcision, which Jews had from the beginning regarded as Judaism's primary mark of identification, for which its mothers and children had sacrificed their lives, and which was considered equal in significance with the Abrahamic offering of Isaac.[10] The last paragraphs of Lawrence Schiffman's *Who Was a Jew?* are appropriate here:

> In retrospect, the *halakhot* . . . were what maintained the

identity of the Jewish people. Had the Rabbis relaxed these standards, accepting either the semi-proselytes or the gentile Christians into the Jewish people, Christians would quickly have become the majority within the expanded community of "Israel." Judaism as we know it would have ceased to exist even before reaching its codification in the Mishnah and the other great compilations of the tannaitic tradition. Christianity would have been the sole heir to the traditions of biblical antiquity, and the observance of the command-ments of the Torah would have disappeared within just a few centuries. In short, it was the Halakhah and its definition of Jewish identity which saved the Jewish people and its heritage from extinction as a result of the newly emerging Christian ideology.

The ultimate parting of the ways for Judaism and Christianity took place when the adherents to Christianity no longer conformed to *halakhic* definitions of a Jew. As these *gentile* Christians, who never converted to Judaism through the legal requirements we have discussed, became the dominant stream in the Christian communities which the Rabbis con-fronted, even in Palestine, the Rabbis ceased to regard the Christians as a group of Jews with heretical views and Christianity as a Jewish sect. Rather, the Rabbis began to regard the Christians as members of a separate religious com-munity, and their teachings as a perversion of the biblical tradition. From then on, Christians and Jews began a long history of interreligious strife which played so tragic a part in medieval and modern history.

The "return" of the convert, in this sense, is not only a return to the original meaning of the One God idea and to the truth of the covenant. It is a healing of the original wound, a suturing of the original rupture, a setting aright of an old historic wrong. Judaism, by its acceptance of right-minded converts, rewinds the historical reel and puts the convert back into the picture of its founding fathers.

HOMECOMING

The writing of this chapter was not only prompted by the undercurrents in the literature we have noted, but was also the result of powerfully articulated sentiments of converts them-selves, who had no way of divining these emotions before their conversion.

Over and over, converts use the same phrases in a shock of self-revelation: "I'm home!" "I've always been a Jew!" If these were only isolated comments, they could safely be attributed to the exuberance of this grand experience—being overcome by the release of emotion after a long, worrisome, and sometimes arduous personal struggle. Such an achievement of cherished goals can bring forth such exclamations of the spirit. But the idea is a recurring theme heard by many rabbis, written in magazines that periodically run stories on converts.

Here are just a few examples—some quoted in part from the testimonies in Part I:

Frances Price, a past president of the sisterhood of Congregation Beth Israel, Camden, New Jersey, wrote in an article in 1958 (*Women's League Outlook*, and then reprinted in *The Jewish Digest*, April 1958):

> It is not as a convert to Judaism, but as a very proud Jewess that I write. Even though I was born into the world of the gentile and have only comparatively recently become a Jew, I hesitate to use the term "convert" since I feel in no way converted to Judaism. What I really feel is that I have "come home." . . . Born and raised in a gentile world, living in a Christian atmosphere, having had the usual schooling in Christianity, I lived a pleasant and satisfying life. . . . My entrance into Judaism dates from the beginning of my small son's religious education. . . . I must admit that it was a purely academic thing with me. What makes a Jew a Jew? How does a Jew think? What are his traditions?
>
> How can I help but raise my head in pride as I pass by the mezuzah on my doorpost and enter the warmth and the beauty of *my* Jewish home, where lives *my* Jewish family?
>
> No, I was not converted. I came seeking. I was informed. I was welcomed. I was home.[11]

Christina Costa, a twenty-four-year-old housewife from Surrey, England, wrote in *The London Jewish Chronicle* in 1980:

> My father had always been irreligious, at least outwardly, but my mother was staunchly Catholic at one time. She was educated in a convent and remained very observant until shortly after moving down south. . . . My brother got married in a Catholic church. My own wedding was in a registry office. By that time, I'd rejected Catholicism, having a few months earlier briefly and unsuccessfully tried to revive my interest in it. My husband believes that religion has the sole purpose

of reinforcing family life, consequently Judaism rather appeals to him. At the moment, his attitude is a bit too academic for him to convert.

My commitment to Judaism at that stage was purely emotional and intuitive. My actual knowledge was woefully thin. . . . But I was still absolutely terrified! Then, as soon as I went through the synagogue doors, I felt I was coming *home*. I know that sounds irrational, but it really was how I felt. One of the first services I attended was Yom Kippur, when I also fasted. That was a very emotional experience. Indeed, my early convictions about Judaism were almost mystical, and it's interesting that I've now come right over to a strongly rational approach.

I intend to go on studying and look forward to becoming more involved in synagogue services. I really feel I've begun to find myself and that this is where I was always meant to be.[12]

Dr. Constance Head is a professor of history and religion and the author of several books. Writing in 1981 (*The National Jewish Monthly*, 3/81), she says:

When I was thirty-nine, I became a convert to Judaism. The event was the culmination of many years of seeking, pondering and trying to force myself to believe the doctrines of Christianity, which I never accepted, yet felt guilty in rejecting. I teach history and religion and have a Ph.D. and a divinity school degree from a Methodist university. I came to Judaism not through marriage. . . . I came not through the influence of friends, for, when I made my decision to seek conversion, I had no close Jewish friends. The nearest Jewish congregation is fifty-three miles from my home. I came into Judaism because, while there is a measure of truth in all the great religions, I believe that Judaism is the truest of them all.

Then, gradually, I began to admit how I really felt. "I guess I'm more Jewish than anything else," I'd say. And when I did, I felt a warm, wonderful glow of rightness. In my heart, I *was* Jewish; only through some accident of birth, I was not born to Judaism.

There is little doubt that, for many converts, Judaism is strange and filled with unknowns. Yet, it is equally true that, for many, conversion is truly a homecoming. Perhaps it is only the stuff of imagination, or wish-fulfillment, or radical optimism, to believe that inside even the most WASPish-looking and-sounding people there may be a Jew hiding shyly, waiting to be asked to step out into his own. Perhaps, too, there are Jews whose Christian bearing and style hints at a soul exiled from its source.

What accounts for the persistent belief on the part of the most far-flung civilizations that they are the true lost Ten Tribes of Israel? I refer not to the overworked imaginations of adventurous spirits, but to masses of people who perform Jewish-style rituals and who believe they will one day come home to their people in Israel. This is the fervent hope of 200,000 members of the Lemba tribe of Zimbabwe, who don't eat pork, or mix meat and milk products and practice circumcision; two million Shinlung tribesman of northeastern India who insist they descend from the tribe of Menashe, just as the Beta Israel, Ethiopian Jews, recognized by the Rabbinate in Israel as authentic Jews, claim descendancy from the biblical tribe of Dan; numerous Japanese who claim to derive from the tribe of Zebulun; the twenty million members of the Pathan in Afghanistan who observe rituals and cherish tribal memories that point strongly to Jewish origins or influence.[13]

We do not believe in a genetic inheritance of acquired characteristics, of course, but we must paraphrase the author of *Bet Elokim*, referred to as Mabit, who was quoted at the beginning of this work.

> The Lord offered the Torah to all the nations, and it was refused by all except the Jews. Now, it is probable that, among all the peoples, there was a minority in every nation that believed the Torah should be embraced. But they could not prevail, because they had to follow the majority. It is impossible that any idea will be accepted unanimously, even for an easy-to-accept plan, let alone one which is difficult, such as the keeping of Torah.

> Now, God did not wish to deny these people their just reward, so He enabled their descendants to fulfill the secret wish of their ancestors who could not fulfill their desires themselves. It is probable that those who have converted to Judaism, were those whose parents wanted to stand at the foot of Sinai when God gave the Torah. This will surely occur when the Messiah arrives, and all the souls who could not come to the original revelation will be brought back to their origins.

S. Y. Agnon, Israel's Poet Laureate, said, when receiving the Nobel Prize for Literature, that he was born in Jerusalem, his beloved city, the spiritual capital of the world. But, by a historic mistake of the Roman Empire, his mother was in Poland when he came into this world. In that sense, perhaps we are all born in the Holy City—and all of us were at Sinai.

The coalescence of the novice Jew's deepest sentiment with the tradition's mature wisdom should be encouraging, if also mystical, to those contemplating becoming Jews. It should be flattering to know that the convert is recouping 1900 years of history, that his or her soul's venture into a new faith is actually a correction of a historical flaw, a vindication of ancestors who lived more than three millennia ago. It should encourage the convert to feel that he or she is a participant in the long march of civilization that is now turning onto a new road, making a sweeping 180-degree turn—declaring that from this generation onward, the family will walk in step with the oldest and most God-intoxicated religion in history. He or she is rejoining a minority in terms of numbers, but a clear majority in terms of the ideas by which mankind functions.

We welcome you as Ruth, the convert, was welcomed by Boaz (Ruth 2:11, 12):

> It hath fully been told me . . . how thou hast left thy father and thy mother, and the land of thy nativity, and art come unto a people that thou knowest not heretofore. The Lord recompense thy work, and be thy reward complete from the Lord, the God of Israel, under whose wings thou art come to take refuge.

It is unquestionably a difficult trip—this converting to a religion like Judaism. But all the same it is a coming home, a returning to roots, a vindication of all that has gone by.

The Jewish people has kept the lights burning—stubbornly trying to illuminate civilization during the long night of its exile—subliminally hoping against hope that the light would draw thinking people to its source.

Welcome home. We just knew you would come back.

Notes to Chapter Twenty-nine

1. The idea for this chapter was first given me by my distinguished friend, Rabbi Hershel Schachter, Rosh Kollel at Yeshiva University, to whom I am deeply indebted. I have since spoken of this theme to many converts

and a look of instant recognition and relief showed in their faces. It is an acknowledgement of the truth. For the germ of this concept, see Talmud, Shabbat 146a.

2. See the comments of Rashi and Nachmanides to these verses.

3. Shabbat 145b.

4. Bava Batra 16a.

5. The subsequent awareness by Adam and Eve of their nakedness and their sexual differences undoubtedly gave rise to the injection of the evil of lustfulness. It should be noted that this is another illustration of the rejection of the "original sin" concept. See Isidore Epstein's comments in his translation of tractate *Shabbat*, Soncino Press, p. 738; and Hertz, *Additional Notes to Genesis,* pp. 195-196, second edition, Soncino Press, 1965; and D. Weiss in *Dor dor vd'dorshav,* II, p. 9, Ziv, Jerusalem, 1963.

6. Note the dispute between the two Amoraim, Rav Acha bar Kahana and Rav Ashi, regarding whether it was the ancestry of the three generations of the patriarchs that removed the *zuhamah,* lustfulness, or their presence at Sinai. On *mazalot,* see Megillah 3a regarding Daniel and his friends, whose mazal they saw, and Rashi that it is not actually they themselves, but their reflection above, i.e. their mazalot. See also the comments of Yosef Lifland in *Gerim Ve'Gerut,* Mossad Ha'Rav Kook, Jerusalem, 1971.

7. Yevamot 47a.

8. See Maimonides, *Mishneh Torah,* Hilkhot Issurei Bi'ah 13:14-17. The word chozer does not generally mean "he turns from," but "he returns"— implying a 180-degree turn, a reversal, a coming back. To wit, see Jastrow on *chazirah* and its four uses.

9. Maimonides, *Mishneh Torah,* Hilkhot Avodat Kokhavim 1:1.

10. An excellent analysis of this age and these problems and a description of the true parting of the ways can be found in Lawrence H. Schiffman's *Who Was a Jew!,* Ktav Publishing House, Hoboken, New Jersey, 1985. Also see Abraham Cohen's *The Parting of the Ways: Judaism and the Rise of Christianity,* published for the World Jewish Congress, British Section, Lincolns-Prager, London, 1954, and Abba Hillel Silver's *Where Judaism Differed,* Macmillan, New york, 1957.

11. As quoted in Max Eichhorn, *Conversion To Judaism,* p. 261. Ktav Publishing House, Hoboken, New Jersey, 1965.

12. *London Jewish Chronicle,* "Coming Home" 1980. (The precise date is not known to the writer at the present time.)

13. This research is headed by Dr. Tudor Parfitt, Professor of Hebrew and Jewish Studies at London University's School of Oriental and African Studies. A descriptive article of Parfitt was done by the *Jerusalem Post Magazine,* April 27, 1990.

APPENDIX 1

(Addendum to Chapter 4)

MOTIVATIONS TO CONVERT:
JETHRO AND OTHERS

The Talmud, Zevachim 116a, referring to three possible reasons for Jethro's "coming," asks: *Mah sh'muah shama u'va?* "What news did he hear that he came and turned proselyte?" What exactly prompted him to "come" to the Jewish people? "Rabbi Joshua said: He heard of the battle with the Amalekites. . . . Rabbi Eleazar of Modim said: He heard of the giving of the Torah and came. . . . Rabbi Eleazar said: He heard about the dividing of the Red Sea and came . . .".

These three reasons have always been high on the list of motivators of conversion for one or another proselyte throughout the ages:

1. The splitting of the sea implies that Jethro realized that, inasmuch as this people deserved to have God intervene in nature to rescue it from disaster, it must be the true religion, and it is therefore of the greatest merit that they be joined. So he came to them. The religion was obviously "successful" and had a future, and it is natural to want to associate with a people protected by God. The widespread acceptance of Christianity and Islam centuries later was their symbol of "success," and they were joined by millions who looked upon that as an indication of God's favor.

2. The victory over Amalek in a vicious war must have captivated the imagination of the ancient world for the utter miraculousness of this event. The Jews surely must have deserved to win. So Jethro "came" and "turned proselyte." This motivation is one of associating with national power, which was the reason why conversions were actively discouraged during the ages of Jewish hegemony in the times of King David and Solomon. The Rabbis were afraid that the authentic reason for conversion would be subordinated to the more convincing practical reason for aligning oneself with victors.

3.   More incredible than either the splitting of the sea or
the triumph in the war with Amalek must have been the
news of the revelation of God at Sinai. The dimensions of
that event were seismic and continue to shake the world
to this day. They surely were the confirming fact that Israel
was protected by God because they were chosen by Him
to be His people. Jethro's hearing of that news must have
been the most convincing argument for his joining the Jewish
people. Of all the reasons, this has the ring of authenticity.
The Sinaitic Covenant was the revelation of the true God,
whose Torah made a convincing case of becoming a constitution for the global society and a moral prescription for
living the good life.

One Midrash (Devarim Rabbah, I:5) holds that when Jethro
"came," he said: "Now I know that God is greater than all
other gods on earth." How could he say "all other gods"?
Perhaps greater than the god Jethro had been serving, but
"all other gods"—as if he knew? The Midrash answers that
Jethro had indeed examined every other religion before he
"heard the news and came" to the Jews. In each he was ordained
and, after he was ordained, he left. One who makes and breaks
commitments is surely not the paradigm of stability that qualifies
one for conversion. I thank my son-in-law, Rabbi Simcha Weinberg of New York, for reminding me of this Midrash.

A number of rabbis do not accept these descriptions and
the attributions of Jethro's lack of pure motivation. They hold
that Jethro was a great man, but believed that his leadership
talents would not be useful if he remained with the Jews in
the presence of giants like Moses and Aaron. Rabbi Eleazar
ha'Moda'i (Yalkut Shimoni 271, to Yitro 18) puts these words
into the mouth of Jethro: "A candle is useless except in the
dark. What good can a candle do between the sun and the
moon? You [Moses] are the sun, and Aaron is the moon. What
should a candle do between the sun and the moon? What
then? I am going back to my country and I will convert all
my countrymen and I will bring them to study, and I will draw
them close under the wings of the Shekhinah."

There were exceptions to this general insistence on converting for the sake of Heaven, and they were unhesitatingly
noted in the Talmud. For example, Hillel the Elder (Shabbat
31a; also see note to Kiddushin, Soncino edition, p. 313, note
3) converted someone who wanted to be a Jew so that he
could earn the title of High Priest and wear the elegant Priestly

garments. The Talmud (Menachot 44a) relates a spectacular story of how Rabbi Chiyya converted a promiscuous woman who fell in love with one of his students, but who genuinely repented of her life-style.

But how could these Sages have converted persons with clearly ulterior motives? The Rabbis answer that those courts were presided over by the greatest scholars of the age and they could be relied upon to correctly evaluate the candidates. If, after intense scrutiny, they decided that ultimately their unworthy motives would be transformed into motives "for the sake of Heaven," the conversion was fully valid.

To this day, a properly constituted Bet Din, is given this very mandate. The members of the Bet Din are obligated to carefully scrutinize all candidates and accept or reject them based solely on their personal, unbiased judgment. Nonetheless, in every country and in every century of its history, the rabbis doggedly insisted on the ideal of pure motive. While it is true that the decision to reject conversion for the purpose of marriage was the decision of one talmudic Sage, that is the generally accepted decision that was kept until our day. One may not initially accept such conversion, although, once having been effectuated, the conversion is accepted as valid. Maimonides codifies this in the law unequivocally in the thirteenth century, and it is replicated in all the codes that follow.

See Chapter 15 for the responsa on this, and Appendix 5.

APPENDIX 2

(Addendum to Chapter 6)

COVENANT: THE SOCIAL CONTRACT AND THE DIVINE CONTRACT

There is yet another lesson to be drawn from the idea of covenant—the Jewish concept of the Social Contract. Contrasting the covenant with God and the Social Contract with man is instructive. The unconditional covenant with God is not a business contract, and the contractual social relationship of people is not modeled on the covenant between God and man. People are tied to one another by a Social Contract, such as that described by Jean-Jacques Rousseau. The Social Contract is based upon simple, utilitarian motives—people must depend on one another and therefore must have mutually respected rights and ties. Now, this contract is the very foundation of society, the sub-structure of all social life.

Thomas Hobbes, in his *Leviathan*, maintains that the formation of a commonwealth is dependent upon the enactment of a covenant, and he holds it to be the foremost natural law after the preservation of life itself. If there is no common fundamental agreement among diverse peoples on how to live together, there can be no unity. Without unity, society relapses into "Natural Right"—people acting savagely to fulfill their personal needs, regardless of their actions' effect upon others. Without this contract, society as we know it could not exist—human predators would stalk the earth in total anarchy. In the language of the *Ethics of the Fathers*, "Man would swallow his neighbor alive." The Social Contract is a conditional and utilitarian one.

But a covenant struck between people that is based on society's relationship with God is qualitatively different. It is not utilitarian. People do not undertake actions only because they work, but because they are right. The covenant is not based on some moral profit-and-loss statement. Nor can it be assumed that the good is desired only for the sake of benefits promised.

It is also not conditional. This means that, though he suffer the slings and arrows of outrageous fortune, man cannot withdraw from the duties which God commanded him. This unconditionality binds God as well, by His own will, so that, even if a person commits behaviors unworthy of the people of God, God is still not free from the force of this covenant. People who relate unconditionally to God should be able to relate to one another in a more elevated manner than that rudimentarily required by the Social Contract.

A consequence of this idea is that, while the relationship between people in the Social Contract is based on *reciprocal rights*, that of the covenant is based on *mutual obligations*. The relations between people who have a compact with God are based upon the fraternal model wherein people are required to treat one another as God's children, all created in the image of God, rather than as dominoes which lean upon one another in a mutually needy relationship.

A person's value is determined not by his usefulness to society, as Plato would have us believe. Rather, as in the Jewish view, each person's fundamental value as a human being derives from being created in God's image. Dignity issues not from one's fellow man, so that a person's value relates only to his or her qualifications, but from an eternal God unconditionally bound to us. This guarantees equal value and therefore equal treatment for all people. It is the reason why the elderly have equal value with the young in western society, and the infirm with the robust. It is why the covenant is the quintessential symbol of Jewish society, the basis of its community structure and the essential expression of its concept of governance. That Jewish understanding is the basis of all social work.

Circumcision articulates this idea in the very terms the Torah uses. The Bible speaks of "cutting" and "binding" the covenant. The Hebrew phrase for establishing a covenant is *koret b'rit*, "cutting" a covenant—a metaphor for at once separating and linking. Circumcision simultaneously symbolizes mutuality (linking) and independence (cutting), which are required for the existence of community on the one hand and freedom on the other. A society that draws its sustenance from the covenant has the potential of constituting itself a "Holy Community," *Kehillah Kedoshah.*

Circumcision is the permanent physical symbol that forever reminds the Jew of the permanence of his relationship with God which is the basis of his relationship to God and to society.

In order to understand the Jewish concept of covenant, one needs to read the works of Daniel Elazar. See, among Elazar's many contributions on the subject, "Some Preliminary Observations on the Jewish Political Tradition" in *Tradition*, 18 (3), Fall 1980.

APPENDIX 3
(Addendum to Chapter 9)

CHRISTIANITY REJECTED CIRCUMCISION AND ACCEPTED IMMERSION

Paul rejected circumcision as a requirement for conversion to Judaism. In strictly practical terms, he had to reject it, because he simply could never convert the world's heathens if he insisted on so difficult an admission procedure. But, in political terms, it presents us with an interesting development. Paul was a total stranger to Jesus, never having met him, and even having persecuted the followers of the Galilean Messiah contender. He rejected much of what was dear to his mentor. But his rejection of circumcision was remarkable. (On this, see Joseph Klausner, *From Jesus to Paul*, ch. V, p. 504, Menorah Publishing, New York, 1978.)

After all, the Jews had not long before suffered martyrdom at the hands of Antiochus Epiphanes who outlawed circumcision, and thereby caused the suicides of numerous mothers with their children. By rejecting this very dearly-held observance, the sign of the covenant, the mark of the Jew, he enraged many of the most intimate colleagues of Jesus. They began to preach a contrary gospel, one that kept the observance of circumcision—and of Shabbat and holidays and kosher food—and referred to it as a "Jewish-Nazarene" gospel (Galatians I:6-12).

With our understanding of the twin concepts required in conversion, what appears to have been a decision based only on practical needs really bespeaks a whole philosophy. Circumcision represents peoplehood. Paul, preaching to heathens who wanted no part of the Jewish tradition, not only could not proffer circumcision as a requirement for practical reasons, he had to obliterate the whole symbol, because it was the antithesis of everything he sought to achieve—a separate peoplehood, a new church, a different religion. But circumcision would mean taking on Jewish peoplehood. The Jewish-Nazarenes, on the other hand, were interested only in adding a Messiah component to the Jewish religion, not replacing it. In addition, having their center in Palestine, not in Syrian Aleppo, their interest was to retain the unity of peoplehood and, therefore, they looked upon circumcision as a vital requirement for joining their people. The break with circumcision was a break with the peoplehood idea, which they believed Jesus wanted as, for example, when he insisted on preaching only to the Jews and not to gentiles. So stunning was Paul's decision that the Jewish Sages, embracing heretofore a wide diversity of practices within the Jewish community, could never countenance such an action and forthwith expelled Christianity from the sacred precincts of the Jewish religion.

Unlike circumcision, however, immersion in a mikveh stands for a relationship which is vertically-oriented between God and the individual—ye'ud and not goral—and that did not cause Paul any difficulty since his emphasis was faith, not community. In time, however, what was an immersion, in Christian terms a "baptism," became a sprinkling of "holy waters," and that proved to be a total distortion, not only of the Halakhah, but of the finely crafted symbol that went from generation to generation since Sarah.

The convert to Judaism should know, therefore, that circumcision is not valuable only because Jews traditionally used it in the conversion protocol, but because halakhically and philosophically no gentile could become a Jew without it. A convert's understanding and accepting of this is his symbol of rejecting Paul's original breakaway and the beginning of the decoupling, in a halakhic sense, from his status as a non-Jew.

APPENDIX 4

(Addendum to Chapter 10)

THE WATER METAPHOR

There is a third instructive aspect to the waters of the mikveh. It is that the creation of the world is bound up with water as its most important element. The creation narrative in the Torah highlights this aspect of the beginnings of the cosmos. (See Sefer Ha'Chinukh, mitzvah 173.)

At first, the earth was empty, desolate and dark, with "God's spirit fluttering on the face of the water." On the second day, the waters were divided, upper from lower. On the third day, the waters were gathered and islands of earth appeared. Water, then, is a key ingredient in the new creation and its dominant presence.

This metaphor of mikveh waters conveys most completely the idea that while circumcision is the component of the ceremony which negates and removes the former status of non-Jew, immersion is that segment which is designed to create the positive new status of Jew—the creation of a Jew paralleling the creation of the universe. There is no doubt that the mikveh symbol is the transforming agent. It is overpowering in its physical suggestiveness—precisely upon emerging from the waters does the convert emerge into a new life. The convert's descent into the water is a reenactment, on the personal level, of the global history of man's original creation. Hopefully for the convert, it is the creation of a new world, into which the convert is now born, and which contains new ideas, makes new demands, and gives rise to new expectations.

If we probe deeper, we find that water relates to the creation of the convert in an even more profound sense. In Jewish sources, the water which covered the earth traces its physical origin to the Garden of Eden, the earthly manifestation of the state of human perfection that preceded the history of humanity (Bekhorot 55a, and also Malbim to Genesis 2:10).

It is worthwhile to read Aryeh Kaplan's *Waters of Eden*, National Cconference of Synagogue Youth, New York, 1976. Much of the discussion of mikveh here was informed by the insights developed by Aryeh Kaplan, and much credit to him for the profound work that he produced in the few years that God granted him life. He notes that, in the very heart of the story of the Garden, there is an unusual biblical verse which describes a river, which the Rabbis say is the tributary of the four rivers then known and, by extension, the source of all the world's water.

> "And a river went out of Eden to water the garden and from there it split and became four headwaters" (Genesis 2:3).

Curiously, the Bible does not return to that verse to continue the thought of what happened to the water. The Rabbis of the Midrash, disturbed by the mysterious, unconnected verse, suggest that Adam repented of his sin, the first, by immersing in that river, and that is why it appears in the midst of the story. (*Pirke De'Rabbi Eliezer* 20 (47b).)

The purpose served by immersing and washing his sins away in that river is that Adam thereby symbolically sought to link himself once again to the source of life, after being expelled from the garden, and to reconnect to the state of perfection, the garden of purity, the roots from which he grew.

In terms of conversion, the symbol is as graphic as it is deep: The waters of the mikveh symbolize a return to the headwaters in Eden, before the split into the four tributaries. It is a coming back to old roots, a return to Torah Judaism before it was split. It is how Adam purified himself, and how we, his descendants, purify ourselves.

APPENDIX 5

(Addendum to Chapter 15)

THE MARRIAGE MOTIVATION: A BRIEF REVIEW

There is a significant source of hope implicit in the very nature of conversion today. It is possibly an opportunity, not only a danger as seen heretofore, that is of significant value in our contemporary situation. The sooner we recognize this, the more effective will be our management of conversion. There are several new factors to consider today:

Starting with Accommodation CAN End with Conviction

If one needs to substantiate this idea on a communal level, the proof is not difficult to find. Which objective thinkers, in possession of advanced scientific, sociological, and psychological knowledge and a host of experiential insights, could have predicted the teshuvah movement of religious return in the late twentieth century—content-filled, freely inspired, and the source for the buoyant optimism of traditional Jewry? Who could have forecast the authenticity and honesty of this generation of youth?

Conversion can often lead to an authentic transformation, even if it begins only as an accommodation. And if that appears to be likely, then flippancy toward the accommodation convert can easily result in a noxious form of spiritual vandalism.

The Changing Content of the Marriage Motivation

Today, couples can freely live together without benefit of religious marriage, or even civil marriage, without fear of communal rejection or even disapproval. If conversion is undertaken, it is usually not for the sole purpose of marriage, because that is no longer the vital condition without which man and woman cannot couple. In addition, sadly in our times, one need not enter conversion in order to satisfy a sexual passion (which was a primary concern of the Rabbis of pre-modern days).

Nonetheless, it is quite true that there are non-Jews desperately seeking a Jewish mate, often in circumstances approaching entrapment. Conversion for such devious purposes is to be frowned upon and strenuously avoided.

Reactions of the Jewish Partner

Further, it is not out of the realm of possibility in our day, that rejecting a candidate for conversion will encourage a non-observing couple to simply slip out of the fold and join a church some time later. In the mobile society of our day, and in the free-for-all religious movement that characterizes our californiated communities, this is not unthinkable or even an exceptional case. Do we want to chance this? While Judaism must refuse to be held hostage by such threats, it is nonetheless a factor that must be weighed along with others. This situation falls under the legal rubric of *sha'at ha'dechak*, "times of emergency." In Jewish law, this is considered equal to an *ex post facto* circumstance which, while it is not ideal, does nonetheless trigger religious conversion. It renders the participant a "lion convert," *ger arayot*, an accommodation convert out of fear, rather than one who converts out of pure motivation.

Intermarriage: The Risk/Benefit Ratio

How much intermarriage are we prepared to risk in order to defend the "pure-motive" idyllic state that we have cherished all through history? It is not an accident, I hold, that Maimonides placed the laws of admission to Judaism purposely within the folds of the laws of prohibited unions, such as intermarriage. The avoidance of one may lead us to the other. Perhaps the concept of conversion can save us from that fate which surely is the most tragedy-filled of all the visions of the Jewish future. This factor surely defines our situation as a "time of emergency," which should qualify the present practice of accepting accommodation converts after the fact of their conversion.

For these reasons and others, Orthodox rabbis often participate in such conversions. Nonetheless, the fundamental *sine qua non*, even of these conversions and regardless of the motivation, is the safe predictability of living a traditional Jewish life, replete with Jewish values, Jewish education for the children, and observance of the whole skein of Jewish practices.

This chapter should serve only for elucidation and not for *P'sak*, the Halakhic decisions of the rabbis. Such decisions are to be rendered only by the local authoritative Bet Din.

A CONVERT'S BIBLIOGRAPHY

What is the critical content of the Jewish religion? A library of books stands in eloquent, but mute testimony to the diversity of answers. They offer the answers, but first they must be opened and asked.

It is not the purpose of this book to convey all Torah in one stellar burst of information—to paraphrase the convert who asked the Sage, Hillel, to teach him all Torah while standing on one foot. But a bibliography can direct the reader to the sources of our religion. A beginning must be made.

What follows is an outline of suggested reading material for converts. It is a reading guide to Judaism that is naturally incomplete, given the huge quantity and diverse quality of books available today. It also makes no pretense to being a recommended reading list for scholars or academics who have the ability and the time to do research. The books are secondary sources that will digest and present the Jewish religion in a way that will make it more accessible to prospective converts and enable them to learn where to find the light.

A bibliography is usually written as a list of books subsumed under one title or another. But there are too many books on the broad subject of Judaism, and they vary in usefulness for converts at their different stages of experience and learning. Therefore, the recommended texts are few and they will be incorporated in short descriptive paragraphs.

Who are the Jews?

One of the finest texts for gentiles who wish to become Jews was written by a layman, not a rabbi. He is Herman Wouk, my old friend, who wrote *This is My God*, now in a new paperback edition by Touchstone (for which I wrote the Study Guide, *I Shall Glorify Him*). It introduces authentic Judaism to the uninitiated in an elegant, contemporary style. The book describes "the Jews in these times," and the meaning of the most definitive term that describes them, "the chosen people." It is a good, popular introduction for non-Jews. It covers the ideas as well as the practice, and it is written by a master communicator and one who is very well versed in his Judaism. Every convert should start here. It has never been out of print since its first publication in 1959.

Why the Jews?

Dennis Prager and Joseph Telushkin provide an answer in their book, *Why the Jews?*, (Simon and Schuster, New York, 1983). A documentation of the Church's anti-Semitism is forthrightly presented in Malcolm Hay's *A Foot of Pride*. Also very readable are books on the subject by authors as diverse as Jean-Paul Sartre and Maurice Samuel, and a sheaf of publications by the Anti-Defamation League.

What Do the Jews Believe?

1. The idea of one God—monotheism—is the cornerstone of all Jewish beliefs. While Christianity is a "monotheistic faith group," it does not hold to the pure and undiluted monotheism of Judaism.

Literature on the Jewish God-concept is not difficult to find. There are many books on the subject, and choosing the right one depends on what is specifically appropriate to the mind of the convert and that can best be determined by the sponsoring rabbi or teacher. A general introduction to it can be found in *This is My God*; a mystical one in Abraham Joshua Heschel's *Man is Not Alone*, published by Farrar, Straus; a philosophical one by Isidore Epstein in *The Faith of Judaism*, Soncino Press, London, 1961, ch. 8 and 9, and by David Bleich in *With Perfect Faith*, Ktav Publishing House, Hoboken, New Jersey, 1985; and in a little, but very lucid, paperback book by Aryeh Kaplan, *The Infinite Light: A Book about God*, published by NCSY/UOJCA, New York, 1984.

2. The difference between the Jewish idea of God and the deviation in Christian theology is well defined in two books— Trude Weiss-Rosemarin, *Judaism and Christianity*, Jonathan David Publishers, Middle Village, New York, 1972, and Abba Hillel Silver, *Where Judaism Differed*, the Jewish Publication Society, Philadelphia, 1957.

3. The prohibition of idolatry sounds like a throwback to primitive times. After all, where is Queequeg mumbling to his wooden statue today? The fact is that idolatry is rampant in our time, masquerading as the true religion of cultists. Caught up in the fervor of the new fads are young men and women of middle-class America, searching for one true God and stumbling on ersatz faiths that satisfy a ravenous emotional hunger. The subject is well-handled by David Berger and Michael Wyschogrod in *Jews and Jewish Christianity*, Ktav Publishing House, Hoboken, New Jersey, 1978.

What are Some of Their Practices?

"A few of the minor mitzvot and a few of the major mitzvot. . . . " This is a curious instruction. One would think that this is the nub of the whole matter. What is Judaism if not a series of God's mandates which man fulfills as cherished ideals? Yet, the whole enterprise of conversion is impossible if we demand, in advance, comprehensive knowledge of this vast storehouse of tradition which is Judaism. **But while we are not obligated to complete the work, we may not desist from making a beginning.**

1. General Books:

The books available on the general subject are too numerous to mention here. A quick review of Jewish information is presented in Louis Finkelstein, *The Beliefs and Practices of Judaism*, Devin-Adair Co., New York, 1952, and in a more interesting format in a two-volume set, Rabbi Alfred J. Kolatch, *The Jewish Book of Why*, Jonathan David Publishers, Middle Village, New York, 1985. Other basic introductions to Judaism include Hayim Halevy Donin, *To Be A Jew*, Basic Books, New York, 1972. Also valuable for the beginner are the three volumes of Richard Siegel, Sharon Strassfeld and Michael Strassfeld,

The Jewish Catalog, Jewish Publication Society, Philadelphia, which are a popular diagrammatic outline of Jewish life. A more academic volume is Gershon Appel, *The Concise Guide to Jewish Laws and Customs*, Ktav Publishing House, Hoboken, New Jersey, 1976, two volumes, and also Abraham Chill, *The Minhagim*, Sepher-Hermon, New York, 1979. Fine introductory primers for converts have recently been published. One such is Lawrence H. Schiffman, *Judaism: A Primer*, Anti-Defamation League of B'nai B'rith, New York, 1985.

2. Specific Subjects:

On immersion: Dr. Norman Lamm, *A Hedge of Roses*, Phillip Feldheim Inc., New York, 1977, for an intellectual apologetic on the subject. A lucid and detailed description of the *laws* of family purity can be found in another excellent English language work on the subject, Dr. Moses Tendler, *Pardes Rimonim: A Marriage Manual for the Jewish Family*, Judaica Press, New York, 1982.

On kashrut: Yacov Lipschutz, *Kashruth*, Art Scroll, Mesorah Publications, Brooklyn, New York, 1972.

On Shabbat: The books by Dayan Grunfeld and Abraham Heschel as noted in this book, plus *Shabbos—A Day Of Eternity*, NCSY/UOJCA, New York, 1976.

On Tefillin: *G-d, Man and Tefillin*, NCSY/UOJCA, New York, 1976.

On mezuzah: *The Mezuzah*, Art Scroll, Mesorah Publications, Brooklyn, New York, 1984.

On ethics: A plethora of recent books on specific subjects within the tradition such as on ethics, philosophy and history are also available. A review of primary sources translated into English can be found in a B'nai B'rith volume, edited by my brother, Dr. Norman Lamm, entitled *The Good Society*, B'nai B'rith Publications, Viking Press, New York, 1974, and in Meyer Waxman, *Judaism: Religion and Ethics*, Yosselof, New York, 1958.

On philosophy: Isidore Epstein, *The Faith of Judaism*, Soncino Press, London, 1960; Norman Lamm, *Faith and Doubt*, Ktav Publishing House, Hoboken, New Jersey, 1971; and Eliezer Berkovitz, *God, Man and History*, Jonathan David Publishers, Middle Village, New York, 1959.

What Literature Have They Produced?

On the Bible, *Tanakh*, there are many books, depending on whether one wishes to use them for study or for reading at services. A good one for the synagogue is *The Pentateuch and Haftorahs*, edited by Joseph Hertz, Soncino Press, London, 1960. For study, one should read either the Art Scroll volumes on the separate books of the Bible, or the Soncino edition of the Bible, London.

On the Prayerbook: *The Authorized Daily Prayer Book*, edited by Joseph Hertz, Soncino Press, 1960; *The Art Scroll Prayerbook*, Mesorah Publications, Brooklyn, New York, 1979; *To Pray as a Jew*, Hayim Halevy Donin, Basic Books, New York, 1980.

On the Oral Law, the Mishnah and Talmud: The following offerings are made, each of them on a different level of depth. Recommendations especially for this category should be made by a teacher who knows both the student and the texts. *Torah: The Oral Tradition, An Outline of Rabbinic Thought Throughout the Ages*, by Noah Aminoah and Yosef Nitzan, World Zionist Organization, Israel, 1983, is an excellent, lucid, pictorial presentation. Also, *The Art Scroll Mishnah Series*, edited by Zlotowitz and Scherman, Mesorah Publications, Brooklyn, New York, 1979; *El-Am Talmud*, edited by A. Ehrman and others, Jerusalem, 1965; *A Guide to a Page of Talmud*, Shefa Institute, Sepher-Hermon, New York, 1978; and *The Essential Talmud*, Adin Steinsaltz, Basic Books, New York, 1977. In 1990, the same author and publisher produced a more comprehensive introduction to the Talmud.

What of Their Recent History?

The preparation for conversion should not omit the following subjects, which may sometime be considered peripheral because they do not directly address the subject of the religion and because they make no action demand which requires commitment and evaluation in terms of acceptance into the Jewish *people*. Nonetheless, they are vital to an understanding of the Jewish people which, as we note many times, is an equal component with the Jewish *religion* in entering the covenant.

1. History

The history of the Jews is a subject treated in an exciting

manner or very tepid. History is not, as Henry Ford called it, "just one damned thing after another." It is the very stuff of our past. Few historians do that past justice. Some books are readable as texts, such as Isidore Epstein, *Judaism: A Historical Presentation*, Penguin Books, Baltimore, Maryland, 1959. Also, the more recent popular volume by a non-Jewish journalist, Paul Johnson, *A History of the Jews*, is superbly done and very accessible to gentiles as they learn about the Jewish people. Historical novels are also an exciting source of Jewish information. There are far too many to list. Ask for recommendations. Perhaps a good place too start is Leon Uris' *Exodus*.

2. Hasidism

Hasidism is an eighteenth-century movement that has forever altered the stream of Jewish history and the quality of Jewish piety. Today's Judaism cannot be fully appreciated by the western mind without understanding Hasidism, and also its numerous counterfeits in the modern world. Insights into that world can be gained from such books as A. J. Heschel's *The Earth is the Lord's*; the anecdotal collection of the Hasidic masters, *Tales of the Hasidim* by Martin Buber, and *The Hasidic Anthology* by Louis Newman (both authors very far from the Hasidic life, but faithful in their presentations); and *Souls on Fire* by Elie Wiesel.

3. The Holocaust

The Holocaust is a qualitatively new experience in Jewish history. Persecution is not; national calamity is not; genocide is. The prospective candidates owe it to themselves to read the literature on the Holocaust, or Sho'ah, in order to understand the nature of Jew-hatred, and to be aware what they must prepare for—though on a far diminished level, we expect. It is not enough to know the statistics of the Holocaust. One should feel the horror of it. The books by Elie Wiesel and Primo Levi and others are available all over the world. A few specific ones: Elie Wiesel, *Night/Dawn/Day*, Jason Aronson, 1985; for non-fiction, among many others, Yaffa Eliach, *Hasidic Tales of the Holocaust*, Oxford University Press, Bantam Books, 1982. There are magnificent documentaries on film, not the least of which is Herman Wouk's *Winds of War*.

Why are They So Tied to the State of Israel?

One simply cannot know Jewish life today without an understanding of the centrality of the State of Israel. The advent of the State is considered by some to be the forerunner of Messianic times, the "beginnings of redemption." Others, equally devoted to the State, think of its birth as miraculous and history-changing and evidence of God's Providence, but without immediate theological consequences. Some very pious people cannot consider it in any way because they are awaiting the miraculous arrival of the Messiah, for only he, not a political movement, is invested with the power of conferring statehood anew upon the Holy Land. The history of Zionism was written and documented by many writers, including Ludwig Lewisohn, Maurice Samuel, and in such texts as Arthur Hertzberg's *The Zionist Idea*, Greenwood Press, Atheneum, New York, 1976, and Walter Lacqueur's *A History of Zionism*, Schocken Books, New York, 1976.

Is Hebrew Reading Necessary to Believing?

In regard to studying the general skein of mitzvot, it is vital to learn to read Hebrew. Understanding is important. But at this stage, rapid mechanical reading is more important. It will enable the convert to attend religious services comfortably. He or she should practice reading the liturgical Hebrew of the prayerbook, emphasizing the major prayers. This will be the first activity as a Jew—becoming responsible to recite prayers immediately after becoming Jewish.

Such is the nature of beginnings that one cannot see the end of the circuitous road that lies ahead—if there is ever a terminus to learning. The convert should plan to make this a life-study, as should all Jews. "The People of the Book" should not settle for less. Good luck.

GENERAL INDEX
Jewish

Day, counting the, 309
Daylight, 169
Dear Abby, 197
Death and mourning, 404-414
    casket, 407
    comforting the bereaved, 411
    cremation, 409
    five stages of mourning, 410
    flowers, 407
    funeral service, 408
    Kaddish, 412
    joyous occasions, 412
    night before, 408
    preparation of remains, 406
    rending the garment, 408
    timing the funeral service, 407
    unveiling, 413
    yahrzeit, 413
    yizkor, 413
Dedicated funds, 178
Democracy, 91
Demography, 274
Denver, 137
Destruction of Temples, 390
Devekut, definition, 31
Dietary laws. See Kosher laws.
Dignity, 433
Disillusionment, 78
Divine Fate, 106, 110, 115
Divine Destiny, 106, 107, 109, 110, 115, 162,
Dogmas, 278
Doubt, dealing with, 294-295
Dukhan, 233

Edward I, King, 390
Egypt, 61
Egyptian bondage, 377
Electricity, 344
Eliezer, 398
Elul, 351
Embalming, 406
England, 44, 129
Enosh, 421
Erev Shabbat, definition, 340
Esau, 148, 330
Ethical living, 136
Ethiopia, 105
Etrog, definition of, 363
Exodus, 110, 377, 378, 384
Eyes of the Bet Din, 62, 133

Faith, xix, 105, 148
    as term for religion, xix
Faith group, 75
Faith and deed, 298-300
Faith and Law, 301
Family, 83
Family origin, 272
Family purity, 268, 402
Fast of Esther, 374
Fast of Gedaliah, 351
Feast of Weeks: Shavuot, 387-390

Feeding the hungry, 313
Ferdinand and Isabella, 391
Fifth Commandment, 248
Finnegan, Edward, 24
First Commandment, 139
First Fruits, 387
First Temple, 275, 391
For the sake of heaven, 82, 84, 206, 208
For the sake of marriage, 85, 229
Forefathers, 220
Foreskin of the heart, 138
Formal process, 73, 119-125. See also Protocol.
    outline, 119
Formal conversion, 235
Four Questions, 90
Fourth of July, 250
France, 275
Franco-German, 60
Fraternalism, 126
French Revolution, 237
Friedman, Dorothy Foster, 21
Full-time Jew, 311

Gehr, Mary Ruth, 53
Gemara kop, 316
Gentile, 78
Gentile celebrations, 245
Gentile family in Jewish celebrations, 254-262
    ushers and bridesmaids 255
Gentile parents at wedding, 254
Gentile couple wishes to convert, 230
Gentiles at the Seder, 258
Ger, xxi, 31, 61
    definition, xxi, 31
Germany, 275
God, 38, 49, 55, 61, 179, 217, 267, 280, 282, 283, 284, 286
    the Creator, 282
    desecration of the Name of, 217
    existence of, 179
    history is meaningful because of, 284
    human being counts, 284
    is One, 282
    Jewish idea of, 280
    the Judge, 283
    personal God, 283
    the Redeemer, 283
    tracing his actions, 286
    transcendental, 49
"God of Our Fathers", 220
God's image, 433
God-Man partnership, 107
Godhood, 126
Godliness, 127
Golden Calf, 109
Goodness, 127
Goy, 5, 22, 23, 63
Grace After Meals, 220, 343, 369
Great authors, 317
Greece, 73
Gregorian calendar, xvii, xviii, 307

Pogrom, 63
Polytheism, 421
Pompeii, 275
Pragmatism, 81
Prayershawl. *See* Tallit.
Prayer experience, 188, 268, 319-322
Prayerbook (Siddur), 54, 221, 319
Pregnant convert, 230
Price, Frances, 15
Priest People, 107, 124, 162, 176
Pro forma, 122
Promised Land, 271
Prophets, 109
Protocol, 73-77, 177
Psyche, 110
Pulpit, 30
Puppet show, 284-285
Pur, 374
Purim, 34, 374-377
  feast, 376
  gifts to needy, 376
  Megillah, 375
  Shalach Manot, 376

Rabbinic authority, 112
Rebecca, 143, 398
Reconstructionist, 55
Rectifying the world, 70
Reform, 8, 10, 19, 20, 25, 30, 55, 120, 157, 199, 328
Religious conduct, 108-109
Religious criteria, 126
Religious divorce, 404
Religious freedom, 91
Religious preference, 81
Religious responsibility, 396
Remarriage, 403
Repudiation of the Law, 302
Responsa, 203-262
Return. *See* Teshuvah.
Returnee (Baal Teshuvah), 83, 352
Revelation, 14, 95, 97, 98, 99, 107, 110, 121, 217, 221, 276, 349, 379, 384, 387, 388, 418, 419
Reward and punishment, 136, 267, 286-289
  bad things happen to good people, 288
  goodness for goodness sake, 287
  problems in the belief of retribution, 288
Ribbono Shel Olam, definition, 30
Right action, 299
Right of intention, 299
Right living, 299
Right, child's, to protest, 193
Roman law, 191
Rome, 73
Rosh Chodesh, definition, 308
Ruth, 68, 75, 82, 389, 427
  name change, 184

S'khakh, definition, 362
Sabbath, xviii, 6, 7, 38, 40, 55, 56, 136, 268, 286, 308, 335-346

definition 335
begins, 340
candles, 370
as Queen, 339
Shabbat Welcome, 341
stopping for Shabbat, 344
Sacrifices, rules of, 109
Salvation, 89
Sanctuary, 157
Sarah, 70, 96, 143, 164
Sarai, 96
Saul, 275
Saving a soul, 70
Scholars' Festival, 385
Sciatic nerve, 332
Scotland, 53
Se'udah Shlishit, 342
Se'udat Mitzvah, 143
Second Temple, 275, 391, 422
Secrets of the Jews, 260
Secularist, 125
Sefer Ha'B'rit, 99
Seleucid Greek, 367
Sephardim, 69, 72
Seven Noahide Laws, 240, 332
Seventeenth of Tammuz, 392
Sexual mores, 227
Sh'lom Bayit, 341
Sh'ma Yisrael, 136, 359, 321
Sha'at Ha'dechak, 438
Sha'atnez, 328
Shacharit, 321, 349
Shaddai, definition, 329
Shailah, definition, 236
Shalach Manot, 376
Shalom Aleikhem, definition, 341
Shamash, 369
Shanah Tovah, 351
Shankbone, 383
Shavuot, 388, 390
She'hecheyanu, 172
Shekhinah, 289, 313, 430
Sheloshim, 249, 410
Shelter to the homeless, 314
Shevarim, 349
Shiksa, 22
Shivah, 249, 408, 410
Shlemut, 154
Shmini Atzeret, 365, 366
Shofar, 349, 350
  definition, 349
Shomer Shabbat, 335
Shtetl life, 318
Shul (synagogue), definition, 6
"Shut the door in the face of converts," xii, 102, 133
Sick parents, 246
Silent Devotion (Amidah), 68, 220, 319, 321, 369
Simchat Torah, 366
Simon the Maccabee, 275
Sinai, 97, 98, 107, 276
Sinaitic Covenant, 95, 97-100, 102, 103,

GENERAL INDEX
Non-Jewish

SOURCES CITED
Jewish

SOURCES CITED
Non-Jewish

TABLE OF AUTHORITIES
Jewish

TABLE OF AUTHORITIES
Non-Jewish